THE COMPOSITION OF MARK'S GOSPEL

BRILL'S READERS IN BIBLICAL STUDIES

VOLUME 3

THE COMPOSITION OF MARK'S GOSPEL

Selected Studies from Novum Testamentum

COMPILED BY

DAVID E. ORTON

BRILL
LEIDEN · BOSTON · KÖLN
1999

This book is printed on acid-free paper.

Cover design: BEELDVORM, Leidschendam

On the cover: The evangelist Mark, Manuscript Patmos, 13th century, evangeliarion, fol. 92 vo. From: Ath. D. Kominis, *Patmos. Die Schätze des Klosters*, Athens: Ekdotike Athenoon, 1988, p. 316.

ISSN 1389-1170
ISBN 90 04 11340 1

PRINTED IN THE NETHERLANDS

CONTENTS

PREFACE

This is the third in a series of publications designed to make previously published journal material available in a more convenient and accessible form. The material presented in this series, then, though it certainly contains some previously neglected but valuable studies alongside established "classic" essays (with which this collection is replete), does not claim to be more than a convenient selection. However, convenience can easily translate into usefulness and indeed use, and many university and seminary teachers will find the selections suitable not only for their personal use, but also for their classes.

The present selection has been made from the best and most useful articles on the literary work of the inventor of the Gospel genre, Mark, to have appeared to date in the journal, *Novum Testamentum*. The seminal—according to Norman Perrin, the "brilliant"—essay on "The Composition of Mark 7.27-9.1 par." by Ernst Haenchen has been included here in the original German. It is the hope of editor and publishers that this will not prove too demanding on the users of this volume. It sets the tone for the discussion of Mark's literary activity in this collection, and provides a springboard for the discussion of Markan composition in the subsequent essays.

The individual essays, which are listed in chronological order of original publication, speak for themselves, and are offered without editorial comment, in conformity with the ethos of the journal. Taken as a whole, the collection illustrates and documents the development of international scholarly discussion on Mark's literary and theological contribution from the first tentative days of redaction criticism.

Readers of German are referred also to the article by Hans-Josef Klauck, "Die erzählerische Rolle der Jünger im Markusevangelium" (NovT 24 [1982]: 1-26), which could not be included in this collection.

DEO
Leiden, 1999

PLACES OF ORIGINAL PUBLICATION

The articles of this book first appeared in *Novum Testamentum*.

Ernst Haenchen, 'Die Komposition von Mk vii 27-ix 1 und Par.,' *NT* vol. VI (1963), pp. 81-109.

J. Norman Perrin, 'The Composition of Mark ix, 1,' *NT* XI (1969), pp. 67-70.

R.H. Stein, 'The Proper Methodology for Ascertaining a Markan Redaction History,' *NT* XIII (1971), pp. 181-198.

John Dominic Crossan, 'Mark and the Relatives of Jesus,' *NT* vol. XV (1973), pp. 81-113.

J. Lambrecht, 'The Relatives of Jesus in Mark,' *NT* vol. XVI (1974), pp. 241-258.

Vernon K. Robbins, 'Summons and Outline in Mark: The Three-Step Progression,' *NT* vol. XXIII (1981), pp. 97-114.

Charles W. Hedrick, 'The Role of 'Summary Statements' in the Composition of the Gospel of Mark; A Dialog with Karl Schmidt and Norman Perrin,' *NT* vol. XXVI (1984), pp. 289-311.

Elizabeth Struthers Malbon, 'Disciples/Crowds/Whoever—Markan Characters and Readers,' *NT* vol. XXVIII (1986), pp. 104-130.

Stephen H. Smith, 'The Literary Structure of Mark 11:1-12:40,' *NT* vol. XXXI (1989), pp. 104-124.

James R. Edwards, 'Markan Sandwiches: The Significance of Interpolations in Markan Narratives,' *NT* vol. XXXI (1989), pp. 193-216.

Michael D. Goulder, 'Those Outside—Mark 4:10-12,' *NT* vol. XXXIII (1991), pp. 289-302.

Stephen H. Smith, 'A Divine Tragedy: Some Observations on the Dramatic Structure of Mark's Gospel,' *NT* vol. XXXVII (1995), pp. 209-231.

DIE KOMPOSITION VON MK vii 27-ix 1 UND PAR.

VON

ERNST HAENCHEN

44 Münster/Westf., Deutschland

I. Mk. viii 27-ix 1

Früher [1]) war man davon überzeugt, daß die Evangelien die Ereignisse des Lebens Jesu so wiedergeben, wie sie sich zugetragen haben. Für den Redestoff hat man freilich längst umgelernt. Daß die Bergpredigt eine Sammlung einst selbständiger Logien ist, wird heute allgemein anerkannt. Auch für die Berichte über Jesu Taten hat man den Anteil der Evangelisten an der Darstellung sehr viel höher einzuschätzen begonnen. Aber an manchen Stellen, die für die vita Jesu besonders wichtig sind, zögert man, dieses Prinzip anzuwenden, so z. B. für die Perikope Mk viii 27-33 [2]). Denn wenn hier das Ereig-

---

[1]) Z. B. H. J. HOLTZMANN: *Die Synoptiker usw* 2. verbesserte u. vermehrte Aufl. Freiburg i. Br. 1892. — Gustav WOHLENBERG, *Kommentar z.N.T.* 2, „Das Evangelium des Markus". Leipzig 1910.

[2]) JOH. WEISS, *Die Schriften d. N.T.*, 2.A. Göttingen 1907, 145-148 „. . . war ihm" (Petrus) „unvergeßlich, daß Jesus in diesem großen Augenblick rätselhaft erregt und abwehrend war, sodaß es fast zweifelhaft schien, ob er sein Bekenntnis annehmen wollte. Wir können das nur so verstehen, daß Jesus von der Art und Weise, wie Petrus sprach, enttäuscht war". — K. L. SCHMIDT, *Der Rahmen d. Geschichte Jesu*. Berlin 1919, 216: „Wir. stehen hier auf dem Boden der ältesten Überlieferung." — E. LOHMEYER, *Das Evangelium des Markus*, Göttingen 1937, 170: "Von hier aus" (der Lehre vom leidenden Menschensohn) „ist auch gegen die erste einleitende Szene ein begründeter Einwand nicht mehr vorzubringen." — J. SCHNIEWIND, *Das NT deutsch*, 1. Bd., „Das Evangelium nach Markus", Göttingen 1937, 110: „. . . von hier aus" (Messias-Geheimnis) „wird es möglich und wahrscheinlich, daß unsere Überlieferung Recht hat, ein besonders entscheidendes Messiasgespräch nach Cäsarea Philippi und an den Beginn der Passion zu legen." — E. HIRSCH, *Frühgeschichte des Evangeliums*, Bd. 1, Tübingen 1941, 91: „Der erste Erzähler ist entweder Petrus selbst oder schrieb auf Grund von Erzählungen, die aus des Petrus Munde stammen." — J. SCHMID, *Das Evangelium nach Markus*, Regensburg, 3.A. 1954, 155: „. . . Damit ist dann auch gesagt, daß die nachfolgende Belehrung der Jünger über das Leiden Jesu und die Leidensnachfolge vom Evangelisten auch zeitlich richtig eingeordnet sind." — W. GRUNDMANN, *Theol. Handkommentar* 2, „Das Evangelium nach Mk.," 2. A. Berlin 1959, 167, ist unsicher: „Verdient die Ortsangabe Beachtung, dann wird man in der Überlieferung einen Kern anerkennen müssen, der bestimmte Tatbestände zutreffend wiedergibt, die

nis im wesentlichen genau so berichtet ist, wie es sich zugetragen
hat, dann würden wir hier in eine der entscheidenden Stunden des
Lebens Jesu unmittelbar hineinblicken, in die Stunde nämlich, da
Jesus zuerst versucht hat, die Jünger auf sein Leiden vorzubereiten.

In der Tat nimmt sich der Versuch, diese Perikope als einen im
wesentlichen zutreffenden Bericht auszulegen, zunächst recht
überzeugend aus. Irgendwo auf dem Weg zwischen Bethsaida [1])
und den Dörfern, die schon zu Cäsarea Philippi gehören, fragt Jesus
die Jünger, wer er nach dem Glauben der Leute eigentlich sei. Die
Antworten gehen auseinander: der (wieder auferstandene) Täufer
oder Elias oder einer von den (alten) Propheten. Aber sie stimmen
doch alle darin überein, daß sie Jesus irgendwie unter die Kategorie
des Prophetischen zu bringen versuchen. Diese erste Frage an die
Jünger verlangte von ihnen nur, über die Stellung anderer zu Jesus
zu berichten. Aber Jesu zweite Frage kommt unausweichlich auf
die Jünger selbst zu: ,,Wer aber meint *ihr*, daß ich bin?''

Die Antwort gibt für die Jünger Petrus:,,Du bist der Christus!''.
Man meint heute vielfach [2]) aus dieser Antwort herauszuhören, daß

---

zu einem wesentlichen Kern zu einem Ereignis in dieser Gegend gehören.''
— Philiph CARRINGTON, According to Mark, Cambridge 1960, 181: ,,Peter
says in effect, that the time has come for him to step into the position of
national leader and hero; Jesus answers that time has come when he must
endure a martyr's death.'' Es ist erstaunlich, was hier alles in den Text
hineingelesen ist.

[1]) BULTMANN *ZNW* 19, 1920, 169 und *Geschichte d. syn. Tradition* 276
zieht zu Unrecht den V. 27a zur vorhergehenden Geschichte, weil Bethsaida
kein Dorf mehr war. Josephus teilt Ant. 18, § 28 darüber mit: ,,Philippus
benannte Paneas . . . Cäsarea; das Dorf Bethsaida aber . . . Stadtrechte ver-
leihend . . . nannte er nach Julia, der Tochter des Kaisers.'' Wer nach der
alten Tradition von Bethsaida sprach, dem lag es nahe, es eine κώμη, ein
Dorf zu nennen. So V. TAYLOR, *The Gospel according to St. Mark*, London
1959, 370. — Die Lesart Βηθανίαν bei D pc it könnte dem Umstand Rechnung tragen, daß Bethsaida im 2. Jht. als Dorf nicht mehr bekannt war.
Darum mußte man einen anderen, ähnlichen Namen eines Dorfes dafür
einsetzen. — BULTMANN 68 hält die ganze ,Nordreise' Jesu für Phantasie.
Aber aus welchem Grunde soll eigentlich die Gemeinde dazu gekommen
sein, Jesus nach Norden wandern zu lassen? — E. STAUFFER, *Jesus, Gestalt
und Geschichte*, Bern 1957, 71, dagegen weiß, daß Petrus das Bekenntnis
am 10. Tischri des Jahres 31 ablegte.

[2]) J. WEISS 148: ,,. . . Jesus von der Art und Weise, wie Petrus sprach,
enttäuscht . . . Aus Gebärde und Ton hat er offenbar nur jenen politischen
Fanatismus herausgefühlt, den er nicht befördern wollte noch konnte.''
Welche Phantasie der Autor besitzt! — HIRSCH 89: ,,Jesus bringt durch
sein Fragen das, was als heimliche Hoffnung im Herzen der Jünger lebt, ans
Licht; aber er gibt dem Christusgedanken einen ganz neuen Inhalt: . . . daß
er der von Gott zu Leiden und Tod bestimmte Menschensohn sei. Erst als

Petrus und die Jünger noch dem jüdischen Messiasideal zuneigen
und vom Messias Glanz und Herrlichkeit, vielleicht sogar die Ver-
treibung der heidnischen Römer und Israels Weltherrschaft erwarten. Darum, so interpretiert man weiter, habe Jesus versucht,
dieses Messiasbild zu reinigen, indem er den Jüngern zum ersten
Mal das Bild des leidenden Menschensohnes vor Augen stellt, in dem
sich die Vorstellung vom Gottesknecht Deuterojesajas und vom
danielischen Menschensohn verschmelzen [1]). Aber wie wenig die
Jünger innerlich reif sind für die Korrektur an ihren Erwartungen,
zeigt die Reaktion des Petrus: er drängt Jesus, nicht diesen Leidens-
weg zu gehen. Dafür muß er nun die harte Abweisung durch Jesus
über sich ergehen lassen, der ihm auf den Kopf zusagt, daß aus ihm
der Versucher, der Satan redet.

An diese wirkliche Szene habe dann der Evangelist einige Einzel-

---

Petrus sich im Sinn des alttestamentlich-jüdischen Inhalts des Bildes vom
Messias gleich gegen den ersten Versuch Jesu wendet, ihnen das neue ...
Christusbild mitzuteilen, erst da fällt das Wort: Du Satan. Dies ist das
wahrhaft geschichtliche, das wahrhaft tiefe Verständnis dieses Abschnitts.''
— Welcher Ausleger hofft nicht das wahrhaft geschichtliche und tiefe Verständnis getroffen zu haben? — E. KLOSTERMANN, *Das Markusevangelium*
4.A. Tübingen 1950, 80: ,,Die Meinung ist hier'' (V. 30) ,,offenbar nicht,
daß Jesus die Aussage des Petrus zurückweist und das Gespräch abbricht,
sondern daß er sie sich zwar gefallen läßt, aber nur für den Kreis der Jünger,
deren Messiashoffnung er gleichzeitig umschmilzt — zu *ihrem* Messiasbild
paßt das Leiden offenbar nicht.'' — Josef SCHMID 155: ,,Dasz die Zwölf
das tiefste Geheimnis von Jesu Wesen noch nicht erfaßt haben, ist wohl
richtig. . . . Korrektur des Messiasglaubens der Jünger.'' — W. GRUNDMANN
169: ,,Darin, daß der Menschensohn wird leiden und verworfen werden
müssen, ist die neue Lehre Jesu enthalten, die das Bekenntnis zu seinem
messianischen Königtum korrigiert.'' *Ebda* 170: ,,Das nationalpolitische
Messiasbild des anerkannten und siegenden Messiaskönigs tritt dem ent-
gegen, was Jesus als apokalyptische Notwendigkeit entworfen hat: das Bild
des leidenden und verworfenen Menschensohnes.'' — G. FRIEDRICH, *ZThK*
53, 1956, 292: ,,Petrus denkt wohl an den gesalbten König der Endzeit.
Mk. viii 30 wird diese Antwort des Petrus abgelehnt. Anstelle der Davids-
sohnerwartung tritt die Gottesknecht-Menschensohn-Christologie.'' Ist von
Petrus der Davidsohn auch nur angedeutet worden?

[1]) Z. B. J. SCHNIEWIND 110: ,,Endlich muß schon im Judentum der
leidende Gottesknecht aus Deuterojesaja mit diesem überweltlichen Messias''
— gemeint ist der kommende Menschensohn — ,,gleichgesetzt worden sein''.
SCHNIEWIND beruft sich dafür auf die Menschensohn-Aussagen des Buches
Henoch; ein m.E. fragwürdiges Zeugnis. SCHNIEWIND fährt fort: ,,Dann
also hätte Jesus die Messias-,,Idee'' keineswegs umgestaltet, aber er hätte
gewußt, daß *er* der Gotteskönig ist, der zum Weltrichter-Menschensohn
erhöht werden wird, zuerst aber leiden und sterben muß. Das Geheimnis
wäre lediglich das ,,Ich bin's''. Lediglich! Dies ,,Ich'' bedeutet nach Jesu
eignen Worten, . . . daß man sich seiner schämt Mk. viii 38. Dies zeigt sich
sofort: V. 31-33.''

sprüche angefügt, die vom Verhalten der Jünger zum Leiden
sprechen. Damit scheint die ganze Perikope viii 27 - ix 1 durchsichtig
geworden zu sein [1]).

Das mit dieser Exegese gewonnene Bild ist zweifellos eindrucks-
voll. Aber sieht man genauer zu, dann merkt man: der Text kommt
nicht ganz zu seinem Recht, und auch die nüchterne Überlegung
findet manches fragwürdig. Zwar daß normalerweise der Jünger
fragt und der Meister antwortet [2]), ist noch kein durchschlagender
Einwand gegen V. 27b, denn von dieser Regel gibt es gut begründete
Ausnahmen [3]). Auch LOHMEYERS Bedenken, ,,Man kann einen
Lehrer oder Propheten nicht fragen, wer er sei, sondern was er
lehre oder verkünde'' [4]), ist ohne Gewicht, ganz abgesehen davon,
daß weder die Jünger noch Jesus an einen Lehrer oder Propheten
eine solche Frage gestellt haben, und daß auch Jesus nicht gefragt
wird, sondern selber fragt. Die Hoffnungen der Leute [5]), welche die
Jünger berichten, zeigen andererseits, daß man damals sehr wohl
fragen konnte: ,,Wer ist Er ?''. Denn damals war die Hoffnung nicht
unerschwinglich, daß in einem Menschen ein höheres Wesen —
vielleicht sogar der große Heilbringer — verborgen sein könne.
Etwas derartiges haben nach Mk. die Leute auch bei Jesus gehofft
und geglaubt. Nur griff ihr Glaube nicht hoch genug, sondern blieb
in der Sphäre des Prophetischen hängen.

Ernster ist schon BULTMANNS Einwand: ,,Wozu fragt Jesus nach
einer Sache, über die er genau so gut orientiert sein mußte wie seine

---

[1]) LOHMEYER 161 hat als erster versucht, den ganzen Abschnitt viii 27-
ix 1 als eine marcinische Komposition zu erklären: ,,Drei Überlieferungs-
stücke sind hier von Mk. zusammengestellt: 1. Die Frage, wer er sei (viii
27-29) . . . 2. Die Verkündigung von der Notwendigkeit des Leidens des
Menschensohnes (viii 30-33). 3. Die Verkündigung von der Notwendigkeit
des Leidens seiner Jünger (viii 34-ix 1). Die Anfügung dieses dritten Teils
zeigt deutlich, daß diese Ordnung unter katechetischem Gesichtspunkt
steht; er zieht aus dem Leiden des Herrn mit Herrenworten die praktisch
gläubige Folgerung für das Verhalten der Gemeinde und ihrer Glieder.''
Nur ist der erste Teil nicht in demselben Sinn eine literarische Einheit wie
die — freilich auch aufgefüllte — kerygmatische Formel des zweiten Teils
und die Spruchsammlung des dritten.

[2]) R. BULTMANN, *Die Geschichte der synoptischen Tradition.* 2.A. Göttingen
1931, 70, 126.

[3]) Z.B. Mk v 30; ix 21.   [4]) LOHMEYER 162.

[5]) LOHMEYER meint 162 fälschlich, ἄνθρωποι bedeutete nicht ,Leute',
sondern ,,gegen Gott gerichtete . . . Menschen''. Freilich bleibt die Erkenntnis dieser Menschen hinter der Erkenntnis der Jünger zurück, ohne daß sie
darum gegen Gott gerichtet wären. LOHMEYER sucht aber den Gegensatz
zwischen den gottwidrigen Menschen und den Jüngern als den ,Begnadeten'
herauszustellen, zu dem ihn die Mt.-Parallele verführt hat.

Jünger? [1]" Darauf sollte man freilich nicht mit K. L. Schmidt antworten, daß offenbar „die Jünger über die Volksstimmung" (!) [2] „besser unterrichtet sind als Jesus selbst. Jesus muß eine Zeitlang die Fühlung mit seinen Jüngern verloren haben, die Jünger müssen von ihm getrennt unter der Bevölkerung gelebt haben." Damit wird phantastisch aus Jesu erster Frage eine ganze uns bisher unbekannte und sonst nicht bezeugte Epoche des Lebens Jesu erschlossen. Viel näher liegt die Erklärung, daß Jesus nicht mit der Tür ins Haus fällt, sondern die entscheidende Frage erst vorbereitet.

Aber ebensogut kann natürlich auch der Evangelist selbst die Szene so geschickt aufgebaut haben. Dafür spricht, daß schon in Mk. vi 14 f. die Frage nach Jesu Wesen erörtert worden war und daß dort — mit nur geringen Änderungen [3] — dieselben Meinungen der Leute aufgetaucht waren, die hier von den Jüngern genannt werden. Mk. hat anscheinend ein und dieselbe Tradition zweimal benutzt.

Wie steht es nun mit der zweiten Frage Jesu? Ganz schlimm erging es ihr bei Wohlenberg [4], der noch dem Rechnung tragen mußte, daß die Jünger nach Joh. i 41 ff. das wahre Wesen Jesu seit der Johannestaufe kannten. Wohlenberg half sich mit der Erwägung: „Wie ein Gemeindepastor, der die Konfirmanden unterrichtet hat und längst weiß, daß sie Kenntnis der christlichen Heilswahrheiten, besonders von der Person und dem Werk des Erlösers besitzen, doch nichts Überflüssiges tut, wenn er sie schließlich in feierlich-ernster Stunde nach ihrer persönlichen Überzeugung fragt und zum Bekenntnis auffordert, so bedeutete es auch nichts Überflüssiges, wenn Jesus seine Jünger fragte, was sie von ihm hielten, und brachte es für ihn nichts Überraschendes, wenn sie antworteten, wie es geschah." Vor 50 Jahren mochten sich noch manche mit dieser Erklärung zufrieden geben, die Jesus zum Pastor und die Szene vor Cäsarea Philippi zu einer Art Konfirmationsfeier umdeutet. Heute gibt es zwar noch Forscher, die sich vorstellen. Jesus

---

[1] Bultmann 276.
[2] K. L. Schmidt, *Der Rahmen der Geschichte Jesu*, Berlin 1919, 216, vergreift sich schon mit dem Gedanken, Jesus frage nach der ‚Volksstimmung', in den Kategorien. Ähnlich Taylor 376.
[3] Mk vi 14: ὁ βαπτίζων, viii 28: τὸν βατπιστήν, vi 15: προφήτης ὡς εἷς τῶν προφητῶν, viii 28: εἷς τῶν προφητῶν... Daß der Täufer in Jesus von den Toten auferstanden sei (Mk vi 14), hätte in viii 28 nicht hineingepaßt; vgl. Mk ix 11.
[4] Wohlenberg 231.

habe mit seinen Jüngern die nachösterliche Theologie eingeübt. Aber weder vom einen noch vom andern steht bei Mk. etwas zu lesen. LOHMEYER hat sich eine andere Erklärung zurechtgelegt: ,,Die Frage setzt voraus, daß Jesus bisher den Jüngern noch nicht gesagt hat, wer er sei. Dieses Eine ist verborgen, und es muß von denen gesagt werden, die er darum fragt, und an ihrem Sagen wird erkennbar, ob sie zu den Begnadeten gehören [1].'' Abgesehen davon, daß Mk. schon in ii 10 und ii 28 Jesus als Menschensohn bezeichnet hat, scheitert diese Erklärung daran, daß sie durch den Mt.-Text beeinflußt ist, wie die Rede von den ,Begnadeten' erweist.

Tatsächlich ist Jesu Frage, wenn sie nicht vom Evangelisten formuliert ist, schwer zu verstehen. Von der angeblichen Pädagogik Jesu ist nichts zu bemerken, denn die Jünger bleiben so unverständig, wie sie waren. Begreiflicher wird alles, wenn wir uns fragen, was der Evangelist mit diesem Zug — der zweiten Frage und ihrer Beantwortung — seinen Lesern sagt. Zunächst einmal müssen wir nämlich beachten: Petrus antwortet als Sprecher für die gefragten Jünger. Das wird dann in Jesu Wort ,,und er bedrohte sie usw.'' besonders sichtbar [2]. Mk. zeichnet den Petrus — anders als Mt.! — nicht als einen einzelnen, der eine besondere Offenbarung empfangen hat, sondern nur als den Jünger, der ausspricht, was alle denken. Zum andern: die Antwort des Petrus zeigt: Die Jünger haben schon während Jesu Erdenleben erkannt, daß er der Christus ist [3]. Damit war die Kontinuität vor und nach Ostern gesichert; Jesus war vor Ostern schon der, als der er sich nach Ostern erwies. Daß auf unsere Geschichte unmittelbar die von Jesu Verklärung folgt, ist kein Zufall. Denn die Verklärungsgeschichte bekräftigt das Jüngerbekenntnis auf ihre Weise.

---

[1] LOHMEYER 163.

[2] Das hat LOHMEYER 162 übersehen. Gewiß antworten hier ,,nicht mehr alle Jünger insgesamt, sonden ein namentlich genannter einzelner, Petrus'', aber daß Petrus nur als Sprecher der Jünger antwortet, zeigt sich dennoch deutlich. Im übrigen muß man bedenken: die drei verschiedenen Aussagen der ,Leute' lassen sich leichter auf eine Mehrheit von Sprechern verteilen, als der Satz ,Du bist der Christus'. Sollen ihn alle unisono sprechen?

[3] J. WEISS 148: ,,. . . zweifellos betrachtet Mk die Jünger oder Apostel schon vom ersten Augenblick, von der Berufung an, als vollkommen messiasgläubige Christen. Insbesondere bei der Mission (vi 7 ff.) gelten sie ihm natürlich schon als Zeugen für den Messias.'' — CARRINGTON 176: ,,The apostles are represented as having reached this stage in the formulation of their faith; and we cannot suppose that it was a new thought, produced on the spur of the moment.''

BULTMANN vermutet, daß es sich hier um eine ins Leben Jesu zurückgetragene Ostererzählung handelt [1]). Dies wird ihm freilich nur möglich, weil er die in Mt. xvi 17-19 überlieferten Worte als den eigentlichen Schluß der Petrusszene ansieht, ,,da eine Stellungnahme Jesu zu dem von ihm provozierten Bekenntnis ursprünglich erzählt gewesen sein muß [2]).'' Über die Mt.-Verse wird später zu sprechen sein. Daß Jesus auf das Bekenntnis mit dem Verbot, die Wahrheit weiter zu erzählen, antwortet, hat freilich nicht nur BULTMANN verwundert. Nur haben andere, wie z. B. O. CULLMANN [3]), daraus gefolgert, Jesus habe zum Petrusbekenntnis geschwiegen, weil er mit diesem Bekenntnis nicht ganz zufrieden gewesen sei.

Aber diese Vermutung kommt aus der anscheinend selbstverständlichen Annahme, daß es sich bei Petrus um ein Messiasbekenntnis gehandelt habe, in dem noch jüdische Irrtümer enthalten waren. In Wirklichkeit ist das Bekenntnis des Petrus ,,Du bist der Christus!'' das Bekenntnis der Christenheit. Der Gedanke, daß das ὁ χριστός im Munde des Petrus noch nicht das richtige ὁ χριστός gewesen sei, ist dem Mk nicht gekommen — und welcher seiner Leser wäre darauf verfallen? Gerade weil es das rechte Bekenntnis ist, braucht Jesus gar nicht dazu ,,Stellung zu nehmen'', sondern kann zu dem weitergehen, was nun gesagt werden muß: Diese Wahrheit muß verborgen bleiben [4]). Natürlich gilt das — ebenso wie das Schweigegebot in ix 11 — nur bis zur Auferstehung Jesu. Aber weil Mk von dieser noch nicht gesprochen hatte, konnte er diese Begrenzung hier auch noch nicht erwähnen. Wenn die Überlieferung über Jesu Erdenleben so wenig von seinem eigentlichen Wesen aussagte, dann lag das für Mk einzig und allein an Jesu Verbot, das rechte Bekenntnis schon zu verbreiten.

---

[1]) BULTMANN 277.
[2]) BULTMANN 276.
[3]) O. CULLMANN, *Petrus*, Zürich-Stuttgart, 2. A. 1960, 206 und 206 A 1. Später vertritt er sogar die Meinung: ,,Vom Vater war Petrus nicht in Cäsarea Philippi inspiriert, wo er im Gegenteil die teuflische Auffassung von ,,Christus'' vertrat, sondern bei einer anderen Gelegenheit, wo er in Jesus den Gottessohn erkannte'', nämlich beim letzten Abendmahl Jesu (293). An dieser kühnen Kombination möchte ich mich auf keine Weise beteiligen.
[4]) Weil sich Jesus weder zu den Meinungen der Leute noch zum Bekenntnis des Petrus äußert, hat man — die Szene wie eine Originalaufnahme des Geschehens behandelnd — in diesem Schweigen Jesu Unzufriedenheit mit beiden Antworten enthalten gefunden. Aber ,,er redete ihnen ernstlich zu, daß sie keinem von ihm sagten'', wäre eine unpassende Erwiderung, wenn Petrus mit seinem Bekenntnis auf falschen Wegen ginge.

Wenn Hirsch den V. 30 streichen [1]) muß, weil er die Leidensankündigung unmittelbar an das Petrusbekenntnis anknüpfen
will, dann gibt er dem Text nicht sein Recht. Mk. läßt in V. 31
wirklich einen neuen Abschnitt beginnen, der freilich seine be-
sonderen Probleme hat. Der Evangelist hatte einmal die schwierige
Aufgabe, das Jüngerbekenntnis im Erdenleben Jesu Wirklichkeit
werden zu lassen. Der eigentliche ‚Sitz im Leben' für ein christ-
liches Bekenntnis war für die Gemeinde des Mk. freilich das Bekenntnis angesichts der Verfolgung; das wird aus V. 34 ff. sehr
deutlich. Aber während des Erdenlebens Jesu konnte es nicht zu
einer solchen Situation kommen (die Verleugnung des Petrus
während der Passion war nur ein Vorspiel dafür). So blieb dem
Schriftsteller keine andere Wahl, als Jesus selbst nach einem solchen Bekenntnis fragen zu lassen. Andererseits mußte er seine
Leser darauf vorbereiten, daß auf Jesus nun die Passion wartete.
Das war umso nötiger, als das gleiche Leiden auch — zum mindesten
als Möglichkeit — vor den Christen stand.

Mk hat sich für diese Aufgabe einer alten kerygmatischen Formel
bedient [2]), die in den Wiederholungen der Leidensankündigung in
Kapitel ix und x wiederkehrt. Diese Formel enthält den feierlichen
Ausdruck ‚der Menschensohn', von dem Jesus in der dritten Person
spricht; sie redet von seiner „Auferstehung" (nicht: „Auferwek-
kung"), und sie benutzt die Wendung „nach drei Tagen" statt
„am dritten Tag". Die Verwertung einer solchen Formel hinderte
den Evangelisten nicht daran, sie kunstvoll zu variieren. Die erste,
sehr ausführliche Wiedergabe dieser Formel an unserer Stelle zählt
die jüdischen Widersacher auf (Älteste, Hohepriester, Schrift-
gelehrte). Sie werden Jesus „verwerfen", d.h. nicht als ὁ χριστός
anerkennen. Zuvor ist umfassend gesagt worden, daß er viel leiden
muß [3]). Dann wird angekündigt, daß Jesus getötet werden und

---

[1]) Hirsch streicht V. 30 wegen des vermeintlichen Widerspruchs zu V. 32.
Dabei versteht er παρρησία als „in aller Öffentlichkeit" und meint, „daß
Jesus bei seiner Lehre 31 andere Hörer als die Jünger nicht ausgeschlossen
hat". Aber wo sollen sie vor dem Herbeirufen der Menge herkommen? —
Wir verstehen Mk. dahin, daß Jesus hier offen ‚das Wort' im Sinne der christ-
lichen Missionsbotschaft geredet habe; vgl. dazu Mk. ii 2; iv 14 ff.; iv 33.

[2]) Grundmann 169: „eine kerygmatische Glaubensformel".

[3]) W. Michaelis, ThWB V 913 vermutet, „viel leiden und verworfen
werden" sei eine alte zweigliedrige Wendung. „Verworfenwerden" beschreibe
die Verwerfung des Menschensohnes durch die Menschen. Dann müsse „viel
leiden" den göttlichen Sinn dieses Geschehens ausdrücken. Das ist u.E.
wenig wahrscheinlich, zumal das Jes. liii 4, 11 gebrauchte סבל in keiner

auferstehen wird; von der Wiederkunft Jesu ist keine Rede. Eine
Beziehung auf Jes. liii hört man nur heraus, wenn man sie vorher
bereits im Ohr hatte. Die zweite Leidensankündigung in ix 30-32
erwähnt das „in die Hände der Menschen übergeben werden",
das Sterben und Auferstehen. Die dritte Leidensankündigung dagegen, in x 32-34, besagt, daß der Menschensohn übergeben wird
den Hohenpriestern und Schriftgelehrten, daß sie ihn zum Tode ver-
urteilen und den Heiden übergeben werden, die ihn verspotten,
anspeien und töten werden; auch hier endet die Aufzählung mit
der Auferstehung. Da παραδίδοσθαι in x 33 zweimal vorkommt
(im Sinne der Auslieferung an die Juden und dann an die Heiden),
ist der Sinn des Wortes in ix 31 nicht ganz deutlich; wahrscheinlich ist aber dort beides gemeint.

Diese Wiederholung der Leidensankündigung prägt sie dem
Leser unvergeßlich ein. Daß die Auferstehung ebenfalls voraus-
gesagt wird, greift freilich über die Passion hinaus und bestätigt
damit, daß eine kerygmatische Formel zugrunde liegt, die an sich
mit dem Petrusbekenntnis gar nichts zu tun hatte. Vermutlich war
sie kürzer als die erste und die dritte Leidensankündigung. Dadurch
daß der Evangelist diese Formel mit den Einzelheiten der Passions-
geschichte aufgefüllt hat, macht er die Leser dessen gewiß, daß Jesus
sein Leiden bis in alle Einzelheiten vorhergewußt hat. Ihn hat also
kein unerwartetes Schicksal ans Kreuz gebracht, sondern er hat
die nahende Passion als von Gott gesandt (δεῖ) Mk viii 31[5]) gehor-
sam auf sich genommen.

Gegen dieses Leiden wendet sich nun — bei Mk wiederum als
Sprecher der Jünger — Petrus. Man hat diesen Einspruch gegen
das Leiden weithin mit der Aussage über den 'Messias' verbunden
und damit die Hypothese von dem noch jüdischen Messiasglauben
des Petrus begründet. Nun bedeutet freilich ὁ χριστός ebenso wie
das Wort 'Messias' selbst: der Gesalbte. Aber Mk spricht eben
nicht, wie Joh. i 41, vom Μεσσίας, sondern sagt ὁ χριστός. Man trägt
in seinen Text etwas Fremdes ein, wenn man das Bekenntnis der

---

Übersetzung mit παθεῖν wiedergegeben wird. Auch die weitere Annahme,
πολλά steht semitisierend für πάντα, ist nicht zwingend. Daß schon „im
ältesten, vor Mk. liegenden Passionsbericht die Vorstellung vom leidenden
Gottesknecht gewesen sein muß", ist nur eine (freilich äußerst beliebte)
Hypothese. In Barn 7, 11 wird πολλά παθεῖν vom Leiden der Christen *vor*
dem Martyrium gebraucht. So scheint es auch in Mk. ix 12 verwendet zu
sein, wo ἐξουδενηθῇ die Tötung selbst meint.

Christenheit „Du bist der Christus!" im Munde des Petrus zum
Ausdruck einer falschen Christuserwartung erniedrigt [1]).
    Die weitere Hypothese, das Wort vom Leiden usw. des Menschen-
sohnes solle eine Korrektur sein, aber beachtet gar nicht, daß
auch die zweite und dritte Leidensankündigung von den Jüngern
nicht verstanden werden. Sie fragen nach ix 11 sogar: „Was heißt
das, ,von den Toten auferstehen?' " Mk. hätte sich also mehr als
ungeschickt ausgedrückt, wenn er mit den Leidensankündigungen
Belehrungen der Jünger Jesu über den rechten Messiasbegriff
hätte geben wollen. Was er tatsächlich zeigt, ist das Unverständnis
der Jünger, das erst durch die Auferstehung selbst behoben wird.
    Natürlich konnte Mk. die innere Spannung zwischen dem Petrus-
bekenntnis — das Jesum zu Recht als den Christus bekennt —
und dem Nichtbegreifen der Leidensankündigung nicht aus der
Welt schaffen. Diese Schwierigkeit wird am deutlichsten darin
sichtbar, daß Petrus so spricht, als hätte er Jesu Wort über die
Auferstehung gar nicht gehört. Das zeigt: die Reaktion des Petrus
paßt nicht zu der kerygmatischen Formel, die Mk. verwendet hat [2]):
er ist hier an seine Grenze als Schriftsteller gekommen.

---

[1]) CULLMANN 200: „Auch Petrus teilte ganz und gar die diabolische
politische Auffassung des Messiasberufes, wie er sie in der Versuchungs-
geschichte vertreten hatte". Das ist eine psychologische Konstruktion, die
weit über das durch den Text Verifizierbare hinausgeht. Daß Petrus aus
Leidensscheu Jesus das Leiden erspart sehen möchte, erklärt das Handeln
des Petrus, wie es Mk. erzählt, ganz gleich, ob man die Szene für historisch
hält oder nicht. Übrigens braucht man ἐπιτιμάω keineswegs mit „schelten"
zu übersetzen, wie es CULLMANN 200 tut — welchen Grund hätte Petrus
gehabt, Jesus zu schelten? Das Wort hat neben ,anfahren', ,tadeln', ,schel-
ten', ,Vorhalte machen' — Bedeutungen, die hier allesamt, genau besehen,
keinen Sinn haben — auch die hier ungleich passendere Bedeutung ,ernst-
haft zureden' (um einem Tun vorzubeugen): W. BAUER, WB 5. A. 599 f. In
viii 30 bedeutet es das ebenfalls; ,schelten' kommt hier gar nicht in Frage.
Daß ἐπιτιμάω in den drei aufeinander folgenden Fällen immer dieselbe
Nuance ausdrückt, ist nicht nötig. — ὕπαγε ὀπίσω μου, σατανᾶ wird nichts
anderes besagen als „weiche von mir, Satan!" in Mt. iv 10, obwohl dort nur
ὕπαγε, σατανᾶ steht; so auch CULLMANN 201 A 1.
[3]) HIRSCH 90 streicht freilich „und getötet werden und nach drei Tagen
auferstehen" als spätere Zutat des Bearbeiters Mk II. HIRSCHS Versuch, den
Wortlaut des Mk.-Textes genau auf Mk I (den ersten Erzähler, wahrscheinlich = Petrus oder einen von dessen Hörern). auf den Bearbeiter Mk II,
der bald darauf das Evangelium im Zeitgeschmack modernisiert habe, und
endlich auf den Redaktor R (der Mk I und Mk II kunstvoll so vereint habe,
daß kaum ein Wort verloren ging) zu verteilen, hat verständlicherweise an
dem Bemühen, das Ganze des Textes als Komposition des Evangelisten zu
verstehen, kein Interesse. Für ihn gibt es eben nur Mk I, Mk II und R,
aber nicht ,den Evangelisten'. Diese Verengung der Auslegung auf die Fest-

Daß Petrus auch hier für die Jünger sprach, beweist das Sätzchen
καὶ ἰδὼν τοὺς μαθητὰς αὐτοῦ in viii 33. Denn wenn man jemanden
heftig anfährt, dann sieht man dabei nicht einen anderen an.
Hirsch hat darum diese Worte dem Redaktor zugeschrieben [1]),
aber als ihren Sinn richtig erkannt, daß Petrus mit seiner Abwehr
des Leidens wieder als der Sprecher der Jünger gezeigt werden soll.
Das besagt aber nicht, daß auch die Jünger aus jüdischen Messias-
vorstellungen heraus gegen das Leiden protestieren, sondern aus der
allgemeinen Scheu des Menschen vor dem Leiden (τὰ τῶν ἀνθρώπων!),
von der selbst die Jünger nicht frei sind (und die Leser ebensowenig!).
Wenn Jesus daraufhin den Petrus einen Saten, einen Versucher
nennt, dann deswegen, weil Petrus vom Ideal des leidlosen Lebens
— nach dem sich alle Menschen sehnen — verführt ist und verführen
will. Er bringt mit dem Traum eines leidfreien Lebens den Christus
wie die Christen in Versuchung.

Denn diese Versuchung steht vor jedem, der Christ ist oder
Christ werden will. Das Leiden ist nicht nur Jesus auferlegt, sondern auch jedem, der sich zu ihm bekennt. Diese Einsicht bindet
die beiden Teile dieses Abschnittes (viii 27-33 und viii 34 - ix 1) zusammen: hier wird die Einheit des Leidens bezeugt, die zwischen
Jesus und seiner Gemeinde besteht. Dem sein Kreuz tragenden
Jesus kann man nur nachgehen, wenn man selbst das eigene Kreuz
trägt [2]).

Diese Verpflichtung zum Leiden gilt allen. Mk drückt das dadurch
aus, daß er den von Petrus auf die Seite genommenen (vgl. προσλα-
βόμενος V. 32) Jesus die Menge samt den Jüngern herbeirufen läßt.
Man hat sich an diesem Zug gestoßen: wie kann Jesus auf einer
Wanderung im fremden und schwachbesiedelten Lande plötzlich
eine Menge herbeirufen [3]), als wäre er noch an dem galiläischen See?
Aber für Mk steht überall, wo Jesus spricht und handelt, eine auf-
merksame Menge im Hintergrund; es bedarf, wie hier in V. 34,
nur eines Rufes Jesu, und schon strömt sie herbei und hört, was

---

stellung der Quellen ist aber keineswegs auf Hirsch beschränkt; sie beherrsch-
te in der vorigen Generation das Feld.

[1]) HIRSCH 91.

[2]) Nach HIRSCH 93 hat erst Mk II das Nehmen des Kreuzes und Nach-
folgen hinzugesetzt. Es sei aus der Q-Fassung Mt. x 38/Lk. xiv 27 hier ein-
gewandert.

[3]) GRUNDMANN 174: ,,situationswidrig'', aus einer Vorlage des Mk. über
nommen. Die Konjektur von A. PALLIS, der ὄχλον durch πέτρον ersetzen
möchte (Notes on St. Mark 27 f.) gehört nicht zu seinen besten.

ihr der Herr zu sagen hat. Insofern ist dieser Einzelzug kein un-
bedachter Mißgriff des Autors; die Situation einer „Lehre für alle"
verlangte von Mk einfach diese Darstellung. Wieder einmal zeigt
sich hier, wie wenig Quellenscheidung der Universalschlüssel ist.

Jesus sagt also allen: Wer, als Jünger des Meisters, hinter ihm
hergehen will, soll sich selbst verleugnen und sein Kreuz tragen und
ihm folgen. Man sollte dieses „er trage sein Kreuz" nicht abschwä-
chen. Es geht nicht darum, wie einst EISLER [1]) gemeint hat, daß
man das Zeichen χ oder τ vielleicht eintätowiert trägt. Wer sich
als Christ selbst verleugnet, gehört nicht mehr sich selbst, sondern
Jesus. Daß er nicht mehr sein eigenes Leben führt, geht soweit,
daß er auch den Tod für Jesus auf sich nimmt. Christ sein — das
sagt Mk. hier mit einem Jesus-Logion — schließt die Hingabe des
Lebens in der Verfolgung ein, also das, was man später Martyrium genannt hat [2]). Nicht daß alle bekennenden Christen am Kreuz
enden wie Jesus — den Zebedaiden Jakobus und Paulus hat man
enthauptet und den Stephanus gesteinigt. Es ist nicht einmal gesagt,
daß man alle Christen bis auf den letzten Mann aufspüren und hin-
richten wird. Aber von jedem Christen ist die Bereitschaft zur Lebenshingabe gefordert, wie sie Jesus vorgelebt hat. Hier wird deutlich
die Lage der nachösterlichen Gemeinde anvisiert; erst sie, und
nicht schon die Jünger vor Ostern, mußten mit einer Verfolgung
wegen des Bekenntnisses zu Jesus rechnen.

Dagegen kann man freilich einwenden: Zur Zeit, da das Mk-Ev
entstand, hat man u.W. die Christen noch nicht allgemein verfolgt,
sondern nur in einzelnen Fällen. Wie verträgt sich damit der Abschnitt Mk. viii 35 ff., wonach Christsein und Martyrium untrennbar
verbunden scheinen? Man wird antworten dürfen: Es kommt nicht
darauf an, ob wir von einer so allgemeinen Verfolgung der Christenheit vor Mk wissen, sondern ob sich zeigen läßt, daß sie damals

---

[1]) R. EISLER: Ἰησοῦς βασιλεὺς οὐ βασιλεύσας, Bd. II 1930, 238 f. Vgl.
auch E. DINKLER, „Zur Geschichte des Kreuzsymbols", *ZThK* 48, 1951,
148-172; ders., „Jesu Wort vom Kreuztragen". *Nt. liche Studien für R.
BULTMANN, Beiheft ZNW* 21, 1954, 110-129. — Joh. SCHNEIDER *ThWB* VII
579 sieht in dem Wort ein plastisches Bild für den, „der . . . ein Nein zu
seinem eigenen Ich gesagt hat (. . .), wobei als letzte Konsequenz die Hingabe des Lebens in den Tod denkbar ist." U.E. ist KÜMMEL, *Verheißung
und Erfüllung*, 3.A. Zürich 1956, 72 im Recht, wenn er an Verfolgungen
denkt, die nicht mehr zur Zeit des Lebens Jesu stattfinden werden.

[2]) CARRINGTON 186: „Incidentally, the theology of a martyr's devotion
to death was not without its antecedents in Judaism" mit Hinweis auf Jos.
BJ VII, § 323-336.

derartige Verfolgungen erwartete. Obgleich wir die Angst der
Christen vor dem, was an gewaltigen Verfolgungen noch vor dem
Weltende über sie ergehen wird, nicht aus geschichtlichen Ereig-
nissen erklären können — daß eine solche Angst vor einer alle
Begriffe übersteigenden Verfolgung bestanden hat, das beweist das
xiii Kapitel des Mk.-Ev.; ' wenn der Herr nicht die Tage verkürzt
hätte . . ., so würde kein Fleisch gerettet werden'', heißt es Mk.
xiii 20.

Von Mk. viii 34 an wird deutlich: Der Evangelist hat, um diese
eine große Forderung der Lebenshingabe zu verdeutlichen, Logien
verbunden, die eine andere Tradition in einem etwas veränderten
Zusammenhang überlieferte. Mt. x, 38 und Lk. xiv 27 lassen den
Spruch vom Kreuztragen auf das Wort folgen, daß die Liebe zu
Jesus größer sein muß als die zu der eigenen Familie. Ähnlich verhält es sich mit Mk. viii 35: neben der Mk.-Fassung findet sich eine
andere (,,Q'') in Mt. x 39 und Lk. xvii 35. Bei Mk verdeutlicht das
Wort, wie sonderbar es sich für einen Christen mit Leben und Tod
verhält: Wer sein (irdisches) Leben retten will, der wird sein Leben
(im Gottesreich) verlieren; wer aber sein (irdisches) Leben ,,um
meinet- und des Evangeliums willen'' verliert, wird sein Leben (im
Gottesreich) erhalten. Hier ist offensichtlich an eine Verfolgung
gedacht, bei der man den einzelnen fragt: ,,Bist du Christ?'', und
ihn hinrichtet, wenn er das bejaht. Daß V. 35 in die Zeit der nachösterlichen Gemeinde gehört, bedarf wohl keines weiteren Beweises.

V. 36 f. — wie V. 35 mit γάρ lose angeschlossen — sollen wohl
das bisher Gesagte erläutern. Vielleicht handelt es sich, wie BULT-
MANN vermutet [1]), bei diesen beiden Versen um einen ursprünglich
profanen Weisheitsspruch, das das hemmungslose Gewinnstreben
des Menschen als töricht erweist [2]). Jedenfalls meint Mk. damit:
,,Was hilft es, wenn ein Mensch die ganze Welt gewinnt und darüber sein Leben im Gottesreich einbüßt? Diesen Verlust kann er
mit nichts ausgleichen.

V. 38 — abermals gibt γάρ einen lockeren Anschluß — ist besonders
wichtig. Schon die frühe Gemeinde hat ihn hochgeschätzt. Das sieht
man an den verschiedenen Formen, in denen er erhalten ist. Lk
hat den Mk-Text in ix 26 benutzt, in xii 8f. aber den Spruch in
einer zweiten Form geboten. Hier folgt die negative Aussage, wie sie

---

[1]) BULTMANN 86. 101 f.
[2]) Die Zerlegung in zwei Sprichwörter (Reichtum hilft im Tode nicht, das
Leben ist der Güter höchstes) bei BULTMANN 86 dürfte unnötig sein.

Mk bietet, erst auf die positive Form. Dasselbe zweigliedrige Logion
finden wir in Mt x 32. Das nur bei Mk vorkommende ‚sich schämen'
meint: etwas für minderwertig und verächtlich halten und darum
nichts mehr damit zu tun haben wollen [1]. Sachlich unterscheidet sich
der Ausdruck nicht von dem üblicheren Wort "verleugnen',
dessen Gegensatz 'bekennen' ist. Dieses ἐπαισχύνομαι begegnet uns
in Herm. Sim. viii 6, 4: „ . . . das sind die Abtrünnigen und Ver-
ächter der Kirche, die in ihren Sünden den Herrn gelästert und sich
überdies des Namens geschämt haben, der über ihnen genannt ist.
Diese sind Gott gänzlich verloren gegangen." Wir finden es aufs
neue im Sim. ix 14, 6: „er trägt sie gern, weil sie sich nicht schämen,
seinen Namen zu tragen" und in Sim. ix 21, 3: „So pflegen auch
die Zweifler, wenn sie von Drangsal hören, aus Feigheit den Götzen
zu opfern, und schämen sich des Namens ihres Herrn." Aber auch
Ignatius gebraucht dieses Verb; in Smyrn x, 2 schreibt er: „ . . . mei-
ne Ketten, . . . deren ihr euch nicht geschämt habt. Auch euer
wird sich nicht schämen . . . Jesus Christus." Wenn man für
dieses 'sich schämen' einsetzt 'verleugnen' (wie es die Q-Fassung
bietet), so zeigt das Logion noch deutlicher seinen Sinn: Ein solches
'verleugnen' oder 'sich schämen' setzt voraus, daß man den Be-
treffenden nach seiner Zugehörigkeit zur Jesusgemeinde gefragt
hat und daß er, um sein Leben zu retten, diese Zugehörigkeit
bestritten hat. Ein solches Bekenntnis vor Gericht, welches das
Leben preisgibt, darf man also nicht mit einem liturgischen Bekennen verwechseln; es meint vielmehr jene Tat, die unmittelbar
das Martyrium bringt.

Hat man sich das einmal klargemacht, dann sieht man die Folgerung: Auch hier steht die Lage der nachösterlichen Gemeinde im
Blick, eine Lage, die für die Jünger während Jesu Erdenleben noch
nicht vorhanden war. Handelt es sich aber in V. 38 um eine prophe-
tische Mahnung innerhalb der nachösterlichen Gemeinde, dann
besagt das zugleich: Jesus und der Menschensohn sind ‚futurisch
identisch'.

Die frühe Gemeinde erwartete, Jesus werde bald — und dann
als ‚Menschensohn' wiederkehren. Während seines Erdenlebens
konnte er noch nicht der Menschensohn gewesen sein. Denn dieser
kommt doch mit den Wolken des Himmels am Ende der Tage zum
Gericht. Darum ließ die frühe Gemeinde Jesus vom ‚Menschen-

---

[1] BULTMANN *ThWB* I 189, 38: „sich schämen einer verdächtigten Person . . ."

sohn' in der dritten Person sprechen; daß andere Menschen den auf
Erden wandelnden Jesus mit ‚Menschensohn' anredeten, war unter
diesen Umständen ausgeschlossen. So erklärt sich die eigentümliche Tatsache, daß — abgesehen von der späten Stelle Apg.
vii 56 — kein anderer von Jesus als dem Menschensohn redet und daß
Jesus selbst — wenn ein Jesuslogion den Menschensohn erwähnt —
von ihm in der dritten Person redet. Diese Redeweise blieb auch
dann erhalten, als man — beim Abklingen der Naherwartung —
auch schon den irdischen Jesus als Menschensohn zu betrachten
begann. Endlich wurde ‚Menschensohn' so etwas wie eine feierliche
Selbstbezeichnung Jesu — gerade durch die Rede vom Menschensohn in der dritten Person wurde diese Feierlichkeit erhöht. Aber
selbst diese Feierlichkeit wurde schließlich nicht mehr empfunden.
Das zeigt z. B. Mt. xvi 13: ‚‚Wer sagen die Menschen, daß der
Menschensohn sei?'' Zu diesen Fällen gehört auch der Gebrauch von
‚Mehrschichtigkeit' der von Mk. benutzten Tradition: die beiden
Erwähnungen des Menschensohns in Mk. viii 31 und viii 38 ent-
stammen nicht derselben Schicht. In viii 31 treffen wir die jüngere
Form, wo schon der irdische Jesus sich in seinem gegenwärtigen
Zustand als Menschensohn bezeichnet, in V. 38 aber die ältere, wo
seine Menschensohnwürde noch in der Zukunft liegt.

Wenn man sich all das vergegenwärtigt, wird man nicht länger
behaupten, Jesus habe in dem Logion V. 38 vom Menschensohn in
der dritten Person gesprochen, ‚‚ohne sich mit ihm zu identifizie-
ren [1].'' Man wird auch nicht mehr versichern: ‚‚Hier finden wir
das einzige Menschensohn-Logion bei Mk. das sich wahrscheinlich
auf Jesu Verkündigung zurückführen läßt'' [2]. Und man wird auch
nicht mehr die ‚Echtheit' dieses Logions damit begründen, daß
dessen Pointe auf der Notwendigkeit und dem Ernst des jetzt
schon beginnenden Gerichts beruhe [3] — diese Pointe gilt ja genau
so, wenn der jetzt auf Erden wandelnde Jesus dereinst als Menschen-

---

[1] BULTMANN, *Theol. d. NT.* Tübingen 1953, 29.
[2] E. H. TÖDT, *Der Menschensohn in der synoptischen Überlieferung.*
Gütersloh 1959, 37.
[3] F. HAHN, *Christologische Hoheitstitel. Ihre Geschichte im frühen Christen-
tum.* Göttingen 1962, 33 ff., bes., 35. Es kommt nicht auf den abstrakten
Gedanken an, daß sich jetzt schon das Gericht vorbereitet, sondern darauf,
worin das geschieht. Mk. meint, daß es sich dabei um das Verhalten in der
Verfolgung handelt. — Bei HAHNS Deutung wird der Menschensohn, obwohl
ein himmlisches Wesen, von Jesus abhängig, eine — sit venia verbo — Art
himmlischer Hausknecht. Vor allem aber: schon der Vordersatz zeigt die
Situation der nachösterlichen Gemeinde.

sohn wiederkehren wird. Es liegt also kein Grund mehr vor, die fu-
turische Identität Jesu und des Menschensohns an dieser Stelle zu
bestreiten.

Wann aber wird Jesus als der Menschensohn zum Gericht wiederkehren? V. ix 1 — ein deutlicher Nachtrag zum vorigen Gedangen-
gang, ohne daß wir ihn deshalb Mk. absprechen müßten! — ver-
sichert, daß einige der hier bei Jesus Stehenden nicht sterben werden, bevor jenes Ereignis eingetreten ist. Daß dieser Vers nicht
vom kommenden Menschensohn, sondern vom kommenden Gottesreich spricht, (vom Kommen der Gottesherrschaft in Kraft, statt
nur in der Gestalt der von der Welt bedrohten Gemeinde), ist un-
erheblich, weil für Mk nicht nur Christus und Menschensohn gleich-
sinnig sind, sondern auch das Kommen des Menschensohnes zum
Gericht mit dem Kommen des Gottesreiches zusammenfällt.

Damit ist deutlich geworden: Mk. viii 27- ix 1 sind eine Komposition des Evangelisten, der keineswegs nur ‚Sammler und Tra-
dent' [1]) war. Freilich hat er sich dabei auf die ihm bkannten Über-
lieferungen gestützt und mit ihrer Hilfe seine theologische Botschaft
ausgesprochen.

II. Mt. xvi 13-28

Mt. scheint zunächst den Mk-Text mit leichten Kürzungen [2]) und
einer gelegentlichen Verdeutlichung wiederzugeben. In Wirklichkeit aber versteht er auch diesen Anfang anders als Mk. Das wird
deutlich, sobald man die größte Veränderung erwägt, nämlich den
aus einer anderen Tradition stammenden Einschub [3]) von V. 17-19.

---

[1]) Martin DIBELIUS, *Formgeschichte des Evangeliums.* Heidelberg 1933
2.A., S. 2: ,,Das literarische Verständnis der Synoptiker beginnt mit der
Erkenntnis, daß sie Sammelgut enthalten. Die Verfasser sind zum geringsten
Teil Schriftsteller, in der Hauptsache Sammler, Tradenten, Redaktoren.''
Während dieses frühen Stadiums der Formgeschichte hatte man noch nicht
genügend in Rechnung gestellt, daß ein Evangelist seine eigene theologische
Botschaft in der Zusammenstellung von Einzellogien ausdrücken kann.

[2]) E. KLOSTERMANN, *Das Matthäusevangelium.* 2.A. Tübingen 1927, 142-
144. — Aus Raummangel können wir weder auf alle diese Einzelheiten eingehen noch die schwer überschaubare Literatur zu Mt. und speziell Mt.
xvi 17-19 berücksichtigen. Th. DE KRUIJF, ‚*Der Sohn des lebendigen Gottes'.
Ein Beitrag zur Christologie des Matthäusevangeliums.* Romae 1962, bringt
p. XI-XVI ein bis November 1959 reichendes Literaturverzeichnis.

[3]) Ad. SCHLATTER, *Der Evangelist Matthäus. Seine Sprache, sein Ziel, seine
Selbständigkeit.* 3.A. Stuttgart 1944 (p. 502-525 gelten unserer Perikope)
setzt die Priorität des Mt. vor Mk. und die historische Zuverlässigkeit des

Vielleicht ist dieser Einschub schon daran schuld, daß sich das
Petrusbekenntnis nicht auf die in Mk. viii 29 genannten Worte des
Petrus beschränkt: „Du bist der Christus", sondern noch hinzu-
fügt: „der Sohn des lebendigen Gottes" [1]. Das dürfte nicht nur
eine ,liturgische' Auffüllung sein, entsprungen aus dem wachsenden
Bestreben einer späteren Zeit, die Würdenamen Jesu zu häufen
und so die Feierlichkeit seiner Nennung zu erhöhen. Vielmehr sagt
uns dieser Zusatz, wie Mt. hier den Begriff „Christus" interpretiert:
Jesus ist der Sohn des lebendigen, d.h. des einen und wahren Gottes.
Damit scheidet für den Mt.-Text die Möglichkeit jener Deutung
des ,Christus' aus, die nicht wenige Exegeten dem Wort im Mk.-
Bericht angedeihen ließen: bei Mt. ist es von Anfang an klar, daß
Petrus das rechte christliche Bekenntnis spricht und nicht ein
durch jüdische Messianitätsvorstellungen heimlich entstelltes [2]).
Außerdem aber greift dieses erweiterte Petrusbekenntnis über das
hinaus, worüber die menschliche Erkenntnis verfügt: es greift in
die göttliche Sphäre hinein.

So hat es jedenfalls Mt. selbst angesehen und es verdeutlicht und
befestigt durch den ,Einschub' von V. 17-19, und zwar zunächst
durch V. 17. Hier preist Jesus den Simon selig, denn diese Erkenntnis der Würde und des Wesens Jesu kann Petrus nicht Menschen
verdanken — ,Fleisch und Blut' —[3]); ihnen ist sie vielmehr schlecht-

---

Mt.-Berichtes voraus. SCHL.s sehr überlegte eigenständige Erklärung des
Textes behält trotz jener Voraussetzungen ihren hohen Wert.

[1]) SCHL. 504 verweist auf Hosea ii 1. Dort, in einer die Drohung Gottes
zu einer Heilszusage umbiegenden Glosse, heißt es: „Dereinst wird die
Zahl der Kinder Israel werden wie der Sand des Meeres . . ., und statt daß
man zu ihnen sagt: "Ihr seid nicht mein Volk!", wird man zu ihnen
sagen: „Söhne des lebendigen Gottes". Die LXX gibt das mit υἱοὶ θεοῦ
ζῶντος wieder. Es ist deutlich, daß der Ausdruck hier nicht die Qualität
eines einzelnen beschreibt, etwa des Messias, sondern die Zugehörigkeit
des ganzen Volkes zu Gott. — Das paßt zu der Gesamtaussage von DE
KRUIJF (s. A I) 3: „Man findet keine eigentümliche, systematische Sohn-
Gottes-Lehre im Alten Testament. Der Ausdruck ,Sohn Gottes' hat keine
besondere Kraft." — Nach O. CULLMANN, *Die Christologie des Neuen Testaments*, Tübingen 1957, 287 bestand für die Urgemeinde von der alttestamentlichen und spätjüdischen Anschauung her kein ersichtlicher Grund, Jesus
als Sohn Gottes zu bezeichnen. — F. HAHN sagt von der Frage des Hohe-
priesters Mk. xiv 61f.: „Dabei ist aber nun nicht wie etwa in Mt. xvi 16 der
Christostitel durch den späteren Gottessohntitel des hellenistischen Christentums erklärt . . ."

[2]) Zur Auslegung dieser Stelle bei CULLMANN s.o. S. 87 A. 3 zu Mk viii 29.

[3]) Fleisch und Blut „steht da, wo der Mensch im Unterschied von Gott
gekennzeichnet wird": SCHL. 505.

hin unzugänglich. Nein, diese Erkenntnis hat Jesu himmlischer Vater dem Petrus offenbart. Das verändert nun aber die Stellung dieses Jüngers gegenüber der, die bei Mk. erkennbar ist, sehr tief. Dort war Petrus der Sprecher der Jünger; sein Bekenntnis war auch das ihre. Hier dagegen nimmt ihn die ihm gewährte Offenbarung aus dem Jüngerkreis heraus; er, der Sohn des Jona [1]), dieser einzelne hat eine einzigartige Stellung bekommen. Wenn er in der Verklärungsgeschichte auch bei Mt. zusammen mit Johannes und Jakobus als einer der drei Hauptjünger erscheinen wird [2]), so steht er doch in unserem Abschnitt einsam und überlegen auf einer höheren Ebene. Das hat nun sogleich eine weitere Folge: bei Mk. viii 27-33 stand Jesus selbst, wie es sich gehört, im Mittelpunkt. Bei der Mt-Parallele ist das nicht mehr der Fall. Mit der Offenbarung um deren willen ihn Jesus selig preist, ist Petrus in den Mittelpunkt getreten, und er behält diese Stellung auch in V. 18f. bei.

Schon damit verbietet sich die Vermutung [3]), Mk. habe durch viii 30 die in Mt. xvi 17-19 erhaltene Tradition verdrängt. Denn die beiden Texte zeichnen jeweils ganz verschiedene Petrusbilder. Das zeigt sich besonders deutlich an dem Stilbruch in Mt. xvi 20 [4]), wo Mt. wieder zum Mk.-Text zurücklenkt.

Ziel und Gewicht von V. 17 dürften damit deutlich geworden sein. Dagegen ist noch nicht geklärt, wie V. 17 mit V. 18 zusammenhängt. Denn V. 17 hat die Seligpreisung des Petrus mit dem begründet, was ihm Gott durch seine Offenbarung gegeben hat. V. 18 setzt zwar die Auszeichnung des Petrus fort, aber in einer ganz neuen Weise. Nicht der himmlische Vater, sondern Jesus selbst ist es nun, der die Begnadung des Petrus fortführt, und mit einem ganz andern Grund.

Rein formal betrachtet könnte V. 16, wo Petrus sagt: ,,Du bist

---

[1]) Joh. i 42 und xxi 15 vertreten mit dem Namen (ὁ)υἱὸς Ἰωάννου eine andere Tradition als hier Mt.

[2]) Mt. xvii 1 ff.

[3]) BULTMANN 277 findet: ,,Die Worte können kaum irgendwo anders als in der palästinensischen Urgemeinde formuliert worden sein, wo man zu Petrus als dem Begründer und Führer der Gemeinde aufsah und dem Auferstandenen die Seligpreisung des Petrus in den Mund legte''. In der Bekenntnisszene kommt ,,auch zum Ausdruck, daß das Ostererlebnis des Petrus die Geburtsstunde des Messiasglaubens der Urgemeinde war, ja die ganze Erzählung wäre dann als eine Ostergeschichte zu bezeichnen, die . . . ins Leben Jesu zurückverlegt worden wäre.''

[4]) Die hymnische Form der Jesusrede weicht wieder dem normalen Erzählungsstil.

Christus" dem V. 18 entsprechen, wo Jesus antwortet: „Und ich
sage dir: Du bist Petrus" [1]). Man hat sogar gemeint, dieser Beiname
— oder eigentlich sein aramäisches Aquivalent כֵּפָא — sei erst hier
dem Petrus verliehen worden. Falls der „Einschub" einheitlich aus
einer schriftlichen Quelle stammen sollte, dann könnte es sich dort
so verhalten haben. Aber Mt. selbst wird schwerlich dieser Meinung
gewesen sein; hat er doch schon in iv 18 und x 2 von „Simon, genannt Petrus" gesprochen [2]). Also wird der Name Petrus hier nicht
neu verliehen, sondern vorausgesetzt und gedeutet: Petrus ist der
Felsen, auf dem Jesus — wie er nun verheißt — die Gemeinde er-
bauen wird. Wir brauchen hier nicht die Belege für die Verwertung
des Begriffs ‚Felsen' und des Wortes ‚bauen' anzuführen. Sie sind
bekannt und können im *Theologischen Wörterbuch* [3]) und in O.
CULLMANNS Buch *Petrus* [4]) nachgelesen werden. Wichtiger ist für
uns jetzt etwas anderes: Jesus spricht in V. 18f. nur von der Zukunft.
Jetzt, während seines Erdenlebens, besteht noch keine ἐκκλησία!
Indem Jesus davon spricht, daß er sie auf dem Felsen Petrus bauen
wird, greift er verheißend voraus in die Zukunft, wo er als der Auferstandene das nun Versprochene erfüllen wird.

Manche Exegeten haben vermutet, wir hätten es hier überhaupt
mit einer Auferstehungsgeschichte zu tun, mit einer nachösterlichen
Geschichte, die Mt. oder ein Vorgänger von ihm in das Erdenleben
Jesu zurückgetragen hat [5]). Wie diese vermutete Geschichte ge-

---

[1]) LOHMEYER, *Das Evangelium des Matthäus*, Göttingen 1956, 263: „Jesu
Erwiderung ist eingeleitet wie Petri Bekenntnis, so heben sich die beiden
Sätze als Mittelpunkt der Überlieferung heraus."
[2]) So argumentiert auch SCHLATTER 506. Dagegen J. SCHMID, *Das Evangelium nach Matthäus*, 4. A. Regensburg 1959, 248: „Da der Beiname Kepha
nur in der hier geschilderten Situation . . . dem Träger des Namens selbst
verständlich wird, so ist es wahrscheinlich, daß seine Mitteilung auch bei
dieser Gelegenheit (und nicht früher) erfolgte." „Der Beiname ‚Fels' soll
das Amt andeuten, für das Simon von Jesus bestimmt wird". Aber SCHMID
gibt 247 zu, daß diese Verse ein Einschub sind.
[3]) Zu πέτρα s. CULLMANN, *ThWB* VII 94-99, zu Πέτρος ebda 99-112. Später
erschien: O. CULLMANN, *Petrus*. 2. umgearbeitete und ergänzte Auflage.
Zürich/Stuttgart 1960, bes. wichtig: ‚Die exegetische Frage von Mt. xvi
17-19' (S. 183-243).
[4]) Zum Bild vom Bauen: MICHEL *ThWB* V 141: ein „eschatologischer
Akt des Christus, eine neue Vollmacht von Gott her: der Messias wird den
zukünftigen Tempel und die neue Gemeinde ‚bauen'.
[5]) BULTMANN 277 f. — Wohl aber könnte man vermuten, daß in jener
Erzählung, aus welcher der Einschub stammt, von dem späteren Konflikt
zwischen Petrus und Jesus ebensowenig etwas stand wie in der lukanischen
Parallele.

nauer ausgesehen hat, das verrät man uns leider nicht. Bescheidener ist eine andere Annahme: der Seligpreisung des Petrus wie dem Felsenwort liege die Tatsache zugrunde, daß Petrus der erste Auferstehungszeuge war [1]. Aber alle diese Quellenfragen sind nicht das Erste, was besprochen werden muß. Zunächst haben wir den Mt.-Text vor uns und müssen herauszubekommen versuchen, was er sagen will.

Er spricht von dem, was Petrus nach Jesu Willen und Vollmacht später einmal sein wird: der Fels, auf dem die Gemeinde errichtet werden wird [2]. Daran schließt sich das andere Wort: Jesus wird ihm die Schlüssel des Himmelreichs geben. Gewiß sind die Schlüssel das Würdezeichen des Verwalters, nicht die Abzeichen des Türhüters [3]. Aber was sie hier besagen, zeigt der nächste Satz, der wiederum selbst vom Schlüsselwort erklärt wird. Binden und Lösen heißt hier nicht „für verboten erklären'' und „frei geben''. Sondern in Verbindung mit dem Schlüsselwort hat der ursprünglich jüdisch-rabbinische Ausdruck [4] einen andern Sinn: Petrus wird bestimmen, wer in das Gottesreich kommen wird! Zwar wird hier die Gemeinde keineswegs mit dem Gottesreich ineinsgesetzt [5]: die Gemeinde ist auf Erden, das Gottesreich aber im Himmel. Die Aufnahme in die Gemeinde ist jedoch die Vorbedingung und Garantie dafür, daß

---

[1] S. oben A. 12 — HIRSCH II 306: „So wie er'' (= Petrus) „der erste ist, der Jesus als den Christus jetzt (17) erkennt, ohne menschliche Anleitung, auf Grund göttlicher Offenbarung, so wird er von Jesus als erster dessen gewürdigt sein, ihn nach dem Tode als Erhöhten und Herrn zu schauen und mit seinem Zeugnis davon der Anfang der nach Charfreitag neu erstehenden Gemeinde werden. Damit . . . haben die Todespforten die Macht verloren, die Gemeinde des Christus zu vernichten.'' Aber das Jesuswort spricht nicht von einem Wiederaufbauen, sondern von einem ersten Bauen.

[2] Die erste Erscheinung Jesu vor Petrus ist rasch vergessen worden. Lukas trägt sie mühsam in die Emmausgeschichte ein: xxiv 34.

[3] J. SCHMID 250: „Der Schlüsselbund . . . ist . . . das Abzeichen des Verwalters, der den Hausherrn vertritt.

[4] SCHLATTER 511: „Der Sprachgebrauch zeigt deutlich, daß ursprünglich die Formel ‘Lösen und Binden' das Handeln des Richters beschreibt. . . .An eine gesetzgeberische Tätigkeit des Apostels hat aber Mt. nicht gedacht.'' „Weil Gottes Recht unantastbar ist, ist das Wort des Apostels nicht nur Freispruch, sondern auch Verurteilung.'' — BILLERBECK I 738 zu Mt. xvi 19: „Die Parallele Mt. xviii 15 ff. läßt keinen Zweifel, daß mit dem ‘Binden' die Ausschließung aus der Gemeinde und mit dem ‚Lösen' die Aufhebung des Bannes gemeint ist''. Aber Petrus habe nicht nur Disziplinargewalt, sondern auch Lehrgewalt bekommen: ebda 739. „Die gleiche Stellung nimmt nach rabbinischer Anschauung Gott den halakhischen Entscheidungen gegenüber ein, die die Rabbinen treffen.''

[5] J. SCHMID Mt. 250.

jemand später in das Gottesreich aufgenommen wird; wer aus der Gemeinde ausgeschlossen wird, der kommt damit eo ipso für das Gottesreich nicht in Betracht. „Extra ecclesiam nulla salus" — das wird schon hier vorausgesetzt, ebenso wie es bereits in Qumran galt. HIRSCH [1]) hat behutsam, aber klar das Verhältnis beschrieben, das hier herrscht, und seinen Grund aufgezeigt: „Es ist das Rückgrat des Bewußtseins der jungen Kirche gewesen, daß sie die Gemeinde der Auserwählten der letzten Tage sei; die Zugehörigkeit zu ihr und das Teilhaben am Gottesreich waren für sie nicht von einander zu trennen. Gliedschaft in der Gemeinde und Ausschluß aus der Gemeinde galt alles beides bei Gott . . ."

Aber hat Mt. diese Worte noch in dieser eindeutigen Bezogenheit des Gottesreiches auf die irdische Gemeinde verstanden? Offenbar nicht. Denn wenn er xiii 24-30 das Gleichnis vom Unkraut unter dem Weizen oder xiii 47-50 das vom Fischnetz erzählt, dann zeigt er damit: So wie er die Gemeinden kennt, sind ihre Mitglieder nicht alle sichere Anwärter auf das Gottesreich [2]). Vielmehr „wird der Menschensohn seine Engel senden, sie werden aus seinem Reich alle sammeln, die Anstoß bieten und wider das Gesetz handeln, und sie in den Feuerofen werfen". Oder, wie es xiii 49 f. heißt: „Sie werden die Bösen mitten aus den Gerechten aussondern und sie in den Feuerofen werfen". Für Mt. fällt also die Christenheit auf Erden nicht mit denen zusammen, die ins Gottesreich eingehen werden. Wohl gilt weiter das „extra ecclesiam nulla salus", aber es besagt nicht mehr: in ecclesia certa salus.

Jedoch auch der Schein, daß Petrus allein bestimmt, wer in die Gemeinde und damit in den Himmel kommt, wird durch Mt xviii 18 zerstört: hier wird den Jüngern — keineswegs nur den Zwölf — zugesagt, daß ihr Binden und Lösen auch im Himmel gelten werde; und aus dem, was diesem Vers vorausgeht, läßt sich leicht erkennen, daß für Mt jede Einzelgemeinde selbständig die Frage entscheidet, ob ein unwürdiges Gemeindeglied ausgeschlossen wird oder nicht. Wir sehen hier den Instanzenweg, der sich herausgebildet hat: zuerst

---

[1]) HIRSCH 307.
[2]) G. BORNKAMM, „Enderwartung und Kirche im Matthäusevangelium" (in: *Überlieferung und Auslegung im Matthäusevangelium*, Neukirchen 1960), 17: Die Kirche ist ein „mixtum compositum". BORNKAMM hat völlig recht, wenn er 42 betont daß Kirche und Gottesreich unterschieden sind, aber doch eng auf einander bezogen, weil die Lehr- und Disziplinarentscheidungen der Kirhce im Gottesreich „ratifiziert" werden, wie es BORNKAMM anschaulich formuliert.

Vermahnung des Sünders durch den, der ihn sündigen sah. Hilft
das nicht, dann eine weitere Vermahnung durch eine kleine Gruppe.
Bleibt auch das erfolglos, dann wird der Fall vor die Gesamt-
gemeinde gebracht, die ἐκκλησία. „Wenn er aber nicht auf die
Gemeinde hört, soll er dir sein wie der Heide und der Zôllner."
Daß hier in Mt xviii 17 eine judenchristliche Gemeinde spricht, die
von Jesu Hinwendung zu den Zöllnern und von der Heidenmission
nichts weiß und wissen will, ist deutlich.

Obwohl also die Schlüssel des Himmelreiches in Mt. xvi 18 dem
Petrus verheißen werden, hat Mt. daraus nicht entnommen, daß nur
Petrus und niemand sonst diese Schlüsselgewalt habe. Es ging Mt.
nicht darum, das Anliegen irgend einer Quelle unverändert zum
Ausdruck zu bringen. Wenn dem Petrus hier die Binde- und Löse-
gewalt verheißen wird und in xviii 18 allen Jüngern = Gemeinden,
dann kann das für Mt. kein Widerspruch gewesen sein. Denn wenn
man den Evangelisten nicht für einen gedankenlosen Sammler hält,
dann dürften xvi 17-19; xviii 15-17, 18 zusammen etwa folgendes
Bild ergeben: Petrus war der erste, der — dank einer göttlichen
Offenbarung — Jesu wahres Wesen erkannte. Diese Erkenntnis
hat die Gemeinde von Petrus geerbt. Dasselbe gilt von der ihm
zuteil gewordenen Verheißung: Petrus ist in xvi 17-19 ein Bild des
von den Gemeinden verkörperten Christentums [1]. An Petrus wird
hier die Seligpreisung ebenso wie die Vollmacht der Christenheit
vorbildlich dargestellt. Von einem einzelnen Nachfolger ist nicht
die Rede und kann es nach der Logik des Mt. ebenso wenig die Rede
sein wie nach der Wirklichkeit: daß Petrus der erste war, der den
Herrn erkennen durfte, läßt sich ja nicht vererben [2]. Insofern ist
und bleibt er der Fels. Aber sein Bekenntnis kann sich die Gemeinde
aneignen und hat sie sich zu eigen gemacht. Insofern ist die göttliche Offenbarung nicht auf ihn allein beschränkt geblieben; insofern hat er Nachfolger — aber nicht nur einen, sondern in jedem
wahren Christen in allen Gemeinden.

Daß in dem Glauben der ersten Gemeinde, die Erwählten zu
sein, und darum Anteil an ihr und Anteil am Gottesreich untrennbar waren, noch ein Problem steckt, sei zum Schluß an einem Anek-

---

[1] Vgl. G. STRECKER, *Der Weg der Gerechtigkeit*, Göttingen 1963, 207.
[2] Von einem Amt des Petrus sagt der Text kein Wort; ebensowenig war
die reformatorische Deutung auf den Glauben des Petrus durch den Text
gedeckt.

dote gezeigt. Wie Josef SCHNITZER [1]) in seinem großen Werk über Savonarola berichtet, hat der Weihbischof Paganotti, der Savonarola und dessen beiden Gefährten vor der Verbrennung die kirchlichen Weihen wieder abnehmen mußte, in seiner Aufregung gesagt: „Ich scheide dich von der streitenden und der triumphierenden Kirche". Alsbald verbesserte ihn der gelehrte Dogmatiker, der Savonarola auch war: „Nur von der streitenden, nicht von der triumphierenden; denn das vermagst du nicht!" Soweit Mt. und Joh. (xxi 23) diese Grenze überschreiten, tut man besser, ihnen nicht zu folgen.

Den in der theologischen Debatte so heftig umstrittenen Vers Mk. viii 38 hat Mt. nicht aufgenommen; dafür steht in x 32 f. die doppelteilige Q-Fassung. Statt eines Äquivalents zu Mk. viii 38 steht (xvi 27) die Beschreibung, wie Jesus bei seiner Wiederkehr als Weltrichter handeln wird: „Denn der Menschensohn wird kommen in der Herrlichkeit seines Vaters mit seinem Engeln, und er wird einem jeden vergelten nach seinem Tun". Dem entsprechend wird nun Mk. ix 1 von Mt. umgeformt: aus dem Gottesreich bei Mk. wird — mit glatterem Anschluß — der Menschensohn. Aber das Gottesreich ist nicht ganz fortgelassen; es erscheint eigenartig mit dem Menschensohn verbunden: „er wird kommen in seinem Reich". Nun ist kein Mißverständnis mehr möglich und ist kein Gegensatz oder Unterschied mehr zwischen dem Gottesreich und dem Reich des Menschensohnes.

III. Lk. ix 18-27

Die Lk-Parallele beginnt gleich mit einem sehr problematischen Vers. Bekanntlich endet vor ihm die große Lücke, die Mk vi 44-viii 26 nicht berücksichtigt. Man hat alle möglichen theologischen und literarischen Gründe für die Weglassung dieses Mk-Stoffes angeführt; aber sie überzeugen nicht. Dazu kommt die Eigenart von Lk ix 18 selbst. Der erste Teil dieses Verses, bis προσευχόμενον κατὰ μόνας (Jesus „war betend allein") [2]) erinnert an Mk vi 46, wo es

---

[1]) J. SCHNITZER — M. FERRARA: *Savonarola*. 2 Bände. 2.A. Florenz 1952.
[2]) HIRSCH 54 übersetzt zu Unrecht: „Und es begab sich, als er für sich allein betete, traten seine Jünger zu ihm usw." — D hat recht geschickt korrigiert: „und es geschah, als sie allein waren . . ." — B* pc f helfen sich, indem sie συνῆσαν mit συνήντησαν ersetzen. GRUNDMANN 190 behauptet (nach CONZELMANN, *Die Mitte der Zeit*, 3.A. Tübingen 1960, 49), die πάντες, zu denen Jesus die Worte von der Leidensnachfolge spricht, könnten nur

von Jesus heißt, er ging auf den Berg um zu beten. Mit dem Wort
ἐπηρώτησεν dagegen beginnt deutlich der Einfluß von Mk viii 27.
Beide Teile passen jedoch nicht wirklich zu einander. Denn συνῆσαν
αὐτῷ heißt nicht ,,sie traten zu ihm'', sondern ,,sie waren bei ihm''.
Aber ,,Als Jesus betend allein war, waren die Jünger bei ihm'' ist
offensichtlich ein verzweifelter Versuch, zwei ganz verschiedene
Situationen mit einander zu verbinden. In der ersten ist Jesus betend
allein; das entspricht Mk vi 46. In der zweiten sind die Jünger bei
Jesus und werden befragt: das ist die Lage von Mk viii 27. Einige
Forscher, so HIRSCH 55 ff. haben in dieser schwierigen Lage sich
für die Vermutung entschieden, daß in dem von Lk benutzten Mk-
Text das Zwischenstück (Mk. vi 46-viii 26) fehlte [1]. Manchem mag
diese Lösung zu mechanisch erscheinen. Dennoch dürfte sie stimmen. Wir haben in den neugefundenen Papyruskodizes [2] Beispiele

---

die Menge sein, ,,die gespeist wurde und noch nicht entlassen wurde''. Aber
mit Lk. 18 beginnt doch eine neue Szene (Jesus allein und dann zusammen
mit den Jüngern). Die wunderbar Gespeisten sind lautlos verschwunden.
Mit πάντας sucht Lk. das unwahrscheinliche Herbeirufen einer Menge zu
ersetzen.

[1]) Schon B. WEISS hat in seinem Kommentar von 1901 (MEYER) vermutet
(was später STREETER, *The Four Gospels* 1924, 176 ff., und HIRSCH 54 f,
aufgegriffen und modifiziert haben), Lk. habe ein defektes Mk-Exemplar
benutzt. K. H. RENGSTORF, ,,Das Evangelium nach Lukas ''*NTdeutsch* 3,
9.A., Göttingen 1962, 120 hat wegen der Übersetzung ,,Und es geschah, als
er für sich allein betete, da waren die Jünger bei ihm'' es nicht für nötig
gehalten, auf die von uns genannten Schwierigkeiten einzugehen. Jesu
Frage solle klären, ob die Jünger bereit sind, mit Jesus nach Jerusalem zu
gehen. — GRUNDMANN 189 glaubt nicht, daß Lk. ein unvollständiges oder
korruptes Mk.-Evangelium'' ,,gehabt hat, sondern eine ,,von späterer Hand
erweiterte Auflage''. — Das verstehe ich nicht: wie soll eine solche (für die
Zeit des Mk. überdies ein sehr fragwürdiger Begriff) zur Tilgung von Mk. vi
48 (vi 47 μόνος scheint in Lk. ix 18 κατὰ μόνας durchzuscheinen) bis viii
26 geführt haben, mit der GRUNDMANN doch rechnet? — Die Erklärung der
großen Lücke bei SCHLATTER 96 (,,das Bestreben zu kürzen''; das Wider-
streben der Jünger gegen Jesu Bereitschaft zum Leiden in Lk. ix 51-56 zeige
sich nicht weniger deutlich als im Widerspruch des Petrus, der darum fortgelassen werden konnte: 98), K. L. SCHMIDT 214 (Lk. wolle die Dubletten
der Speisungsgeschichte — hat er sie als solche erkannt? — vermeiden,
welche die erstrebte Periodisierung hinderten), J. SCHMID 167 (dem Lk. sei
,,der Schauplatz selbst eines so hochwichtigen Ereignisses . . . unwichtig,''
und er mußte ihn ungenannt lassen, weil er für den ersten Hauptteil
seines Werkes (bis ix 50) Galiläa als Schauplatz festhalten wollte) oder Taylor
(Lk wollte Jesus nur im jüdischen Land wirken lassen) können alle den
Bruch in Lk. ix 18 nicht erklären.

[2]) Im P 66 fehlen 4 Seiten Text: Joh. vi 11-35, genau eine Lage. Bei P 75
ist nicht nur der Anfang und das Ende des (aus einer einzigen riesigen Lage
bestehenden) Kodex verloren gegangen, sondern auch die vier innersten
Blätter mit dem Text von Lk. xviii 18 - xxii 4.

dafür genug, daß Lagen am Anfang und Ende, aber auch in der Mitte fehlen. Darum ist diese Erklärung sehr wahrscheinlich. Man kann für sie noch eine weitere Erwägung anfügen. Als das Lk-Ev geschrieben wurde, gab es nicht viele Exemplare des Mk in den Gemeinden — Mk war weniger verbreitet als die späteren Evangelien des Mt und Lk. Die Aussicht, von einer Gemeinde das Exemplar eines Mk-Ev zu erwerben, war also äußerst gering. Besaß dagegen eine Gemeinde noch ein altes und unvollständiges Exemplar, dann läßt es sich eher begreifen, daß sie es einem interessierten Privatmann überließ.

Lk hat das Petrusbekenntnis gegenüber dem Mk-Text leicht erweitert, indem er zu χριστόν noch das Wort θεοῦ fügte; die Mk-Form wird ihm zu kahl vorgekommen sein. Weiter hat Lk die Worte καὶ ἤρξατο διδάσκειν mit einem einfachen εἰπὼν ὅτι ersetzt und damit die Leidensankündigung angefügt. Ebenso wie Mt spricht er von der Auferstehung τῇ τρίτῃ ἡμέρᾳ (V. 22), (nur D [Mcion] haben die Formel μετ᾽ ἡμέρας τρεῖς wieder eingesetzt). In V. 23 (= Mk viii 34) hat D, nur von a und l begleitet, καὶ ἀράτω τὸν σταυρὸν αὐτοῦ fortgelassen. Diese Stelle ist offenbar nicht mehr recht verständlich gewesen. C𝕽 al it sy^s haben sich damit geholfen, daß sie hinter ,,sein Kreuz" einfügten: ,,täglich" und es damit auf die täglichen Mühen und wohl auch auf die Schikanen bezogen, denen die Christen ausgesetzt waren. D hat dieses 'täglich' an 'verleugne sich selbst' angeschlossen und damit eine Mahnung zur täglichen Selbstverleugnung hergestellt. Dagegen hat er Mk viii 38 — nur ohne die Worte ,,in diesem ehebrecherischen und sündigen Geschlecht" — übernommen, allerdings den Schluß für unser Gefühl verdorben, indem er Jesus in einer dreifachen Herrlichkeit kommen läßt bei der Parusie: in der eigenen, in der des Vaters und in der der heiligen Engel. Daß D a e l sy^c Or nur ἐμούς ohne λόγους lesen, ist ohne Bedeutung: das Auge eines Schreibers kann leicht von der ersten Endung zur zweiten übergehen. In V. 27 (= Mk ix I) hat D τὴν βασιλείαν τοῦ θεοῦ ersetzt durch τὸν υἱὸν τοῦ ἀνθρώπου ἐρχόμενον ἐν τῇ δόξῃ αὐτοῦ. Hier läßt sich der Einfluß des Mt-Textes spüren.

Aber wichtiger als alle diese Änderungen ist, daß Lk. den Einspruch des Petrus gegen Jesu Leidensankündigung und die scharfe Zurückweisung, die er durch Jesus erfährt, fortgelassen hat [1]). Ver-

---

[1]) Vielleicht hat die Mk.-Tradition mit dem scharfen Tadel des Petrus durch Jesus dazu beigetragen, daß eine andere aufkam, die eine Seligpreisung des Jüngers durch Jesus enthielt. Lk. hat diese zweite offensichtlich noch

mutlich hat er diesen Zug der Geschichte — einen so harten Tadel
soll sich Petrus unmittelbar nach seinem Bekenntnis zugezogen
haben? — für unwahrscheinlich und unerbaulich gehalten.

Auf den ersten Blick gehen der Mt.- und der Lk.-Text in diesem
Punkte weit auseinander. Aber Mt. hat mit der vorweggenommenen
Seligpreisung des Petrus den folgenden Tadel entschärft, während
Lk. — dem wohl ein Mt. xvi 17-19 entsprechender Text nicht zur
Verfügung stand — den anstößigen Passus einfach gestrichen hat.

IV. Das Johannesevangelium

Das 4. Evangelinm bietet keine genaue Entsprechung zu Mk viii
27-ix 1. Dennoch haben gewisse Teile dieses Abschnitts Ebenbilder
bei Joh.

Alle drei Synoptiker bringen am Schluß dieser Perikope die
Worte: ,,die den Tod nicht schmecken werden'' [1]); Joh schreibt
viii 52: ,,Wenn jemand mein Wort bewahrt, wird er den Tod nicht
schmecken in Ewigkeit''. Mk viii 35 mit seinen Parallelen in Mt xvi
25 und Lk ix 24 und die Q-Fassung Mt x 39; Lk xvii 33 kehren
— freilich in johanneischer Sprache! — in Joh xii 25 wieder: ,,Wer
sein Leben liebt (ὁ φιλῶν), verliert es, und wer sein Leben in
dieser Welt haßt, bewahrt es zum ewigen Leben''.

Die wichtigste Berührung mit unserer Perikope aber findet sich
in der johanneischen Form des Petrusbekenntnisses in Joh. vi 66-71.
Als Jesus nach der ,,harten Rede'' in der Synagoge von Kapernaum
von vielen seiner Jünger verlassen wird, fragt er die Zwölf: ,,Wollt
ihr etwa auch gehen?'' Darauf antwortet 'Simon Petrus' — auch
er ist hier der Sprecher der Jünger, an die sich Jesus in seiner Antwort wenden wird —: ,,Herr, zu wem sollen wir gehen? Du hast
Worte des ewigen Lebens. Und wir haben geglaubt und erkannt,
daß du der Heilige Gottes bist.'' Auch hier kann man sagen, daß
Jesu Frage das Bekenntnis der Jünger 'provoziert', das freilich
nicht den Christustitel enthält [2]). Jesus antwortet ihnen, den

---

nicht gekannt. RENGSTORF 120f. hat in seinem für einen weiteren Leserkreis
bestimmten Werk die Frage nicht behandelt, warum Lk den Tadel des
Petrus verschweigt.

[1]) In Spruch 1 des Thomasevangeliums (80, 12-14) klingt wohl Joh. viii
51 nach: ,,Wer die Bedeutung dieser Worte findet, wird den Tod nicht
schmecken''. Spr. 85 (95, 33 f.): ,,Wäre er'' (Adam) ,,würdig geworden,
<hätte er> den Tod nicht <geschmeckt>.''

[2]) BULTMANN, *Das Evangelium des Johannes*, Göttingen 1941, 343 A. 6.
vergleicht das johanneische Petrusbekenntnis mit dem synoptischen: ,,Die

Jüngern: ,,Habe ich nicht euch zwölf auserwählt? Und von euch ist einer ein Teufel". Erklärend fügt der Evangelist hinzu, damit sei Judas Σίμωνος 'Ισκαριώτου gemeint gewesen. In dieser Überlieferung wird wie bei Mk kurz nach dem Jüngerbekenntnis einer als Teufel bezeichnet. Aber es ist nicht mehr Petrus, sondern der Verräter Judas [1]).

V. Das Petrusbild der vier Evangelisten in dieser Perikope

Es lohnt sich, nach dem Petrusbild in dieser Perikope bei den vier Evangelisten zu fragen. Bei Mk. spielt Petrus in diesem Ab-

---

Motive der johanneischen Fassung sind dort" (bei den Synoptikern) ,,wohl vorgebildet: das Bekenntnis ist die Antwort auf Jesu Frage; es wird gegen das abgehoben, was die ,Leute' sagen. Aber erst bei Johannes treten diese Motive deutlich heraus, weil das Bekenntnis aus einer bestimmten Situation erwächst und das Ärgernis überwindet." Allerdings ist nach BULTMANN Joh. 345 der Sinn dieser johanneischen Verse ,,der, zu zeigen, daß selbst für denjenigen, der aus dem Kreis der Ungläubigen in den Kreis der μαθηταί vordrang, und der auch das Ärgernis überwand, das diesen Kreis bis auf Zwölf verkleinerte, keine Sicherheit gegeben."

Dazu zwei Bedenken. 1. Es ist immer unwahrscheinlicher geworden, daß Joh. die Synoptiker oder auch nur einen von ihnen benutzt und gekannt hat. P. GARDNER-SMITH, St. John and the Synoptic Gospels, Cambridge 1938, 36, gibt für die Unabhängigkeit des Joh. in dieser Episode folgende Gründe an: ,,. . . to say that these verses represent ,a rewriting of the Marcan account' is to go far beyond the evidence. The only real point of contact is the belief that Peter understood the Lord's Person best, and that was probably the conviction of the early Church. Again, although the phrase ,the Holy One of God' is Marcan, Mark puts it into the mouth of a demoniac, a fact which would not comment it to the Fourth Evangelist. Lastly, the reference to Judas at the end of the discourse may be significant in view of the synoptic references to Judas at the Last Supper. But at the most it indicates that John had the current accounts of the Last Supper at the back of his mind when he composed this discourse, it does not prove literary dependence on any one of our Gospels. It may be, and probably is, quite accidental."

2. Joh. kennt die von BULTMANN hier vorausgesetzte Lehre von der Entscheidung nicht. Jesus ist es, der die Zwölf ,erwählt' hat; es ist keiner ,,in den Kreis der Zwölf vorgedrungen". Daß auch der Verräter — als zukünftiger Verräter — in den Augen des Joh. miterwählt worden ist, kann man kaum leugnen: Judas ging verloren als der υἱὸς τῆς ἀπωλείας, ,,damit die Schrift erfüllt werde" (Joh. xvii 12). Joh. liegt nichts an einer existentialen Anthropologie, sondern an der Christologie und der Lehre von dem Gott, der alles nach seinem Willen lenkt und vor dem die Herzen der Menschen sind wie Wasserbäche.

[1]) Manche Personen gewinnen im Lauf der Evangelientradition einen bestimmten Charakter, der ihnen alle ihnen entsprechenden Züge zuführt. Vgl. für Judas die Entwicklung der Salbungsgeschichte bei Mk. xiv 6, bei Mt. xxvi 8 und endlich bei Joh. xii 4-6..

schnitt eine verhältnismäßig geringe Rolle. Er ist der Sprecher des Zwölferkreises. Als solcher bekennt er Jesus als den Christus. Aber im Vordergrund steht der dem Leiden entgegengehende Jesus (der darum den vor dem Leiden des Herrn zurückschreckenden Petrus hart anfahren muß) ¹) und die Gemeinde, die ebenfalls dem Leiden nicht ausweichen darf, wenn sie durch das Bekenntnis zu Jesus mit in das Todesleiden gerissen wird.

Die Bearbeitung durch Lukas wirkt am flachsten: er macht aus

---

¹) Von einem gegen Jesus aufbegehrenden jüdischen Messiasglauben sagt Mk nichts, und die frühesten Kommentare — Mt xvi 22: ἵλεώς σοι, κύριε· οὐ μὴ ἔσται σοι τοῦτο (,,Davor wolle dich Gott bewahren! Das möge dir nicht widerfahren!''), und syˢ: ὁ δὲ Σίμων Πέτρος ὡς φειδόμενος αὐτοῦ εἶπεν αὐτῷ — zeigen, welches Motiv man hinter dem ἐπιτιμᾶν (,,ernstlich zureden'') des Petrus fand: Mitleid. Er wollte Jesus schonen und ihm das Leiden ersparen. Wenn Jesus den ihm von Gott gegebenen Auftrag darin gefunden haben sollte, das über den Gottesknecht und über den Menschensohn in der Schrift Gesagte vereinend zu verwirklichen, so war nicht zu erwarten, daß die Jünger ganz für sich zum selben Ergebnis gekommen waren. D.h. aber: Falls man die Szene als einen historisch zutreffenden Bericht nimmt, bleibt es unbegreiflich, daß Jesus den Petrus und die andern Jünger nicht belehrt hat, sondern mit einer — bei Mt noch etwas erläuternd erweiterten — harten Ablehnung beantwortet, die für die Jünger nichts klären konnte.
Man kann freilich einwenden: ein den Petrus so schwer belastendes Jesuswort könne die Gemeinde nicht selbst gebildet haben; hier liege älteste Tradition vor, da außer Petrus niemand Jesu Wort gehört habe (HIRSCH 91). Aber diese Behauptung ist durch den Text nicht gedeckt. So wird man sich besser helfen, wenn man im Mk.-Text nicht gleichsam einen Dokumentarfilm der Szene sieht, sondern höchstens das Ereignis und sein Ergebnis auf das knappste Maß zusammengepreßt denkt, wie sie in der Erinnerung und dem Verständnis der Gemeinde weiter lebten. Dann ist man aber nicht mehr so weit von der Vermutung entfernt, daß Mk. hier eine Gemeindetradition weitergibt, der es entscheidend um zweierlei ging: 1. um den Anstoß, daß Jesus am Galgen sterben mußte, 2. um den weiteren Anstoß, daß die Christen ebenfalls zur Hingabe des Lebens bereit sein müssen.
HIRSCH 91 streicht ἀλλὰ τὰ τῶν ἀνθρώπων, weil nicht ,menschlich', sondern nur 'satanisch' das Gegenwort zu 'göttlich' sein könne. Aber der Versucher (σατανᾶς, σκάνδαλον) packt — so sehen Mk und Mt die Lage — den Menschen gerade bei ihrer Schwäche (τὰ τῶν ἀνθρώπων): sie wollen sich das Leid ersparen. Die Lehre Jesu in V. 24-27 über das notwendige Leiden der Jünger erklärt nicht im mindesten, warum Jesus selbst leiden muß, sondern ist ein Gebot, das im Grunde jenes von Gott gewollte Leiden Jesu (δεῖ) diskussionslos voraussetzt.
Die Versuche, schon in der Zeit Jesu eine Lehre vom leidenden Messias zu finden, sind — abgesehen von der Fragwürdigkeit der Belege — im Grunde ein Bumerang: war diese Lehre schon im Judentum bekannt und verbreitet, dann wurde der Widerspruch der Jünger gegen Jesu Leiden vollends unverständlich. Im übrigens sollte man nicht immer die heutige Gelehrsamkeit und ihre Ergebnisse schon bei den im NT handelnden Personen voraussetzen. Vgl. jetzt auch M. RESE, ZThK 60, 1963, 21-41.

der Bereitschaft zum Martyrium das willige Tragen der Lasten, die
der Alltag bringt, und läßt die ganze Szene, die den Petrus belastet,
fort.

Matthäus hat durch die Aufnahme von V 17-19 eine Art Gegen-
gewicht zu dem Tadel geschaffen, der Petrus so bald darauf trifft.
Daß er jetzt Offenbarungsempfänger und im nächsten Augenblick
‚Satan' sein kann, zeigt, wie ungesichert auch der Christ lebt, und
wie ganz er auf Gott angewiesen ist.

Johannes unterscheidet sich von den Synoptikern darin, daß er
das ewige Leben in Jesu Wort geschenkt sieht. Aber das hindert
nicht, daß einer von den zwölf Auserwählten, die alle Jesu Wort
hören, ein διάβολος ist, und zeigt die erschreckende Unbegreiflichkeit
des göttlichen Handelns.

So kann ein und dieselbe Perikope bei den vier Evangelisten in
dem Dienst sehr verschiedener Aufgaben stehen: Aufforderung zum
Martyrium (Mk.), geduldiges Ertragen des alltäglichen Kreuzes
(Lk), den Umschlag vom Offenbarungsempfänger zum ‚Satan'
(Mt.), — doch nicht sichernde — Hören des göttlichen Wortes
aus Jesu Mund als der Zugang zum ewigen Leben (Joh.).

THE COMPOSITION OF MARK ix 1

BY

NORMAN PERRIN

Chicago

ERNST HAENCHEN's brilliant essay "Die Komposition von Mk viii 27-ix 1" in this Journal (Vol. VI [1963], 81-109) raises afresh the question of the origin of Mark ix 1. HAENCHEN himself hints that he would regard it as a Markan composition, but does not go into the question of its origin in any detail.

There have been a number of different viewpoints expressed recently in connection with the saying. W. G. KÜMMEL has argued that it is an authentic saying of Jesus [1]), A. VÖGTLE sees it as having been formed in the pre-Markan tradition from a genuine saying of Jesus referring to the destruction of the Temple, now found at Mark xiii 30 [2]), and a number of scholars regard it as a prophetic *Trostwort* in the face of the delay of the Parousia [3]). The present writer previously regarded it as an authentic *Jesus-wort* [4]) but further research has led him to a change of view.

A study of the pericope Mark viii 27-ix 1, under the tutelage of the *Haenchen* article, helps us to see that ix 1 serves a clear and definite purpose in terms of the pericope as a whole. The church for which Mark is writing has been warned that, as the way of the Master led to the cross, so may that of the disciple. Specifically, the church faces the threat of persecution, and the individual member must be prepared for the very real possibility of martyrdom.

---

[1]) W. G. KÜMMEL, *Heilsgeschehen und Geschichte* (Marburg: N. G. Elwert, 1965), pp. 464 f. (= *Zeit und Geschichte. Dankesgabe an Rufold Bultmann zum 80. Geburtstag*, pp. 39 ff.).

[2]) A. VÖGTLE, "Exegetisches Erwägungen über das Wissen und Selbstbewusstsein Jesu", *Gott in Welt. Festgabe für Karl Rahner*, ed. J. B. METZ et al. Freiburg: Herder, 1964), I, 608-667, esp. 642-647.

[3]) Most important, perhaps, G. BORNKAMM, "Die Verzögerung der Parusie", *In Memoriam Ernst Lohmeyer*, ed. W. SCHMAUCH (Stuttgart: Evangelisches Verlagswerk, 1951), pp. 116-126, esp. 116-119. Other recent representatives of this view are given by W. G. KÜMMEL, *op. cit.*, n. 51.

[4]) N. PERRIN, *The Kingdom of God in the Teaching of Jesus* (London: S. C. M. Press and Philadelphia: Westminster Press, 1963), pp. 137 ff.

Those who may become apostate in that hour are warned of the consequence of this (viii 38), and those who hold fast are assured that they have only to endure, their reward will be near (ix 1). So the two sayings form a climactic antithesis of warning and promise which brings the pericope to its close. The question we have to answer is whether Mark has adapted sayings from the tradition to serve his purpose here, or whether he has created the sayings himself. We shall restrict ourselves to a discussion of the question in connection with the second saying [1]).

A careful scrutiny of Mark ix 1 reveals that it has three distinct features which call for explanation: it has some Markan characteristics, it is related in form to Mark xiii 30, and it is related in content to Mark viii 38. Its Markan characteristics are the reference to "seeing" the Parousia, which is a feature of Mark (ix 1; xiii 26; xiv 62) [2]) and the use of "power" and "glory" in this connection (viii 38; ix 1; x 37; xiii 26) [3]). It is related to Mark xiii 30 in form: both begin with the solemn asseveration ἀμὴν λέγω ὑμῖν, continue with a ὅτι clause containing the promise and use the same emphatic form of negation (οὐ μή + subjunctive). It parallels Mark viii 38 in that it concludes with a reference to the eschaton "coming".

The feature with which we begin our investigation is the relationship in form to xiii 30. This seems too close to be accidental and, since exactly the same apocalyptic promise is contained in each saying, the two must be held to be variants of one another. But xiii 30 belongs to its present context very closely; the "these things" clearly refers to the whole sequence of signs, portents and events with which the apocalyptic discourse, xiii 5-27, is concerned, and the saying itself finally answers the question of the disciples which provides the narrative setting for the discourse, xiii 3f. Moreover, it is entirely characteristic of apocalyptic in general

---

[1]) We may be permitted to say that we would regard viii 38 as a Markan adaptation of a saying like that now found in Luke xii 8 f.

[2]) Matthew follows Mark on each occasion. Luke transforms the first into a non-parousia reference and omits the "seeing" in the third (Luke xxii 69). Matthew nowhere has the verb in connection with the parousia except in dependence on Mark, nor has Luke.

[3]) There is no such use in Luke independent of Mark and only one in Matthew. Matt. xxv 31 begins the parable of the sheep and the goats: "When the Son of man comes in his glory, and all the angels with him, then he will sit on his glorious throne". In view of Matt. xix 28 (". . . in the new world, when the Son of man shall sit on his glorious throne" [no parallels].) this looks like a combination of Matthaean and Markan characteristics.

and the use of μέχρι for "until" is non-Markan. It may therefore be held that the saying was composed to bring to an end the pre-Markan apocalyptic discourse, which probably once had a form xiii 3-27, 30. The ἀμὴν λέγω ὑμῖν is almost certainly a characteristic of Jesus' way of speaking [1]), but its presence here is most probably a mark of early Christian prophecy, perhaps in imitation of the dominical style which had established itself in the tradition. The suggestion that the saying was originally a genuine saying of Jesus which originally referred to the destruction of the Temple and the fall of Jerusalem, and which has been adapted to serve its present purpose in the apocalyptic discourse [2]), is probably to be rejected. We have absolutely no evidence that the saying ever existed in any form other than that which it now has, and its present form fits its function as ending the discourse so perfectly that it seems likely that it was composed for this purpose. Furthermore, there is no single dominical feature about the saying except the solemn introduction, which could be, as we have suggested it may be, prophetic imitation of a dominical style. In a case such as this, where an early Christian prophet is certainly offering to his church an apocalyptic discourse in the name of the risen Lord, the imitation of the dominical style would be perfectly natural.

IX I, on the other hand, has the distinctively Markan characteristics to which we called attention above, and it also has ἕως for "until," the usual Markan word. This would seem to indicate that it is a Markan variant of the apocalyptic saying now at xiii 30. Further, the "This generation will not pass away" has become "some standing here will not taste death", a phrase reminiscent of a commonplace of Jewish apocalyptic (cf. IV Ezra vi 25f.). This is a change readily explicable on the basis of the function of the saying in the pericope viii 27-ix I, i.e., as a promise to a limited and specific group of people, those members of the church who will remain stedfast under the threat of persecution. These considerations would seem to indicate that ix I is a Markan product, modelled on the saying ending the apocalyptic discourse which Mark knew and was to use later.

The remainder of the saying can readily be accounted for on the

---

[1]) J. Jeremias, "Kennzeichen der ipsissima vox Jesu", *Synoptische Studien* (Wikenhauser Festschrift [München: Karl Zink, 1953]), pp. 86-93.
[2]) V. Taylor, *Gospel According to St. Mark* (London: Macmillan, 1952), p. 521, followed by A. Vögtle, *op. cit.*, p. 647.

hypothesis that Mark has produced it to serve its present function in the pericope. The use of "Kingdom of God" to describe the eschaton as promise is paralleled in Mark i 15, which itself is a Markan editorial summary of the message of Jesus [1]). The verb "to come" connected with it is explicable as a deliberate echo of that same verb in viii 38, if, as we are suggesting, ix 1 was composed as the promise antithetical to the warning in that saying. Moreover, on this basis we can account for the otherwise difficult ἐληλυθυῖαν. It will be remembered that C. H. DODD wanted to translate this to give the meaning that the hearers of Jesus afterwards came to recognize that the Kingdom had in fact come in the ministry of Jesus [2]). The subsequent discussion, however, tended to establish the fact that the reference could only be to a future event in which the people would become aware of something that had just happened, not that had long existed [3]). Such a reference matches perfectly the function of the saying in the Markan pericope, indeed, as a deliberate contrast to the aorist of viii 38 the perfect of ix 1 becomes very effective.

We suggest, therefore, that Mark ix 1 is a saying produced by Mark on the model of xiii 30 as the promise antithetical to the warning contained in viii 38, rather than a Markan adaptation of a genuine saying of Jesus or a *Trostwort* from early Christian prophecy.

---

[1]) N. PERRIN, *op. cit.*, pp. 200 f.
[2]) C. H. DODD, *Parables of the Kingdom* (London: Nisbet & Co., 1936), p. 54.
[3]) N. PERRIN, *op. cit.*, p. 67, with references.

THE PROPER METHODOLOGY FOR ASCERTAINING A MARKAN REDACTION HISTORY

BY

Dr. ROBERT H. STEIN

St. Paul Minnesota

During the past two decades two new emphases have dominated the investigation of the gospel materials. One of these is the "new" quest of the historical Jesus. Receiving its initial impetus from the now famous lecture of KÄSEMANN [1]), investigators have sought to establish some sort of continuity between the historical Jesus and the Christ of the kerygma. In so doing the "new" quest hopes that it possesses certain bulwarks [2]) which will protect it from the errors of the nineteenth century quests. The second new emphasis in gospel studies is the "redaktionsgeschichtlich" [3]) investigation of the gospels. Whereas form criticism generally thought of the Evangelists as collectors and scissors and paste men, BORNKAMM [4]), CONZELMANN [5]), and MARXSEN [6]) demonstrated that they were more than this. Each Evangelist was a theologian in his own right and possessed a theological purpose for writing his gospel. As a result there has been much investigation of the particular theologies of Matthew, Mark, and Luke. Although there has been a great deal of "redaktionsgeschichtlich" investigation, the question of methodology has frequently been glossed over. Yet a proper methodology is necessary. This is especially true with regard to "redaktionsgeschichtlich" investigation of Mark. The purpose of this article is to list some of the means by which we can ascertain a Markan redaction history.

It is evident from the start that the investigation of a Markan

---

[1]) "The Problem of the Historical Jesus," *Essays on New Testament Themes.*
[2]) See JOACHIM JEREMIAS, *The Problem of the Historical Jesus,* pp. 15 f.
[3]) See the author's article, "What is Redaktionsgeschichte?", *JBL,* 88 (1969), pp. 45-56, for a definition of this term.
[4]) BORNKAMM's work is contained in *Tradition and Interpretation in Matthew* which he co-authored with G. BARTH and H. J. HELD.
[5]) *The Theology of St. Luke.*
[6]) *Mark the Evangelist.*

redaction history is much more difficult than the investigation of a Matthean or Lukan one [1]). The reason for this is twofold. First of all Mark nowhere expressly states his purpose for writing his gospel [2]). Secondly, we do not possess any of the sources which Mark used, whereas for Matthew and Luke we possess Mark, their main source [3]), and we can construct, to a certain extent, the "Q" source which they used. In the case of Mark, however, we lack any such source which will serve as a standard for comparison. Yet such a standard is necessary. We must be able to ascertain what the sources of Mark were like or else our ability to ascertain a Markan redaction history will be severely limited, for before we proceed to the latter investigation, we must ascertain the Markan redaction and this can only be done by comparing Mark with the sources he used. How then are we to determine what the sources which were available to Mark were like? If we could go back in time and look over the shoulder of the Evangelist to see what his sources were like (let us assume for the sake of our illustration that the sources of Mark were all written), our task would be considerably easier. Unfortunately no such possibility exists. Nevertheless it is possible, although difficult, by means of form-critical investigation to re-construct to a certain extent the pre-Markan tradition. Having done this, we then can see how Mark joined, arranged, modified, selected, etc. the traditions available to him. Mark has made our task more complicated, however, because he has "markanized" the traditions, both oral and written, which were available to him. He has done this by retelling the traditions in his own words and in his own style. This is unfortunate because it makes the separation of the Markan redaction from the pre-Markan tradition all the more difficult.

The primary purpose of this article is to list the various ways in which Mark has edited the materials available to him. By the investigation of this editorial redaction we can then ascertain a Markan redaction history. We cannot, of course, describe in detail the various areas of redaction, so that we shall have to content ourselves with simply listing them. Up to the present time this has not been done, and it is a pressing need [4]).

---

[1]) This was clearly seen and stated already in 1908 by FIRMIN NICOLARDOT in his *Les procédés de rédaction des trois premiers évangélistes*, p. 215.

[2]) Contrast Luke i 1-4 and John xx 31.

[3]) The present writer believes that Matthew and Luke used a copy of Mark very much like the one we possess.

[4]) GEORG STRECKER in his article, "The Passion- and Resurrection

A. *The Markan Seams*

One of the means most often used to ascertain a Markan redaction history is the investigation of the Markan seams [1]). It was because the region of Galilee was so frequently mentioned in the Markan seams that LOHMEYER [2]), R. H. LIGHTFOOT [3]), and MARXSEN [4]) argued for a unique Galilean emphasis and stress on the part of Mark. BEST [5]) in his work argued from the frequency with which the terms διδάσκαλος, διδαχή, and διδάσκειν appear in the Markan seams that the evangelist desired to portray Jesus as a teacher rather than as an exorcist. The importance of the seams for ascertaining a Markan redaction history has been recognized by almost all of the scholars interested in the investigation of the "third" *Sitz im Leben* of Mark [6]). The reason for this is that apart from certain pre-Markan complexes [7]) the material used by Mark existed as isolated pericopes. Although these pericopes must have had introductions of some sort, they did not possess seams uniting them to one another. In order to join these pericopes together Mark had either to create the seams we find in his gospel or rework the original introductions which introduced the isolated pericopes. There may have been occasions when the introductions to the isolated pericopes would have served as seams, but frequently this would not have been so.

One means then by which we can ascertain a Markan redaction history is by the investigation of how Mark joined together the various materials available to him. The cement he used to bind

---

Predictions in Mark's Gospel," *Interp.*, 22 (1968), p. 423 n. 5, states, "The methodological problem of redaction criticism has not yet been worked [for Mark] in a clear presentation and remains a matter of urgent importance."

[1]) MARXSEN, p. 23, writes, "We grasp Mark's share of the work and thus his actual achievement (as well as that of the other evangelists) not in the material primarily but in the 'framework'." Cf. also ERNEST BEST, *The Temptation and the Passion*, p. 63, "The most obvious place to look for Mark's hand is in the words, phrases, sentences which join together the various incidents of the Gospel."

[2]) *Galiläa und Jerusalem*, p. 26.

[3]) *Locality and Doctrine in the Gospels*, p. 112.

[4]) MARXSEN, *op. cit.*, pp. 54 f.

[5]) BEST, *op. cit.*, pp. 71-2.

[6]) See EDUARD SCHWEIZER, *Das Evangelim nach Markus*, pp. 4-5; S.E. JOHNSON. *The Theology of the Gospels*, p. 21; WALTER GRUNDMANN, *Die Geschichte Jesu Christi*, p. 15; KLAUS KOCH. *The Growth of the Biblical Tradition*, p. 59; etc.

[7]) We mean here "pre-Mark's Gospel" complexes. It may be that Mark himself was the author of certain of these complexes.

these materials together reveals something of his own particular theological emphasis. Since we now recognize that the Evangelists were not scissors and paste men but theologians, it is obvious that the investigation of the way the Evangelists cemented together the various isolated materials available to them must reveal something of their unique theological interests [1]).

B. *The Markan Insertions*

Another means by which we can ascertain a Markan redaction history is by the investigation of the Markan insertions or "Zwischenbemerkungen". Two insertions that have frequently been discussed in this regard are Mark xiv 28 and xvi 7. LOHMEYER [2]) has argued that these two insertions by Mark refer to the parousia rather than the resurrection, and MARXSEN [3]) has argued from them that Mark wrote his gospel to urge his readers to flee to Galilee in order to await the imminent parousia. Other scholars have also recognized the importance of investigating the Markan insertions [4]). It is quite evident that when the Evangelist inserts a statement into some tradition he does so in order to comment upon or explain that tradition to his reader. The investigation of this comment will therefore reveal something of the Evangelist's particular theology, for the Evangelist evidently thought that he needed to explain the tradition to his readers, and this explanation will frequently reveal his own theological interests and emphases.

C. *The Markan Summaries*

In the Gospel of Mark there frequently appear statements which summarize Jesus' activity, message, or fame. These summaries are extremely important for the investigation of a Markan redaction history. Various scholars have pointed out the importance of the summaries for the "redaktionsgeschichtlich" investigation of Mark [5]). It is almost certain that the summaries found in Mark did

---

[1]) For a discussion of the various means for ascertaining a Markan seam, see the author's article, "The 'Redaktionsgeschichtlich' Investigation of a Markan Seam," *ZNW*, 61 (1970), pp. 70-94.

[2]) LOHMEYER, *op. cit.*

[3]) MARXSEN, *op. cit.*, pp. 75 f.

[4]) See BEST, *op. cit.*, p. ix; SCHWEIZER, *op. cit.*, p. 5; KURT FRÖR, *Wege zur Schriftauslegung*, p. 254; etc.

[5]) See BEST, *op. cit.*, p. 64; SCHWEIZER, *op. cit.*, p. 5; WILLI MARXSEN, "Redaktionsgeschichtliche Erklärung der sogenannten Parabeltheorie des Markus," *ZTK*, 52 (1955), p. 258; etc.

not circulate independently during the oral period. This is especially
true with regard to such brief summaries as Mark i 28, 39; ii 13;
and vi 6 b. Since these summaries are not part of a pericope, for they
are seldom essential to any pericope, their brevity makes their
independent existence highly questionable. Most probably therefore
they were composed by the Evangelist.

It has been argued that these summaries often contain traditional
material. This is certainly true with regard to the larger summaries
such as Mark i 14-15; iii 7-12; vi 53-56; ix 30-32; and x 32-34. Yet,
even if these summaries contain traditional material, they are still
helpful for our investigation because Mark had to compose them.
In other words, in these summaries Mark did not simply write down
a traditional pericope. He personally composed these summaries
and selected the particular material that he wanted to insert into
them. The summaries are therefore especially important for our
investigation because even if they contain traditional material Mark
had to create or compose them. They did not exist before him. He
has selected, according to his own particular interests, those pieces
of tradition that were important to him. His selection of material
here is far more important than his selection of the individual
pericopes that he wished to include in his gospel, because the latter
did not require an amount of creative activity comparable to the
creation of the various summaries out of diverse traditional material.

D. *The Markan Creation of Pericopes*

It has already become evident that certain parts of the Gospel
of Mark are due to the creative activity of the Evangelist. This has
been apparent in our discussion of the Markan seams, insertions,
and summaries. If we could demonstrate that Mark created certain
pericopes, this would be extremely helpful in ascertaining a Markan
redaction history [1]. The question that faces us, however, is not
whether Mark created certain pericopes appearing in his gospel
(perhaps he did and perhaps he did not) but whether we are able to
demonstrate that such and such a pericope was in fact the creation
of Mark. This is the rub! If we seek to prove that Mark created a
certain pericope, we are faced with five possibilities: (1) It was

---

[1] PAUL WINTER in his article, "Markus xiv 53 b, 55-64 — Ein Gebilde des
Evangelisten," *ZNW*, 53 (1962), pp. 260-66, seeks to do just this. He states
on p. 263, "Kein Traditionselement, auch kein sekundäres, sondern schrift-
stellerische Absicht liegt der Erzählung in Mc. xiv 53 b, 55-64 zugrunde."

historically true; (2) It has an historical basis but was reworked by Mark; (3) It was created by the community; (4) it was created by the community and reworked by Mark; and (5) It was created by Mark. Historical criticism may be able to separate the first possibility from the remaining four, but the separation of the fifth possibility from the third, and especially the second and fourth possibilities is extremely difficult and probably impossible. It seems best therefore to look elsewhere than in the creation of various pericopes by the Evangelist for a means for ascertaining a Markan redaction history.

E. *The Markan Modification of the Material*

Another means by which we can ascertain a Markan redaction history is by observing how the Evangelist modified the traditions he received. We have already referred to the modification of certain traditions by the creation or reworking of certain seams, insertions and summaries. Here we are not concerned with the modification of the tradition in these areas. We are concerned rather with the changes made by the Evangelist to the pericopes and sayings he received in order that he might stress his own particular point of view. We would distinguish between a Markan insertion and a Markan modification of the material. The former refers to an additional statement which the Evangelist has inserted into the material, whereas the latter refers to the changing of the audience, the situation, certain words, etc. in the tradition in order to make the tradition say what he wanted it to.

The great difficulty facing us is that we must first ascertain the pre-Markan tradition, so that by comparing it with Mark we can determine the Markan redaction. Thereupon we can investigate the redaction in order to ascertain the redaction history of the Evangelist. The difficulty of ascertaining the pre-Markan tradition is not to be minimized. The "markanizing" of the pericopes by the Evangelist makes our task more difficult because some of our guides such as the vocabulary and style are not absolute but only relative, i.e. a Markan vocabulary and style here as well as in the investigation of the seams, insertions, and summaries does not assure us of a Markan redaction but only of the possibility of such a redaction [1]).

---

[1]) JAN LAMBRECHT in his *Die Redaktion der Markus-Apokalypse*, p. 89, rightly comments, "Die gleiche Ansicht wird mit Recht ferner vorbringen, dass das *Markinische* eines Textes nicht ipso facto auf eine 'creatio' oder auf eine 'unhistorische Wiedergabe' schliessen lässt. Es ist doch (noch einmal!)

The situation is not entirely hopeless, however, because several additional means of detecting the Markan modification of the tradition are available. These are:

1. *The Comparison of Mark with Matthew and Luke*

A frequent method used to ascertain the Markan modification of the tradition is to compare Mark with the other Synoptic Gospels [1]). By such a comparison it is hoped that we can ascertain the pre-Markan tradition. This is a difficult procedure because in general the changes made by Matthew and Luke to their Markan source reveal primarily a Matthean and Lukan redaction history and not a Markan one [2]). There are times, however, when an agreement between Matthew and Luke against Mark may point to an older form of the tradition than contained in Mark. It may be in such an instance that Mark has modified the tradition which he received and that Matthew and Luke agree against Mark because they both reject the Markan modification in favor of the pre-Markan tradition with which they were both familiar. An example of this may be Mark xiv 62 and parallels. A difficulty presents itself here, however. Could it be that the tradition Mark used already contained this "modification" whereas the tradition with which both Matthew and Luke were familiar did not ? If this is the case, we are dealing with different forms of the tradition and not a Markan redaction history [3]).

---

normal und natürlich, das bei der Niederlegung des Traditionsgutes Markus spontan seinen Eigenen Stil schreibt! Es kann ohne weiteres zugegeben werden, dass die oft hervorgehobene markinische Wortwahl und seine Stileigenheit allein diese Frage nicht entscheiden können".

[1]) JOHANNES SCHREIBER in his article, "Die Christologie des Markusevangeliums," *ZTK*, 58 (1961), p. 154, states, "Wo Matthäus oder Lukas oder gar beide Evangelisten den Markustext in einem bestimmten Punkt, womöglich über das ganze Evangelium hin, ändern, liegt sehr wahrscheinlich eine theologische Aussage des Markus vor, die sie ablehnen. Dieser Grundsatz gilt besonders dann, wenn festgestellt werden kann, dass ihre eigene Theologie der des Markus in diesen Punkt widerspricht." Cf. also MARXSEN, *Mark the Evangelist*, p. 124, who states with regard to his investigation of the term εὐαγγέλιον, "If we can establish that the synoptic material as a whole is not aware of the term εὐαγγέλιον (except for passages where Mark gives it or which are dependent on Mark), that at least indicates that the evangelist quite probably introduced the term into the tradition."

[2]) Because of this SCHREIBER (see above n. 1) is not entirely correct. When the particular theological viewpoints of Matthew and Luke clash with Mark, their change of Mark reveals not so much a Markan redaction history as a Matthean and Lukan one.

[3]) The greatest single weakness of LOHMEYER's work is that he did not sufficiently distinguish between the Galilean tradition allegedly used by

It is not necessary to limit our investigation of the Markan modifications to the Matthew-Luke agreements against Mark. There are times when an Evangelist apparently changes Mark because he was familiar with a tradition that is more primitive than the tradition found in Mark [1]). In such an instance he may witness to a pre-Markan tradition and thus reveal the Markan redaction. The account of the wicked husbandmen in Luke (and the Gospel of Thomas) is seen by Jeremias [2]) as being more primitive than the account in Mark xii 1-11. If this is true, the difference between the account in Mark and the account in Luke may be due to the "redaktionsgeschichtlich" interests of the Evangelist [3]).

It would appear therefore that the comparison of Matthew and Luke with Mark is a valid method by which we can ascertain the Markan modification of the tradition. We must, however, keep uppermost in our minds the following considerations: (1) The changes of the Markan account by Matthew and Luke witness primarily to a Matthean and Lukan redaction history rather than a Markan one; (2) The changes made by Matthew and Luke may witness to their favoring a different tradition rather than the tradition Mark used and, if this is true, we are dealing primarily with form-critical problems and not "redaktionsgeschichtlich" ones and (3) The alleged modification should possess a typically Markan vocabulary, style, and theme and should be in agreement with the general Markan scheme.

Mark and the evangelist's own particular emphasis. Because of this we must conclude that although LOHMEYER at times alluded to the "redaktionsgeschichtlich" interests of the evangelist he was primarily concerned with the second *Sitz im Leben* or the form-critical investigation of the tradition. (See MARXSEN, *op. cit.*, p. 28 n. 38.) It could, of course, be argued that if Mark possessed a Galilean tradition and a Jerusalem tradition and chose the one over the other that this would reveal his own theological emphasis. (This LOHMEYER in fact did. See LOHMEYER, *op. cit.*, p. 98). It would be difficult if not impossible, however, to demonstrate that an evangelist possessed both traditions and chose one over the other.

[1]) JOACHIM JEREMIAS, *The Parables of Jesus*, (1963), pp. 70 f., even compares Mark with the Gospel of Thomas in order to arrive at the more primitive tradition.

[2]) *Ibid.*

[3]) Unfortunately JEREMIAS does not investigate the significance of the Markan redaction here, but this is not his purpose. This is a good example of how some form critics once they ascertain the evangelists' redaction set aside the redaction and investigate only the tradition.

2. The Investigation of "Misformed" Pericopes

According to form criticism there existed certain "rules" or "laws" which supervised the transmission of the gospel pericopes during the oral period. These "laws" tended to give to the oral material a particular shape and form. Divergencies from this pure form may be due to the modification of the pericopes by the Evangelist. If a pericope therefore contains material that would have been difficult to transmit during the oral period, this may be due to a Markan modification of the pericope. An example of this is Mark xi 27-33. The anacoluthon of verse 32 would have been impossible to transmit orally. It is therefore probably due to the hand of Mark. It would seem therefore that when a pericope is sufficiently "misformed," so that it would not have been able to be repeated as such during the oral period, we can legitimately claim that this pericope has undergone modification by the hand of the Evangelist.

3. The Investigation of the Inconsistency Between Mark's Account and What Actually Happened

One of the first attempts to ascertain a Markan redaction history, the attempt by WREDE, sought to do so by demonstrating an inconsistency between what Mark records and what actually happened [1]). Yet if by critical historical investigation this can actually be demonstrated, what have we in fact proven? We have demonstrated that there is an inconsistency between the first and third *Sitz im Leben* OR between the first and the second *Sitz im Leben*. Merely demonstrating an inconsistency would not, however, demonstrate that this inconsistency is due to the modification of the tradition by the Evangelist. It may very well be due to a pre-Markan modification. On the other hand such a demonstration is helpful in raising the possibility that such an inconsistency is due to the Evangelist, and if we were to discover a "consistent" inconsistency which portrays a Markan vocabulary, style, theme, etc. then the Evangelist may very well be the cause of this inconsistency [2]).

---

[1]) *Das Messiasgeheimnis in den Evangelien*, pp. 46 f. and 15.

[2]) Another method sometimes used to ascertain a Markan redaction history is to observe the way Mark used "Q". (So NICOLARDOT, *op. cit.*, pp. 215-6; WILHELM LARFIELD, *Die Neutestamentlichen Evangelien*, pp. 251 f.; BENJAMIN WISNER BACON, *The Gospel of Mark*, pp. 156 f.; FREDERICK C. GRANT, *The Gospels: Their Origin and Their Growth*, p. 87; etc.). It would appear quite certain, however, that Mark did not know "Q", (see BURNETT

F. *The Markan Selection of Material*

Another way in which the evangelist reveals his theological emphases is by means of his selection of material [1]. It must be admitted from the start that Mark need not have chosen every pericope in his gospel because it contained his particular theology or point of view. He may have included some simply because they were well known. Others stood in complexes that would have required him to excise them if he wanted to exclude them from his gospel, and Mark apparently was inclined to use these complexes as whole units, so that the pericopes in such units appear in Mark even if they do not necessarily contain his own particular point of view or even conflict with his scheme. It should not be surprising therefore if occasionally we find in Mark material contradicting somewhat his own particular emphases [2]. Nevertheless in general the selection of material made by Mark must of necessity reveal something of his own particular theological interests.

G. *The Markan Omission of Material*

If the selection of material reveals something of the Evangelist's theological emphases, we can expect that the gospel traditions which he chose to omit from his gospel will also reveal something of his particular theological emphases. There is, however, a major difficulty in the use of this means for ascertaining a Markan redaction history. Whereas we know what Mark chose to include in his gospel, we do not have any certain way of knowing what he chose to exclude. We simply do not know what sources and materials Mark possessed [3].

HILLMAN STREETER, *The Four Gospels*, pp. 186-91; PAUL FEINE, JOHANNES BEHM, and WERNER GEORG KÜMMEL, *Introduction to the New Testament*, p. 55; and BURTON H. THROCKMORTON, "Did Mark Know Q", *JBL*, 67 (1948), p. 327) so that this method is not valid.

[1] See SCHREIBER, *op. cit.*, p. 155; GRUNDMANN, *op. cit.*, p. 15; BEST, *op. cit.*, pp. 103-11; KURT FRÖR, *Biblische Hermeneutik*, p. 246; JOACHIM ROHDE *Rediscovering the Teaching of the Evangelists*, p. 14; JOHNSON, *op. cit.*, p. 21; ANTON VÖGTLE, "Was Heisst „Auslegung der Schrift"?", *Was Heisst Auslegung der Heiligen Schrift*, p. 53; FRANZ-JOSEF STEINMETZ, "Literaturbericht", *Geisteb*, 42 (1969), p. 64; etc.

[2] The position of Mark ii 19-20 seems contrary to the general scheme. According to the Markan scheme we would expect to read of this reference to Jesus' death after Mark viii 31 f. The reason that it appears "out of place" in Mark is no doubt due to the fact that it was already found in the pre-Markan complex of Mark ii 1-iii 6.

[3] BEST, *op. cit.*, p. 103, sees this problem clearly. He states, "If we knew that Mark had a great amount of material about the teaching of Jesus, say

As a result it is more difficult to ascertain a Markan redaction
history from what we do not find in the Gospel of Mark. Nevertheless this method does give some hints as to areas of the tradition
which Mark chose not to stress. An example of this is the few
exorcisms recorded in Mark. In his work, *The Problem of History
in Mark*, JAMES M. ROBINSON sought to demonstrate that Mark
desired to portray Jesus as a Victor over Satanic powers. If this
were the intention of Mark, however, we might expect to find a
greater number of exorcisms in Mark. The lack of such stories
weakens Robinson's thesis. One cannot place an inordinate amount
of weight on this argument, however, because we do not know how
many exorcism stories were available to Mark. This is, of course,
the great unknown that weakens any argument based upon the
Markan omission of material.

H. *The Markan Arrangement of the Material*

It has been recognized by many scholars that the arrangement
which Mark gave to his material is due in part to his own particular
theological emphasis [1]). The investigation of the Markan arrangement is of great importance in ascertaining a Markan redaction
history. We are not concerned here primarily with the question of
literary style but of the theological emphasis that results from the
arrangement of the material. We must be aware at the start that a
theological purpose need not lie at the root of every Markan
arrangement. At times an arrangement may be due to topical or
even geographical considerations. Furthermore to a certain extent
there existed a pre-Markan arrangement of certain material. The
extent to which this is true is debated. Certainly, however, the work

---

a 'copy' of Q and only three exorcism accounts, and chose to omit most of
the teaching and put in all three exorcisms, this would obviously lead us to
conclude that for him exorcisms were most important. Equally had he at
his disposal only the teaching of Jesus which he has inserted and a hundred
exorcism stories from which he selected the present three then we would
come to quite a different conclusion about the importance of the exorcisms
for Mark. Unfortunately we are not in a position to draw either conclusion."

[1]) See NICOLARDOT, *op. cit.*, p. 216; ROHDE, *op. cit.*, p. 14; VÖGTLE, *op.
cit.*, p. 53; T. A. BURKILL, *Mysterious Revelation*, p. 5; MARXSEN, "Redak-
tionsgeschlichtliche . . .," p. 258; SCHREIBER, *op. cit.*, p. 155; BEST, *op. cit.*,
pp. 112-33; LEANDER E. KECK, "The Introduction to Mark's Gospel," *NTS*,
12 (1966), p. 369; SCHWEIZER, *op. cit.*, p. 5; STEINMETZ, *op. cit.*, NORMAN
PERRIN, *What is Redaction Criticism?*, p. 1; and GRUNDMANN, *op. cit.*, p. 15,
who states, "Die Stellung einer Pericope im Kontext ist häufig der älteste
Kommentar, der ihr gegeben wird."

of John the Baptist, the baptism of Jesus, the call of the disciples, and perhaps the temptation were already associated before Mark with the beginning of Jesus' ministry. As for the Lord's Supper, Gethsemane, the betrayal, the trial, the crucifixion, and the resurrection, these events were already arranged before Mark at the end of Jesus' ministry because they had of necessity to come at the end. If the temporal designation that we find in Mark ix 2 was in the pre-Markan tradition, then the transfiguration and the confession of Peter may also have been associated together before Mark.

Over thirty years ago C. H. DODD sought to demonstrate that a pre-Markan order of the gospel events existed along the lines of Acts x 37-41 [1]). Dodd's thesis has been much criticized [2]). If, however, his thesis is correct, this would further limit the freedom of Mark in arranging his material. The existence of certain pre-Markan complexes also limited the freedom of the Evangelist to place the pericopes found within them wherever he desired because they were already bound in these complexes. The extent to which these complexes existed and the question of whether Mark himself composed any of them is difficult to answer. What is clear is that certain did exist and that Mark did not therefore have a completely free hand in the arrangement of the material found in them.

Nevertheless much of the material available to Mark could be arranged in accordance with his own particular theological purposes. Several means by which Mark reveals his own theological emphases are:

1. *The Arrangement of the Individual Pericopes*

Mark was free to a certain extent to place the individual pericopes and sayings wherever he desired. An example of this is Mark viii 27-x 52. This concentration of teaching material was almost certainly not connected to the passion sayings before Mark [3]). The systematic arrangement of this material clearly indicates that Mark has collected this material and arranged it to make a theological point. Each instance of a passion saying reveals the following pattern:

---

[1]) "The Framework of the Gospel Narrative," *ExpT.*, 43 (1932), pp. 396-400.
[2]) The most important criticism of DODD's thesis is DENNIS ERIC NINEHAM's article, "The Order of Events in St. Mark's Gospel — an Examination of Dr. DODD's Hypothesis," *Studies in the Gospels*, pp. 223-39.
[3]) See HARALD RIESENFELD, "Tradition und Redaktion in Markusevangelium," *Neutestamentliche Studien für Rudolf Bultmann*, p. 160; SCHWEIZER, *op. cit.*, p. 124; and WALTER GRUNDMANN, *Das Evangelium nach Markus*, p. 217.

Passion Saying	Disciples Err	Theme of Discipleship
Mark viii 31-2	Mark viii 33 (Peter errs)	Mark viii 34-ix 1 Discipleship Involves suffering like Christ [1])
Mark ix 30-2	Mark ix 34 (The Twelve err)	Mark ix 33-37 Discipleship Involves serving like Christ [2])
Mark x 32-4	Mark x 35 f. (James and John err)	Mark x 42-5 Discipleship Involves serving like Christ [3])

It seems clear that Mark has given to his materials a distinct arrangement. By his arrangement he seeks to stress that discipleship involves following the Crucified One. Discipleship involves an *imitatio Christi*.

2. *The Placing of One Pericope Inside Another*

There are a number of instances in Mark where we find one pericope inserted into the framework of another. The following are such instances:

Mark iii 22-30	into	Mark iii 19b-21 and 31-35;
Mark v 25-34	into	Mark v 21-24 and 35-43;
Mark vi 14-29	into	Mark vi 6b-13 and 30 f.;
Mark xi 15-19	into	Mark xi 12-14 and 20-25; and
Mark xiv 3-9	into	Mark xiv 1-2 and 10-11 [4]).

It is quite probable that a Markan arrangement is witnessed to in several of these instances, for the frequency of occurrence argues against all of these being pre-Markan. In order to ascertain a redaction history from such a "sandwich", we must first of all establish whether this "sandwich" is due to the hand of Mark. The question then must be raised as to whether both incidents took place at the same time or were located in the same place. If either of these two questions is answered in the affirmative, it is questionable if we can assert that there is any "redaktionsgeschichtlich" significance in the arrangement. Another question that must then be raised is whether these two incidents were placed together simply because they deal with a similar theme. If this is true, the arrangement may

---

[1]) Note v. 34 ἀράτω τὸν σταυρὸν αὐτοῦ and v. 35 ὃς δ᾽ ἂν ἀπολέσει τὴν ψυχὴν αὐτοῦ ἕνεκεν ἐμοῦ καὶ τοῦ εὐαγγελίου . . . .

[2]) Note v. 35 ἔσται πάντων ἔσχατος καὶ πάντων διάκονος.

[3]) Note v. 43 ἔσται ὑμῶν διάκονος, v. 44 ἔσται πάντων δοῦλος, and v. 45 ὁ υἱὸς τοῦ ἀνθρώπου οὐκ ἦλθεν διακονηθῆναι ἀλλὰ διακονῆσαι . . . .

[4]) Possibly Mark xiv 55-65 into Mark xiv 53-4 and 66-72 as well as Mark xv 16-20 into Mark xv 6-15 and 21-32 might also be considered examples of this "sandwiching".

be due primarily to topical rather than theological considerations. Finally it must be borne in mind that a Markan redaction history can only be ascertained from such a "sandwich" if in some way the inserted pericope interprets or is interpreted by the pericope into which it has been inserted. A possible example of this is Mark xi 12-25. By this "sandwich" Mark may be interpreting the cleansing of the temple by means of the pericope about the cursing of the fig tree. By this arrangement the cleansing of the temple, which originally may have referred to a reformation (see verse 16), is now apparently portrayed as an act of judgment [1]).

3. *The Geographical Scheme of Mark*

The uniqueness of the geographical scheme in Mark has been seen by many scholars as being due to a Markan redactional emphasis [2]). Actually the Markan scheme may be due to any of three reasons: (1) Mark never fully mastered his material and decided that only one short period of ministry in Jerusalem had in fact taken place. It is evident that Mark's own material contradicts this [3]). Jesus must have been in Jerusalem more than once, but Mark may not have known this [4]). (2) Since the tradition associated most of Jesus' teaching and healing ministry with Galilee and his passion with Jerusalem, Mark used the Galilee-Jerusalem scheme as a convenient literary device to group his material. (3) Mark decided to use the

---

[1]) It is quite possible that in our account the figs symbolize Israel (cf. Hosea ix 10; Jeremiah xxiv; xxix 17) and the destruction of the fig tree symbolizes judgment (cf. Hosea ii 12 and Isaiah xxxiv 4). See A de Q Robin, "The Cursing of the Fig Tree in Mark xi. A Hypothesis," *NTS*, 8 (1962), pp. 276-81. By his "sandwiching" these two incidents, Mark causes the theme of judgment in the fig tree pericope to "rub off" on the cleansing pericope. Schweizer, *op. cit.*, p. 130, rightly gives to this section of Mark the title, "Das Ende des Tempels Israels und der Aufbruch Gottes zu den Heiden." The cleansing of the temple is for Mark an act of judgment in which Jesus rejected Israel. The proximity of Mark xii 1-11, whose placement in the midst of a collection of controversy stories (Mark xi 27-33 and xii 13-37) is surely Markan, also indicates that Mark seeks at this point in his gospel to stress the divine judgment of Israel.

[2]) See Lohmeyer, *op. cit.*, Lightfoot, *op. cit.*; Marxsen, *Mark the Evangelist*, pp. 54-116; Best, *op. cit.*, pp. 174 f.; Feine-Behm-Kümmel, *op. cit.*, p. 65; G. Boobyer, "Galilee and Galileans in St Mark's Gospel," *BJRL*, 35 (1953), pp. 334-48; etc.

[3]) See Mark x 46 f.; xi 2 f.; xiv 3, 13 f., 49; and xv 41.

[4]) Best, *op. cit.*, p. 112, raises this possibility. This question is intimately related to the question of whether Mark created the one year cycle of Jesus' ministry or whether John created the three year cycle. Or were there two traditions? These questions may be unanswerable.

Galilee-Jerusalem scheme to stress a particular theological point.
The geographical scheme found in Mark may be of great importance
for our study and reveal a Markan redaction history. This still has
not been fully demonstrated, however, and the theological significance of this scheme is far from clear.

I. *The Markan Introduction*

It is evident from the other three gospels that the introductions
to these gospels are extremely helpful in revealing the theological
purpose and emphasis that each writer brought with him in the
writing of his gospel. It is only reasonable to expect the same to be
true in the case of Mark. During the oral period the various pericopes
circulated independently and in certain complexes. In writing his
"life of Christ" Mark had to begin somewhere. Where he would
begin and how he would begin had to be his decision. The introduction of his gospel must therefore reveal something of his purpose
in writing [1]. We shall only mention here two possible "redaktionsgeschichtlich" emphases of the Evangelist contained in his introduction. Mark apparently seeks to stress in his introduction that Jesus
is the fulfillment of the Old Testament prophecies. He does this by
the two prophecies which introduce the gospel and by his description
of the Baptist [2]. Mark also apparently seeks to stress that the
coming of the Christ inaugurated a new era in salvation history.
The Markan "Heilsgeschichte" is sufficiently developed that a clear
distinction is even made between the period of imminence, i.e. the
coming of Elijah *redivivus* [3], and the actual appearance of the

---

[1] KECK, *op. cit.*, p. 352, laments that "almost never does the introduction
figure in discussions of Mark's purpose." He goes on to say on p. 353, "Mark
assumed his contemporary readers (in contrast with modern scholars) did
not have the whole of his work in mind when they began, and that therefore
the opening paragraph was his opportunity to orient them to what he wanted
to say and how he wanted to say it."

[2] Note also the term πεπλήρωται in Mark i 15. MARXSEN, *op. cit.*, p. 42,
and ALFRED SUHL, *Die Funktion der alttestamentlichen Zitate und Anspielungen
im Markus-Evangelium*, p. 131, deny this. SUHL maintains that Mark does
not portray the Baptist as the fulfiller of the Old Testament prophecies,
but that his coming is simply "Schriftgemäss." But what is the difference?
JAMES M. ROBINSON, *The Problem of History in Mark*, p. 24, is certainly
more correct when he states, "The fact that the ministry of John is seen from
the viewpoint of fulfillment is confirmed by an analysis of the Markan presentation of John. This presentation is characterized by a remarkable correlation
of prophecy (vv. 2-3) and history (vv. 4-8)."

[3] Cf. Mark i 6 with 2 Kings i 8 and Zechariah xiii 4 and Mark ix 11-13
with Malachi iii 1 and iv 5.

Kingdom in the coming of Jesus [1]), for it is only after the Baptist disappears from the scene (see Mark i 14) that Jesus proclaims the new age (Mark i 15). It is evident therefore that the investigation of the Markan introduction will be an important means for ascertaining a Markan redaction history.

J. *The Markan Conclusion*

Even as the introduction of a man's work is important for ascertaining his purpose in writing so also is the conclusion of his work. The purpose for which a man writes is usually revealed in some way by the way he ends his work. This is certainly true in the case of John (cf. John xx 31) [2]), Matthew (cf. Matthew xxviii 19-20), and Luke (cf. Luke xxiv 49) [3]). We should be able to assume *a priori* that this is also true in the case of Mark. With Mark, however, we encounter a major problem. The basic problem is the classic question of where Mark originally ended. Since the work of LIGHTFOOT on this question [4]), the view that Mark originally ended at Mark xvi 8 has gained support [5]). There are, however, several reasons for still maintaining that the original ending of Mark is lost [6]). Because of

[1]) The term ἐγγίζειν which appears in the Markan summary, Mark i 14-15, can mean both "to come near" and "to arrive". What is crucial for our investigation is not what Jesus may have meant by this term but what Mark meant by it. Mark sees the Baptist as the coming Elijah who is to prepare men for the kingdom. With his coming the kingdom is near. With the coming of the Christ the kingdom is not merely "near", for it was already "near" in the coming of the Baptist. For Mark the coming of the Christ meant that the kingdom had arrived. This is evident by: the fulfillment of the Old Testament prophecies concerning the coming of the "new age" (see above p. 195 n. 2); the presence of a new teaching (see Mark i 21-22 and 27 b which are a Markan seam and insertion); the defeat of hostile powers (see Mark i 27b); the forgiveness of sins (see Mark ii 1-12, especially v. 10; and Mark i 4-5); etc.

[2]) This is true regardless of whether John originally ended at chapter twenty or twenty-one.

[3]) In the case of Luke the "conclusion" serves as an "introduction" to his next work.

[4]) LIGHTFOOT devoted the first two chapters of his work to this question.

[5]) See FEINE-BEHM-KÜMMEL, *op. cit.*, p. 72, for a list of some of the scholars who take this position.

[6]) Briefly some of these are: (1) although LIGHTFOOT has found examples in which a Greek sentence ended in γάρ, there is no example of any work ever having ended in this manner. (2) BRUCE M. METZGER in his *The Text of the New Testament*, pp. 228 f., has pointed out that the term φοβεῖσθαι is never used absolutely in Mark except in this instance, if the gospel originally ended at Mark xvi 8. (3) Since Mark xiv 28 and xvi 7 point to a future resurrection appearance of the risen Christ in Galilee and no such appearance is recorded in our present form of the gospel, the gospel must have originally contained such an account which unfortunately is now lost.

the confusion as to the ending of Mark, it would appear that rather
than clarifying for us the "redaktionsgeschichtlich" emphases of
the Evangelist, our present conclusion to the Gospel of Mark still
remains an enigma and offers little assistance in the investigation
of a Markan redaction history.

K. *The Markan Vocabulary* [1])

The religious language that a man uses often helps reveal something of his particular theological emphasis and stress. A sermon
by a minister of existentialistic conviction would be characterized
by a specific vocabulary; a sermon by a minister whose main
concern lay in the area of social action would be characterized by
another; and a sermon by a minister of fundamentalistic persuasion
would be characterized by still another. To be sure much that they
would say would involve similar terms and phrases, but again and
again certain specific words and phrases would arise which would
betray their own particular emphasis. Matthew reveals something
of his own particular theological emphasis by his frequent use of
such terms as πληροῦν, ῥηθέν, and γέγραπται. Mark does likewise by
his frequent use of such terms as: διδάσκειν — διδάσκαλος — διδαχή,
κηρύσσειν εὐαγγέλιον, ἐξουσία, δύναμις — δύνασθαι, θαμβεῖσθαι — θαυμάζειν — ἐκπλήσσεσθαι, δεῖ, παραδίδοναι, ἀκολουθεῖν, πίστις — πιστεύ-
ειν, λόγος, and σώζειν. These terms furthermore often appear in the
seams, insertions, and summaries. What their significance is for
understanding a Markan redaction history is, of course, beyond the
limits of this article. What is important for us here is to note that
the investigation of the vocabulary, itself, will be a useful means for
ascertaining a Markan redaction history.

L. *The Markan Christological Titles*

Closely related to the investigation of the Markan vocabulary is
the investigation of the Markan Christological titles. The importance
of such an investigation is evident, because the theology of Mark,
like the theology of the entire New Testament, is Christocentric.
It would seem therefore that the titles which Mark gave to Jesus
would be of utmost importance in understanding what the Evange-

---

[1]) We are not concerned here with the investigation of the vocabulary in
order to ascertain whether a seam, insertion, etc. is Markan. We are concerned here with what the vocabulary which Mark uses reveals as to his
theological interests.

list thought, believed, and desired to stress concerning the "pioneer and perfector of our faith". When one furthermore observes the freedom with which Matthew and Luke alter the titles Mark gave to Jesus [1]), it would appear that Mark also probably changed the titles he found in his sources. This being so, the titles used of Jesus both in the pericopes and in the seams will reveal the Christological preference of Mark, and this preference will be a theological preference and not merely an aesthetic one. The investigation of the Christological titles used by Mark will therefore be a helpful means for ascertaining a Markan redaction history.

Conclusion

In concluding our brief discussion of the various means for ascertaining a Markan redaction history it must be pointed out that not all the means mentioned are of equal value. Some of them, such as the investigation of the creation of pericopes, the omission of material, and the conclusion are of little, if any, value. Other means, such as the investigation of the seams, insertions, and summaries, the modification of the material, the selection of material, the arrangement of the material, the introduction, the vocabulary, and the Christological titles, are of great value [2]). The pursuit of a Markan redaction history is a difficult task, but it is not an impossible one. In the past errors have been made because a proper methodology was not followed. By using a proper methodology, such as we have outlined above, it is hoped that some of these errors may be avoided in the future.

---

[1]) See BEST, *op. cit.*, pp. 160-1. For a discussion of the alteration of the title, Son of Man, in the Gospel tradition, see the article by JOACHIM JEREMIAS entitled "Die älteste Schicht der Menschensohn - Logien," *ZNW*, 58 (1967), pp. 159-72.

[2]) In certain instances these means overlap, for the investigation of the Markan introduction will involve the investigation of the seams, insertions, summaries, modification, arrangement, etc. found in the introduction.

MARK AND THE RELATIVES OF JESUS

BY

JOHN DOMINIC CROSSAN
Chicago

The purpose of this article is to investigate certain sections of Mark's gospel where he is referring to the relatives of Jesus: their arrival in conjunction with the Beelzebul controversy (iii 20-35); the rejection of Jesus in his home town (vi 1-6); and, as a tentative hypothesis, the activity of certain women at the death, burial, and resurrection of Jesus (xv 40, 47; xvi 1). The method to be used is that of redactional criticism and it will seek: to separate tradition from redaction in a verse by verse analysis so that redactional verses as well as redactional additions to traditional verses can be clearly isolated; to see what overall tendencies emerge from this redactional activity for the three units under consideration; and, finally, to suggest the purpose of all this editorial work concerning Jesus' relatives against the general background of the gospel [1].

It might be useful to summarize certain "principles" for ascertaining redactional activity in Mark which can be placed here at the start although they were actually determined in the process of the analysis itself. The methodological basis of the investigation is: that can be most probably judged as redactional which (1) creates some awkwardness, discrepancy, contradiction, impropriety etc., by its presence—be this formal or material, linguistical

---

[1] The theory of the method is well known: cf., for example, R. H. STEIN, "What is Redaktionsgeschichte?" *JBL* 88 (1969) 45-56, and more fully in his 1968 Princeton doctoral thesis, *The Proper Methodology for Ascertaining a Marcan Redaktionsgeschichte* (U. Microfilm/Xerox), cf. *DissAbstr* 29 (1968-9) 2797-A. But, in practice, and apart from error in the analysis of the redactional *activity*, there is a far greater possibility of error in the synthesis of the redactional *purpose*: cf. the criticism of W. MARXSEN, *Mark the Evangelist*, trans. J. BOYCE *et al.* (Nashville/New York: Abingdon Press, 1969) in J. ROHDE, *Rediscovering the Teaching of the Evangelists*, trans. D. M. BARTON ("The New Testament Library"; Philadelphia: Westminster Press, 1968) 23-25, 113-140 (esp. pp. 136-140). The methodological "cautions" necessary in practice are well outlined in Q. QUESNELL, *The Mind of Mark* ("Analecta Biblica", 38; Rome: Pont. Bib. Inst., 1969) 46-55.

or logical, stylistic or conceptual; *and* (ii) this awkwardness is signalled as such by its absence (removal?) in the parallels of Matthew and/or Luke, and sometimes even by scribal changes in the Markan textual tradition; *and* (iii) the presence of this awkwardness serves to promote some recognizable redactional purpose in the theology of Mark and may even be expressed in predominantly Markan language or style. The simultaneous presence of all three points is highly persuasive in determining the presence of editorial work by the final redactor because it negates the possibility that the awkwardness stemmed from the tradition and was simply copied thence by Mark but not by Matthew or Luke. This would be true whether one is working on a two source hypothesis or on the theory of a common source for the three synoptics: in the former Mark has created the awkwardness for his own purpose and leaves it there since literary polish does not interest him (luckily for the exegete), and Matthew and Luke both delete it because of style, lack of interest, or opposition; in the latter case it is still unlikely that the awkwardness came from the tradition and was retained only by Mark since its presence serves a wider Markan purpose. These three points are especially useful in studying places where Mark has tampered internally with traditional material rather than created new verses from whole cloth. In such creations one may only have the second and third point to go on unless the very presence of the newly created verse develops some contextual awkwardness.

I. The Redactional Activity of Mark

This section will investigate the three pericopes verse by verse to isolate the editorial work of Mark from the received tradition. His purpose in all this will be a second problem.

A. Mk. iii 20-35.

What is the compositional and functional relationship of iii 20 to iii 21 and of these to iii 22-30 and iii 31-35? The status of iii 20-21 shows very significant differences in recent English translations. The Nestle-Aland text puts all of iii 20-35 in one paragraph. The *RSV* follows it in not putting iii 20-21 as a separate unit but placing minor paragraph breaks at iii 20-27, 28-30, 31-35. But the *JB* separates iii 20-21 as an individual paragraph with its own heading: "His relatives are concerned about Jesus." The *NEB* also unites iii 20-21 as a separate sub-paragraph. It will be argued that even if iii 20 is transitional in location and function it is to be related to the preceding rather than the following verses in content, and that iii 21 is to be taken with the following iii 22-35 rather than the preceding iii 20.

(1) iii 20. This verse is a redactional creation of Mark because: (i) there is a discrepancy between the singular *erchetai* and the plural *aytoys* and this is smoothed out by the former verb being changed to *erchontai* in the Markan textual tradition itself—if the reverse had happened to focus all interest on Jesus one would expect *ayton* as well; (ii) there are no equivalents to iii 20 in the parallel positions of Mt. ix 32; xii 22; Lk. xi 14; (iii) the language and style "suggests that Mark is writing freely without the aid of a source" [1]; and (iv) it contains a Markan pattern whose presence dictates its content. In all the vocations recorded by Mark he has a four-point sequence: Jesus is by the sea, the election of the disciple(s) by Jesus, Jesus and the disciple(s) are together in a house, and their eating together is mentioned. So for the first four in i 16a, 16b-20, 29, 31; for Levi in ii 13, 14, 15, 16; and for the Twelve in iii 7-9, 13-19, 20a, 20b. It seems that Mark wishes to conclude the elections with the mention of a *common* meal, or at least of its impossibility (cf. also vi 31): thus, for example, he has *diēkonei aytois* in i 31, which Mt. viii 15 told with *aytǭ* in the interests of a different symbolism. The conclusion is that iii 20 is a redactionally created connecting verse with regard to its position. But connection could have been effected quite adequately by *kai* or *kai eythys* and connection does not therefore determine content. It is this content with its mention of the common meal that makes iii 20 the conclusion of iii 13-19 rather than the opening of a separate unit as iii 20-21 [2].

(2) iii 21. When iii 21 is read as a unit with iii 20 it is somewhat strange: on the one hand the problem is not just Jesus' asceticism

---

[1] V. TAYLOR, *The Gospel according to St. Mark* (2nd ed.; New York: St. Martin's Press, 1966) 235.

[2] Already noted in C. H. TURNER, "Marcan Usage: Notes, Critical and Exegetical, on the Second Gospel," *JTS* 25 (1923-4) 377-386: "St. Mark has rounded off his story of the call of the Twelve by the summary statement... Then begins a new paragraph, verses 21-35, dealing with two alternative explanations offered by those who criticized the new teacher's work: *elegon ʿoti Exestē, elegon ʿoti Beelzeboyl echei*" (p. 384).

but a group (*aytoys* in iii 20) problem, and on the other hand Jesus himself seems quite able to handle such a group problem in vi 31. Once again iii 21 has no parallels in Mt. ix 31-32; xii 21-22 or Lk. xi 13-14 before their Beelzebul incidents, or in Mt. xii 45-46 or Lk. viii 18-19 before their account of the family pronouncement. The language and concepts of iii 21 are characteristically Markan. The *akoysantes* as a prelude to coming to Jesus appears in ii 1; iii 8; v 27; vii 25; x 47, but is absent from the synoptic parallels in all cases but the last one where a blind man is concerned (x 47 = Mt. xx 30 = Lk. xviii 36). The phrase '*oi par' aytoy* is used only here in the NT. The closest usage is the neuter *ta par' aytēs* of Mk. v 26 and *ta par' aytōn* of Lk. x 7 [1]). The verb *kratēsai* followed by a name or pronoun in the strong sense of holding someone by coercion is used by Mark eight times: of the Baptist (vi 17), of Jesus (xii 12; xiv 1, 44, 46, 49) and of the enigmatic "young man" in Gethsemane (xiv 51). In the other synoptics: Matthew has it seven of these eight times but has no parallel to Mk. xiv 51; however, he only uses it himself three times (xviii 28; xxii 6; xxvi 57 may be still under the influence of xxvi 55 = Mk. xiv 49); and Luke never has it in his parallels to Mark nor does he ever use it himself. The verb *exestē* is used four times by Mark, but of amazed reaction to Jesus (ii 12; v 42; vi 51) rather than of Jesus' own state (iii 21). In the synoptics: Mt. xii 23 has it once, and Luke uses it twice apart from Mark (ii 47; viii 56 = Mk. v 42; xxiv 22). The conclusion is that iii 21 is just as much a redactional creation as was iii 20. But if iii 20 concluded the preceding section, iii 21 must inaugurate the following pericope and this raises the question why Mark has prefaced it to the controversies in iii 22-35.

It has long been recognized that iii 21 should be connected to iii 31-35 [2]), even though this has also been resisted since it is hardly flattering to Jesus' relatives and hence seems unlikely to have been Mark's intention [3]). It has been argued that: (i) the

---

[1]) The translation accepted here is "his relatives" (*JB*) or "his family" (*NEB*) rather than merely "his friends" (*RSV*). Cf. V. TAYLOR, *op. cit.*, p. 236 for a summary of the problem; and also H. RIESENFELD, "*para*", *TDNT* V, 730-731. The final decision on the translation of iii 21 probably depends more on exegesis of all of iii 21-35 than on grammar alone.

[2]) For example, R. BULTMANN, *The History of the Synoptic Tradition*, trans. J. MARSH (New York/Evanston: Harper & Row, 1963) 29: "It seems impossible to doubt that vv. 20 f., and 31-35 belong together."

[3]) The tradition has always found it difficult to understand this of Jesus' relatives: Matthew and Luke have no parallels to Mk. iii 21, and part of the

'oi par' aytoy of iii 21 are not the relatives of Jesus in iii 31-35;
(ii) the *kratēsai ayton* of iii 21 refers back to the *ochlon* of iii 20 [1]);
(iii) the *elegon* of iii 21 is impersonal ("it was said . . .") [2]). But:
(i) *'oi par' aytoy* cannot refer to the Twelve for the *aytoys* of iii 20
can hardly be the *akoysantes* of iii 21, and neither can they be
Jesus' followers or disciples in a wider sense because the *ochlos*
of iii 20 is presumably the *ochlos* of iii 32 and these are approved
as *'oi peri ayton* in iii 32, 34; and (ii) even if this is grammatically
possible and syntactically likely, Mark always uses *krateō* in the
literal sense of grasp or arrest and not in the metaphorical sense of,
say, restraining a crowd by persuasion; and (iii) even if it is imper-
sonally recorded, it is clear that the *'oi par' aytoy* concur in the
judgment enough to act upon it. But the real question is not whether
iii 21 is flattering or not or even whether it is historical or not,
but whether Mark intended to connect iii 21 with iii 31-35 and
what was his purpose in doing so.

The literary technique of "sandwiching" a pericope between the
start and finish of another pericope has been noted as a standard
Markan redactional device [3]). Thus the presence of iii 22-30 between
iii 21 and iii 31-35 would be due to Mark's redaction and this
"sandwich" device. But while this may describe the end-product, it
is not at all clear that it describes the literary process. It seems
much more likely that Mark prefixed iii 21 to the already united
complex of iii 22-27, 31-35 than that he deliberately inserted
iii 22-27 between the separated units of iii 21 and iii 31-35. In

Markan textual tradition replaced the family (*'oi par' aytoy*) with the
scribes (*akoysantes/ēkoysan peri aytoy 'oi grammateis kai 'oi loipoi*).

[1]) Cf. the discussion in J. E. STEINMUELLER, "Jesus and the *'oi par' aytoy*
(Mk. 3, 20-21)," *CBQ* 4 (1942) 355-359; P. J. CANNON, "Could Mark Employ
ayton in 3, 21 Referring to *ochlos* in 3, 20?" *CBQ* 15 (1953) 460-461; A.
WIMMER, "Apostolos quosdam exisse, ut Jesum domum ducerent (Mc.
iii 20s)," *VD* 31 (1953) 131-142; F. SPADAFORA, "Il greco degli Evangeli,
esegesi di Mc. 3, 20s," *Lateranum* 28 (1962) 126-147.

[2]) C. H. TURNER, *loc. cit.*, p. 384: " 'for it was reported that He was out
of His senses,' " because of "Mark's fondness for the impersonal plural".
But J. C. DOUDNA, *The Greek of the Gospel of Mark* ("*SBL* Monograph
Series", Vol. 12, 1961) 6 gives the *legoysin* of ii 18 as the only example in
Mark of the impersonal "plural actives restricted to matters of common
report and opinion".

[3]) É. TROCMÉ, *La formation de l'Évangile selon Marc* ("Études d'Histoire
et de Philosophie Religieuses," 57; Paris: Presses Universitaires de France,
1963) 66. Examples would be the presence of v 25-34 between v 21-24 and
v 35-43 or of vi 14-29 between vi 7-13 and vi 30-31.

either case Mark's addition of iii 21 has drastically changed the nature of the confrontation in iii 31-35 by putting it on a par with the controversy concerning Beelzebul.

The reasons for considering iii 22-27, 31-35 a pre-Markan unity are as follows. In Lk. 11 there is a sequence involving an exorcism (xi 14), the Beelzebul accusation (xi 15-23), the warning of the seven devils (xi 24-26), and the blessing of his mother which Jesus rejects in favor of the blessedness of those "who hear the word of God and keep it" (xi 27-28). Similarly in Mt. xii is a sequence of exorcism (xii 22-23), accusation (xii 24-32), the seven devils (xii 43-45), and the Matthean parallel to Mk. iii 31-35 (xii 46-50). The literary activity of the synoptics could be summarized as follows [1]. Both Matthew and Luke had (i) Mark's combination of Beelzebul accusation and family confrontation; and (ii) the Q-text which combined exorcism, accusation, seven devils, and the woman's blessing. Matthew conflated them in accepting the exorcism, accusation, seven devils (from Q), and the family meeting (from Mk.). Luke also accepted them both, but separately: he kept the Q sequence in xi 14-28 and placed the family meeting as a very fitting conclusion to his parable chapter; thus the interpretation of the sower parable in Lk. viii 11-15 with its repeated mention of hearing the word of God (viii 11, 12, 13, 14, 15) is given a fitting climax in viii 19-21 by Luke's excellent relocation of Mark's familial debate. But because of this combination of Beelzebul accusation and the statement of Jesus concerning obediential relationship to God rather than biological relationship to himself in the Q basis for Mt. xii and Lk. xi; and because of the common theme of doing the will of God in Mk. iii 35 and practicing

---

[1] J. LAMBRECHT's Dutch article in *Bijd.* 29 (1968) 114-150, 234-258, 369-393 has been abstracted by the author himself in *NTA* 13 (1968-9) # 191, 584, 880. It is now available, with a four page English summary, as *Marcus Interpretator: Stijl en Boodschap in Mc. iii 20-iv 34* (Brugge/-Utrecht: Desclée de Brouwer, 1969). He argues that Mk. iii 20-35 is based on the Q text behind Mt. xii and Lk. xi. Tentatively, not knowing Dutch, this writer would ask: (i) if Mark knew Q why did he change the *pasa basileia* of Q: Mt. xii 25 = Lk. xi 17 into his own *kai ean basileia* in iii 24; or (ii) why did he change the rhetorical question *pōs stathēsetai* of Q: Mt. xii 26 = Lk. xi 18 into his assertion *oy dynatai stēnai* in iii 26. These can hardly be ideological changes and, unless Mark is more interested in stylistic changes of a minor nature, they remain unexplained on the hypothesis of his use of Q. But it seems also clear that Mark and Q were extremely close to one another on this pericope.

the word of God in Lk. xi 28, both being compared with mere familial bonds, it seems necessary to presume that Mark found the Beelzebul controversy in iii 22-27 and family meeting in iii 31-35 already united in his own source.

But such consecutive positioning in no way equates the two confrontations as being similar inimical encounters. The tradition which had placed them together had presumably no intention of such equation. The Markan redaction prefaced his own iii 21 to this complex and immediately the accidental juxtaposition of iii 22-27 and iii 31-35 takes on very different overtones. The accusation concerning Beelzebul in iii 22 mentions: personages, their departure to come to Jesus, and their statement (*elegon 'oti*). The redactional iii 21 shows a formal similarity to this: personages, their departure to come to Jesus, and their statement (*elegon gar 'oti*). This formal similarity in the inimical accusations of iii 21 and iii 22 links them together and prepares for the reaction of Jesus to each, in inverse order from the necessities of the redactional activity rather than from chiastic elegance, in iii 23-30 and iii 31-35. Hence the end-product is two accusations and two rebuttals in an abb'a' schema but this is accidental rather than intentional because Mark (i) did not freely create the schema; nor (ii) did he "sandwich" iii 22-30 between the unity of iii 21, 31-35. What he did was both minimal and effective: he prefixed iii 21 to the accepted sequence of iii 22-27, 31-35 and he phrased its accusation in formal similarity with that of iii 22. Since this is the first major redactional action of Mark in this complex it will serve as a guide towards other redactional touches within iii 22-35. In fact every other change will flow from this linking and equating of the two accusations in iii 21 and iii 22. From all this it is clear that it was not Mark's intention to place iii 20-21 as a unity in which the problem of Jesus' lack of food (iii 20) cause his relatives to come to assist him (iii 21).

(3) iii 22. In his handling of the traditional datum of the accusation redactional touches show up in the Markan version of the statement, the source, and the wording of the attack. All three present unusual features which are absent from the synoptic parallels but which seem necessary for Mark's purpose.

Both Mt. ix 32-33 = xii 22-23 and Lk. xi 14 precede this accusation with a specific exorcism and give the attack as a counter-charge to the admiration of the people. In this case it seems most likely that Mark's source had some such preface as well and that we can argue for its presumed removal [1]). By omitting it Mark lets the attack stand against exorcism as a repeated phenomenon of Jesus' ministry (i 24-26, 32, 34; iii 11) which has just been promised to the Twelve as well (iii 15). The attack is against the power of exorcism itself.

The next difference is in the source of the accusation. In Mt. ix 34 = xii 24 it stems from the Pharisees; in Lk. xi 15 it is simply from some of the crowds [2]). But in Mk. iii 22 it is from the quite unusual "scribes who had come down from Jerusalem". This is a quite emphatic designation of their office, their authority, and their arrival in Galilee. Whatever was in his source (Pharisees?) this designation is redactionally Mark's and combines two themes. The first is that of the scribes as one of the major groups, if not *the* main group, opposed to Jesus in Mark. The redactional verse in i 22 [3]) places the inaugural teaching (*edidasken, didachē, didaskōn*) in sharp and immediate contrast with that of *'oi grammateis*. Later, in ii 16, *'oi grammateis* seems to have been forced into the context to create the unique phrase, "the scribes of the Pharisees." This would be another redactional touch to link the scribes more expressly with the controversies of Mk. ii [4]). After i 22; ii 6, 16, the next times Mark mentions the scribes he qualifies them as scribes who have come from Jerusalem, here in iii 22 and in vii 1. Once again this latter designation is totally absent from the synoptic parallels of Mt. xv 1 (Pharisees and scribes)

---

[1]) R. BULTMANN, *op. cit.*, p. 13: "the discussion presupposes an exorcism preceding it, and no story original to the tradition would be likely to begin with a reference to some activity of Jesus in quite general terms."

[2]) This difference between Pharisees in Matthew and (some of) the crowds in Luke appears elsewhere as well: compare Mt. iii 7 with Lk. iii 7, where the attitude to the crowds in Lk. iii 10 seems much milder; or Mt. xii 38 with Lk. xi 16, 29; or Mt. xvi 1 with Lk. xii 54. Presumably the Q original behind Mt. xii 24 = Lk. xi 15 had Pharisees and Luke simplified the account by omitting the specific reference.

[3]) Textual indications of the combination of the redactional i 21-22 with the given i 23-28 appear in the *kai eythys* repeated in i 23 after i 21, and the second mention of the synagogue in i 23 after i 21. The scribes are not mentioned in the parallel Lk. iv 32, and Mt. vii 29 has the comparison at the end of the Sermon on the Mount.

[4]) In the parallels Mk. ix 11 has "the Pharisees," Lk. v 30 has "the Pharisees and the scribes". Later Markan textual tradition also changed it to "both the scribes and the Pharisees".

and Lk. xi 37 (a Pharisee). This mention of Jerusalem is the second
note introduced into the traditional datum by Mark. Apart from
the single positive usage in iii 8, all other times where Jerusalem
appears in Mark place it in an atmosphere of threat to Jesus
(x 32, 33; xi 1, 11, 15, 27; xv 41). Jerusalem is the place whence
opposition comes to Jesus or to which he must go towards his
death. It is Mark who has redactionally specified the charge as
stemming from these scribes who have come down from Jerusalem
in iii 22.

The exact wording of the accusation is also different in Mk.
iii 22 as compared to Mt. ix 34; xii 24; Lk. xi 15. In Mark there
is an unusual combination of demonic collusion and demonic
possession which can hardly be considered as exactly the same
thing. The accusation in the Q text was that Jesus could cast out
devils *en Beezeboyl (tǫ) archonti tōn daimoniōn*, as Mt. xii 24 = Lk.
xi 15. Once again it is Mark who has changed his tradition. In itself
this attack in Q explained Jesus' power by suggesting demonic
assistance and this is not *per se* a statement that Jesus is possessed.
It is not such in either Matthew or Luke but it is such in Mark.
It was seen earlier that Mk. iii 21 modelled the familial accusation
of madness on the traditional accusation of demonic collusion in
iii 22. Within the second accusation Mark has created a split so
that it is now a double (contradictory?) attack: demonic possession in iii 22a and demonic assistance in iii 22b. By this split the
material closeness of the two accusations is heightened: (i) *'oti*
Jesus is insane in iii 21; (ii) *'oti* Jesus is possessed in iii 22a; (iii)
'oti Jesus is in demonic collusion in iii 22b. By his redactional
creation of the possession accusation in iii 22a Mark intended to
link the two accusations together not only formally but also materially: it is an easier step from insanity to possession than it is
from madness to demonic assistance. His change in the wording
of the second accusation is a continuing part of his equating of
the twin attacks and his preparation to hurl iii 28-30 against both
relatives and scribes together.

(4) iii 23. The *proskalesamenos aytoys* is strange: who are these
unidentified people? who needs to be called? It is hardly the accusers who are presumably present. Both Mt. xii 25 and Lk. xi 17
lack this phrase and have Jesus answer immediately to his accusers
(*aytois*). Yet *proskalesamenos* is a standard redactional connective

in Mk. iii 13; vi 7; vii 14; viii 1, 34; x 42; xii 43 and all of this would indicate that iii 23 comes from Mark's editorial activity. But the formal "calling" serves only to draw attention to the following *en parabolais* which is also lacking in Mt. xii 25 and Lk. xi 17. For Mark alone Jesus first speaks *en parabolais* in this intensely inimical context. This redactional phrase links the complex of iii 21-35 with the succeeding chapter where Jesus teaches *en parabolais* (iv 2). An exploration of this linkage would exceed the purpose of this article and it will suffice to conclude that iii 23a is redactionally Markan and is created to point forward to iv 1-34 [1]).

The rest of iii 23 is also from Mark. Three arguments can be given for this. First, the form of the answer of Jesus is a double metaphor (city, house) which counters with a *reductio ad absurdum* [2]) and Mk. iii 24-25; Mt. xii 25; Lk. xi 17 witness to this stylized reaction. The presence of iii 23b spoils this formal structure. Secondly, this intervention between accusation and counter by *reductio ad absurdum* is rendered more striking in that the term for the prince of evil is changed from Beelzebul to Satan. This is in keeping with the interest in Satan shown earlier by Mark in i 13 [3]), and later in

---

[1]) If this general conclusion is correct the Markan understanding of Jesus' speech *en parabolais* must begin with iii 20-35 and not just with iv 1-34. For example: those who are addressed *en parabolais* (iii 23 = iv 11) may find it impossible to find forgiveness: *oyk echei aphesin* in iii 29 and *mēpote* . . . *aphethę* in iv 12, where neither of the parallel citations from Is. vi 9-10 in Mt. xiii 13 and Lk. viii 10 have any mention of forgiveness; and the distinction of those who are *exō* (the relatives in iii 31, 32) and those who are *peri ayton* (the others in iii 32, 34) is repeated in the *peri ayton* of iv 10 and the *exō* of iv 11, and once again the synoptic parallels are indicative: the *peri ayton* of Mk. iii 32, 34 is absent from Mt. xii 49 = Lk. viii 21 and neither the *peri ayton* nor the *exō* of Mk. iv 10-11 is present in Mt. xiii 10-11 = Lk. viii 9-10. In other words, these links between iii 21-35 and iv 10-11 would indicate that the blind and the deaf, the unrepentent and the unforgiven of iv 10-12 have been explicitly exemplified previously in iii 21-35.

[2]) R. BULTMANN, *op. cit.*, pp. 39-54 discussing the reply-form from controversy dialogues in synoptic and rabbinic sources notes "the reply to the attack follows more or less a set form, with special preference for the counter-question or the metaphor, or even both" (p. 141). It is quite possible that both the double image of divided kingdom and household ("metaphor") and reference to Jewish exorcists (= "counterquestion") in the Q text of Mt. xii 25-17 and Lk. xi 17-19 were united at a very early stage of the tradition.

[3]) In the temptation accounts in Mt. iv and Lk. iv the ordinary term is *diabolos* (Mt. iv 1, 5, 8, 11 = Lk. v 2, 3, 6, 13) with *'o peirazōn* in Mt. iv 3. But Mt. iv 10 has *'ypage, satana* which is not present in the parallel Lk. iv 8. Most likely it is placed here to link with the *'ypage, satana* of Mt. xvi 23 which comes from Mk. viii 33. Hence only Mark tells of the inaugural

iv 15 [1]). Thirdly, there is no parallel mention of Satan in Mt. xii 25 or Lk. xi 17. The use of the term Satan will be seen again in iii 26 and it can be left until there to decide whether Mark has introduced the term into the tradition in both iii 23b and iii 26 or has simply expanded its usage from iii 26 into iii 23b.

(5) iii 24-25. The counter-argument of Jesus appears in exact parallelism in Mark with only small changes in the order or the tenses of the verbs—if the text is correct on these points. The presence of the phrase *pasa basileia*, of (*dia*) *meristheisa*, and of *erēmoytai* in Mt. xii 25a = Lk. xi 17a would indicate that Jesus' counter argument was also present in Q. The changes in the rest of the verse in Mt. xii 25b = Lk. xi 17a would be explained by the fact that (i) Luke abbreviated the full semitic parallelism by making his xi 17b no more than a subsidiary part of xi 17a; while (ii) Matthew expanded the parallelism from *basileia//oikia* to *basileia//polis ē oikia* [2]). Hence the present text of Mk. iii 24-25 can be taken as untouched tradition and the Q version behind Mt. xii 25 and Lk. xi 17 must have been very similar to it.

(6) iii 26. So far the tradition shows in iii 22b (the Pharisees named?) and in iii 24-25. There is quite close formal similarity between Mk. iii 24, 25 and iii 26 as well as certain minor differences in the latter verse: *kai ei* for *kai ean*; the introduction of *anestē* . . .

---

temptation in terms of Satan. For further discussion, cf. J. M. ROBINSON, *The Problem of History in Mark* ("SBT," No. 21; Naperville, Ill.: Allenson, 1957) 30-31, 35-36, and also E. BEST, *The Temptation and the Passion: The Markan Soteriology* ("Society for NTS: Monograph Series"; Cambridge: C. U. Press, 1965) 10-15.

[1]) In the parallels Mt. xiii 19 has *῾o ponēros* and Lk. viii 11 uses *῾o diabolos*. This could be another word-link between iii 21-35 and iv 1-34 (cf. note 1 on p. 90).

[2]) The reason for Matthew's insertion of *polis* could be a direct allusion to Jerusalem, just as he forced an allegorical allusion to its destruction into the parable of the great supper in xxii 7 as against Lk. xiv 20; cf. also Mt. iv 5; v 35; xxi 10, 17, 18 (these three are not in Mk. xi 11-12); xxvii 53; xxviii 11. This seems a more likely solution than the hypothesis that Q had *basileia//polis* and Mark had *basileia//oikia*, whence Matthew conflated (quite usual) and Luke preferred an abbreviated Mark over Q (rather unusual): cf. B. H. STREETER, *The Four Gospels: A Study of Origins* (London: Macmillan, 1924) who argues that Mark and Q overlap at certain points (pp. 186-191) and that when this happens Matthew and Luke differ with regard to both text and context so that Matthew conflates Mark and Q but retains the context of Mark while Luke chooses the text and context of Q: cf. pp. 186-191, 210-211.

kai; and the concluding *alla telos echei*. If iii 26 is Markan one would have to presume that he modelled it on the format of the tradition in iii 24, 25. But there is also evidence that the text behind Mt. xii 26b = Lk. xi 18b held some more precise application of the preceding metaphors to the case in hand: *pōs stathēsetai 'ē basileia aytoy* would be from the Q text. Because of this it seems more likely that the application to Satan was already present in the pre-Markan tradition of iii 26 as also in the Q text (*aytoy*!). It could also be concluded that Mt. xii 26a has been influenced by the earlier mention of Satan in Mk. iii 23. Luke, who is staying closer to the Q basis than is Matthew, had to insert his xi 18a to make the transition back from Satan to Beelzebul. The mention of Satan in iii 26 is traditional and iii 23 was an extension of this for emphasis on Satan. The tradition is now iii 22b, 24-26.

(7) iii 27. This verse is also from the pre-Markan tradition. As usual when Mark and Q overlap, Luke prefers to follow Q (cf. p. 91, note 2 above) and this is clear in most of the Beelzebul pericope but especially in xi 21-22. Mt. xii 29, with *pōs* picking up the earlier *pōs* of xii 26b, is almost verbatim the text of Mk. iii 27, while Lk. xi 21-22 is quite distinct. Both the pre-Markan and the Q tradition had the image of the looted house. All of Mk. iii 24-27 came to Mark in his received tradition.

(8) iii 28-29. The saying in iii 28-29 raises two major problems: (i) was some form of this logion already appended to the complex in the pre-Markan tradition; (ii) if not, what has Mark done to the saying besides placing it in its present position? The formulation is extremely awkward: in the *panta aphethēsetai* as against the *oyk echei aphesin*; the distribution and division of *panta . . . ta . . . 'osa*; and *tois 'yiois tōn anthrōpōn*. And while these three points are absent from the synoptic parallels, they themselves represent smaller difficulties of their own: the redundancy of Mt. xii 31 and 32, especially of xii 31b = 32b; and the shift from "says a word against" in Lk. xii 10a to "blasphemes against" in xii 10b. It will be argued here that Mark created this saying himself on the basis of another logion still fairly visible in the Q text behind Mt. xii 32 and Lk. xii 10a despite their present combinations of both Mk and Q in varying ways and degrees. The linguistic evidence is that Mk. iii 28-29 is a variation on the Q type text and not vice versa because the earlier stage of the tradition is represented by the

phrase "speak a word against" (Q: Mt. xii 32; Lk. xii 10a) and not by the expression "blaspheme against" (Mk. iii 28-29: Mt. xii 31; Lk. xii 10b) [1]). The original Q text and the text behind Mark stated that "to speak a word" against the Son of Man could be forgiven, but "to speak a word" against the Holy Spirit was unforgivable. It could have represented an assurance that those who opposed Jesus, the Son of Man, on earth could still find forgiveness as long as they did not persist in this also after the resurrection because that would be to oppose the Holy Spirit [2]). The Q form with this balanced "speak a word against" is still quite visible in Mt. xii 32. It is less visible in Lk. xii 10 as only xii 10a is from Q ("speak a word against") and the parallel xii 10b ("blaspheme against") is from Mk. iii 29. In outline:

$$
\begin{array}{lll}
\text{Mk. iii 28} & = \text{Mt. xii 31a} & \\
\text{Mk. iii 29} & = \text{Mt. xii 31b} & = \text{Lk. xii 10b} \\
\text{Q (a)} & = \text{Mt. xii 32a} & = \text{Lk. xii 10a} \\
\text{Q (b)} & = \text{Mt. xii 32b} &
\end{array}
$$

Mark's own theology would not have allowed him to accept the premises of this piece of tradition. For him Jesus is Son of Man even on earth (ii 10, 28) [3]) but he is also endowed with the Spirit on earth (i 8, 10, 12) and to blaspheme against one is to blaspheme against the other. This indeed is precisely the point he is trying to make in this entire pericope. So he had to take the Q type logion and completely and very crudely redo it in his own characteristic language. He removed any reference to Jesus as Son of Man by the contorted phrase *panta aphethēsetai tois 'yiois tōn*

---

[1]) This accepts completely the arguments against Wellhausen's thesis that the form in Mark is prior to Q (cf. R. BULTMANN, *op. cit.*, p. 131) given in H. E. TÖDT, *The Son of Man in the Synoptic Tradition*, trans. D. M. BARTON ("The New Testament Library"; Philadelphia: Westminster Press, 1965) 312-318.

[2]) Cf. H. E. TÖDT, *loc. cit.* On iii 28-29 as basically an authentic saying of Jesus, cf. J. G. WILLIAMS, "A Note on the 'Unforgivable Sin' Logion," *NTS* 12 (1965) 75-77; that it is not authentic but stems from "an early, ecstatic Christianity, which ... accepted no limitations upon its actions in the Spirit, even to the extent of exalting the witness of the Spirit over the test of the kerygma" (p. 365) is argued in R. SCROGGS, "The Exaltation of the Spirit by Some Early Christians," *JBL* 84 (1965) 359-373.

[3]) On the importance of these sayings for Mark's concept of Jesus' earthly authority cf. N. PERRIN, "The Son of Man in the Synoptic Tradition," *BR* 13 (1968) 3-25, and "The Creative Use of the Son of Man Traditions by Mark," *UnSemQR* 23 (1968) 357-365.

anthrōpōn, ta 'amartēmata kai 'ai blasphēmiai 'osa ean blasphē-mēsōsin. On the language: *'amartēma* never appears again in the synoptic tradition; the noun *blasphēmia* and the verb *blasphēmeō* never appear in the synoptic tradition except under Markan influence [1]; and even the verb *aphiēmi* followed by *'amartia* or *'amartēma* seems quite strongly Markan in the synoptic tradition [2].

These redactional changes effected by Mark in his iii 28-29 lead up to the final one which is the addition of *alla enochos estin aiōnioy 'amartēmatos* in iii 29b. This does not add any real content to the preceding *oyk echei aphesin eis ta aiōna.* There is mention of this in the Q version in Mt. xii 32 which ends *'oyte en toytǭ tǭ aiōni oyte en tǭ mellonti.* But it seems best to consider Mk. iii 29b (*alla . . .*) as a redactional addition because: (i) it is redundant with iii 29; (ii) the redundancy is smoothed out in Mt. xii 32b and so this could be from Mark and not from Q; (iii) Lk. xii 10b has solved the redundancy by omitting it completely which might indicate that it was in no way present in the Q text; (iv) the use of *'amartēma* again, as in iii 28. The reason for the addition would have been emphasis by repetition.

Of the two questions proposed earlier concerning iii 28-29 one has now been answered: Mark himself changed from a logion very similar to that in Q to the present awkward saying in his iii 28-29. But he also did something much more significant. The different locations of the Q logion in Mt. xii 32 (connected to Beelzebul controversy) and in Lk. xii 10 (no such connection) would indicate that the connection was not made in Q and that, as usual when Mark and Q overlap in content, Matthew has kept the context of Mark while Luke has accepted that of Q. In other words it is Mark who has placed iii 28-29 in its present association with and application to the Beelzebul controversy. In this he was followed

---

[1] The noun *blasphēmia* is in Mk. iii 28 = Mt. xii 31; Mk. vii 22 = Mt. xv 19; Mk. xiv 64 = Mt. xxvi 65, and the use of the noun in Lk. v 21 is from the verb in Mk. ii 7. The verb *blasphēmeō* is in Mk. ii 7 = Mt. ix 3; Mk. iii 28-29 = Lk. xii 10; Mk. xv 29 = Mt. xxvii 39, and the use of the verb in Mt. xxvi 65 is from the noun in Mk. xiv 64. Lk. xxii 65 is probably relocated there (!) from Mk. xiv 64, and Lk. xxiii 39 is most likely under the influence of Mk. xv 29.

[2] It is used five times in Mark and all Matthew's uses and half of Luke's come thence: Mk. ii 5, 7, 9, 10 = Mt. ix 2, 5, 6 = Lk. v 20, 21, 23, 24. But Lk. vii 47, 48, 49; xi 4 are not from Mark.

by Matthew but not by Luke. Mark introduced it into iii 22-27, 31-35 and he prefaced it with his first use of the solemn *amēn legō 'ymin* which when followed by *'oti* is a predominantly Markan use of the assurance [1]). In summary: Mark knew a traditional logion quite similar to the Q saying in Mt. xii 32 and concerning the Son of Man; he could not accept its disjunction between Son of Man and Holy Spirit; he changed Son of Man (= Jesus) into sons of men (= men) and changed "speak against" into "blaspheme against" so that to blaspheme Jesus was to blaspheme the Spirit; he added a repeated warning of the eternal sanction in iii 29b; and finally and most importantly, he placed this logion, very awkwardly but very effectively redacted, in its present central position between iii 22-27 and iii 31-35.

(9) iii 30. The presence of this phrase is somewhat unexpected and there is no parallel to it at the end of Mt. xii 32 [2]). Secondly, it was seen earlier that the real accusation was demonic collusion and not demonic possession (Q: Mt. xii 24 = Lk. xi 15) and that Mark brought in the idea of demonic possession himself in iii 22 with *'oti Beezeboyl echei*. Thirdly, the phrase *(to) pneyma (to) akatharton* is exclusively Markan in the synoptic tradition with all other uses deriving from his own [3]). Accordingly, this must be considered as another redactional touch from Mark himself. It tends to confirm the preceding analysis of iii 28-29: when Mark inserted this redacted logion into its new position he needed both the prologue of *amēn legō 'ymin 'oti* and the epilogue of *'oti elegon, pneyma akatharton echei* to adapt it to its new context. Finally,

---

[1]) Mark uses the phrase thirteen times: nine with *'oti*, four without; Matthew uses it thirty-one times: eleven with *'oti* (of which four are from Mark), twenty times without; Luke uses it six times: four are with *'oti* (of which one is from Mark), and twice without *'oti*.

[2]) It is possible that Lk. xi 18b is derived from Mk. iii 30 and that Luke found it necessary to effect a smoother transition between the accusation in xi 15, the first answer in xi 16-18, and the second answer in xi 18b-19. The awkwardness of the transition would have come from Q but was ignored by Mt. xii 26-27.

[3]) Mk. i 23, 26, 27 = Lk. iv 33; iii 11 = Lk. vi 18; iii 30; v 2, 8, 13 = Lk. viii 29; vi 7 = Mt. x 1; vii 25; ix 25 = Lk. ix 42. Lk. iv 36 reversed the positions of noun and adjective, and the only non-Markan usage in the synoptic tradition also appears as *to akatharton pneyma* in the Q text of Mt. xii 43 = Lk. xi 24. The transition from insanity to possession is simple: cf., for example, how the *daimonion echeis* of Jn. vii 20; viii 48 is translated as, " 'You are mad' " in the former verse and as, " 'You are . . . possessed by a devil,' " in the latter one in *JB*.

the phrasing of iii 30 with *'oti elegon* looks back to both the accusations of iii 21 with *elegon 'oti* (madness) and iii 22a with *elegon 'oti* (possession). The two redactional accusations of madness from the relatives and of possession from the Jerusalem scribes which were combined by Mark with the traditional accusation of demonic collusion find alike their solemn rebuttal in the redacted logion of iii 28-30. For Mark the indictment of iii 28-30 is so placed and so phrased as to accuse both the family of Jesus and the scribes of Jerusalem.

(10) iii 31-34. It has already been argued that the sequential position of iii 22b, 24-27 and 31-35, and possibly even some intervening pericopes, was already present in Mark's source. This in no way established the inimical context for their combination which Mark himself created by prefacing iii 21, by changing iii 22b, and by his development and relocation of iii 28-30. But is there any evidence of internal changes in the accepted tradition concerning the arrival of the relatives in iii 31-34. There is, first of all, a far less friendly atmosphere in Mark as compared with Matthew or Luke. On their arrival in Mk. iii 31 the family *exō stēkontes apesteilan pros ayton kaloyntes ayton*. This is surely somewhat peremptory and the synoptic parallels are much more gentle: Mt. xii 46 qualifies it with *eistēkeisan exō zētoyntes aytǭ lalēsai*, and Lk. viii 19 explains it even more sympathetically by noting *oyk ēdynanto syntychein aytǭ dia ton ochlon*. To wish to speak to Jesus or to seek to get through the crowd to Jesus is, at very least, more polite than what is recorded in Mk. iii 31. It seems that Mark wished to contrast the different attitudes by means of location: the relatives are outside (*exō*) and they are standing (*stēkontes*) in iii 31, 32, while the crowd is seated (*ekathēto, kathēmenoys*) around Jesus (*peri ayton*) twice repeated in iii 32, 34. Neither Matthew nor Luke mention this double note concerning those seated around Jesus. This draws attention to an even more striking Markan phenomenon. There is no mention of any disciples as such or of the newly elected Twelve. The relatives are not contrasted with these but with the *ekathēto peri ayton ochlos* (iii 32) and *toys peri ayton kyklǭ kathēmenoys* (iii 34). This is quite different in the synoptics: Mt. xii 46 has no parallel to iii 32 nor does Lk. viii 19; and Mt. xii 49 uses *toys mathētas aytoy*, while Lk. viii 21 dissolves the entire concrete situation into a statement of abstract truth. Mark is clearly placing

the relatives outside with regard to the crowd inside. They are in the most complete isolation, not just from the official disciples but from the crowd itself. Hence Mark has a scene unique in the synoptic tradition—a crowd seated around Jesus in a circle [1]).

(11) iii 35. This verse is a separate problem. One notices immediately that the fourfold repetition of *'ē mētēr kai 'oi adelphoi* in iii 31, 32, 33, 34 is changed to *adelphos moy kai adelphē kai mētēr* in iii 35. Matthew follows Mark rather closely but may have originally reduced the fourfold repetition to three, if his xii 47 should be omitted, but he retained the changed order of the family in the final verse (xii 50). Luke drastically excises Mark's redundancy and discrepancy by cutting the four down to two mentions of *mētēr kai adelphoi* in his viii 19-20 and then making his final verse follow this same *mētēr kai adelphoi* in viii 21. This discrepancy in Mark draws attention to the problem of the relationship of iii 35 to iii 31-34. As this latter unit stands it comes to an adequate pronouncement conclusion in iii 34: those seated in a circle around Jesus are certainly his followers in some sense or at least his listeners and as such they are his real family. At present iii 35 simply renders this point more abstractly clear and relevant to other situations. But if this means that iii 31-34 and iii 35 were originally separate units, is it Mark who first joined them together and did he create this iii 35 in the process? The answer, somewhat tentatively, is that Mark himself created and appended iii 35 to iii 31-34. The idea of *to thelēma toy Theoy* never appears again in the synoptic tradition: in Mt. vi 10; vii 21; xii 50; xviii 14; xxi 31; xxvi 42 and Lk. xi 2; xxii 42 it is always the Father's will that is in question. But the will of God is mentioned frequently in the pauline corpus, for example, Rom. i 10; xii 2 etc. In the synoptic parallels to Mk. iii 35 there is *to thelēma tou patros moy toy en oyranois* in Mt. xii 50, and Luke combined both Mk. iii 35 and iv 33 into his own viii 21 with *logon toy theoy akoyontes kai poioyntes*. This is far from being very conclusive but Mk. iii 35a could be another indication of influence from the pauline tradition in Mark and so composed by Mark himself [2]). But the reason for his creation of iii 35 appears

---

[1]) The term *kyklǭ* is only in Mk. iii 34; vi 6, 36 = Lk. ix 12, and *kathēmai peri* of Jesus appears only here.

[2]) Cf. W. MARXSEN, *op. cit.*, p. 147: "Mark's Gospel is the confluence of two streams coursing through primitive Christian preaching. One is

more securely and more clearly in iii 35b. The phrase *adelphos moy kai adelphē kai mētēr* specifies more exactly the vaguer *mētēr kai adelphoi* of the tradition and prepares the pericope to link more closely with the other places where the relatives will appear: in vi 3 where mother, brothers, and sisters will again be noted and even named, and possibly even in xv 40, 47; xvi 1 where some of the names appear again but with no relationship to Jesus given. Even more significant is the link forged between iii 35 and x 29-30. In x 29 there is a list of seven "abandonments" which the followers of Jesus are expected to make. The sequence is: *oikian, adelphoys, adelphas, mētera, patera, tekna, agroys.* In x 30 Mark wished to keep this seven-fold number and still add in the warning of "persecutions" as well. But he retained intact the sequence of *adelphoys, adelphas, mētera* and removed the following *patera* from the sequence. That this is somewhat unusual is clear from the synoptic parallels: Mt. ix 29 reorders the list into the expected order: *adelphoys, adelphas, patera, mētera.* Lk. xviii 29 rephrases the sequence completely. But Mark's intention was to have Jesus' rejection of brother-sister-mother in iii 35 so stated as to be explicitly and verbally paradigmatic for that of his followers in x 29-30. This intended Markan usage for iii 35b explains why he created the verse and placed it here in conclusion to iii 31-35.

In summary: Mark received from his sources iii 22b, 24-27 and iii 31-34 in close relationship; he also received but separately a version of iii 28-29a close to the Q text of that logion. His redactional activity involved the placing of iii 21-22a before iii 22b, 24-27, 31-34 so that the two accusations of iii 21 and iii 22 were formally and materially quite similar. Jesus refuted the accusations inversely in iii 23-27 and iii 31-34 and the centrally placed indictment of iii 28-30 was worded and located to attack both relatives and scribes. The final redactional touch was the creation of iii 35 so that the relatives of Jesus with whom Mark is interested are: mother, brothers, and sisters.

B. Mk. vi 1-6.

The second pericope concerning the relatives of Jesus is vi 1-6

---

conceptual-theological, represented, e.g., by Paul. The other is kerygmatic-visual, using the so-called material of the synoptic tradition," and also p. 216: "Mark ties together the two 'strands' of primitive Christian preaching."

and the problem is, once again, to isolate tradition and redaction before discussing intention.

(1) vi 1-2a. There is an obvious discrepancy between the positive reaction of the *exeplēssonto* in vi 2a and the *eskandalizonto* in vi 3. This raises the immediate suspicion that there may be a juxtaposition of tradition and redaction at work. Since (i) vi 1-2a has close linguistic links to i 21b-22, 27 and (ii) since these latter are redactional insertions it can be concluded that (iii) vi 1-2a and its positive response represents the redaction whose content is not in complete harmony with the Markan received tradition in vi 3.

The importance of Jesus as teacher is indicated very early in Mark's work [1]). The redactional intrusion of this theme into the traditional miracle story in i 23-28 draws immediate attention to the theme. In the opening of i 21-22 there is a discrepancy between the plural *eisporeyontai* in i 21a and the textually uncertain singular *eiselthōn* in i 21b. The traditional plural opening, "They went as far as Capernaum" (i 21a), had its normal ending in the plural, "leaving the synagogue they went" (i 29). Both the synoptic parallels and the Markan textual tradition indicate awareness of this plural (i 21a), singular (i 21b), plural (i 29) problem. For i 21: there are only singulars in the parallels of Mt. iv 13 or Lk. iv 31, and the *eiselthōn* is lacking in some of the Markan textual tradition [2]). For i 29: both Mt. viii 14 and Lk. iv 38 have the singular, and the plural *exelthontes ēlthon* appears in the singular in some of the manuscripts. The suggested explanation is that the material framed by the *eythys* of i 21b and i 23 is a Markan redactional insertion. This insertion explains also the double mentions of "synagogue" in i 21b (redaction) and i 23 (tradition). Once again Lk. iv 31, 33 deletes the former usage and simplifies the duplication. This means that Mk. i 21b-22 is redactional and so is the triple emphasis (*edidasken, didachę, didaskōn*) on Jesus as teacher, and as a teacher over against the scribes. The next redac-

---

[1]) E. BEST, *op. cit.*, notes the importance of *didaskein* and *didachē* especially in "seams between incidents, where we are most likely to see the hand of Mark" (p. 71), and he concludes that, "Mark leaves us with the impression that the main activity of Jesus was teaching... much more... than 'healing' or 'exorcism' " (p. 72).

[2]) Cf. C. H. TURNER, "Marcan Usage: Notes, Critical and Exegetical, on the Second Gospel," *JTS* 26 (1924-5) 15, and 28 (1926-7) 153.

tional change to be noted is i 27. In the traditional form of the miracle story one is expecting at i 27 the reaction of the people to the miracle itself [1]). This is indeed present in i 27b, but in i 27a their amazement is directed to the *didachē kainē kat' exoysian* before the demons are mentioned. This is another Markan redactional touch to stress Jesus as teacher and not just or even primarily as miracle-worker. Once again the parallel to i 27 in Lk. iv 36 has smoothed out the phraseology with *tis 'o logos 'oytos, 'oti en exoysiạ kai dynamei* etc.

The purpose of these detailed remarks on i 21b-22, 27 is to prepare for the argument that Mark redacted vi 1-2a with a view to this inaugural i 21b, 22, 27. There is the mention of the disciples who follow Jesus in vi 1. They never appear again in the pericope and are ignored in vi 6b, yet their mention in vi 1 recalls the following of i 16-20, 21, 29. The situation of teaching in the synagogue on the sabbath in vi 2 recalls i 21 and the *exeplēssonto* of vi 2 reiterates the same verb in i 22. Finally, the object of their astonishment is similar in i 27 as in vi 2b: teaching and authority (power) or wisdom and miracle. But in i 23-28 the reaction of the crowd was positive and admiring and all Mark did in i 21-22, 27 was to specify this admiration as being directed to both teaching and miracle and in that order. As he opens the pericope in vi 1-2a he has recalled the situation and the language of this Capernaum acclaim but only to have it contradicted by the *eskandalizonto* to follow in vi 3b. For now it will suffice to note this discrepancy: the redactional introduction in vi 1-2a points towards the positive admiration but the traditional comment in vi 2b-3 indicated scandal and rejection.

(2) vi 2b-3. The "scandal" caused by the contrast between Jesus' known origins and his evident knowledge and/or power appears here, in Lk. iv 16-30, and in Jn. vi 42. In Luke Nazareth has been elevated to the status of inaugural and prophetic rejection symbolic of all the future. Two points should be noted: (i) the initial reaction is quite favorable and their wonder in no way presumes rejection: *ethaymazon epi tois logois tēs charitos . . . oychi 'yios estin Iōsēph 'oytos* (iv 22). It is only after Jesus puts the derisive proverb(s) concerning doctor and prophet in their mouth

---

[1]) R. BULTMANN, *op. cit.*, pp. 209-210: "*didachē kainē kat' exoysian . . .* conflict with the point." (p. 209).

in iv 23-24 and goes on the attack in iv 25-27 that the mood becomes, quite understandably, ugly in iv 28-30. This serves to heighten the already noted discrepancy between the *exeplēssonto* and the *eskandalizonto* in Mk. vi 2, 3 where no reason for the change in attitude is indicated; (ii) the contrast is between the power of his word and his known background, but only Joseph is mentioned so that Lk. iv 22 can hardly be derived from Mk. vi 3. In the case of Jn. vi 42 the clash is between claims of heavenly origin and known human background: " 'Surely this is Jesus son of Joseph' they said. 'We know his father and mother,' " but while Joseph is named, both parents are mentioned. Whatever relationship might exist between Lk. iv 22 and Jn. vi 42 it is obvious that there are traces of some contrast between genealogy and genius present in the tradition outside of Mark. It is to be assumed from this that Mark found vi 2b-3 in his received tradition. As it stood there it would have listed relatives of Jesus who were still significant in the community (*'ōde pros 'ēmas*) and also served to challenge a believing, i.e., a non-scandalous, answer to the question of the initial *pothen* [1]). The only remaining problem is whether Mark has changed this given tradition in vi 2b-3 in any way.

There is one problem in comparing Mk. vi 3 and the otherwise quite parallel text of Mt. xiii 55-56. Mk. vi 3 has *oych 'oytos estin 'o tektōn 'o 'yios tēs Marias*, but Mt. xiii 55 reads *oych 'oytos estin 'o toy tektonos 'yios; oych 'ē mētēr aytoy legetai Mariam*. Even in the Markan textual tradition there are important witnesses, which include P[45], that have a version closer to that of Matthew. The difficulty arises from the fact that, "it is contrary to Jewish custom to describe a man as the son of his mother, even when the father is no longer living, except in insulting terms ..." [2]). One might answer that Mark intends to protect the virgin birth, even obliquely on the lips of the unbelieving inhabitants of Jesus' home town, but this is hardly persuasive because: (i) he shows no other explicit interest in the virgin birth; (ii) he indicates no difficulty with the ambiguous *adelphos* and *adelphai*; (iii) even Lk. iv 22 and Jn. vi 42 find no dogmatic problems with having the inimical questioners presume Joseph as the named father. Yet, on the other hand, Mt.

---

[1]) Q. QUESNELL, *op. cit.*, p. 167 notes concerning Mk. viii 4: "the *pothen* tradition of the Old Testament—the question which can receive two answers, and one of the answers is 'From the Lord.' "

[2]) Cf. V. TAYLOR, *op. cit.*, pp. 299-300 for a fuller discussion.

xiii 55 is the more expected way of putting it: the son is identified by the father. But even here it must be noted that the father is not named but only his profession given (*toy tektonos*) while the mother is named. So Mt. xiii 55 is still different from Lk. iv 22 and Jn. vi 42.

It was seen earlier that the traditional sequence of "mother and brothers" in Mk. iii 31, 32, 33, 34 had been redactionally changed to "brother, sister, mother" in iii 35, so that "sister" was the chosen addition rather than, say, "father". This was explained as a Markan preparation for x 29-30 where it is the "father" who is dropped from x 29 in x 30 while "brothers, sisters, mother(s)" are retained in both verses. From this handling of iii 31-35 and x 29-30 it must be concluded that Mark is positively uninterested in the father of Jesus while being quite interested in his mother, brothers, and sisters. It is this phenomenon which suggests a solution to the problem of Mk. vi 3 in relation to Mt. xiii 55. The argument is that: (i) the questioning reaction of the home-town in the basic tradition noted Jesus' profession, Jesus' father and mother by name, and Jesus' brothers and sisters; (ii) the name of Joseph, as the most normal and important way of denoting human origins, was retained in the abbreviated tradition behind Lk. iv 22 and Jn. vi 42; (iii) it was deliberately erased by Mark himself as part of the positive uninterest just noted; (iv) Mt. xiii 35 in following Mark does not accept this strange genealogical note and so changes Jesus' profession (*'o tektōn*) into an indication of paternity (*'o toy tektonos 'yios*) which makes the minimal change necessary in his source—but still does not name the father; (v) the textual variant in Mark would be under the influence of Matthew's correction and possibly also feeling the strangeness of the Markan designation and/or the impropriety of Jesus as a carpenter. Mark's redactional change in vi 2b-3 was the removal of Jesus' named father from the text.

(3) vi 4. In the Oxyrhynchus papyri there is a saying of Jesus [1]: "A prophet is not acceptable in his own country, neither does a physician work cures on those who know him." It also appears

---

[1] From the translation by J. JEREMIAS of Pap. Ox. I, 31-36 in E. HENNECKE & W. SCHNEEMELCHER, *New Testament Apocrypha*, trans. R. McL. WILSON (2 vols.; London: Lutterworth Press, 1963) I, 109.

in the Gospel of Thomas [1]): "No prophet is acceptable in his village, no physician heals those who know him." There is a variation on this parallel proverb in broken form in Lk. iv 23: "Physician, heal yourself", and iv 24: "No prophet is ever accepted in his own country." In Jn. iv 44 only the first half appears: "there is no respect for a prophet in his own country". Because of all this the proverb behind Mk. vi 4 must be accepted as pre-Markan tradition and the only question is whether he may have made any redactional changes in accepting it from his sources. There is an obvious tendency in the tradition to hold on to the "prophet" part of the double proverb and to let the "physician" part fade away. The reason would be the obvious closer application of the former title: thus the form in the two extra-canonical sources is in good parallelism, while the physician part is changed in Lk. iv 23, and dropped entirely in Jn. iv 44. This same process is apparent in Mk. vi 4 where no physician is mentioned but only a prophet.

All of this serves to high-light the main problem in Mk. vi 4 where the prophet is honored save *en tē patridi aytoy kai en tois syggeneysin aytoy kai en tē oikia aytoy*. The difficulty is that (i) the parallelism of prophet/own country and physician/own household has not only been broken by the elimination of physician, which is not surprising, but that (ii) the format has been expanded into prophet/own country, own relations, own house, and that (iii) this is quite strange because in the context *oikia* could not just have meant walls and furniture but must have meant primarily one's relatives so that their explicit presence is redundant. The parallel in Mt. xiii 57 seems to have appreciated this and lacks any mention of the *kai en tois suggeneysin aytoy* of Mk. vi 4. The tradition itself had already moved the double proverb towards a shorter form: prophet/own country (own house), but the new insertion in Mk. vi 4 can best be explained as deliberate Markan redaction which Matthew did not follow or accept. In other words the indictment which the tradition left impersonal by noting only the "house(hold)" is rendered personal by Mark's mention of the "relatives". And, most importantly, this redactional addition in vi 4 is so located that the tradition had just furnished the reader with a named list of Jesus' relatives in the preceding vi 3. This

---

[1]) The translation of *GT* 31 is from A. GUILLAUMONT *et al.*, *The Gospel according to Thomas* (Leiden: Brill/New York: Harper, 1959) 21.

means that the list of personages in vi 3 has been turned from respectful indication in the tradition to specific indictment in the redaction

(4) vi 5-6. This verse presents the same dichotomy of positive and negative as seen earlier between vi 2 and vi 3 [1]). The opening statement that, "he could work no miracle there", in vi 5a is immediately specified with, "though he cured a few sick people by laying his hands on them", in vi 5b. Also there is a certain proverbial expectation of lack of honor given in vi 4 which makes the wonder of Jesus concerning their lack of faith in vi 6 somewhat anomalous. It is possible, of course, to consider vi 5a as simply a very strong but still to be qualified negative, just as it is possible to explain the earlier contradiction of vi 2-3 as being the two stages of a reaction that went from initial astonishment to ultimate rejection. But once again the parallel in Mt. xiii 58 seems to have sensed the problem and reads, "and he did not work *many* miracles there because of their lack of faith". This not only removes the improprieties of Mark's *oyk edynato* and *ethaymasen* with regard to Jesus but smoothes out the clash between the *oydemian* and the *ei mē*. Does the strangeness of vi 5-6 represent a fusion of tradition and redaction?

In the language of vi 5b-6 there are three expressions which are predominantly Markan in the synoptic tradition: (i) *arrōstos* appears only in vi 5 and vi 13, and in Mt. xiv 14 where it is probably under the influence of Mk. vi 13; (ii) the idea of *epitheis tas cheiras* in cures of Jesus is in Mk. v 23; vi 5; vii 32; viii 23, 25; it is twice in Lk. iv 40; xiii 13; but in Mt. xix 13, 15 only under influence from the *titheis* of Mk. x 16; (iii) *apistia* is in Mk. vi 6 = Mt. xiii 58 and Mk. ix 24. This is hardly very apodictic or even conclusive but if vi 5a is tradition and vi 5b-6 is redaction the discrepancy between them arises from the same literary combination as seen earlier between vi 1-2a (redaction) and vi 2b-3 (tradition). This would still leave the question of why Mark would have wanted to add vi 5b-6 redactionally?

The traditional datum of vi 1-6 was the pericope of vi 2b-4a. 4c-5a and (i) it named Jesus' relatives with intentions only of

---

[1]) These were noted but left unexplained in R. H. LIGHTFOOT, *History and Interpretation in the Gospel* ("Bampton Lectures 1934"; New York & London: Harper & Bros., 1935) 188, note 2.

respect; (ii) posed the *pothen* question which was intended to evoke the proper answer from the believing hearer; (iii) noted the problem, experienced presumably in the church's missionary activity, of rejection among one's own people and of the difficulty of miracles in such a situation. Mark took over this with one basic intention in mind: to turn the list of relatives into a list of those who greeted Jesus without respect. This was effected primarily by his insertion of vi 4b but also by mitigating somewhat the negative judgment against the wider circles of Jesus' fellow townsmen: hence the positive redactional frames of vi 1-2a (*exeplēssonto*) and vi 5b (*ei mē oligois . . .*). So specified the final accusation of *apistia* in vi 6a which amazes Jesus [1]) is pointed more precisely towards the relatives and not just against the town in general or the country at large. One should probably consider vi 6b, *kai periēgen tas kōmas kyklō didaskōn*, as the final redactional step in this process and as the close of vi 1-6 rather than the start of the next pericope or even the connective transition to it. This heightens the culpability of the relatives. Not only did Jesus have at least some success in his home town apart from them, but he continued teaching in the surrounding area. This is the force of the *kyklō* which (i) is used in Mk. iii 34; vi 6, 36 (= Lk. ix 12), and not again in the synoptic tradition; (ii) is omitted in Mt. ix 35 although he has the rest of Mark's phrase. But Mark's statement is that Jesus who finds belief round about (vi 6b) and even some positive reaction in his home town (vi 1-2a, 5b) finds only *apistia* and himself *atimos* from his relatives.

C. Mk. xv 40, 47; xvi 1.

This final section is offered as an hypothesis and an extremely tentative one at that. To grant it even this status one would need to have been persuaded by the two preceding sections that Mark has gone considerably out of his way to express redactionally the strongest disapproval against the relatives of Jesus.

The problem arises from the discrepancies between the three lists of women in xv 40 at the cross, in xv 47 at the burial, and in xvi 1 at the empty tomb after the resurrection. The texts are as follows:

---

[1]) The only other time *thaymazō* is used of Jesus is with regard to *pistis* in Mt. viii 10 = Lk. vii 9!

Maria ʿē Magdalēnē	ʿē de Maria ʿē Mag-dalēnē	Maria ʾē Magdalēnē
kai Maria	kai Maria	kai Maria
ʿē Iakōboy toy mikroy		ʿē Iakōboy
kai Iōsētos	ʿē Iōsētos	
mētēr		
kai Salōmē		kai Salōmē
(xv 40)	(xv 47)	(xvi 1)

It has been suggested [1]) that these divergencies arise from (i) a tradition which mentioned only Mary of Magdala and Mary of Joses in xv 47, and (ii) a second tradition which named only Mary of Magdala, Mary of James, and Salome in xvi 1, and (iii) the simple combination of these two strands to form the names of Mary of Magdala, Mary of James and Joses, and Salome in xv 40. This is a quite effective even if somewhat mechanical solution. It leaves certain questions unanswered: (i) why did Mark want to conflate xv 47 and xvi 1 into xv 40 and thereafter show no interest in harmonizing xv 57 and xvi 1 in line with this inaugural conflation; (ii) if he combined "Mary of Joses" from xv 47 with "Mary of Joseph" from xvi 1 in this rather mechanical way might it not have been expected to result in the sequence "Mary of Joses and James" rather than the reverse. These are by no means unanswerable objections but they are sufficient to ask if any other hypothesis is possible and, specifically, whether we might be dealing not with a mechanical conflation of traditions but with a combination of received tradition and subsequent redactional activity by Mark himself.

The discrepancy present in the three Markan texts is even more apparent in comparison with the presence and naming of these women in the other gospels. The parallels to Mk. xv 40, 47; xvi 1 in Mt. xxvii 56, 61; xxviii 1 and Lk. xxiii 49, 55; xxiv 1 all agree in mentioning the presence of women at the cross, the burial, and the empty tomb, but they disagree concerning their names and, more significantly, in how their names are handled. In Mt. xxvii 56 the names are: Maria ʿē Magdalēnē kai Maria ʿē toy Iakōboy kai Iōsēph mētēr, kai ʿē mētēr tōn ʿyiōn Zebedaioy. This is basically the same as Mk. xv 40 and the changes can be explained as Matthean redaction. For example, the mention of the mother of the sons of

---

[1]) V. TAYLOR, op. cit., pp. 651-653.

Zebedee instead of Salome need not be an identification but could be a substitution similar to, but much more gracious than, that in Mt. xx 20 (*'ē mētēr tōn 'yiōn Zebedaioy*) as against Mk. x 35. But the next two times these names appear in Mt. xxvii 61 and xxviii 1 all traces of the Markan discrepancies are absent and the women appear simply as *Maria(m)* *'ē Magdalēnē kai 'ē allē Maria* in both cases. The Lukan situation is even simpler. No names are given until xxiv 10 even though their presence is noted as in Mark. They are identified only at the moment they report their experience at the empty tomb to the apostles. They are named as: *'ē Magdalēnē Maria kai Iōanna kai Maria 'ē Iakōboy kai 'ai loipai syn aytois.* As with the case of Mt. xxvii 56 the naming of Joanna may be under the influence of Lk. viii 3 and hence redactional rather than independent tradition. But what is clear is that the problem of the names within the three Markan texts themselves is totally eliminated in Luke and completely smoothed over in Matthew. Once again these two points—a problem in the Markan text which is absent from the parallels of Matthew and Luke, serve to raise the question: is some deliberate Markan redaction causing the problem and can this be associated with more general Markan redactional activity and intention elsewhere?

There is also a tradition of the presence of certain women near the cross in Jn. xix 25. This text agrees with Mk. xv 40 in that: (i) both gives the names of three women [1]); (ii) both mention Mary of Magdala; (iii) both mention another Mary. They disagree in that: (i) Mark notes the presence of other (*en 'ais*) besides those named; (ii) John places Mary of Magdala last and Mark puts her in first place; (iii) the other Mary (same person?) is designated differently in Mark and John. But Jn. xix 25 is enough to indicate that there is pre-Markan tradition behind Mk. xv 40. There is no presence of the women at the burial in John presumably because his burial is performed most adequately and there is no trace of the synoptic hasty burial which necessitates the return of the women for the fuller anointing on Easter morning. However, in Jn. xx 1, 11 he agrees with Mark again to the extent that the presence of Mary of Magdala (and cf. plural in xx 2) is noted at

---

[1]) In Jn. xix 25 the absence of a *kai* before *Maria 'e toy Klōpa* and the presence of one before *Maria 'e Magdalēnē* would indicate that *adelphē tēs mētros aytoy Maria* . . . is one person cf., for example, *ton adelphon ton idion Simōna* in Jn. i 41.

the empty tomb. Hence in both Mk. xv 40; xvi 1 and Jn. xix 25; xx 1, 11 the death of Jesus on the cross and the finding of the empty tomb are linked by the presence of the same witness(es) and this may well indicate the function of the naming of the women in the tradition. This indicates a closer bond between xv 40 and xvi 1 and the comparative isolation of xv 47. But xv 40 and xvi 1 agree in naming the women as: Mary of Magdala, Mary (the mother) of James, and Salome. The only difference is the presence of the *kai Iōsētos* in xv 40 but not in xvi 1. And it is this mention of *Iōsētos* which reappears in the isolated text of xv 47. The tentative hypothesis offered to explain these literary pheonmena is:

(i) the pre-Markan tradition had only Mary of Magdala, Mary the mother of James, and Salome at the cross *and* at the tomb; (ii) Mark himself added *kai Iōsētos* in xv 40 and also created the new verse of xv 47 [1]) to repeat *'ē Iōsētos* again; (iii) with Joses added in twice, he left xvi 1 untouched and the abbreviation from the earlier *Maria 'ē Iakōboy toy mikroy mētēr* (xv 40) to the shorter *Maria 'ē Iakōboy* (xvi 1) is the normal eradication of the redundant and was probably already in his received tradition (cf., for example, Mt. xxviii 56, 61). If this hypothesis is correct Mark wished to introduce the name of Joses and to emphasize that the Mary in question is the mother of James and Joses. This in its turn would be a deliberate link with the relatives of Jesus in vi 3 where Jesus is *adelphos Iakōboy kai Iōsētos* [2]). What, then, would this pointing

---

[1]) With regard to content xv 47 does not supply much new: (i) *etheōroyn* recals the *theōroysai* of xv 40; (ii) *poy tetheitai* prepares for the *'opoy ethēkan* of xvi 6; (iii) the use of the double article in *'ē Maria 'ē Magdalēnē* is unique in the NT, which uses either *Maria 'ē Magdalēnē* or, once in Lk. xxiv 10, *'ē Magdalēnē Maria*. This unusual form could be explained as redactional rather than traditional. Its presence in xv 47 also resulted in the double article in part of the Markan textual tradition for xvi 1.

[2]) V. TAYLOR, *op. cit.*, p. 598 denies the identity of James and Joses in vi 3 and xv 40: "it is difficult to identify them. They are clearly not the brothers of Jesus (vi. 3), for Mark would not have designated Mary the Virgin in this roundabout way." This presumes *adelphos* in vi 3 denotes blood-brother (cf. pp. 247-249). But if Jn. xix 25 has a Mary (wife) of Clopas as an *adelphē* of Mary the mother of Jesus (cf. note 1, p. 107), this *adelphē* is hardly blood-sister unless both sisters have the same name. Is it not possible that there is a single woman Mary, wife of Clopas, mother of James and Joses, and a cousin of Mary? In any case this article does not presume that Mark's genealogical knowledge of Jesus' family is any more accurate than his geographical knowledge of Jesus' country. The argument is that Mark intends to equate the James and Joses in vi 3 and xv 40, 47; xvi 1. What this has to do with historical accuracy is a separate question.

up of the identity of Mary as a relative of Jesus have to do with the other inimical notes concerning the relatives in iii 21-35 and vi 1-6?

In order to suggest an explanation certain positions concerning the end of the Markan gospel will be accepted as the necessary background—if these are incorrect a new explanation would have to be sought. It is accepted that: (i) the originally intended ending of Mark's work is xvi 1-8 and there is no lost ending [1]); (ii) the intention of this ending was to state that the message of xvi 7 never got back to "the disciples and Peter", and that the call to leave Jerusalem for Galilee—whether this was for post-resurrectional apparition [2]), or for the start of the Gentile mission [3]), or for the final parousiac reunion [4]), was never communicated to them. In a word, the Jerusalem church was not "where" it was supposed to be by the will and summons of its Lord. To this accusation Mark has added a final point: (iv) once again the relatives of Jesus, and not just some Galilean women, have failed him and

---

[1]) B. H. STREETER, op. cit., pp. 335-344 argues for either an unfinished work or a lost ("almost immediately": p. 338) ending. R. H. LIGHTFOOT, Locality and Doctrine in the Gospels (New York & London: Harper & Bros., 1938) 1-48 proposes that it "may have ended and been meant to end at xvi 8" (p. 48); cf. also his The Gospel Message of St. Mark (Oxford: Clarendon Press, 1950) 80-97. The question is still under debate: E. LINNEMANN, "Der (wiedergefundene) Markusschluss", ZTK 66 (1969) 255-287 finds the original ending in Mk. xvi 1-8; Mt. xxviii 16-17; Mk. xvi 15-20, but R. P. MEYE, "Mark xvi 8-The Ending of Mark's Gospel", BR 14 (1969) 33-43 claims xvi 1-8 was the original ending with its "central emphasis that the word of Jesus is being fulfilled in the resurrection events" (p. 43).

[2]) For example, R. BULTMANN, op. cit., p. 285: "So xvi 7 is just as much as xiv 28 put by Mark into the passage from tradition, to prepare the way for a Galilean appearance of Jesus"; or W. G. KÜMMEL, Prophecy and Fulfilment ("SBT," No. 23; Naperville, Ill.: Allenson, 1957) 77-79: "Jesus will appear after his resurrection to his disciples in Galilee" (p. 79).

[3]) G. H. BOOBYER, "Galilee and Galileans in St. Mark's Gospel," BJRL 35 (1952-3) 334-348; D. F. EVANS, "'I will go before you into Galilee,'" JTS 5 (1954) 3-18 concludes: "We have to choose between these two in interpreting the end of Mark's gospel as we have it. Either "he anticipates you into Galilee, and there, in the parousia, you will see him," or 'he is leading you to the Gentiles; it is there you will behold him.'" J. SCHREIBER, "Die Christologie des Markusevangeliums. Beobachtungen zur Theologie und Komposition des zweiten Evangeliums," ZTK 58 (1961) 154-183: "Markus versteht die Landschaft Galiläa nach Jes. viii 23 als das Galiläa der Heiden." (p. 172).

[4]) E. LOHMEYER, Galiläa und Jerusalem ("FRLANT," N.F. 34; Göttingen: Vandenhoeck & Ruprecht, 1936); R. H. LIGHTFOOT, Locality and Doctrine in the Gospels (New York & London: Harper & Bros., 1938) 49-65, 73-77, 106-126; W. MARXSEN, op. cit., pp. 54-116; N. Q. HAMILTON, "Resurrection Tradition and the Composition of Mark," JBL 84 (1965) 415-421.

are directly and causally involved in the failure of the Jerusalem community to "receive" the call of the Risen Lord. This is clearly not intended as a literal statement concerning the historical silence, be it temporary or permanent, of these women, but as a symbolic statement concerning the failure of the Jerusalem church and of the relatives of Jesus.

II. The Redactional Purpose of Mark

In moving from redactional action to redactional intention the possibility of exegetical subjectivity is greatly increased, but one can hardly avoid the interpretative question already broached at the end of the preceding section: what does this polemic against Jesus' relatives mean to Mark? Even if there was some pre-Markan evidence of tension between Jesus and his relatives in the tradition (cf. Jn. vii 2-5 as a possibility), it is Mark himself who: (i) equated their attempt to restrain Jesus as one insane with the accusation of the Jerusalem scribes that he was possessed (iii 21-35); and (ii) mentioned the relatives by name and then added that these also did not honor him (vi 1-6); and possibly (iii) named one of Jesus' relatives among the women who failed to give the Lord's summons to the Jerusalem community.

Recent studies on Mark's gospel have stressed the Christological controversy which is at its core and have argued that the Christology which Mark opposed is exemplified by the attitudes of the disciples while the true Christology is revealed in the Markan Jesus himself [1]. But even if one agrees that: "It was the purpose of the evangelist to teach the Christians of his day a true Christology in place of the false Christology which he felt they were in danger of accepting. The method he chooses is that of a most carefully constructed narrative in which the false Christology is put on the lips of the disciples and the true Christology on the

---

[1] For example, A. Kuby, "Zur Konzeption des Markus-Evangeliums," ZNW 49 (1958) 52-64 contrasts Mk. i 16-8, 21 where "Die Jünger erkennen Jesus nicht als den Messias", and viii 22-14, 72 where "Die Jünger haben Jesus erkannt und verstehen ihn nicht" (pp. 63-64); J. Tyson, "The Blindness of the Disciples," JBL 80 (1961) 261-268; J. Schreiber, loc. cit.; T. Weeden, "The Heresy that Necessitated Mark's Gospel," ZNW 59 (1968) 145-158 who expands Kuby's two points into three more convincing ones: "imperceptivity (i 16-8, 26) to misconception (viii 27-xiv 9) to rejection (xiv 10-72)." Cf. also his Claremont doctoral thesis of the same title in 1964, DissAbstr 28 (1967-8) 4262A-3A.

lips of Jesus" [1]), there is still the question of why Mark would have chosen the *disciples* as the villains of his Christological controversy. Is the debate merely a doctrinal one within the Markan community in which Jesus' disciples are arbitrarily chosen to personify the heretical position or, at very most, are chosen because the Markan heretics claim them as their own authorities [2]). It would seem that Mark would have needed more than this to equate Jesus' disciples and his own heretics. There are two points which argue that the Markan polemic is not only a conflict within the Markan community over doctrine but also a manifesto from the Markan church, in whole or in part, against the jurisdictional and doctrinal hegemony of the Jerusalem church [3]).

The first point is that the villains of the Markan theology are not just the disciples in general but the inner three, Peter, James, and John in particular. The special new names [4]) and the special revelation which Jesus gives only to them makes their utter failure all the more obvious and culpable: for example, Peter (x 28) and James and John (x 35) in the context of ix 30-x 45, or their sleeping in Gethsemane in xiv 32-42 [5]). To focus the failure of the disciples

---

[1]) N. Perrin, "The Son of Man in the Synoptic Tradition," *BR* 13 (1968) 21 = "The Creative Use of the Son of Man Traditions by Mark," *UnSemQR* 23 (1968) 357. On this false Christology as a *theios anēr* theology cf., besides the works cited in the last note J. M. Robinson, "The Recent Debate on the 'New Quest' ", *JBR* 30 (1962) 198-208, esp. pp. 203-204, and his, "The Problem of History in Mark, Reconsidered", *UnSemQR* 20 (1965) 131-147, esp. pp. 135-138.

[2]) T. Weeden, *op. cit.*, p. 155 suggests: "In all likelihood the Markan heretics claimed that their position went back to the disciples themselves."

[3]) Already argued in É. Trocmé, *op. cit.*, pp. 100-109, and repeated in K. Tagawa, *Miracles et Évangile* ("Études d'Histoire et de Philosophie Religieuses", 62; Paris: Presses Universitaires de France, 1966) 174-185: "Marc adresse sa critique à l'Église de Jérusalem" (p. 180).

[4]) Only in Mark are all three apostles (i) given new names; (ii) mentioned as the first three; (iii) renamed by the same phrase: *epethēken . . . onoma*: compare iii 16-17 with Mt. x 2, and Lk. vi 14; in Acts i 13 Peter, James, and John are also in first place. The convoluted nature of Mk. iii 16-17 could be explained if the naming in 16a and 17b were placed redactionally as frames to the given names in 16b-17a.

[5]) Their failure in xiv 34, 38 (*grēgoreite*) and xiv 37, 40 (*'eyriskei/'ēyren aytoys katheydontas*) is heightened by the fact that along with Andrew, they (named in xiii 3 but not in Mt. xxiv 3 = Lk. xxi 7) had been warned *grē-goreite* (xiii 35, 37) lest the Lord *elthōn . . . 'eyrē 'ymas katheydontas* (xiii 36). The guilt of Simon Peter is especially emphasized (as the *thyrōros* of xiii 34 ? which is not in the parallels) in that Jesus withdraws his new name: *kai legei tǭ Petrǭ, Simōn, katheydeis?* which is only in Mk. xiv 37 and not in Mt. xxvi 40 and Lk. xxii 46. Peter then denies Jesus (xiv 54-72), and his

in general on the three in particular and most especially on Peter can hardly be derived merely from a desire to personify the heretics within the Markan community. It seems rather to point towards the Jerusalem mother-church where the importance of Peter, on the one hand, and of an inner three, on the other, is witnessed to by such a text as Gal. ii 7-10. And in Gal. i 19 and ii 9 it is James, the brother of the Lord, who is noted especially in the Jerusalem church. Hence the Markan polemic against the disciples of Jesus points beyond the heretics in the Markan community to the Jerusalem church especially with regard to Peter and the idea of an inner three (be it Peter, James, and John or James, the brother of Jesus, Cephas, and John).

Secondly, the animosity of Mark to the relatives of Jesus points likewise against the Jerusalem church because it is there that James, the brother of the Lord, becomes important. In Acts i 14 the Jerusalem community includes "Mary the mother of Jesus, and . . . his brothers". James is especially noted in Acts xii 17; xv 13; xxi 18; 1 Cor. xv 7; Gal. i 19; ii 9, 12 and Jas. i 1, and his brother Jude is mentioned in Jude i 1 (cf. Mk. vi 3) [1]). The polemic against the disciples and the polemic against the relatives intersect as a polemic against the doctrinal and jurisdictional hegemony of the Jerusalem mother-church although, of course, this was most likely all provoked by heretics within the Markan community. But to oppose them Mark had to write not only a doctrinal warning against heresy but a jurisdictional manifesto against Jerusalem.

If this conclusion is accepted some minor points in the pericopes studied above may also become clearer. The father of Jesus, Joseph, may not have been mentioned in iii 31-35, been removed in vi 3, and been removed from x 30 because he held no place in the Jerusalem community and was thus of no interest to Mark [2]). Nazareth

---

final appearance in Mk. xvi 7 is in second place: "the disciples and Peter." The only other place in the NT where Peter is not mentioned in first place when his name is cited is in Jn. i 44 which is presumably under the influence of the sequence in i 40-41. The order in xvi 7 is extremely unusual.

[1]) There is no need to presume a "caliphate" of Jesus' relatives in the Jerusalem community. On this cf. the negative conclusions of H. VON CAMPENHAUSEN, "The Authority of Jesus' Relatives in the Early Church," *Jerusalem and Rome*, ed. C. L. Lee ("Facet Books: Historical Series," 4; Philadelphia: Fortress Press, 1966) 1-19.

[2]) Compare the suggestion of J. M. ROBINSON, *The Problem of History in Mark* "SBT", No. 21; Naperville, Ill.: Allenson, 1957) 81, note 1, that it is omitted because "God is the father of Jesus".

was never named in vi 1-6 and this could be because the *patris* Mark was interested in was Jerusalem and not Nazareth [1]). Finally, the reason why Mark chose to name the opponents of Jesus in iii 22 and vii 1 as scribes who had come down from Jerusalem becomes clearer. Such a title could apply to Jewish opponents of Jesus during his lifetime but it could also apply to Jewish-Christian opponents of Mark. Mt. xiii 52 shows that it was possible to think of a "scribe who becomes a disciple of the kingdom of heaven". The scribes who came from Jerusalem in iii 22 and vii 1 may represent another pointing of the polemic of Mark against the Jerusalem community whence scribes still come down to regulate the other communities [2]).

The conclusions can now be placed in summary form. Mark has redacted the tradition in iii 21-35 and vi 1-6 and possibly in xiii 40, 47; xvi 1 as well so that there is severe opposition between Jesus and his relatives: they have blasphemed against the Holy Spirit; they have dishonored Jesus and are without faith in him; and they are directly involved in the failure of the Jerusalem community to receive his resurrectional summons to Galilee. This Markan condemnation reflects the polemic of the Markan community against the Jerusalem mother-church not only as a doctrinal debate (against the disciples) but also as a jurisdictional debate (against the relatives) as well. The two facets of the polemic met already in the fact that not only the disciples in general but the inner three and Peter himself in particular had become the focal target of Mark's criticism. But it closed most precisely with the Jerusalem authority in attacking the relatives whose relationship to Jesus gave their doctrinal positions such unassailable force.

---

[1]) A different interpretation is given in E. GRÄSSER, "Jesus in Nazareth (Mark vi 1-6a). Notes on the Redaction and Theology of St. Mark," *NTS* 16 (1969) 1-23.

[2]) For example in Acts xv 1 where trouble is caused by *tines katelthontes apo tēs Ioydaias*, or in Gal. ii 12 where it stems, more specifically, from *elthein tinas apo Iakōboy*. Both cases concern fidelity to Mosaic observance under pressure from Jewish Christians in Jerusalem.

THE RELATIVES OF JESUS IN MARK

BY

J. LAMBRECHT S.J.

Leuven

The Markan gospel presents us with several groups of people who are, at certain times and places, obviously hostile to Jesus: scribes, Pharisees (Pharisees and scribes, Pharisees and Herodians), the Jerusalem council, Jesus' fellow townsmen, and his relatives. In this paper we wish to draw attention to the last category, or more precisely, to the way in which the evangelist Mark presents them to his readers. Hence our title: The Relatives of Jesus in Mark. Last year a study appeared in *Novum Testamentum*, written by J. D. CROSSAN, with a similar title: Mark and the Relatives of Jesus [1]. In this study CROSSAN investigates three passages: Mk iii 20-35; vi 1-6; and the texts mentioning the women at the cross (xv 40-41) and at the tomb (xv 47; xvi 1). He analyses first in great detail Mark's redactional activity; in a second shorter section, whose thesis, however, is a more debatable one, he elaborates upon Mark's redactional purpose.

It is our intention to show (1) that Mark was more dependent upon traditions still recoverable to a certain degree and at the same time editorially more active than CROSSAN seems willing to accept, and (2) that the Markan redactional purpose may be explained differently from what CROSSAN described as a double polemic: "a doctrinal warning against heretics within the community" and "a jurisdictional manifesto against the hegemony of Jerusalem." It will also become clear that in order to show what Mark exactly means by the relatives of Jesus Mk iii 20-21, 31-35 is the only important passage.

I. CROSSAN'S FINDINGS

1. With regard to the first passage, Mk iii 20-21, 31-35, Mark's redaction must be studied together with his handling of the Beelze-

---

[1] J. D. CROSSAN, "Mark and the Relatives of Jesus," *Novum Testamentum*, 15 (1973), 81-113. Cf. H.-H. SCHROEDER, *Eltern und Kinder in der Verkündigung Jesu. Eine hermeneutische Untersuchung* (Theol. Forschung 53), Hamburg-Bergstedt, 1972, pp.110-124, whose search for Jesus' intention, however, manifests a different methodological approach.

bul controversy (iii 22-30) since the Beelzebul incident was probably already linked in Mark's sources to a pericope on Jesus' relatives (the pre-Markan unity of iii 22b, 24-27 and 31-34; cf. the
sequence of Lk xi 14 = Mt xii 22-23: exorcism; Lk xi 15-23 = Mt
xii 24-32: accusation; Lk xi 24-26 = Mt xii 43-45: seven devils; and
Mt xii 46-50: relatives, see Lk xi 27-28: woman blessing Jesus'
mother). Mark creates vv. 21-22a. The relatives are of the opinion
that Jesus is out of his senses. This negative judgment should be
read in the light of the first accusation of the Jerusalem scribes:
Jesus has Beelzebul in him. The two utterances are similar in form.
Mark's literary activity makes a parallel between relatives and
scribes. Since in the Markan view both v. 21 and v. 22 lead up to
the discussion, Jesus reacts first to the accusation of the scribes
(iii 23-27) and then to the initiative of his relatives (iii 31-35). The
inverted order is due to the sequence in Mark's sources. Materially
speaking vv. 28-30 are part of the Beelzebul discussion. V. 30
is purely redactional; it repeats the accusation of v. 22b which
itself is a redactional doubling of v. 22c. Vv. 28-29 are related to a
traditional saying (Q, cf. Mt xii 32 and Lk xii 10a), but the Markan
redaction here has been very thorough: no more distinction between
speaking against the Son of Man and against the Holy Spirit
because in the redactor's mind, the earthly Jesus possessed the
Spirit (cf. i 8, 10, 12). Mark gave the logion a central position and
since in his opinion the relatives as well as the scribes did not
acknowledge in Jesus the presence of the Spirit, the conclusion in
vv. 28-29 concerning the unforgivable sin is meant for both [2]).
Of the verses 31-35, tradition is contained in vv. 31-34 and v. 35
is redaction. As has been stated already, in the Markan sources
the tradition of the relatives was linked with that of the Beelzebul
incident, but the distance and hostile attitude characteristic of the
relatives stem from Mark's rewriting so that iii 31-35 continues
the trend of the redactional v. 21. The Markan v. 35 shows that
Mark wanted to include the sisters into Jesus' family (cf. vi 3 and
x 29-30). Taken together, in iii 21-35 the Markan redaction intended
to equate the relatives of Jesus with the culpable scribes; Mark made
them participants in the scribes' accusation of Jesus. A result is that

---

[2]) Cf. e.g. E. TROCMÉ, *La formation de l'évangile selon Marc*, Paris, 1963,
p. 108: "Si donc les scribes venus de Jérusalem ont commis un péché qui ne
pourra jamais être effacé, la famille de Jésus a fait autant, laisse entendre notre
évangéliste."

kinsmen and 'true' relatives, those who do the will of God, are now extreme opposites.

In vi 1-6 the Markan editorial activity consists in adding vv. 1-2a and vv. 5b-6 and inserting the phrase "and among his own kin" into v. 4. By this redaction two changes are effected. The negative attitude which the fellow townsmen manifested in Mark's tradition is somewhat tempered. And the relatives who in the traditional v. 3 were mentioned in a neutral way are now included among those who do not accept Jesus.

CROSSAN himself admits that his redaction-hypothesis concerning xv 40-41, 47; xvi 1 is "an extremely tentative one." Mark would have considered the second of the women whose names are known through tradition (Mary Magdalene, Mary the mother of James, and Salome, cf. xv 40; xvi 1) a relative of Jesus [3]). This can be concluded from his addition of the 'brother' Joses (see xv, 40, 47; cf. vi 3). These women ("not just some Galilean women" but relatives!) did not transmit to the disciples the Lord's command to leave for Galilee (cf. xvi 7-8). Does Mark say by this that relatives are causally involved in the failure of 'Jerusalem' to receive the call of the Risen Lord?

2. "Mark has redacted the tradition in iii 21-35 and vi 1-6 and possibly in xv 40, 47; xvi, 1 as well so that there is severe opposition between Jesus and his relatives: they have blasphemed against the Holy Spirit; they have dishonored Jesus and are without faith in him; and they are directly involved in the failure of the Jerusalem community to receive his resurrectional summons to Galilee" [4]). What is the redactional purpose of that deliberately negative picture of Jesus' relatives? CROSSAN in his dealing with this question starts by mentioning a thesis which nowadays is widely accepted. Mark writes in an actualizing way; he fights against the dangers of a false christology; he does so by means of a narrative in which Jesus presents the true doctrine while the disciples are unwilling to accept it. Through these disciples Mark aims at his fellow Christians: what is said of the slowness and blindness of the disciples is a warning to them.

CROSSAN corrects and completes this basic insight. More than the disciples in general the privileged inner circle of the three,

---

[3]) In footnote 2 of p. 108, *art. cit.*, the author tries to show that the mother of James and Joses could be another person than the mother of Jesus.

[4]) *Art. cit.*, p. 113.

Peter, James, and John, are described in a very negative fashion. Does this not point to the 'three' who, after Easter, were leading the Jerusalem church for a period of time ? And was it not in the same Jerusalem that the relatives of Jesus, first James and later Simeon and the grandsons of Judas, were governing the Church ? The polemic against the disciples and against the relatives is conducted by Mark with a twofold purpose. The Markan polemic contains a doctrinal warning intended for failing believers (exemplified by the disciples) within the local community *and* it is a protest against the Jerusalem jurisdictional and doctrinal hegemony (symbolized by the relatives and the disciples). Within this framework of editorial tendencies other details can be explained. Because the father of Jesus held no place in the Jerusalem community, Joseph is nowhere mentioned in the Markan gospel; because it was Jerusalem that was in power, Jesus' home town in ch. vi is not indicated by its name Nazareth; and because Jerusalem sent inspectors to the other churches, the scribes, according to Mark's view, have to come from Jerusalem (iii 22; vii 1).

II. Critical Remarks and Personal Reflexions

The method *qua* method used in Crossan's study is a valid one [5]). Crossan's insight into the sources of Mark may be adopted globally. In addition to many pertinent observations he convincingly indicated that Mark's editorial activity changed a possible pre-Markan tension between Jesus and his relatives into explicit opposition and that the editor made use of a tradition of accusing opponents (presumably Pharisees) for this purpose. A critical discussion could start with the so-called Markan polemic against the relatives. Is the equation of relatives and scribes so radical and complete as Crossan maintains ? ἔλεγον . . . ὅτι ἐξέστη in v. 21b [6])

---

[5]) On pp. 81-82, *ibid.*, Crossan indicates three 'principles' for ascertaining redactional activity in Mk: (1) the presence of some awkwardness in the text, (2) its absence in the parallels of Matthew and/or Luke (or in post-Markan textual changes) and (3) the presence there of Markan language and theology. "The simultaneous presence of all three points is highly persuasive in determining the presence of editorial work by the final redactor" (p. 82). Crossan may be overestimating the value of the second 'principle'. Matthaean and/or Lukan differences from Mark which presumably are caused by Q influence may be more significant.

[6]) We should mention here two recent attempts to eliminate the offensive character of v. 21. The translation of H. Wansbrough, "Mark 3, 21 — Was Jesus out of his mind ?", *New Testament Studies*, 18 (1971-72), 233-235, is as

and ἔλεγον ὅτι Βεελζεβοὺλ ἔχει in v. 22b have a symmetrical structure which is certainly intended by Mark. Indeed ἐξέστη cannot be interpreted as being caused by the people's excitement and the forced ascetism of Jesus, both mentioned in v. 20. Yet some data stand in the way of a simple identification of the attitudes of each party. ἔλεγον of v. 21b as contrasted with that of v. 22b does not imply an accusation openly expressed; it only gives the motivation of the initiative of οἱ παρ' αὐτοῦ: they were of the opinion that.... Besides, v. 21b is separated from the accusation in v. 22b by v. 22a which introduces a new scene.

---

follows: "When they heard it, his followers went out to calm it down, for they said that it was out of control with enthusiasm" (p. 235). Referring to G. HARTMANN, Mk 3, 20f., *Biblische Zeitschrift*, 11 (1913), 249-279, SCHROEDER, *op. cit.*, p. 111, translates in a similar way as WANSBROUGH: "Seine Jünger (sc. die mit ihm im Hause sind) hörten (sc. von dem andrängenden Volk) und gingen hinaus, um es zurückzuhalten; denn sie sagten: 'Es ist ausser sich'." SCHROEDER's arguments are: (1) οἱ παρ' αὐτοῦ is not a technical term for 'relatives'; παρά + gen. would indicate here descent, origin and the οἱ in that case cannot point to mother or brothers; (2) where the vague phrase οἱ παρ' αὐτοῦ is used, the persons meant are always named before (cf. Sus. 30-33); (3) there would be a tension between v. 21 where the relatives act in a rather strong way, and vv. 31-35 where their appearance seems to be rather harmless. (4) The anticipatory usage of παρά + gen. instead of παρά + dat. (before going out the friends are with Jesus) is not unknown in Greek; (5) the scene depicted in iii 20-21 should be read in the light of iii 9-10; (6) the synoptic usage of ἐξίστημι generally connotes astonishment on Jesus' deeds.

In spite of all this we continue to prefer the interpretation which holds that in v. 21 the relatives of Jesus go out to seize him because they think that he is out of his mind. Our chief reason is, as stated already in the text, the obvious parallelism between v. 21b and v. 22b which cannot but be intended by the editor. As to SCHROEDER's arguments: (1) even in examples given by him the παρά in οἱ παρ' αὐτοῦ is not to be pressed; we admit that the expresssion οἱ παρ' αὐτοῦ in Mk iii 21, especially before ἐξῆλθον, is somewhat strange; it would seem to us that παρά here has nothing to do with ἐξῆλθον; (2) it is not to be excluded that Mark uses in v. 21 this rather vague expression precisely in order to avoid the explicit naming of mother and brothers in such a context; (3) when vv. 31-35 are read in continuation of vv. 20-21, the arrival of the relatives is appropriately motivated; (4) this possible explanation can be dismissed; (5) is there a reference to iii 9-10 ? It should be stressed that αὐτόν in iii 21 can hardly point back to the crowd of v. 20. In addition to the fact that Jesus (αὐτοῦ) is clearly the most natural antecedent, Mark never refers to ὄχλος with αὐτόν (after writing ὄχλος there are seventeen cases where he even continues with the plural); (6) ἐξίστημι occurs four times in Mark. The subject in ii 12 and v 42 is the people, in vi 51 the disciples. The meaning is 'to be amazed, astonished'. In all three passages, however, a marvelous deed of Jesus precedes; this would not be the case in iii 21. Further, in Mk κρατέω is never used in the sense of 'to restrain'. Moreover, it would be unusual that ἀκούσαντες is said of disciples who hear about something that happens in their presence!

Further, ἔξεστη is a statement which, after all, sounds more vague and weaker than the blasphemous charges in v. 22. CROSSAN does not say clearly who the αὐτούς of v. 23a are, but he does suggest, incorrectly, we feel, that they are not the scribes [7]). Related with this is his view that Jesus' severe judgment in vv. 28-29 is also meant for the relatives. But actually, only the scribes formulated the really culpable accusation (cf. its redactional repetition in v. 30); vv. 28-29 function as the end and climax of Jesus' apology which is addressed to the accusers—*they* are the most obvious antecedent of αὐτούς in v. 23a. And the overtones in vv. 31-35 show Jesus keeping aloof rather than condemning.

1. We will have to return later to the puzzling question of what this polemic against Jesus' relatives meant to Mark. A few critical notes concerning CROSSAN's evaluation of Mark's editorial work should be given first. The numerous redactional changes as well as the typical structure resulting from them seem to prove a good deal of Markan activity *and* the use of sources which differ slightly or not at all from those provided by a reconstructed Q text [8]). Before we consider the structure of the two united pericopes in ch. iii we shall discuss iii 22-30 and iii 20-21, 31-35 separately.

a) iii, 22-30. No need to deal again with the omission by Mark of the exorcism (cf. Mt xii 22-23 = Lk xi 14), the doubling of the accusation in v. 22b and 22c. CROSSAN and others treated those items sufficiently. But in vv. 23b-26 Markan redaction is definitely more recognizable than CROSSAN presumes [9]). To the accusation that Jesus casts out the demons with the assistance of Beelzebul, Jesus in Q at first replies indirectly by stating that such a charge is absurd. Q begins with a general assertion: every kingdom divided against itself is laid waste, house falls upon house. Then comes the application to Satan's kingdom (cf. Lk xi 17-18). Mark, however, articulates that answer in a different way. Satan's kingdom is no more mentioned by him in v. 26; in vv. 24-25 'kingdom' and 'house' (= household) are two independent metaphors, while

---

[7]) *Art. cit.*, p. 89: "... hardly the accusers who are presumably present."

[8]) The following pages make use of the study we published in Dutch, with a four page English summary, *Marcus Interpretator. Stijl en boodschap in Mc. 3, 20-4, 34*, Brugge-Utrecht, 1969 (= *Bijdragen*, *29*, 1968, pp. 114-150, 234-258, 369-393). We refer to it for full discussion and bibliography.

[9]) Cf. *art. cit.*, p. 91: "... the present text of Mk iii, 24-25 can be taken as untouched tradition."

in Q, house (= building) was only an illustrative feature of the kingdom's destruction. The two comparisons (cf. ἐν παραβολαῖς, v. 23a) are framed: v. 23b raises the introductory challenging question and v. 26 drives the point home. CROSSAN writes: "The presence of iii 23b spoils this formal structure" [10]). By structure he means here the double metaphor (kingdom, house) of what is called a 'stylized reaction' in iii 24-25. But Mark's source (cf. Q) probably never possessed a double metaphor and Mark himself is working out his own abb'a'-pattern [11]):

vv. 23b-26:

a πῶς δύναται σατανᾶς σατανᾶν ἐκβάλλειν;
 b καὶ ἐὰν βασιλεία ἐφ' ἑαυτὴν μερισθῇ,
   οὐ δύναται σταθῆναι ἡ βασιλεία ἐκείνη·
 b' καὶ ἐὰν οἰκία ἐφ' ἑαυτὴν μερισθῇ,
   οὐ δυνήσεται ἡ οἰκία ἐκείνη στῆναι.
a' καὶ εἰ ὁ σατανᾶς ἀνέστη ἐφ' ἑαυτὸν καὶ ἐμερίσθη,
   οὐ δύναται στῆναι
   ἀλλὰ τέλος ἔχει.

In vv. 23b-26 Mark undoubtedly expanded his source. After that, before writing v. 27, he probably leaves out tradition (cf. Lk xi 19-20, 23 = Mt xii 27-28, 30), and in redacting v. 27 he abbreviates the received tradition. The rather compact character of v. 27 with its varying repetition of τὰ σκεύη αὐτοῦ διαρπάσαι and τὴν οἰκίαν αὐτοῦ διαρπάσει seems to be a result of editing. Mark wanted to summarize the idea contained in the short but colourful Q parable which Luke -albeit in his own wording- transmitted to us (cf. Lk xi 21-22).

After the logion of scattering-gathering (Lk xi 23 = Mt. xii 30) Q offered the story of the seven devils (Lk xi 24-26 = Mt xii 43-45). The phrase πνεῦμα ἀκάθαρτον (Lk xi 24 = Mt. xii 43: τὸ ἀκάθαρτον πνεῦμα) in the redactional v. 30 may be evidence that Mark was

---

[10]) *Ibid.*, p. 90.

[11]) Once this intentional structure is recognized, objections such as those raised by CROSSAN, *art. cit.*, p. 186, n. 1, in relation to our analysis have no more relevance. "Stylistic changes of a minor nature" have a compositional function indeed, but the new structure itself serves a new 'ideological' outline. The author admits: ". . . it seems also clear that Mark and Q were extremely close to one another on this pericope (= Beelzebul controversy)." We would prefer instead of Mark: *the Markan source.*

acquainted with that section of Q [12]). He omitted it, or it might be more appropriate to say that he replaced it by his own version of another Q-tradition: the unforgivable sin (vv. 28-29; cf. Lk xii 10 = Mt xii 32). In Mark's composition the saying obtains a new context; the blasphemy against the Holy Spirit is now explicitly related to the concrete accusation of the scribes. CROSSAN rightly mentions Mark's radical interpretative rewriting [13]). But he did not notice that the same Mark in rewriting and expanding the passage of the Q source as he did, effected a second abb'a'-schema. Its formal similarity with that of vv. 23b-26 is hardly accidental.

vv. 28-29:

ἀμὴν λέγω ὑμῖν ὅτι

a   πάντα ἀφεθήσεται τοῖς υἱοῖς τῶν ἀνθρώπων,

  b   τὰ ἁμαρτήματα καὶ αἱ βλασφημίαι

          ὅσα ἐὰν βλασφημήσωσιν·

  b'   ὃς δ' ἂν βλασφημήσῃ

εἰς τὸ πνεῦμα τὸ ἅγιον,

a' οὐκ ἔχει ἄφεσιν εἰς τὸν αἰῶνα,

ἀλλὰ ἔνοχός ἐστιν αἰωνίου ἁμαρτήματος.

CROSSAN underlines the Markan inclusive character of v. 30 [14]). However, v. 30 is not so completely and purely Markan. The verse seems to be a return to a clause of the source which had been passed over: ὅτι λέγετε ἐν Βεελζεβοὺλ ἐκβάλλειν με τὰ δαιμόνια (Lk

---

[12]) Cf. CROSSAN, *art. cit.*, p. 95: ". . . the phrase (τὸ) πνεῦμα (τὸ) ἀκάθαρτον is exclusively Markan in the synoptic tradition with all other uses deriving from his own." See also n. 3 on the same page: ". . . the only non-Markan usage in the synoptic tradition also (= Lk iv 36) appears as τὸ ἀκάθαρτον πνεῦμα in the Q text of Mt xii 43 = Lk xi 24." The Q passage in our opinion was the basis of Mark's use of the term in iii 30.

[13]) We question CROSSAN's statement on p. 94, *art. cit.*: '. . . the noun βλασφημία and the verb βλασφημέω never appear in the synoptic tradition except under Markan influence." βλασφημία and βλασφημέω are certainly favourite words of Mark. But this does not exclude the possibility that they are borrowed from Q; cf. the verb in Lk xii 10. Or do we have to accept that it was Luke who wrote in xii 10 the term under Markan influence? Although Luke locates the Beelzebul passage in another context (ch. xi) according to Q, he did know Mk iii 22-30 and Markan influence there is possible. But what about Lk xii 10? In that saying the first half reads "speak against the Son of Man." According to Q this speaking is not blasphemous in opposition to that against the Spirit: the distinction made by Q seems to be responsible for the new different term in the second half: βλασφημέω (already in Q!).

[14]) *Ibid.*, pp. 95-96.

xi 18c; probably present in Q) [15]). Mark places the clause outside the apology; the direct discourse has to disappear and ἔλεγον clearly refers back to the double ἔλεγον of vv. 21b and 22. The phrase πνεῦμα ἀκάθαρτον and, possibly, the idea of possession are taken by the redactor from Q (Lk xi 24-25 = Mt xii 43-45).

b) iii 20-21, 31-35. The introductory redactional v. 20 definitely points forward to v. 21. The absolute ἀκούσαντες of v. 21 provides the link of the two verses effectively [16]). This should be stated against CROSSAN who otherwise rightly stresses the Q impact upon the formulation and the meaning of v. 21b. We already made a critical reservation concerning his conclusion on the equation of relatives and scribes.

Did Mark limit his editorial activity in vv. 32-34 to a few changes which underline the inimical attitude of the relatives: their standing outside and their calling Jesus from outside while the crowd is sitting around him? [17]) And on the other hand is v. 35 purely Markan? [18]) We should first repeat CROSSAN's initial observation: the place of our pericope in Mk after the Beelzebul discussion is the same as in his source [19]). If this assumption is right we may ask whether in the Markan source the pericope was that of the woman who blessed Jesus' mother (cf. Lk xi 27-28, probably also in Q). Taking this position as an hypothesis we can explain not only the sequence, but also the content of v. 35a, which is presumably a Markan version of a Q saying that Luke writes as follows: μακάριοι οἱ ἀκούοντες τὸν λόγον τοῦ θεοῦ καὶ φυλάσσοντες (xi 28) [20]). In that saying Jesus criticizes the exaltation of mere biological

---

[15]) For a fuller discussion of this hypothesis, see LAMBRECHT, *op. cit.*, pp. 38-39.

[16]) CROSSAN, *art. cit.*, pp. 82-83, disagrees, but his evidence for his so-called Markan 'pattern', a four-point sequence: (1) Jesus is by the sea, (2) the election of the disciple(s) by Jesus, (3) Jesus and the disciple(s) are together in a house, (4) and their eating together is mentioned (i 16a, 16b-20, 29, 31; ii 13, 14, 15, 16; iii 7-9, 13-19, 20a, 20b) does not convince. On p. 84 he discusses the usage of ἀκούω "as a prelude to coming to Jesus" in ii 1; iii 8; v 27; vii 25; x 47. In all these passages, however, the verb ἀκούω has an object (ὅτι . . ., direct object, περί. . .). The absolute ἀκούσαντες of iii 21 clearly supposes the information of iii 20.

[17]) *Ibid.*, pp. 96-97.

[18]) *Ibid.*, pp. 97-98.

[19]) *Ibid.*, pp. 85-87, 96 and 98. But see our hesitation in LAMBRECHT, op. cit., pp. 29, 46-47, 65, 97.

[20]) Cf. CROSSAN, *art. cit.*, p. 86: ". . . the common theme of doing the will of God in Mk iii, 35 and practicing the word of God in Lk xi, 28 . . ."

relationship to himself. Was this not the tradition, we ask, which
Mark, in a very creative way, elaborated into the scene of an actual
family meeting ? [21]) If one still hesitates to accept such a thorough
manner of editing traditional materials, the redacted verses 20-21
illustrate quite convincingly how Mark is able to create a new
scene, to change and to stress one definite idea [22]) ! On such an
assumption v. 31 would be the Markan continuation of v. 21. V.
32 is to a great extent repetition of v. 31, but it pictures a sympa-
thetic crowd (ὄχλος) which the redactor already mentioned in v. 20.
Here, however, it seems also to be suggested by his source: cf.
Lk xi 27 with (γυνὴ) ἐκ τοῦ ὄχλου (see also xi 14). In Q the woman's
reaction was a kind of 'choral ending', an exclamation full of admiration for Jesus' apology, a blessing of the earthly mother,
corrected immediately by Jesus' blessing of obediential relationship.
Owing to Markan redaction, vv. 20-21, 31-35 have become an
independent, self-contained composition, the two parts of which
are separated by the Beelzebul controversy, making its progressive
action more relevant. Not only Jesus' mother, but also other
relatives are present and active. They think that Jesus has gone
insane. They hear that he went home where people are gathering
and they go out to seize him. Meanwhile a confrontation takes place
between Jesus and the scribes who accuse Jesus of demonic collusion and demonic possession. After that confrontation mother
and brothers arrive, stand outside and send for him. The crowd
sits around him and passes the message on to Jesus. Jesus answers:
Who are my mother and my brothers ? He looks over the crowd
seated around him and says: Here they are ! For whoever does the
will of God is my brother, and sister, and mother [23]).

---

[21]) Cf. R. BULTMANN, *Die Geschichte der synoptischen Tradition*, Göttingen,
⁷1967, p. 29: "... der Inhalt des Logions V. 35 sollte in einer idealen Szene
abgebildet werden ..." It is not v. 35, however, which is original but possibly
a Q saying (cf. Lk xi 28); not the anonymous community who composed the
scene ('Gemeindebildung') but the evangelist Mark.

[22]) For a different opinion, see the recent article of B. RIGAUX, "Sens et
portée de Mc 3, 31-35 dans la mariologie néotestamentaire," in: *Maria in
Sacra Scriptura*, Vol. IV: *De Beata Virgine Maria in Evangeliis synopticis*,
Romae, 1967, p. 541: "L'historicité de la démarche des parents de Jésus n'est
mise en doute par personne." Cf. SCHROEDER, *op. cit.*, pp. 116-124; BULTMANN
op. cit. p. 29: "... das Motiv von V. 21 ... beruht offenbar auf guter alter
Tradition." RIGAUX distinguishes "au niveau des faits" in v. 21 and vv. 31-35
"deux démarches distinctes" (p. 544)!

[23]) We do not take as evident that μήτηρ καὶ ἀδελφοί in vv. 31-34 is tradi-

In view of the evidence of that all-pervading redactional activity
it seems superfluous to postulate for iii 20-21, 31-35 another source
than that which must have been present in Q and of which Lk xi
27-28 probably is a fairly faithful transmission. Yet we should
keep in mind that Lk xi 27-28 is possibly *not* a Q text. In that case
Mk iii 31-35 may either be still more redactional than we presumed
or contain some non Q tradition (a saying or/and incident). Vv.
20-21 at any rate are redactional.

c) iii 20-35 and its structure. Mk iii 20-35 manifests itself as a
well-constructed, stylized unity. Looking at the redactional process only, i.e., the way Mark used his sources, one should speak of
receiving and omitting tradition, of rewriting, abbreviating or
expanding, of prefixing vv. 20-21 and inserting a Q saying (vv.
28-29) from a different context. But was Mark not interested in
the final result ? Mk iii 20-35 as it stands has a central unit (vv.
22-30) and another unit at the periphery, divided into two parts
(vv. 20-21, 31-35). Jesus' apology (vv. 23b-29) within the central
pericope is framed by the attack of the scribes: its factual wording
(v. 22) and the redactional repetition referring back to it (v. 30).
The heart of the apology is the statement of v. 27: Jesus explains
here what 'casting out' precisely means and how the exorcist
has to proceed. This central metaphoric saying is surrounded by
two structurally similar sections: vv. 23b-26 and vv. 28-29. They
display the same abb'a'-pattern. All this would build up to the
following overall structure:

---

tional while only ἀδελφός — ἀδελφή — μήτηρ is redactional (cf. vi 3, tradition ?)
The expansion to three terms (+ sisters) as well as the inversion of the
sequence in v. 35 may well be occasioned by the fact that v. 35 functions as
the solemn concluding saying. A discussion on the "brothers and sisters of
Jesus" or on the absence of the father of Jesus in iii 31-35 and vi 3 (see the
redactional difference between x 30 and x 29, cf. CROSSAN, *art. cit.*, p. 98) is
beyond the scope of these pages. Even after reading the recent study of E.
GRÄSSER, "Jesus in Nazareth (Mc 6, 1-6a). Bemerkungen zur Redaktion und
Theologie des Markus," in: E. GRÄSSER, A. STROBEL, R. C. TANNEHILL, W.
ELTESTER, *Jesus in Nazareth*, Berlin, 1972, pp. 24-25, I cannot eliminate the
possibility that the silence on Joseph in Mk is somehow related with the
Christian theologoumenon of the Virgin Birth. See the balanced conclusion
of RIGAUX, *art. cit.*, pp. 534-535; on pp. 548-549 he even ends his summary as
follows: "C'est là une porte ouverte qui pourrait conduire à une perspective
marcienne plus accueillante pour la relation Jésus-Marie." Another open
question: Who are James and Joses of xv 40 (cf. xv 47; xvi 1) and who is
Mary their mother ?

A   Jesus at home and the initiative of the relatives (vv. 20-21)
B   The accusation of the scribes (v. 22)
C   Jesus' apology (vv. 23-29):
   a   Refutation (vv. 23b-26)
   b   The binding-logion (v. 27)
   a' Judgment (vv. 28-29)
B' Repetition of the accusation (v. 30)
A' Arrival of the relatives and the proclamation of true kinship
   by Jesus (vv. 31-35) [24]).

Since 'sandwiching' (ABA') is a favourite Markan literary technique used also elsewhere in his gospel, one can hold without much risk of illusion that the tendency to structurize, noticeable in iii 20-35, is not accidental. Such a fine and reflexive composition cannot but confirm the basic insight that was found from time to time during the analysis of the text. The role of Markan redaction in iii 20-35 is very considerable. Joined with other reflexions this evidence does not encourage attempts to discover different and more 'Markan' sources than those we could, with a fair degree of probablility, admit as present in Q.

d) The two remaining passages which CROSSAN uses in order to describe Mark's concept of the relatives of Jesus can be dealt with only very summarily. One is hardly able to forget or minimize the numerous uncertainties which are inherent to CROSSAN's hypothesis concerning xv 40, 47; xvi 1 [25]). Are we so sure that the naming of 'Joses' in xv 40, 47 has been added by Mark ? [26]) Would it not be more logical in CROSSAN's line of thought that the 'mother of James and Joses' is at the same time the mother of Jesus ? [27]) And is the step to identify the women = (among whom) relatives = Jerusalem not much too risky ? Still, it seems likely that Mark writing the names of James in xv 40; xvi 1 and of Joses in xv 40, 47 wanted to refer back to vi 3.

With regard to the passage vi 1-6 Mark may well have added the

---

[24]) Full elaboration in LAMBRECHT, *op. cit.*, p. 80. E. SCHWEIZER, *Das Evangelium nach Markus*, Göttingen, 1967, p. 45, rightly notes: "Kaum irgendwo tritt die Komposition des Markus so stark hervor wie hier."

[25]) *Art. cit.*, pp. 105-110.

[26]) L. SCHENKE, *Auferstehungsverkündigung und leeres Grab. Eine traditionsgeschichtliche Untersuchung von Mk 16, 1-8* (Stuttgarter Bibelstudien 33), Stuttgart, 1968, pp. 20-30, e.g., provides us with a different redactional explanation.

[27]) See note 23.

phrase καὶ ἐν τοῖς συγγενεῦσιν αὐτοῦ καὶ ἐν τῇ οἰκίᾳ αὐτοῦ (v. 4) [28]). Between that insertion and the presumably traditional vi 3 there is now a discrepancy, for in vi 3 nothing suggests that the relatives belong to those who take offense at Jesus. By inserting the phrase into vi 4, Mark wanted to point back to iii 20-21, 31-35. The reader should remember the information given there. He should know that also the relatives were resisting Jesus [29]). But as for Jesus' family, more than this cannot be found in Mark's redaction of vi 1-6. The rather complicated effort of CROSSAN to explain different features as a partial but intentional whitewash of the fellow townsmen and, simultaneously, as a denigration of the relatives [30]) leaves us unconvinced.

2. In spite of all these critical remarks and uncertainties, the fact remains that Mark, by means of his editorial and creative dealing with the traditional materials, has presented the relatives of Jesus, his mother, brothers and sisters, in an explicitly unfavourable fashion. The opposition between Jesus and his relatives appears to be more severe than any that could be traced in his sources. What was Mark's redactional purpose? Hardly an exclusively esthetical and structural one only!

a) We found that according to CROSSAN Mark's controversy is a more or less hidden polemic not only against Jerusalem-minded fellow Christians within his church but also *ad extram* against the Jerusalem leaders themselves. For CROSSAN, thus, the relatives of Jesus are not so much historical figures from the past; they rather symbolize the actual authorities in Jerusalem [31]). Admittedly, in Mark's mind Jerusalem is more than a neutral geographical name; the whole composition and content of his gospel prove this.

---

[28]) According to CROSSAN, *art. cit.*, pp. 100-103, only "and among his relatives."

[29]) For an outstanding analysis, see GRÄSSER, *art. cit.* He discusses the redactional intention of vi 4 on p. 25.

[30]) *Art. cit.*, pp. 98-105.

[31]) Cf. *ibid.*, pp. 110-113. Others before CROSSAN defended similar ideas See e.g. S. G. F. BRANDON, *Jesus and the Zealots. A study of the Political Factor in Primitive Christianity*, Manchester, 1967, pp. 274-277, or TROCMÉ, *op. cit.*: Mark is "un auteur assez passionnément dressé contre la famille du Seigneur et par conséquent contre Jacques" (p. 105); "un ennemi déclaré de Jacques, frère du Seigneur, chef unique de l'Eglise de Jérusalem pendant de longues années . . ." (pp. 108-109); and ". . . l'auteur de Marc mène dans cette partie de son livre une véritable campagne contre la famille de Jésus, c'est-à-dire surtout contre Jacques" (p. 107).

But the question is whether besides the historical events including Jesus' passion and death, other (still actual) situation and tensions within the church known to us through the Pauline letters, the Acts of the Apostles and later extrabiblical traditions, played a role in the formation of Mark's ideas on Jerusalem. Does the redactional notice "scribes who come down from Jerusalem" (iii 22; vii 1) contain an allusion to the way the Jerusalem leaders in Markan time exercised their authority ? Surely, all this is far from impossible. Yet its hypothetical character should always be kept in mind.

Markan polemic against 'Jerusalem' cannot be explained without referring to the equally Markan Galilee-theme. Was, as it has been frequently argued, the postpaschal missionary activity among the Gentiles responsible for Mark's rather schematic geographical outline in which 'Galilee' then represents the Gentiles ? This does not have to be excluded, but another more understandable factor should also be taken into account when one wants to interpret Mark's specific geography. Later, because of their temporal remoteness, the complex historical facts are easily simplified and major data among them may become somewhat a symbol. Galilee was, historically speaking, an important scene of Jesus' earthly activity; in Mark, however, Galilee becomes, if not the only scene, certainly the main one, and, moreover, since thematically stressed, Galilee obtains as such a symbol-status for that activity. Jesus suffered and died in Jerusalem. The same process of simplification seems to be at work: for Mark, Jerusalem has also a symbolic value; already by itself it points to an opposition to Jesus.

b) It is still more hazardous to consider the Markan view on relatives and Mark's picture of the inner circle of three disciples as elements of that hypothetical polemic [32]). As for the three disciples, leaving out the fact that the apostle James (James the Greater) does not belong to the three "reputed pillars" (cf. Gal. ii 9) of the Jerusalem church, it is nowhere apparent that they constitute a purely negative symbol. On the contrary: the later believers are also 'disciples', though, of course, they have to avoid the unbelief and failures of the historical disciples.

That the evangelist Mark presented the relatives as severe opponents during Jesus' life in order to express his personal or his community's opposition to the hegemony of relatives in the Jeru-

---

[32]) *Art. cit.*, pp. 111-112.

salem church is not to be denied *a priori*. This possible explanation, however, is rather far-fetched and, therefore, deserves serious consideration only if a more realistic interpretation cannot be found and other evidence recommends it. Such evidence may be provided by the knowledge we have about the long and hard struggle within the early Church. But in the light of the date of the gospel and changed conditions the question may be raised whether it is not better not to associate the evangelist Mark too personally with that struggle. R. RUETHER writes in a rather synthetic and thematic study: "The underlining of the tradition of the infidelity of the family of Jesus in the synoptics would then have historical roots in the late-comer status of the family, but possibly enjoyed a revival and continuation in the tradition because of later party animosities between the conservative Jewish Christians in Jerusalem and diaspora Christianity, both in its Petrine (diaspora Jewish) and Pauline (gentile) branches" [33]). We should perhaps modify her judgment. For his rewriting and 'staging' of traditional data concerning relationship and family (cf. Lk xi 27-28, Q ? But see also Mk x 29-30; Mt x 37 = Lk xiv 26 and the related passage in Mk viii 34-38), Mark may ultimately have been dependent upon such a 'revival and continuation' of party animosities indeed; but no so much in his own days as in a former time [34]). Thus even given that dependence, the question remains: What was the purpose of Mark himself ?

c) Mark has portrayed in his gospel a manifold opposition to Jesus. Resistance, infidelity or misunderstanding: it all points

---

[33]) "The Collision of History and Doctrine: The Brothers of Jesus and the Virginity of Mary," *Continuum*, 7 (1969), pp. 98-99.

[34]) Cf. T. A. BURKILL, *New Light on the Earliest Gospel. Seven Markan Studies*, Ithaca-London, 1972, pp. 237-238. The author, however, reckons perhaps too easily with a possible historical basis. "The materials are arranged and adapted in such a manner as to suggest that the evangelist is here giving expression to the philosophico-theological doctrine that the promised Messiah had to be rejected by his own nation before God's new offer of salvation through the crucified Christ could be freely proclaimed. Of course this does not exclude the possibility that iii 20-21, 31-35 and the *logion* of vi 4 took their rise in a conflict which actually occurred between the historical Jesus and his next of kin; nor does it exclude the possibility that these items of the tradition had been utilized by representatives of the new faith who resented the leadership of James at Jerusalem and the dynastic principle his presidency introduced among the Jewish-Christians sectaries of metropolitan Judea. But as they now stand within the framework of St. Mark's gospel, the passages in question are intimately bound up with the evangelist's philosophy of history . . ." (p. 237).

to the imminent passion and cross; in Mark's view it is inherent
to the whole earthly life of Jesus and it will also be the destiny of
his followers. That opposition, of course, has been historical; after
all Jesus was crucified. But Mark antedates it (cf. iii 6), he underlines it, he extends it: not only Pharisees, scribes, Herodians, the
fellow townsmen and the Jerusalem authorities, but also the people
(cf. e.g. 'those outside', iv 11) and the relatives of Jesus. Moreover,
he accentuated redactionally in an extremely frank way the
misunderstanding, the dullness, and unfaithfulness of the disciples.

Of course, for Mark too, there are gradations. The unbelief of
the townsmen (cf. vi 6) is not to be put on the same level as the
mortal hostility of the Pharisees which already appears in iii 6,
nor with the plotting of the chief priests and the scribes in xii 12 and
xiv 1-2, nor, on the other hand, with the 'hardened hearts' of
the disciples (cf. viii 17). Not all the scribes (cf. xii 28-34), not
all members of the council (cf. xv 42-46) are enemies. And we
argued above that according to Mark's picture the attitude of the
relatives cannot be identified in a drastic way with that of the
accusers of iii 22. In Mk the crowd seems to be neutral at times;
in iii 31-35 the people sitting around Jesus represent the true
relatives, but elsewhere they are without understanding and just as
'those outside' they seem to symbolize the obdurate Jews of the
later Markan days.

The Twelve in Mk never are such a symbol ! They may be slow
and blind, but for Mark and his readers they remain the (first)
disciples. D. J. HAWKIN rightly states: "The disciples are made
to be figures of the church" [35]); he rightly disagrees with J. B.
TYSON and T. J. WEEDEN according to whom "Mark ... wishes
his readership to identify themselves not *with* but *against* them" [36]).
The relatives of Jesus, however, do not stand on the side of the
disciples; they belong to the unbelieving Israel. Generally speaking,
for Mark they are privileged children of Israel whom Jesus had to
invite and to call first (cf. vii 27) before salvation was offered to the

---

[35]) "The Incomprehension of the Disciples in the Marcan Redaction,"
Journal of Biblical Literature, 91 (1972), p. 497.

[36]) *Ibid.*, p. 493. He refers to J. TYSON, "The Blindness of the Disciples
in Mark," *Journal of Biblical Literature*, 80 (1961), 261-268; T. J. WEEDEN,
"The Heresy That Necessitated Mark's Gospel," *Zeitschrift für Neutestamentliche Wissenschaft*, 59 (1968), 145-168. Cf. T. J. WEEDEN, *Mark. Traditions in
Conflict*, Philadelphia, 1971.

Gentiles [37]). They neither understood nor accepted Jesus. And Mark did not want his readers to identify themselves with these relatives [38]).

d) The preceding paragraph not only points to Mark's view on salvation history (cf. 'children of Israel') but also to his *negative* paraenesis (cf. relatives *versus* readers). Yet, the explanation we have developed is not altogether satisfactory. What was it, after all, that induced Mark to place Jesus' mother and relatives in an unfavourable light ? His *positive* paraenetical intention may provide us with the whole truth. We should remember that Mark knew several traditional data which illustrate the radical demand for following Jesus or becoming a disciple by insisting on the inevitable family implications.

In viii 34 Mark uses a tradition which can be found in Lk xiv 27 = Mt x 38 (Q). It is not impossible that the same source offered him also the saying of Lk xiv 26 = Mt x 37 where "hating his own father and mother, brother and sister" is openly spoken of [39]). Anyhow, Mk i 20 and x 29-30 point out that the disciple has to leave his relatives [40]). In Mk xiii 12 Jesus announces sharp divisions within the family [41]). Moreover, Mark was acquainted with the tradition that mentioned so clearly the opposition of Jesus' fellow townsmen (cf. vi 1-6). And we saw that he probably knew the traditional verses in which, according to Luke's wording (xi 27-28), it is explicitly stated that keeping the word of God exceeds physical motherhood.

It would seem that all this information available to Mark brought him to 'create' the incident of iii 20-21, 31-35. Here mother and brothers are portrayed as not understanding Jesus and, to a certain degree, as opposite to him (cf. the Markan insertion into vi 4) [42]). But what matters is that we should fully realize that in doing so Mark's intention was not to provide his readers with better or complementary historical information concerning Jesus' mother

---

[37]) Cf. GRÄSSER, *art. cit.*, p. 34; RIGAUX, *art. cit.*, pp. 546-548.

[38]) But see note 23.

[39]) For a discussion on the original Q text of Lk xiv 27 = Mt x 38 and Lk xiv 26 = Mt x 37, see e.g. S. SCHULZ, *Die Spruchquelle der Evangelisten*, Zürich, 1972, pp. 430-431 and pp. 446-447.

[40]) Cf. Mt viii 21-22 = Lk ix 59-60 (Q).

[41]) For Mark's dependence upon Q (cf. Mt x 35-36 = Lk xii 52-53), see J. LAMBRECHT, *Die Redaktion der Markus-Apokalypse. Literarische Analyse und Strukturuntersuchung* (Analecta Biblica 28), Rome, 1967, pp. 136-138.

[42]) Cf. Lk ii 41-52; John ii 1-12; vii 1-13.

and brothers, but to instruct his fellow Christians on what in his view 'true' kinship really means: to do God's will (iii 35), to deny oneself and take up the cross (viii 34), and, being called, to leave one's relatives (x 29-30). Becoming a disciple one has at any rate to reckon with division within the family (iii 20-21, 31-35; xiii 12).

It cannot be doubted that the Markan 'staging' of the incident (iii 20-21, 31-34) heightens considerably the impact of Jesus' teaching (iii 35). And we can safely add that Jesus' teaching and Jesus' example in Mk iii must have met the actual needs of the Markan church.

SUMMONS AND OUTLINE IN MARK:
THE THREE-STEP PROGRESSION

BY

VERNON K. ROBBINS

University of Illinois at Urbana-Champaign

One of the most well-known features of Mark is the three-fold repetition of the prediction of the passion by Jesus in Mark viii 31; ix 31; x 33-34. By means of this repetition, Mark viii 27-x 45 contains a unified structure that gives the section a central position in the theology of Mark. Recent analysis has shown a more subtle three-part progression in this section of Mark [1]. Each one of the passion predictions itself stands within a unit characterized by three parts (viii 27-30, 31-33, 34-ix 1; ix 30-32, 33-34, 35-50; x 32-34, 35-41, 42-45). This paper contains the proposal that the three-step progression evident in the context of each of the passion predictions is also present in scenes throughout the Gospel where Jesus calls disciples. These scenes are constituted by a three-step rhetorical sequence that features Jesus summoning disciples as the final step.

FRANS NEIRYNCK's study of repetitive phrases in Mark is highly responsible for our ability to see and understand the three-step progression that stands within the Marcan narrative. His study of Mark not only lists dual expressions but also twenty-three "series of three" that characterize the Marcan narrative [2]. At the most primary level of composition, three people, things, or phrases occur in a series in which the author connects the second and third items to the first by means of the simple conjunction καί. At a second level, the series of three structures the dramatic progression of an entire

---

[1] For analysis of the structure of viii 27-x 45, see NORMAN PERRIN, "Towards an Interpretation of the Gospel of Mark," *Christology and a Modern Pilgrimage* (ed. H. DIETER BETZ; Claremont: NT Colloquium, 1971) 7-30; *The New Testament: An Introduction* (New York: Harcourt Brace Jovanovich, 1974) 155-158.

[2] FRANS NEIRYNCK, *Duality in Mark: Contributions to the Study of the Markan Redaction* (BETl XXXL; Leuven: Leuven University Press, 1972) 110-112.

episode. Analysis in this paper is designed to reveal a three-step progression within a span of material two or three pericopes in length. Within this span of material, Jesus is portrayed by means of a three-step progression that reaches its conclusion in an explicit summons of people into discipleship. The model units for the three-step summoning progression exist in viii 27-ix 1; ix 30-50; x 32-45, and the key to the unit is the explicit summoning of disciples in the final part.

After an analysis of the three-step progression in Mark at the level of the three simple items, the level of the single episode, and the level of two or three pericopes; we will suggest that the three-step progressions that cover two or three pericopes form interludes in the narrative that establish the basic outline for the Marcan narrative. These interludes are characterized by a rhetorical progression that draws the previous action of the narrative to a conclusion in the same context in which it inaugurates the action that will transpire in the succeeding section. Moreover, we will suggest that these interludes establish an image of Jesus that mediates between Israelite traditions about Yahweh and the prophets and Graeco-Roman traditions about disciple-gathering teachers. In the Gospel of Mark, therefore, the three-step summoning interlude features Jesus in a role that merges the authority of Yahweh and the prophets with the authority of ethical teachers who embody the system of thought and action they teach to others.

THE SIMPLE SERIES OF THREE AND THE THREE-PART STRUCTURE OF EPISODES

At the most primary level of composition, the author of Mark reveals an interest in series of threes. In sixteen instances, three people, three things, or three phrases occur in a series in which the author connects the second and third items to the first by means of the simple conjunction καί.

(1)   iii 32: ἡ μήτηρ σου καὶ οἱ ἀδελφοί σου [καὶ αἱ ἀδελφαί σου] [3])
(2)   iii 35: ἀδελφός μου καὶ ἀδελφὴ καὶ μήτηρ

---

[3]) καὶ αἱ ἀδελφαί σου is present in A D 700 etc. but absent from א B C K L W Δ Θ Π etc. It is quite possible that καὶ αἱ ἀδελφαί σου was added in later MSS by means of mechanical expansion; see BRUCE M. METZGER, A Textual Commentary on the Greek New Testament (New York: United Bible Societies, 1971) 82.

(3, 4)   iv 8, 20: εἰς τριάκοντα καὶ ἐν ἑξήκοντα καὶ ἐν ἑκατόν [4])

(5, 6, 7) v 37; ix 2; xiv 33: τὸν Πέτρον καὶ (τὸν) Ἰάκωβον καὶ (τὸν) Ἰωάννην

(8)   vi 4: ἐν τῇ πατρίδι αὐτοῦ καὶ ἐν τοῖς συγγενεῦσιν αὐτοῦ καὶ ἐν τῇ οἰκίᾳ αὐτοῦ

(9)   vi 21: τοῖς μεγιστᾶσιν αὐτοῦ καὶ τοῖς χιλιάρχοις καὶ τοῖς πρώτοις τῆς Γαλιλαίας

(10)   ix 5: τρεῖς σκηνάς, σοὶ μίαν καὶ Μωϋσεῖ μίαν καὶ Ἠλίᾳ μίαν

(11)   xvi 1: [ἡ] Μαρία ἡ Μαγδαληνὴ καὶ Μαρία ἡ [τοῦ] Ἰακώβου καὶ Σαλώμη

(12)   viii 31: ὑπὸ τῶν πρεσβυτέρων καὶ τῶν ἀρχιερέων καὶ τῶν γραμματέων

(13)   xi 27: οἱ ἀρχιερεῖς καὶ οἱ γραμματεῖς καὶ οἱ πρεσβύτεροι

(14)   xiv 43: παρὰ τῶν ἀρχιερέων καὶ τῶν γραμματέων καὶ τῶν πρεσβυτέρων

(15)   xiv 53: πάντες οἱ ἀρχιερεῖς καὶ οἱ πρεσβύτεροι καὶ οἱ γραμματεῖς

(16)   xv 1: οἱ ἀρχιερεῖς μετὰ τῶν πρεσβυτέρων καὶ γραμματέων καὶ ὅλον τὸ συνέδριον

The final example of the primary form of the series of three, xv 1, reveals the potential for the third part in the series to be climactic. In contrast to the constructions in viii 31, xi 27, xiv 43, and xiv 53; the construction in xv 1 collapses "chief priests and elders" into one group so the series can end with "the whole sanhedrin."

Another form of the three-part series in Mark establishes contrasts between the parts. In this form, both δέ and καί are used to construct the series. Two examples of this stand out at the primary level of the form. The most simple example is present in viii 28:

οἱ δὲ εἶπαν αὐτῷ λέγοντες ὅτι Ἰωάννην τὸν βαπτιστήν,
καὶ ἄλλοι Ἠλίαν,
ἄλλοι δὲ ὅτι εἷς τῶν προφητῶν

In Mark vi 14-16, this three-part progression is used in a narrative context that calls for expansion of the first part. A careful examina-

---

[4]) Possibly this triad should be read ἓν τριάκοντα καὶ ἓν ἑξήκοντα καὶ ἓν ἑκατόν, as it appears in D f¹³ 1365 1546 Lect it^(a,aur,b,(c),d,f,(f2),i,l,(q),r1) vg syr^p cop^(sa,bo) goth Diatessaron^a. See Metzger, *Textual Commentary* 83.

tion of Mark vi 14-16 shows how the author can use principles of two-part and three-part composition within the same context:

Καὶ ἤκουσεν ὁ βασιλεὺς Ἡρῴδης,
   (φανερὸν γὰρ ἐγένετο τὸ ὄνομα αὐτοῦ),
   καὶ ἔλεγον ὅτι [5]) Ἰωάννης ὁ βαπτίζων ἐγήγερται ἐκ νεκρῶν,
   καὶ διὰ τοῦτο **ἐν**εργοῦσιν αἱ δυνάμεις **ἐν** αὐτῷ.
   ἄλλοι δὲ ἔλεγον ὅτι Ἠλίας ἐστίν·
   ἄλλοι δὲ ἔλεγον ὅτι προφήτης ὡς εἷς τῶν προφητῶν.
ἀκούσας δὲ ὁ Ἡρῴδης ἔλεγεν· ὃν ἐγὼ ἀπεκεφάλισα Ἰωάννην, οὗτος ἠγέρθη.

This display shows a typical instance of two-part and three-part composition in Mark. In the center of this unit stands a three-part progression printed in bold type. The central three-part portion is framed by two-part repetition (spaced) that refers to Herod hearing about the things that were happening [6]). Since the narrative leads up to Herod's execution of John the Baptist, the first part of the three-part series is expanded when first mentioned, then reiterated at the end of the unit (underlined with a single line). This context which intermeshes dual and triple composition also contains a compound verb followed by the same preposition (ἐνεργοῦσιν ... ἐν) [7]), poetic repetition of a substantive (προφήτης ... προφητῶν), repetition of the antecedent (οὗτος/ὅν ... Ἰωάννην) [8]), and a γάρ clause [9]). The result of this construction is the climactic statement at the end that Herod perceived Jesus to be John the Baptist, whom he himself beheaded, raised from the dead.

In Mark, a three-part progression may provide the basic structure for an entire scene. The denial of Peter contains an excellent example (xiv 66-72):

---

[5]) ℵ A C K L Δ Θ Π f¹ f¹³ plus many Greek minuscules and many versions contain καὶ ἔλεγεν ὅτι. The reading καὶ ἔλεγον ὅτι appears to be primary, however, on the basis that ἔλεγον likely became ἔλεγεν to agree with ἤκουσεν. See METZGER, *Textual Commentary* 89.

[6]) This feature is called the "insertion" technique by JOHN R. DONAHUE, *Are You the Christ?* (SBLDS 10; Missoula: SBL, 1973) 241.

[7]) NEIRYNCK, *Duality* 75.

[8]) NEIRYNCK, *Duality* 86.

[9]) C. H. BIRD "Some γάρ clauses in St. Mark's Gospel," JTS 4 (1953) 171-187; E. J. PRYKE, *Redactional Style in the Marcan Gospel* (SNTSMS 33; Cambridge: Cambridge University Press, 1978) 126-135.

(1) ἔρχεται μία τῶν παιδισκῶν . . .

    καὶ ἰδοῦσα . . . ἐμβλέψασα αὐτῷ λέγει . . .

       ὁ δὲ ἠρνήσατο λέγων . . . (xiv 66-68)

(2) καὶ ἡ παιδίσκη ἰδοῦσα αὐτὸν

    ἤρξατο πάλιν λέγειν . . .

       ὁ δὲ πάλιν ἠρνεῖτο (xiv 69-70a)

(3) καὶ . . . **πάλιν** . . . **ἔλεγον** . . .

    ὁ δὲ ἤρξατο ἀναθεματίζειν καὶ ὀμνύναι . . . (xiv 69-71)

    (. . . τὸ ῥῆμα ὡς εἶπεν αὐτῷ ὁ Ἰησοῦς . . . τρίς με ἀπαρνήσῃ) [10]

In this series, which spans seven verses of text, some of the characteristics appear that reveal the nature of larger literary units constructed in three parts in the Marcan narrative. First, the series begins with a verb of movement in the narrational framework (ἔρχεται); second, the series emphasizes interaction that occurs by means of seeing someone and speaking to him (ἰδοῦσα . . . ἐμβλέψασα αὐτῷ λέγει; . . . ἰδοῦσα αὐτὸν ἤρξατο πάλιν λέγειν; . . . πάλιν . . . ἔλεγον); third, the verbal interaction in the sequence comes to a climactic finish in emphatic speech. In the third item, therefore, the repetition of "denied" gives way to "began to invoke a curse on himself and to swear." This sequence reveals the author's interest in the third part of an expanded form of the series of three. While special emphasis on the third item seems not to be characteristic of the series at the primary level (a third item is sufficient to bring a sense of completeness), the third item in the expanded form is customarily characterized by emphatic speech. In this instance, Peter's statements of denial reach a point of pronouncing a curse upon himself and swearing that he has no knowledge whatsoever of Jesus (xiv 71) [11].

When the expanded form of a three-part literary unit features Jesus as the main actor (rather than Peter as in xiv 66-72), the final part of the sequence features summons and command on the

---

[10] See Mark xiv 30; cf. NEIRYNCK, *Duality* 112.

[11] For a detailed discussion of the story of Peter's denial, see KIM E. DEWEY, "Peter's Curse and Cursed Peter," *The Passion in Mark* (ed. W. H. KELBER; Philadelphia: Fortress, 1976) 96-114; "Peter's Denial Reexamined: John's Knowledge of Mark's Gospel" (SBLSP 1; Missoula: Scholar's Press, 1979) 109-112; WOLFGANG SCHENK, *Der Passionsbericht nach Markus* (Gütersloh: Gerd Mohn, 1974) 215-223; DETLEV DORMEYER, *Die Passion Jesu als Verhaltensmodell* (NTAbh 11; Münster: Aschendorff, 1974) 150-157.

lips of Jesus. An excellent example is present in Mark xiv 35-42, the prayer in Gethsemane:

(1) καὶ προελθών ... καὶ προσηύχετο ... καὶ ἔλεγεν ...
καὶ ἔρχεται
καὶ εὑρίσκει ...
καὶ λέγει ... (xiv 35-38)

(2) καὶ πάλιν ἀπελθὼν προσηύξατο ... εἰπών ...
καὶ πάλιν ἐλθὼν εὗρεν ... (xiv 39-40)

(3) καὶ ἔρχεται τὸ τρίτον
καὶ λέγει αὐτοῖς,
"Are you still sleeping and taking your rest?
It is enough;
the hour has come;
the Son of man is betrayed into the hands of sinners;
Rise, let us be going;
See, my betrayer is at hand."

This example illustrates the manner in which the author's narrational framework establishes a pattern in the expanded form of the three-part literary unit. The basic actions of Jesus unfold in three steps, and the final step introduces the dramatic conclusion to Jesus' action in the form of emphatic speech that summons and commands. The theme of summons and command may or may not be present in the first or second parts of the sequence, but the final part features Jesus as one who speaks with authority to those who seek a serious relationship with him.

THREE-PART PROGRESSION IN MARK viii 27-x 45

The repetition of the suffering-dying-rising sayings in Mark viii 31; ix 31; x 33-34 reveals three-fold composition at two levels in the Marcan narrative. On the one hand, the material from Mark viii 27 to x 45 is constructed in an overall pattern of three. The three passion predictions establish a framework for a lengthy amount of material and provide a dramatic progression to the third saying in the series. The progression reaches its highpoint in the lengthiest and most dramatic form of the saying in x 33-34:

"Behold we are going up to Jerusalem, and the Son of man will be delivered to the chief priests and the scribes, and they will condemn him to death, and deliver him to the Gentiles; and they will mock him, and spit upon him and scourge him, and kill him; and after three days he will rise."

While the first two passion predictions contain 25 and 17 Greek words respectively, the final one in x 33-34 contains 40 Greek words as it brings Jesus' description of the passion events to its most emphatic and full expression.

At yet another level, however, the passion predictions reveal a technique of literary composition that extends throughout the Gospel. Each of the sayings resides in a three-part literary unit that reaches its climax in a statement that Jesus summoned (προσκαλέομαι), called (καλέω or φωνέω), or sent (ἀποστέλλω) his disciples. The first unit, viii 27-ix 1, reveals the three-part progression in this manner:

(1) Καὶ ἐξῆλθεν ὁ ᾽Ιησοῦς καὶ οἱ μαθηταὶ αὐτοῦ . . .
καὶ . . . ἐπηρώτα τοὺς μαθητὰς αὐτοῦ λέγων αὐτοῖς . . .
καὶ αὐτὸς ἐπηρώτα αὐτούς . . .
καὶ ἐπετίμησεν αὐτοῖς . . . (viii 27-30)

(2) Καὶ ἤρξατο διδάσκειν αὐτούς . . .
καὶ παρρησίᾳ τὸν λόγον ἐλάλει . . .
ὁ δὲ ἐπιστραφεὶς καὶ ἰδὼν τοὺς μαθητὰς αὐτοῦ ἐπετίμησεν Πέτρῳ
καὶ λέγει . . . (viii 31-33)

(3) Καὶ προσκαλεσάμενος τὸν ὄχλον σὺν τοῖς μαθηταῖς αὐτοῦ
εἶπεν αὐτοῖς . . .
καὶ ἔλεγεν αὐτοῖς . . . (viii 34-ix 1)

The spaced portions of the narrational framework indicate a three-part progression that reaches a climax in the statement that Jesus summoned (προσκαλέομαι) the multitude with his disciples. The first part of the sequence begins with a statement that Jesus was going from one place to another, and it explicitly mentions the presence of the disciples with Jesus. The second part features a shift that creates the setting for more intensive interaction between Jesus and his disciples. The third part portrays Jesus summoning the multitude with his disciples, and this narrational comment sets the stage for a series of sayings in which Jesus teaches the implications of discipleship to those whom he summons. The sayings that follow in Mark viii 34-ix 1 are some of the most memorable and most often quoted sayings from the Gospel of Mark.

A three-part literary structure of a parallel nature is found in Mark ix 30-50, the setting of the second passion prediction. The narrational framework presents the sequence in this manner:

(1) Κἀκεῖθεν ἐξελθόντες παρεπορεύοντο . . .
    καὶ οὐκ ἤθελεν ἵνα τις γνοῖ·
    (ἐδίδασκεν γὰρ τοὺς μαθητὰς αὐτοῦ
        καὶ ἔλεγεν αὐτοῖς . . . (ix 30-32)
(2) Καὶ ἦλθον . . . καὶ . . . ἐπηρώτα αὐτοῖς . . .
    ὁ δὲ ἐσιώπων,
    (πρὸς ἀλλήλους γὰρ διελέχθησαν ἐν τῇ ὁδῷ τίς μείζων) (ix 33-34)
(3) Καὶ καθίσας ἐφώνησεν τοὺς δώδεκα
    καὶ λέγει αὐτοῖς . . .
    καὶ . . . εἶπεν αὐτοῖς . . .
    ὁ δὲ Ἰησοῦς εἶπεν . . . (ix 35-50)

Again a three-part sequence leads to a final part where Jesus calls
the disciples and instructs them about discipleship. The first part
portrays Jesus traveling from one place to another, and the disciples
are explicitly mentioned as present with Jesus. The second part
features interaction between Jesus and the disciples that sets the
stage for the third part. The third and final part features Jesus
calling (φωνέω) the Twelve and urging them to understand the
responsibilities of discipleship. As the third part in viii 27-ix 1
features a series of sayings in which Jesus teaches about discipleship, so the third part in ix 30-50 features Jesus teaching the
disciples the intricacies of responsible discipleship.

Mark x 32-45, the three-part literary unit that provides the
setting for the final passion prediction, brings the section to a
dramatic conclusion. The structure of the final unit is analogous to
the structure of the first two:

(1) Ἦσαν δὲ . . . ἀναβαίνοντες . . . καὶ ἦν προάγων αὐτοὺς ὁ Ἰησοῦς
    . . .
    καὶ παραλαβὼν πάλιν τοὺς δώδεκα
        ἤρξατο αὐτοῖς λέγειν . . . (x 32-34)
(2) Καὶ προσπορεύονται αὐτῷ . . . λέγοντες αὐτῷ . . .
    ὁ δὲ εἶπεν αὐτοῖς . . . οἱ δὲ εἶπαν αὐτῷ . . .
    ὁ δὲ Ἰησοῦς εἶπεν αὐτοῖς . . . οἱ δὲ εἶπαν αὐτῷ . . .
    ὁ δὲ Ἰησοῦς εἶπεν αὐτοῖς . . . (x 35-40)
(3) Καὶ ἀκούσαντες οἱ δέκα ἤρξαντο ἀγανακτεῖν . . .
    καὶ προσκαλεσάμενος αὐτοὺς ὁ Ἰησοῦς
        λέγει αὐτοῖς . . . (x 41-45)

Again in this unit the first part indicates the movement of Jesus, and the presence of the Twelve with Jesus is explicitly mentioned in the narrational framework. The second part creates interaction between Jesus and his disciples that sets the stage for the concluding part of the literary unit. The third and final part features Jesus summoning (προσκαλέομαι) his disciples to him and stating to them a sequence of dramatic sayings that summarizes the entire section from viii 27 to x 45.

In parallel with the individual scenes in Mark that feature three parts, the three-part units in viii 27-x 45 reach their highpoint in a final part that emphasizes the authoritative status of Jesus as a teacher. After an initial part that explicitly mentions the presence of the disciples with Jesus as he is moving from one place to another, a second part sets the stage for the final part where Jesus summons (προσκαλέομαι) or calls (φωνέω) his disciples and teaches them about the nature of discipleship.

THREE-PART INTERLUDES IN THE OUTLINE OF MARK

It has been recognized for many years that the term προσκαλέομαι (to summon) is used with special frequency in the Gospel of Mark [12]). The term occurs not only in viii 27-x 45 but also throughout the narrative as a means of introducing a scene in which Jesus challenges, instructs, and commands those who gather around him [13]). Especially, the term accompanies Jesus' appointment of select people to be his disciples, Jesus' commissioning of the disciples to perform certain tasks, and Jesus' instruction of the disciples in the details of the discipleship role. Analysis of the settings in which special summoning occurs reveals the presence of three-part scenes equidistantly spaced throughout the Gospel [14]). These three-part scenes function as interludes that establish the narrative program on the basis of interaction between Jesus and his disciples. These interludes bring themes and activities from the preceding narrative to a conclusion in the same context in which they introduce themes

---

[12]) HENRY B. SWETE, *The Gospel According to Mark* (3d ed.; London: Macmillan, 1909) xlix; VINCENT TAYLOR, *The Gospel According to Mark* (2d ed.; London: Macmillan, 1966) 343; KARL-GEORG REPLOH, *Markus-Lehrer der Gemeinde* (SBM 9; Stuttgart: Katholisches Bibelwerk, 1969) 44; PRYKE, *Redactional Style* 51, 137; HOWARD C. KEE, *Community of the New Age* (Philadelphia: Westminster, 1977) 52-53.

[13]) Mark iii 13, 23; vi 7; vii 14; viii 1, 34; x 42; xii 43.

[14]) Mark i 14-20; iii 7-19; vi 1-13; viii 27-ix 1; x 46-xi 11; xiii 1-37.

and activities that direct the narrative program in the next section of the Gospel. These interludes function, therefore, as formal transitional scenes that divide the narrative on the basis of sequential stages of interaction between Jesus and his disciples.

The first stage of interaction begins with the three-part interlude in Mark i 14-20. In this interlude between the temptation of Jesus in the wilderness (i 12-13) and his first appearance in a synagogue (i 21-28), Jesus' command to all people to repent and believe on the basis of the imminence of the Kingdom of God reaches its climax in the calling of four men into a teacher/disciple relationship. In the final part of the interlude, the reader for the first time encounters the term καλέω (to call) as the author narrates the calling of James and John:

(1) ... δὲ. ... ἦλθεν ὁ 'Ιησοῦς ...
    κηρύσσων ...
    καὶ λέγων ... (i 14-15)
(2) Καὶ παράγων ... εἶδεν ...
    καὶ εἶπεν αὐτοῖς ὁ 'Ιησοῦς ...
        καὶ εὐθὺς ἀφέντες ... ἠκολούθησαν αὐτοῦ (i 16-18)
(3) Καὶ προβὰς ... εἶδεν ...
    καὶ εὐθὺς ἐκάλεσεν αὐτούς,
        καὶ ἀφέντες ... ἀπῆλθον ὀπίσω αὐτοῦ (i 19-20)

Not only is this interlude the first context in which a summons to discipleship occurs, it is the first setting in the narrative in which Jesus is attributed with direct speech. By means of this speech, Jesus announces the Kingdom of God, issues a general command to all people to repent and believe in the gospel, then calls individuals to follow him. This three-part sequence introduces the essential dynamic that accompanies Jesus throughout Mark and establishes the major sections in the narrative. The essential dynamic concerns the movement of Jesus to various places to teach and show people the meaning of the Kingdom of God in word and deed. This activity creates interaction with individuals whom Jesus summons into discipleship. When individuals are summoned into discipleship, they have specific responsibilities which they are asked to perform and to understand. After this interlude in which the first four disciples are called, therefore, three-part literary units systematically occur to inaugurate new stages of interaction between Jesus and his disciples.

The second three-part literary unit of this nature occurs in iii 7-19. This unit contains the first occurrence of προσκαλέομαι in the linear progression of the narrative. The construction of the unit is as follows:

(1) Καὶ ὁ Ἰησοῦς μετὰ τῶν μαθητῶν αὐτοῦ ἀνεχώρησεν . . .

   καὶ πολὺ πλῆθος . . . [ἠκολούθησαν] [15]) . . .

   πλῆθος πολὺ . . . ἦλθον πρὸς αὐτόν (iii 7-8)

(2) καὶ εἶπεν τοῖς μαθηταῖς αὐτοῦ . . .

   (πολλοὺς γὰρ ἐθεράπευσεν . . .)

   καὶ . . . ἐπετίμα αὐτοῖς . . . (iii 9-12)

(3) Καὶ ἀναβαίνει . . . καὶ προσκαλεῖται . . . καὶ ἀπῆλθον πρὸς αὐτόν,

   καὶ ἐποίησεν δώδεκα . . .

       καὶ ἐπέθηκεν ὄνομα . . .

       καὶ ἐπέθηκεν αὐτοῖς ὀνόμα[τα] . . . (iii 13-19)

In analogy with the three-part literary units in viii 27-x 45, this unit begins with reference to the travel of Jesus, and the presence of the disciples with Jesus is explicitly mentioned. The second part features Jesus directing the action of his disciples in a context that creates the stage for the third part in which he summons twelve disciples for the purpose of preparing them to perform the preaching and healing activities characteristic of his mode of action.

The third three-part unit with these features occurs in vi 1-13. The structure of the unit is as follows:

(1) Καὶ ἐξῆλθεν ἐκεῖθεν, καὶ ἔρχεται . . .

   καὶ ἀκολουθοῦσιν αὐτῷ οἱ μαθηταὶ αὐτοῦ.

       καὶ . . . ἤρξατο διδάσκειν . . . (vi 1-3)

(2) Καὶ ἔλεγεν αὐτοῖς ὁ Ἰησοῦς . . .

   καὶ οὐκ ἐδύνατο ἐκεῖ ποιῆσαι οὐδεμίαν δύναμιν . . .

       καὶ ἐθαύμαζεν διὰ τὴν ἀπιστίαν αὐτῶν (vi 4-6)

(3) Καὶ περιῆγεν τὰς κώμας κύκλῳ διδάσκων

   καὶ προσκαλεῖται τοὺς δώδεκα

   καὶ ἤρξατο αὐτοὺς ἀποστέλλειν δύο δύο,

       καὶ ἐδίδου αὐτοῖς ἐξουσίαν . . .

       καὶ παρήγγειλεν αὐτοῖς . . .

       καὶ ἔλεγεν αὐτοῖς . . .

           καὶ ἐξελθόντες . . . (vi 7-13)

---

[15]) For the status of ἠκολούθησαν in the text, see LEANDER E. KECK, "Mark 3:7-12 and Mark's Christology," JBL 84 (1965) 345-348; METZGER, *Textual Commentary* 79-80.

In this interlude again, the disciples are explicitly mentioned as present with Jesus when he goes out (ἐξέρχομαι) from the region in which he has been active, even though the disciples play no role in the first and second parts of the interlude. Jesus' rejection in the first part, however, creates the setting for his direct response to the crowd in the second part and his special summons to the Twelve in the third part. On the basis of his rejection and his response to that rejection in the first and second parts, Jesus summons the Twelve with explicit instructions concerning their preaching and healing activities, ending with explicit instructions for them to follow when they encounter rejection (vi 11).

The fourth interlude containing a three-part rhetorical progression that reaches its climax in Jesus' summoning of his disciples occurs in Mark viii 27-ix 1, which has already been discussed above in the section on viii 27-x 45. Again the disciples are explicitly mentioned in the narrational framework that refers to Jesus coming out (ἐξέρχομαι) of one place into another (viii 27). Also, after an intermediary scene of special interaction (viii 31-33), the final part features Jesus summoning (προσκαλέομαι) his disciples, and in this instance also the crowd, to teach them the central principle of discipleship, i.e., that he who wishes to save his life must accept a form of discipleship in which he is willing to lose his life (viii 34-37). This interlude inaugurates the narrative program that continues through x 45. The teaching introduced in viii 27-9:1 reaches its climax in the third passion prediction, interaction, and summons in x 32-45.

Three-part interludes ending with a summons to the disciples occur systematically in the narrative from i 14-x 45. The frequency of the units increases once the first passion prediction occurs since the narrative program that follows the first prediction features Jesus continually engaging his disciples in conversation about discipleship in the midst of teaching that reiterates the assertion that he will be killed in Jerusalem. Once the stage of the intensive teaching about suffering, rejection, death, and resurrection ends (x 45), the occurrence of three-part interludes ending with a summons to the disciples is less obvious.

It does appear, however, that two interludes after x 45 have been influenced by the three-part compositional schema that is evident in the material from i 14 through x 45. The first interlude that appears to be influenced by the schema occurs in x 46-xi 11 and reaches its climax in the entry of Jesus into the Jerusalem Temple. The unity of x 46-xi 11 has often been overlooked because of the chapter division that was imposed between the healing of blind Bartimaeus and the sending of the two disciples to bring the colt [16]). There is actually no narrative break between x 46-52 and xi 1-11. When Bartimaeus receives his sight and begins to follow on the road (x 52), Jesus continues on the way until he sends two of his disciples to get the colt on which he rides into Jerusalem (xi 1-3). The interlude proceeds much like vi 1-13 which ends with Jesus' sending of the Twelve out to perform specific tasks he asks of them. In the third part of x 46-xi 11, Jesus commissions the disciples to participate directly in the process by which both he and they enter Jerusalem. The three-part structure of the interlude is as follows:

(1) Καὶ ἔρχονται ... καὶ ἐκπορευομένου ... καὶ τῶν μαθητῶν
αὐτοῦ καὶ ὄχλου ἱκανοῦ ...
... ἐκάθητο ... καὶ ἀκούσας ... ἤρξατο κράζειν καὶ λέγειν ...
καὶ ἐπετίμων αὐτῷ ...
ὁ δὲ πολλῷ μᾶλλον ἔκραζεν ... (x 46-48)

(2) Καὶ στὰς ὁ Ἰησοῦς εἶπεν ...
καὶ ἀποκριθεὶς αὐτῷ ὁ Ἰησοῦς εἶπεν ...
καὶ ὁ Ἰησοῦς εἶπεν αὐτῷ ... (x 49-52)

(3) καὶ ὅτε ἐγγίζουσιν ... ἀποστέλλει δύο τῶν μαθητῶν αὐτοῦ
καὶ λέγει αὐτοῖς ...
καὶ εἰσῆλθεν εἰς Ἱεροσόλυμα εἰς τὸ ἱερόν ... (xi 1-11)

Again the narrational comment in the first part of the interlude (x 46-48) explicitly refers to the disciples' presence with Jesus as he comes out (ἐκπορεύομαι) of one location to another place (x 46). In parallel with iii 7-8, the first part of the interlude features the attempt to get to Jesus for the purpose of receiving healing from

---

[16]) A number of interpreters have been aware that the section on Jesus' teaching in Jerusalem begins with Mark x 46-xi 11. See GUSTAV WOHLENBERG *Das Evangelium des Markus* (Kommentar zum Neuen Testament 2; Leipzig: Diechert, 1910) 290-293; FRIEDRICH HAUCH, *Das Evangelium des Markus* (ThHK 2; Leipzig: Diechert, 1931) VII-IX; ALFRED KUBY, "Zur Konzeption des Markusevangeliums," ZNW 49 (1958) 63-64; PHILIP CARRINGTON, *According to Mark* (Cambridge: University Press, 1960) VII; FERDINAND HAHN, *Mission in the New Testament* (SBT 47; London: SCM, 1963) 111-120; cf. VERNON K. ROBBINS, "The Healing of Blind Bartimaeus (Mark 10:46-52) in the Marcan Theology," JBL 92 (1973) 224-243.

him. While the central material in iii 7-8 is bracketed by πολύ πλῆθος ... πλῆθος πολύ, the material in x 46-48 is bracketed by the cry, "'Υἱὲ Δαυὶδ ('Ιησοῦ), ἐλέησόν με." As in iii 7-8 the presence of the great multitude creates the setting for the third part in which Jesus summons "those whom he himself wanted" out of the large number of people who are following him, so in x 46-48 the presence of the people who hear Bartimaeus cry out to Jesus as the Son of David sets the stage for the third part in which they themselves cry out to Jesus, "Blessed be the coming kingdom of our father David." In the second part of the interlude, Jesus tells the crowd to call (φωνέω) Bartimaeus, and they call him using language that is characteristic only of Jesus in the previous narrative [17]). Since this call results in Bartimaeus' following along with the disciples and the crowd in the second part of the interlude, the narrational comment at the beginning of the third part omits a special summons in the context of the sending of two disciples to procure the colt for the entrance. As Jesus sends out two disciples (cf. vi 7), the stage is set for emphatic speech by Jesus that inaugurates the program of action that transpires in the next section of the Gospel.

The second interlude beyond x 45 that appears to be influenced by the three-part schema is the famous "Marcan Apocalypse," xiii 1-37. This chapter contains prophetic and apocalyptic material that functions as a farewell discourse in a setting similar to the Graeco-Roman temple dialogue [18]). As R. PESCH has shown, xiii 1-37 is an interlude that forms a transition between Jesus' teaching in the Temple (xi 12-xii 44) and the arrest, trial, death, and resurrection of Jesus (xiv 1-xvi 8) [19]). The interlude shows evidence of three-part composition at various levels. Firstly, the overall scene is introduced by two parts (xiii 1-2, 3-4) [20]) that lead into a third part featuring direct statements by Jesus (xiii 5-37). This framework suggests the influence of the three-part schema present throughout the narrative. Secondly, the statements by Jesus fall into three basic sections of material: the birth pangs of the new age (xiii 5-23), the

---

[17]) Mark ii 9, 11; iii 3; v 41; vi 50.

[18]) DAVID E. AUNE, "The Prophetic Role of Jesus," forthcoming in *Prophecy and Early Christianity* (Grand Rapids: Eerdmans, 1980).

[19]) RUDOLF PESCH, *Naherwartungen: Tradition und Redaktion in Mk 13* (Kommentare und Beiträge zum alten und neuen Testament; Düsseldorf: Patmos, 1968) 70-73.

[20]) See PESCH, *Naherwartungen* 83-106; W. H. KELBER, *The Kingdom in Mark* (Philadelphia: Fortress, 1974) 111-113.

closing scene of the eschatological drama (xiii 24-27), and the need
for vigilance on the part of believers (xiii 28-37) [21]. Thirdly, the
three-fold structure is present in units of small and intermediate
size, with smaller three-fold sections within overarching three-fold
sections. The three-part dimension is indicated by means of repetition: xiii 5-23: βλέπετε ... βλέπετε ... βλέπετε; xiii 9-13: παρα-
δώσουσιν ... καὶ παραδιδόντες ... καὶ παραδώσει; xiii 24-27: ἐν
ἐκείναις ταῖς ἡμέραις ... καὶ τότε ... καὶ τότε; xiii 32-37: γρηγορῇ
... γρηγορεῖτε ... γρηγορεῖτε. The structure of the unit, therefore,
is as follows:

(1) Καὶ ἐκπορευομένου αὐτοῦ ... λέγει αὐτῷ εἷς τῶν μαθητῶν
    αὐτοῦ ...
    καὶ ὁ Ἰησοῦς εἶπεν αὐτῷ ... (xiii 1-2)
(2) Καὶ καθημένου αὐτοῦ ...
    ἐπηρώτα αὐτόν ... (xiii 3-4)
(3) ὁ δὲ Ἰησοῦς ἤρξατο λέγειν αὐτοῖς,
    βλέπετε ...
    βλέπετε ...
        παραδώσουσιν ...
        καὶ παραδιδόντες ...
        καὶ παραδώσει (xiii 9-13)
    βλέπετε ... (xiii 5-23)
    Ἀλλὰ ἐν ἐκείναις ταῖς ἡμέραις μετὰ τὴν θλῖψιν ἐκείνην ...
    καὶ τότε ...
    καὶ τότε ... (xiii 24-27)
        περὶ δὲ τῆς ἡμέρας ἐκείνης ἢ τῆς ὥρας ...
        βλέπετε ἀγρυπνεῖτε ... ἵνα γρηγορῇ
        γρηγορεῖτε οὖν ...
        γρηγορεῖτε (xiii 32-37)

Like the previous three-part interludes, this unit begins with specific
reference to disciples in the context of Jesus' travel out of the area
(ἐκπορεύομαι) in which the preceding action was located. In contrast
to the scenes in viii 27-x 45 where the disciples would not initiate
interaction until the second part, disciples initiate the questioning
in both the first and second parts of xiii 1-37. The initiative of the

---

21) PESCH, Naherwartungen 107-181; T. A. BURKILL, New Light on the
Earliest Gospel: Seven Markan Studies (Ithaca and London: Cornell University Press, 1972) 256; KELBER, Kingdom 114-128.

disciples in the first and second parts creates the setting, then, for the third part in which Jesus exhorts and instructs Peter, Andrew, James, and John at length by means of direct speech. Also in contrast to the previous interludes, the narrational comment leading into the third part does not contain προσκαλέομαι, καλέω, φωνέω, or ἀποστέλλω. Instead, the author uses another favorite narrational comment, ἤρξατο λέγειν αὐτοῖς [22]), to introduce the speech in which he summons, exhorts, instructs, and commissions his disciples.

The verse immediately after xiii 1-37 shifts abruptly to a temporal reference: "It was now two days before the Passover and the Feast of Unleavened Bread" (xiv 1). Examination of the other interludes indicates that four of the six are immediately succeeded by a temporal reference. The narration after i 14-20 locates the episode "on the sabbath" (i 21: τοῖς σάββασιν); the narration after viii 27-ix 1 locates the episode "after six days" (ix 2: μετὰ ἡμέρας ἕξ); the narration after x 46-xi 11 locates the episode "on the next day" (xi 12: τῇ ἐπαύριον); and the narration after xiii 1-37 locates the events "two days before the Passover and the Feast of Unleavened Bread" (xiv 1: ἦν . . . τὸ πάσχα καὶ τὰ ἄζυμα μετὰ δύο ἡμέρας) [23]).

The presence of temporal statements immediately after these three-part units raises the possibility that each unit functions like an interlude, a period of interaction in which linear progression in the narrative becomes subordinate to a rhetorical progression that reaches its climax in a summons by Jesus to his disciples. The rhetorical progression portrays Jesus moving out from one location with his disciples and entering into interaction that creates the setting for a specific challenge to the person who will accept the role of disciple. Immediately after the interlude that ends with a summons, the narrative program begins with a specific temporal reference. Within the interlude itself, however, rhetorical progression linked with itinerant movement dominates the sequence. For this reason, specific temporal references are absent from the narrative framework as the three parts unfold.

---

[22]) See PRYKE, Redactional Style 81.

[23]) The first specific temporal reference after iii 7-19 occurs in iv 35 (ἐν ἐκείνῃ τῇ ἡμέρᾳ ὀψίας γενομένης), which is likely to be suggestive for the interpretation of iii 20-iv 34. Immediately after iii 7-19, however, the narrative shifts to a later time when "he came to a house" (iii 20: ἔρχεται εἰς οἶκον). Likewise, immediately after vi 1-13, the narrative abruptly shifts to King Herod's thoughts about Jesus and King Herod's actions with John the Baptist.

Conclusion

The analysis of series of three in Mark, therefore, leads the interpreter to three-part literary units that reach their highpoint in a setting where Jesus summons or commissions disciples. Characteristically, these units begin with explicit reference to the presence of the disciples with Jesus as he travels out (ἐξέρχομαι, ἐκπορεύομαι) of one place to another. The second part, then, involves Jesus in interaction that sets the stage for the third part which begins with a narrational comment that Jesus summons (προσκαλέομαι), calls (καλέω, φωνέω), or sends (ἀποστέλλω) his disciples.

The presence of these units in the Marcan narrative from i 14 to x 45 appears quite evident. After x 45, it appears that the three-part rhetorical progression has also influenced the composition of x 46-xi 11 and xiii 1-37. This analysis suggests the following outline for the Gospel of Mark:

Introduction i 1-13

Section 1	i 14-15, 16-18, 19-20	Jesus: Proclaiming the Gospel of God and Summoning
	i 21-iii 6	Initial Stage of the Teacher/ Disciple Relationship
Section 2	iii 7-8, 9-12, 13-19	The Son of God: Casting out Demons and Healing
	iii 20-v 43	Special Instruction and Awareness of Special Powers
Section 3	vi 1-3, 4-6, 7-13	The Prophet: Rejection of the Wonder-Working Teacher
	vi 14-viii 26	Performance of Duties within Discipleship
Section 4	viii 27-30, 31-33, 34- ix 1	The Son of Man: Suffering, Death and Resurrection
	ix 2-x 45	Struggle over the Central Dimensions of the Teacher's Value System
Section 5	x 46-48, 49-52, xi 1-11	The Son of David: Powerful Teaching in Jerusalem
	xi 12-xii 44	Addressing General Issues in Public Forum

Section 6   xiii 1-2, 3-4, 5-37   The Teacher Prepares His
                                      Disciples for His Absence
                                      and Return as Son of Man
              xiv 1-xv 47   Unwillingness to Accept the
                                      Necessity of the Arrest,
                                      Trial, and Death of the
                                      Teacher
Conclusion   xvi 1-8

While the ramifications of this outline for the Gospel of Mark must be pursued in other settings than this article, suffice it to say that these interludes carry the reader through the complete cycle of relationships between a teacher and his student-disciples in Graeco-Roman culture. The stages of discipleship introduced by these interludes reflect the intersection of Jewish traditions about prophet-teachers with Graeco-Roman traditions about itinerant preacher-teachers who gather student-disciples and systematically transmit a system of thought and action to them until death takes them away [24]. The stage in which a "following" relationship is initiated and the stage in which such a relationship is ended have a heritage in both Israelite and Graeco-Roman tradition. The intermediate stages that present the teaching-learning process, however, appear to be dominated by Graeco-Roman cultural influences upon Judaism and Christianity during the Hellenistic period. In Mark iii 7-xii 44, the disciples go through stages of interaction with Jesus that are characteristic of the cycle of relationships that student-disciples experience with people like Socrates and Apollonius of Tyana.

In conclusion, this outline suggests that the Gospel of Mark stands at the interface of Jewish and Graeco-Roman traditions, reflecting impulses both from traditions attached to Israelite leaders like Moses and Elijah and impulses from Graeco-Roman traditions about itinerant preacher-teachers who gather student-disciples around them. The convergence of these impulses leads to the composition of a narrative in which the teacher-Messiah Jesus systematically summons, instructs, and commands people much like Yahweh summons, instructs, and commands in Israelite tradition and much like itinerant preacher-teachers summon, instruct, and command people in Graeco-Roman tradition.

---

[24] For an excellent survey of itinerant preacher-teachers in the Mediterranean world, see WALTER L. LIEFELD, *The Wandering Preacher as a Social Figure in the Roman Empire* (Unpublished Ph. D. Dissertation; New York: Columbia University, 1967).

THE ROLE OF "SUMMARY STATEMENTS"
IN THE COMPOSITION OF THE GOSPEL OF MARK:
A DIALOG WITH KARL SCHMIDT
AND NORMAN PERRIN

by

CHARLES W. HEDRICK
Southwest Missouri State University, Springfield, Missouri 65804

In his New Testament introduction, Norman Perrin argues that Mark has assembled several independent collections of traditional material and arranged them so as to form the first connected narrative of the ministry of Jesus. These units are: The Passion Narrative (14:13-16:8); a cycle of miracle stories (Chapters 5 and 7); a cycle of controversy stories (Chapter 2); a collection of parables (4:1-9, 13-34); two cycles of stories arranged on the basis of the following motifs: feeding, crossing the lake, controversy with the Pharisees and teaching concerning bread (6:30-7:23, 8:1-21); and the apocalyptic discourse (chapter 13).[1] Mark "structured" these materials into a "continuous" narrative by the use of geographical references and summary reports. Where geographical references and summary reports coincide, one is able to identify "natural" divisions in the literary structure of the Gospel. There are three such divisions: 1:14-15, 3:7-12, 6:6b. In addition to these three summary reports, and along with the geographical references, Mark also employs two transitional giving of sight stories (8:22-26, 10:46-52), so as to form two further divisions to the structure of the Gospel. A final compositional technique of the evangelist is his

---

[1] Norman Perrin, *The New Testament: An Introduction* (New York/Chicago/San Francisco/Atlanta: Harcourt/Brace/Jovanovich, 1974) 145-47. Perrin's use of the summary statements in Acts (*The New Testament*, 205-6) also needs to be examined in the light of *all* such statements in the book. Each of Perrin's major divisions for the structure of the book ends with a summary statement (Acts 2:43-47, 5:42, 9:31, 12:24, 15:35, 19:20). Perrin, however, has noted only a few of a much larger collection of summaries in the book (4:4, 5:12-16, 6:7, 8:1b-4, 8:25, 8:40, 11:19, 14:24-28, 16:5, 18:22-23, 19:8-10). Note that Perrin's first summary statement Acts 2:43-47 may actually begin at 2:40. Other travelogs (20:1-6, 20:13-16, 21:1-7, 21:15-17) should also be studied in connection with the summary statements.

inclusion of introductory statements to the apocalyptic discourse (13:1-5a) and to the Passion Narrative (14:1-2, 10:12).

Hence, on the basis of these observations, Perrin breaks down the literary structure of Mark as follows:

1:1-13	Introduction
1:14-15	Transitional Markan summary
1:16-3:6	First major section: The authority of Jesus exhibited in word and deed
3:7-12	Transitional Markan summary
3:13-6:6a	Second major section: Jesus as Son of God and as rejected by his own people
6:6b	Transitional Markan summary
6:7-8:22	Third major section: Jesus as Son of God and as misunderstood by his own disciples
8:23-26	Transitional giving-of-sight story
8:27-10:45	Fourth major section: Christology and Christian discipleship in the light of the passion
10:46-52	Transitional giving-of-sight story
11:1-12:44	Fifth major section: the days in Jerusalem prior to the passion
13:1-5a	Introduction to the apocalyptic discourse
13:5b-37	Apocalyptic discourse
14:1-12	Introduction to the passion narrative (with intercalation 14:3-9)
14:13-16:8	The passion narrative[2]

The purpose of this paper is to challenge Perrin's understanding of summary statements as transitional structural devices in Mark's Gospel. It will proceed by examining the number, character, and function of all such summary statements in Mark and will then

---

[2] In an earlier article Perrin has incorrectly written the division for the third major section as 6:7-8:22 and incorrectly indicated the transitional giving-of-sight story as 8:23-26: "Towards an Interpretation of the Gospel of Mark," *Christology and a Modern Pilgrimage: A Discussion with Norman Perrin* (Claremont, CA: No publisher, 1971) 5; compare *The New Testament*, 147. The clarification of the literary structure of Mark has been a concern of recent New Testament scholarship. See Eduard Schweizer, "The Portrayal of Faith in the Gospel of Mark," *Int* 32 (1978) 387-99; Vernon K. Robbins, "Summons and Outline in Mark: The Three Step Progression," *NovT* 23 (1981) 98-114; and for a discussion of other recent research see Joanna Dewey, *Marcan Public Debate: Literary Technique, Concentric Structure and Theology in Mark 2:1-3:6* (SBL dissertation Series 48; Chico, CA: Scholars Press, 1980) 13.

compare them to similar narrative devices in Philostratus, *The Life of Apollonius of Tyana*.

Perrin recognizes summaries at 1:14-15, 21-22, 39; 2:13; 3:7-12; 5:21; 6:6b, 12-13, 30-33, 53-56; 10:1.[3] Karl Schmidt was the first to call attention to these Markan summary reports (*Sammelberichte*) and to analyze them in connection with the evangelist's literary method.[4] Later C. H. Dodd, *in general* following Schmidt, argued that by placing the summary statements found in Chapters 1-6 end to end one is able to identify a traditional outline of the Galilean ministry of Jesus, much like Dibelius identified in the preaching of the church in Acts.[5] Hence, it appears to Dodd that the structure of Mark is dictated by a schematic outline of the ministry of Jesus that Mark had received from the tradition. Dodd's list of summaries does not completely agree with Schmidt's list.[6] Dodd lists Mark 3:7b-19, 6:7 and 6:30 as summaries, while Schmidt regards Mark 3:7-12, 6:6b and 6:30-33 as summaries. Nor does Dodd discuss as summaries Mark 5:21, 6:53-56 and 10:1, which Schmidt clearly regards as summaries. Perrin, on the other hand, appears to follow Schmidt closely with no (published) independent analysis of his own of the summary reports.[7]

Recently the summary statements in Mark have been made the subject of a monograph by Wilhelm Egger.[8] Egger finds summary statements at 1:14-15, 21-32, 32-34, 39, 45; 2:1-2, 13; 3:7-12; 4:1-2; 6:6b, 30-34, 53-56; 10:1.[9] This list omits two passages iden-

---

[3] Perrin, *The New Testament*, 147. It is striking that most of the summary statements appear in Mark 1-6. Only three appear outside these chapters: 9:30-32, 10:1 and 10:32. Trocmé's identification of a summary statement at 12:38 appears to be an error (*The Formation of the Gospel of Mark* [Philadelphia: Westminster, 1975 (French 1963)] 29). See below for a discussion of 9:32 and 10:32 as summary statements.

[4] Karl Schmidt, *Der Rahmen der Geschichte Jesu: Literarkritische Untersuchungen zur ältesten Jesusüberlieferung* (Berlin: Trowitzsch, 1919). See Schmidt's index (page 320) for his listing of the summaries.

[5] C. H. Dodd, "The Framework of the Gospel Narrative," *New Testament Studies* (Manchester: University Press, 1967 [it originally appeared in 1932]) 1-11.

[6] For a criticism of Dodd's position see Trocmé, *Formation*, 28-31. It is curious to me that Trocmé did not criticize Dodd for ostensibly *following* Schmidt's work (Dodd, "The Framework of the Gospel Narrative," 7) and yet failing to use *all* the summaries in his analysis and even changing with no discussion three of those he did use (see in particular Trocmé, *Formation*, 29).

[7] Perrin, "The Interpretation of the Gospel of Mark," *Int* 30 (1976) 122.

[8] Wilhelm Egger, *Frohbotschaft und Lehre: Die Sammelberichte des Wirkens Jesu im Markusevangelium* (Frankfurt: Knecht, 1976).

[9] Ibid., 2.

tified by Schmidt-Perrin as summaries: 5:21 and 6:12-13; and includes four passages not so identified by Schmidt-Perrin: 1:32-34, 45; 2:1-2; 4:1-2. His book is the first analysis to be devoted completely to a study of the summaries and the first form-critical analysis of the summaries. Like Perrin, he also regards the summaries as providing the primary structural framework for the narrative that constitutes Mark's Gospel.[10]

Schmidt does not define formally what he means by "*Sammelberichte*" but he appears to regard them as general statements composed or created by the evangelist out of traditional pericope introductions and conclusions[11] for the purpose of tying together diverse episodic pericopae so as to include them in a broader narrative framework.[12] Hence, the summary statements describe the activities of Jesus on a broader and more general scale.[13] The topographical and chronological facts contained in them have no significance for the development of the history of Jesus.[14] While it is not noted by Schmidt, the summary statements show a preference for the Greek imperfect tense, a verbal form expressing continuous, repeated or customary action in the past. The use of this verbal form is to be expected, if the author wished to imply a broader ministry for Jesus than is shown by the individual episodes of the Gospel.[15] One also finds in the summary statements the use of cer-

---

[10] Ibid., 19-20 and 162-63.

[11] Schmidt, *Der Rahmen*, 82, n. 2

[12] Ibid., 105-6.

[13] Ibid., 13 and 106.

[14] Ibid., 160, 105, 238. See Dodd's valuable brief summary of the character of these "summary statements" ("The formation of the Gospel Narrative," 2-3). See also the brief assessment by H. J. Cadbury, "The Summaries in Acts," in: *The Beginnings of Christianity*, I, *The Acts of the Apostles* (F. J. Foakes Jackson and Kirsopp Lake, eds.; 5 vols.; London: Macmillan, 1933), 5. 394-402.

[15] The conscious use of the imperfect tense by the author of Mark has also been noted by Wilhelm Egger (*Frohbotschaft und Lehre*, 1, 28 and 30; cf. also id. "Die Verborgenheit Jesu in Mark 3:7-12," *Bib* 50 [1969] 468). Although Egger observes that the imperfect is used to describe the activities of Jesus in the summaries, this verbal form also occurs regularly to describe the activities of other characters in the narrative.

   Mark 1:21-22:   He was teaching (ἐδίδασκεν); they were marveling (ἐξεπλήσσοντο); he was teaching (ἦν διδάσκων—periphrastic imperfect).

   Mark 1:39:   He came preaching (ἦλθεν κηρύσσων; but the editors may not be correct and the variant may be the preferred reading: ἦν κηρύσσων καὶ ἐκβάλλων) in their synagogues (συναγωγὰς αὐτῶν) in all Galilee.

tain turns of expression that invite the assumption that Jesus's ministry was far more extensive than the narrating of the individual episodes by themselves would imply.[16]

Perrin understands the summary reports as a significant part of Mark's conscious compositional activity. Indeed, for Perrin they form the basic "pegs" of Mark's overall literary structure.[17] Schmidt, on the other hand, sees them as literary devices that tie together individual pericopae rather than providing the basic literary structure for the document. According to Schmidt, their significance for the overall Gospel is that they broaden, widen or expand the ministry of Jesus beyond the borders of the individual particularized narratives which constitute the dominant feature of Mark's Gospel.[18]

When one examines the summary reports of Schmidt-Perrin one discovers that they are *on the whole* comprised of generalized and

---

Mark 2:13: All the crowd was coming (ἤρχετο) to him and he was teaching (ἐδίδασκεν) them.

Mark 3:7-12: A great multititude from Judea, Jerusalem, Idumea, around the Jordan and Tyre and Sidon having heard what he was doing (ἐποίει) came to him....And the unclean spirits, when they were beholding (ἐθεώρουν) him, were falling down (προσέπιπτον) and were crying (ἔκραζον); and he was silencing (ἐπετίμα) them.

Mark 5:21: And he was (ἦν) near the lake.

Mark 6:6b: And he was going around (περιῆγεν) the villages teaching.

Mark 6:12-13: And they were casting out (ἐξέβαλλον) many demons and were anointing (ἤλειφον) and were healing (ἐθεράπευον) many sick.

Mark 6:30-33: For many were coming (ἦσαν ἐρχόμενοι) and going ([ἦσαν] ὑπάγοντες) and they were having no leisure (εὐκαίρουν) to eat.

Mark 6:53-56: *Wherever he was entering* (εἰσεπορεύετο) into villages or cities or country places, they were laying (ἐτίθεσαν) the sick in the market places and they were imploring (παρεκάλουν) him; and as many as touched the fringe of his garment were being healed (ἐσῴζοντο).

Mark 10:1: And crowds again gathered to him, and as his custom was, he was teaching (ἐδίδασκεν) them.

The only summary statements not using the imperfect are Mark 1:14-15, 28.

[16] See Egger, *Frohbotschaft und Lehre*, 1 and 164-65. Egger has argued that the summaries have a three-part construction whose elements usually follow the same order (*Frohbotschaft und Lehre*, 27-30).

[17] See Egger's discussion of others who hold to this same understanding of the function of the summaries (*Frohbotschaft und Lehre*, 19-23). See also Vincent Taylor (*The Gospel According to St. Mark* [London: MacMillan, 1959] 165) who also regards 1:14-15 as "one of the summary statements (*Sammelberichte*) which determine the outline of the Gospel."

[18] See in particular Schmidt, *Der Rahmen*, 13.

non-specific statements usually having no essential connection with preceding or succeeding pericopae. Most of them give a brief summary description of some aspect of *Jesus's ministry*. The use of such vague turns of expression has the practical effect of relieving the author of the burden of detail. They do not appear to be *literary* summaries in the narrow sense that they catch up in a brief single statement the essence of a *broader literary segment* that precedes or follows, like good introductory or concluding sentences to paragraphs. Indeed, on the whole, they seem to stand alone, completely independent of the particularized pericopae that surround them. They introduce *new* information into the narrative in a general and non-specific manner.

Mark 1:14-15[19] is an independent passage that introduces new concepts into the narrative. It has no essential, or immediately obvious, connection with the preceding pericope on the temptation of Jesus (Mark 1:12-13) or the following pericope on the call of Andrew, Simon, James and John (Mark 1:16-20). The issue of Jesus's preaching is not introduced in the Gospel until 1:38-39, the only other reference to Jesus preaching in the immediate context.[20] Nor does Mark 1:14-15 seem to serve as a "transition" from Mark 1:1-13 to a first major segment, Mark 1:16-3:6, at least not in the narrow sense that it provides a smooth transition from John's preaching to Jesus's preaching, since what Perrin has identified as the first major section contains only one other reference to the preaching of Jesus. Mark 1:14-15 is a concise *summary* of the content of the preaching of Jesus, the only one in the Gospel. Its position at the beginning of Jesus's ministry affects the reader's view of the entire narrative. It invites the reader to supply the "general content" of Mark 1:14-15 as the substance of Jesus's message, wherever Jesus is described as preaching or teaching (such as at 1:21-22, 27, 38-39, 45; 2:2, 13; 3:14; 4:1-34; 6:2, 6b, 12, 34; 10:1; 11:18; 12:35, 38; 13:10). This technique relieves the author of the necessity of repeating the "message" each time Jesus is described as addressing audiences. Unless otherwise informed, the reader would assume (or Mark appears to *intend* that he assume) on the basis of the summary

---

[19] See Schmidt's discussion, *Der Rahmen*, 32-35; and cf. Egger, *Frohbotschaft und Lehre*, 39-64.

[20] Other references to the preaching of Jesus and his disciples in Mark are 3:14, 6:12, 14:9, [16:15.20]; there is a reference to the kerygma of John in 1:4, 7. See also Mark 2:2 where Jesus "speaks the word to them."

at 1:14-15, that Jesus is preaching and teaching about the Kingdom of God. Hence, this summary statement does not appear to be a structural "peg" around which the author "suspends" segments of material. On the contrary, it is better understood as a compositional or narrative device by which the author attempts to influence the character of the entire narrative. Its supposed function as a structural "peg" that provides a transition from the preaching of John the Baptist (1:1-13) to the ministry of Jesus is an illusion produced by the abrupt break between the Baptist material and the ministry of Jesus, as well as the summary character of 1:14-15. The functional role of 1:14-15 is to provide overall cohesion to the entire narrative with respect to the teaching and preaching of Jesus.

Mark 1:21-22[21] at first may seem to be an essential part of the miracle story that follows (1:23-27). Compare 1:22 (teaching as one "who had authority") and 1:27 (teaching with authority); 1:21 (synagogue) and 1:23 (their synagogue). But Schmidt has argued convincingly that Mark 1:21b-22 is a summary report that has been partially constructed with reference to the miracle story that follows. The statement itself relates a general response to a generally described activity. It seems to imply more than one occasion on which Jesus taught in the synagogue.

Mark 1:39[22] is another general statement about the character and breadth of the ministry of Jesus. It stresses both the preaching and miracle working ministry, incorporating the emphases of both 1:14-15 and 1:32-34. Mark apparently used the saying of Jesus on preaching in 1:38 as an occasion for expanding the ministry of Jesus beyond the particular episodes that describe in greater detail his activities in the rest of the Gospel.

Mark 2:13[23] has no essential connection with the preceding pericope on the healing of the paralytic (2:3-12) that ostensibly takes place "at home" in Capernaum (2:1) or with the following brief pericope on the call of Levi (2:14) at an undisclosed geographical location. Mark 2:13 describes Jesus's change of location and characterizes the ministry of Jesus as a teaching ministry that draws crowds. The adverb πάλιν (again) and the transitional

---

[21] See Schmidt, *Der Rahmen*, 50; and Egger, *Frohbotschaft und Lehre*, 146-49.

[22] See Schmidt's discussion, *Der Rahmen*, 59-60, and Egger, *Frohbotschaft und Lehre*, 73-79.

[23] See Schmidt, *Der Rahmen*, 82 and Egger, *Frohbotschaft und Lehre*, 151-53.

phrase "as he passed on" (παράγων) further highlight the separation of 2:13 from its context.

Mark 3:7-12,[24] according to Perrin, is a transitional summary between Mark's first major section (1:16-3:6) and his second major section (3:13-6:6a). As a summary in the narrow sense, it fails to catch up the essential features of the first section that Perrin characterizes as "the authority of Jesus exhibited in word and deed." It admirably summarizes the healing and exorcising ministry of Jesus that appears through the section (1:23-26, 29-31, 32-34, 40-44; 2:1-2; 3:1-5), but it fails to incorporate the preaching and teaching ministry of Jesus that Mark specifically incorporates at 1:14-15, 21-22, 27, 38-39, 45; 2:2, 13, 18-22, 23-28. And it seems to contradict what Perrin understands to be the major emphasis of a second major section (3:13-6:6a) "Jesus as Son of God and rejected by his own people," since it describes the success of Jesus's ministry and his great popularity among the crowds in his homeland. What the pericope does do is to expand the activities of Jesus beyond the narrow confines of particularized episodes. Its generality invites the reader to view the particular narrative events described in more detail in the Gospel as examples of a broader and more extensive ministry.[25]

Mark 5:21[26] simply describes Jesus's change of location and characterizes his ministry as a popular one that drew a large crowd. The statement is somewhat in tension with 5:24 which appears to introduce unnecessarily another great crowd in order to accommodate 5:31 where the crowd plays a necessary role in the second pericope that follows 5:21. Mark 5:21 seems designed to move Jesus from the "other side" of the lake (5:1-20) and to reaffirm the popularity of his ministry among the people, since he had experienced only mixed success on the "other side" (5:17).

Mark 6:6b,[27] Perrin argues, is a Markan summary that serves as a

---

[24] See Schmidt, *Der Rahmen*, 104-8 and Egger, *Frohbotschaft und Lehre*, 91-111.

[25] However, see L. E. Keck ("Mark 3:7-12 and Mark's Christology," *JBL* 84 [1965] 341-58) who argues that 3:7-12 concludes a section begun at 1:16. He regards the passage as a traditional summary expanded by Mark and not created *de novo* by the evangelist. Keck's position is specifically challenged by T. A. Burkill ("Mark 3:7-12 and the Alleged Dualism in the Evangelist's Miracle Material," *JBL* 87 [1968] 409-17).

[26] See Schmidt, *Der Rahmen*, 146. Egger rejects this passage as a summary statement (*Frohbotschaft und Lehre*, 2).

[27] See Schmidt, *Der Rahmen*, 158-60 and Egger, *Frohbotschaft und Lehre*, 153-55.

transition between the second (3:13-6:6a) and third (6:7-8:21) major sections of the Gospel. The theme of the third section is "Jesus as Son of Man and misunderstood by his own disciples." Mark 6:6b does allude to Jesus's teaching, and the motif does appear in section two (Mark 4:1-34) and in section three (Mark 7:1-23; 8:11-21), but 6:6b fails to do justice to Jesus's ministry of healing and exorcisms which appears to be a dominant emphasis in both sections. 6:6b seems actually only to serve the function of expanding the breadth of the ministry of Jesus. With this statement it would appear that Mark wants to give the impression that the individual incidents he narrates are really only illustrative of what was happening on a much broader scale.

Mark 6:12-13[28] is a summary statement of the activities of the disciples of Jesus further expanding Jesus's ministry with their own preaching, exorcising and healing. The verses have no connection with the intercalated verses on John the Baptist (6:14-29) that immediately follow and actually describe the disciples as going beyond what they were commanded to do in 6:7, where they were only given authority over unclean spirits. The purpose of the verses does not seem to be to summarize the pericope Mark 6:7-11 nor to anticipate Mark 6:30 but rather to summarize the mission of the Twelve (Apostles, 6:30) as event. Hence, it adds new information in a general and nonspecific way about the ministry of the Twelve, rather than summarizing old information that precedes or follows in the narrative.

Mark 6:30-33,[29] while recognized by Schmidt as a summary report, may actually be only an expanded introduction to the feeding of the 5,000 (6:34-44). Mark 6:34 builds upon 6:30-33 (or 6:30-33 anticipates 6:34). Compare 6:34a, "As he went ashore" to 6:32, "they went away in the boat"; 6:34b, "he saw a great throng" to 6:33, "many saw them going ... and got there ahead of them." In 6:35 one is clearly into the pericope of the feeding of the 5,000 which does have some connection to 6:30-34. Compare 6:35, "this is a lonely place" to 6:31a, "Come away to a lonely place" and 6:32a "went away to a lonely place"; compare "and buy themselves something to eat" to 6:31b "had no leisure to eat." The

---

[28] See Schmidt, *Der Rahmen*, 162-63. Egger rejects this passage as a summary statement (*Frohbotschaft und Lehre*, 2).

[29] See Schmidt, *Der Rahmen*, 188. Egger (*Frohbotschaft und Lehre*, 121-31) also extends the passage so as to include Mark 6:34.

only attempt at generalizing in the verses 6:30-33 is the statement they came from "all the towns" (6:33), and the teaching of "many things" (6:34). If it is a summary report, it probably should be extended to include 6:34.

Mark 6:53-56[30] seems to summarize neither the preceding pericope (6:45-52) nor the following pericope (7:1-13). It describes Jesus's change of location, emphasizes the popularity of Jesus's healing ministry and considerably expands the breadth of that ministry beyond the specific examples of healing described in detail by Mark. The passage seems intended to create the impression that the healing ministry of Jesus, illustrated by Mark with certain specific incidents, was being practiced by Jesus throughout all Galilee. No particulars are given. Those who are healed are un-named, no descriptions of their infirmities are provided, and details of the particular incidents are simply omitted.

Mark 10:1[31] begins the trip from Galilee to Jerusalem (10:1-52). It seems clear that the reader is to understand this section as a journey from Galilee to Jerusalem and hence we have here a major shift in both setting and location of the ministry of Jesus. Compare 10:17a, 32, 46a and 11:1. The author clearly wants to create the impression of a trip incorporating all of Mark 10:1-52. Hence, Mark 10:1 does not appear to be only a summary report in the sense of the others that we have just examined, but it seems also to function as the literary introduction to the compiled narrative of the trip from Galilee to Jerusalem. This summary does represent an attempt by the author at providing a broader literary structure for his individual narrative units. Yet it also provides a general summary of the character of the ministry of Jesus. One notes in the travel narrative that with the exception of 10:46-52 Jesus is described as primarily "teaching" (10:1b). The topics are: on marriage and divorce (10:2-12); on entering the Kingdom (10:13-16); on the danger of possessions (10:17-31); the teaching on the cross (10:32-34); the teaching on the nature of discipleship (10:35-45). Mark 10:46-52 may be intended to function as an example of the importance of faith.[32] Hence, Mark 10:1 serves much like other

---

[30] See Schmidt, *Der Rahmen*, 194-96 and Egger, *Frohbotschaft und Lehre*, 134-42.

[31] See Schmidt, *Der Rahmen*, 238 and Egger, *Frohbotschaft und Lehre*, 155-56.

[32] Perrin regards this pericope and 8:22-26 as transitional giving of sight stories; they function according to his theory as major structural shifts in the structure of the narrative.

literary introductions and conclusions in Mark's Gospel (4:1-2a, 33-34; and 13:1-5a).

Both Schmidt and Perrin, however, seem to have overlooked several additional passages in the Gospel that have the same summary character as the verses that have just been discussed: 1:5, 28, 32-34, 45; 2:1-2, 15; 4:33-34; 6:1; 9:30-32; 10:32. Of these Egger has identified as summary statements 1:32-34, 45 and 2:1-2 but has overlooked the rest.

Mark 1:5[33] should also be considered a Markan summary statement because of the exaggerated claims made for the popularity of John's ministry (*all* Judea and *all* the people of Jerusalem were baptized by John), the general description of his activities, and the general similarity of the statement with other summaries.[34] Its function is to describe the widespread popularity of the Baptist's ministry without involving the author in the recounting of detailed incidents. The two main verbs in the sentence (ἐξεπορεύετο—they were going out; ἐβαπτίζοντο—were being baptized) are cast in the imperfect tense, stressing repeated or usual action in past time.

Mark 1:28[35] in its present position appears to be the conclusion to the miracle story 1:21-27 but it really has no evident essential connection to that pericope. In fact, as has been recognized, the connection between 1:21-27 and 1:29-31 would be even better *without* 1:28.[36] When read in the light of the other summary reports, 1:28 reflects the same characteristics. Bordering on exaggeration, it describes the popularity of Jesus in general nonspecific terms as having spread "everywhere," in all the surrounding region of Galilee.

Mark 1:32-34[37] is another general statement about the character

---

[33] Schmidt, *Der Rahmen*, 21, 51.

[34] See in particular Mark 1:28, 32-34.

[35] See Schmidt, *Der Rahmen*, 51; Schmidt sees a close connection of the verse with the pericope 1:21-27. He notes, however, that others have understood the verse differently. See particularly note 3; J. Weiss takes the verse to be an addition of the evangelist that "anticipates the following narratives with respect to time (zeitlich)," *Die Schriften des Neuen Testaments neu übersetzt und für die Gegenwart erklärt* (4 vols; Göttingen: Vandenhoeck & Ruprecht, 1917²) I: 85. With this hint from Weiss it is unclear why Schmidt failed to see the similarity between 1:28 and the other summary statements.

[36] See Gustav Wohlenberg, *Das Evangelium des Markus* (Leipzig; A. Deichert, 1910) 62.

[37] See Schmidt, *Der Rahmen*, 57-58. Egger also identifies this passage as a summary statement; cf. *Frohbotschaft und Lehre*, 64-73.

and breadth of the ministry of Jesus. It describes other healings and exorcisms by Jesus in a general schematic way. No particulars are given. Those who are healed are unnamed, no descriptions of their infirmities are provided, and the details of the particular incidents themselves are simply glossed over. Mark wishes to indicate that the particular healings such as Mark 1:21-27 and 1:29-31 were repeatedly happening on a much broader scale.[38] Through the use of the imperfect the author stresses the continued appeal of Jesus to the masses (ἔφερον—"they continued bringing to him"; ἦν ἐπισυνηγμένη—[periphrastic imperfect]—"the whole city was gathering") and his continued refusal to allow the defeated demons to identify him (ἤφιεν). Through the use of certain adjectives πάντας, ὅλη, πολλούς, πολλά) he stresses the unbridled success of Jesus's ministry.

Mark 1:45[39] is also better understood as a summary report. It has posed problems for translators who have generally taken the subject of 1:45a (ἤρξατο) to be the healed leper, and the subject of 1:45b (αὐτὸν δύνασθαι) to be Jesus. The Greek is obscure leading translators to translate αὐτὸν δύνασθαι as "Jesus could." When one compares the character of 1:45 to the other summary reports it becomes clear that the subject of 1:45a is really Jesus[40] and that 1:45 has no essential connection to the healing pericope that precedes. The statement really refers to the preaching (χηρύσσειν) of Jesus (cf. 1:14-15; 4:3-9, 14-33) and not to the healed leper spreading the news of his healing. The use of the imperfect suggests that Jesus was (ἦν) in the desert because of his unparalleled popularity: for the people continued coming to him (ἤρχοντο) "from everywhere."

Mark 2:1-2[41] transcends the parameters of the narrow event

---

[38] Taylor (*Mark*, 180) does not think it is a summary statement like Mark 3:7-12 but rather a story about Jesus connected with a particular place and time which records things recalled "at the close of a memorable day."

[39] See Schmidt, *Der Rahmen*, 67-68. Schmidt must have noticed the similarity between 1:45 and 1:39. See also J. Weiss, *Die Schriften des Neuen Testaments,* 88. Egger (*Frohbotschaft und Lehre*, 79-82) also identifies this passage as a summary statement.

[40] I think this has been conclusively shown by J. K. Elliott; see "The Conclusion of the Pericope of the Healing of the Leper and Mark 1:45," *JTS* 22 (1971) 153-57; "Is ὁ ἐξελθών a title for Jesus in Mark 1:45?" *JTS* 27 (1976) 402-5; "The Healing of the Leper in the Synoptic Parallels," *TLZ* 34 (1978) 175-76.

[41] Schmidt, *Der Rahmen*, 78-79. Egger (*Frohbotschaft und Lehre*, 149-51) also identifies this passage as a summary statement.

described in the pericope 2:3-12 and in reality is intended to characterize the great popular appeal of Jesus's preaching activity to the masses. So many came together that there was not even room at the door and yet Jesus continued preaching as he usually did (ἐλάλει). The two summary statements, 1:45 and 2:1-2, together create the impression that Jesus's appeal as preacher and healer covered the entire region (1:45, countryside; 2:1-2, cities and villages).

Mark 2:15[42] is a statement that seems intended to describe the great popularity of Jesus and his wide acceptance among the masses. It has the same general character and function as 2:13 preceding it. It serves to have Jesus change location, and it provides the context for the pericope that follows (2:16-17). In this case the statement makes an excellent transition from the call of Levi (2:14) to the following pericope on Jesus eating with tax collectors and sinners (2:16-17). Note in 2:14 "follow me" and in 2:15 "for there were many who followed him." In 2:16 note "eating with sinners and tax collectors" and in 2:15 "many tax collectors and sinners were sitting with Jesus and his disciples." The author uses the imperfect to stress the usual or customary character of the events: tax collectors and sinners were usually reclining with Jesus (συνανέκειντο); there were (ἦσαν) many of these and they were following him (ἠκολούθουν).

Mark 4:33-34[43] is clearly a Markan summary statement that is tied very closely to a broader *literary* context. These two verses function as a literary conclusion to the Markan chapter on parables whose literary introduction is found in 4:1-2.[44] It is striking that

---

[42] Schmidt, *Der Rahmen*, 82-85; Schmidt does describe 2:15b ("For there were many who followed him") as an addition of the evangelist (p. 84).

[43] See Schmidt, *Der Rahmen*, 126-32.

[44] See Schmidt, *Der Rahmen*, 126-28. Mark 4:1-2a may also be a summary statement, and Egger (*Frohbotschaft und Lehre*, 111-19) so regards it. In my judgment, however, it appears that the author intends it to provide a literary setting for the collection of parables that follow. Mark does not seem to have the customary practice of Jesus in view nor does he imply in these verses a wider circulation of Jesus's activities. 4:1-2a decribes a specific occasion on which Jesus taught the crowd in parables. Unlike other summaries, 4:1-2a is closely connected with the events of the following narrative and is not easily separated from its context, while 4:33-34 clearly transcends the parameters of a single specific event. Nevertheless compare 4:1-2a to 1:21-22, 2:1-2, 2:13 and 5:21.

Likewise whether or not Mark 3:19b-21 is to be thought of as a summary statement in part depends on how one analyzes the passage 3:19b-35. Does 3:31 pick up again with the scene introduced in 3:21? Opinions are divided (see Schmidt, *Der*

Perrin does *not* regard 4:33-34 as a summary statement since it is unquestionably what he considers the other summary statements to be: a statement summarizing a broad literary segment. One wonders why Mark 4:1-34 should not be regarded as a major division of Mark's literary structure, since Mark so carefully sets it off with literary introduction and conclusion similar to the apocalyptic discourse, whose literary introduction Perrin does regard as introducing a major literary division of Mark's structure. All verbs in 4:33-34 are cast in the imperfect tense to stress that the usual and customary practice of Jesus is to teach in parables.

Mark 6:1[45] also describes an activity of Jesus in a general and non-specific manner, as do the other summaries. 6:1a describes Jesus's change of location from some indefinite location beside the lake of Galilee in the region of Galilee (5:21) to his "own country" (6:1). In 6:1b, the addition of the brief statement, "and his disciples followed him," may be a compositional technique that serves to introduce the disciples, who appear to be a major motif in 6:1-52. The elements in the section are: 6:1-6a, Jesus rejected by his own countrymen; 6:7-11, the call and commissioning of the Twelve (disciples?); 6:14-29, the interlude on John the Baptist;[46] 6:30-34, summary; 6:35-44, the feeding of the 5,000 (served by the disciples) and 6:45-52, the ignorance of the disciples. The summary 6:53-56 may serve in part to offset the negative features of Jesus's rejection by his own countrymen and his disciples' lack of faith.

Mark 9:30-32, like Mark 1:14-15, is a concise summary of Jesus's instructions to his disciples relative to his coming passion. Etienne Trocmé identified Mark 9:30 *only*, in this passage, as one of the summary statements that "accompany isolated sayings attributed

---

Rahmen, 122-23). Schmidt analyzes the passage 3:20-35 as three separate pericopae (3:20-21, 22-30, 31-35). Others regard 3:22-35 as an intrusion into the narrative unit 3:20-21 + 31-35. While the three pericopae may originally have been independent, it does appear to me that there are grounds for regarding their present organization as forming a conscious literary unit. For example, 3:22-30 seems to be connected to 3:21b and 3:31-35 does build on 3:20-21. It would appear that 3:20-21 forms the literary setting for the entire segment. Hence, I am not inclined to regard 3:20-21 as a summary statement. It is not easily separable from its immediate context and seems to provide the setting for a particular incident rather than describing customary actions of Jesus over broad geographical areas and general time frames.

[45] Schmidt, *Der Rahmen*, 152-57.

[46] This section is out of logical order. Its logical position would have been in some connection to 1:14b.

to Jesus."[47] However, it would seem that the entire passage is a generalizing summary. It describes the character of Jesus's instructions to his disciples on a trip throughout Galilee. No *specific* occasions are described. It was while passing through Galilee ostensibly on *repeated* occasions that Jesus taught his disciples about his forthcoming passion. Compare Mark 8:31 where Mark implies that Jesus instructs his disciples about the passion on a *particular* occasion. Mark's use of the imperfect in 9:30-32 suggests that the instruction about the passion occurred on several different occasions: He was passing (παρεπορεύοντο) through Galilee; he was teaching (ἐδίδασκεν) his disciples; he was saying (ἔλεγεν); they were not understanding (ἠγνόουν); they were fearing (ἐφοβοῦντο). Trocmé regards the summary statements as being composed by Mark "to give his gospel more coherence." Trocmé is correct if by that he means that Mark intends the statement to expand the activities of Jesus, as opposed to providing a structural "peg" for a literary framework. The statement does not appear to tie together episodes rather it seems to create the impression of depth and movement, both geographical and temporal, in which one reads the episodes in Mark as highlights of a more extensive ministry.

Mark 10:32 also has been identified by Trocmé as another of the summaries.[48] In this case, it does appear that Mark intends to structure 10:1-52 as a trip from Galilee to Jerusalem (see above) and 10:32, along with 10:1, 17a, 46a and 11:1, provides the literary structure for the individual episodes that constitute this "trip." The imperfect tense used in the statement emphasizes an iterative action and thereby contributes to the impression of movement: were going up (ἦσαν ἀναβαίνοντες); Jesus was going before them (ἦν προάγων); they were amazed (ἐθαμβοῦντο); they were afraid (ἐφοβοῦντο).

What seems to be emerging from this analysis is that the summary statements are generalized non-specific descriptions of the ministry of Jesus intended to expand it beyond the few typical episodic incidents described in the Gospel. They are not summaries in the narrow sense that they summarize episodes that precede or follow in the narrative, rather they summarize new activities over broad general geographical areas and indefinite periods of time. The action narrated in the summary is clearly distinguishable from

---

[47] Trocmé, *Formation*, 29; see also Schmidt, *Der Rahmen*, 217-19.
[48] Ibid.

that narrated in the episodes. While one might argue that the summaries supply cohesion in various ways to an episodic and poorly integrated narrative, evidence for the summaries providing a basic structural framework for the Gospel is still lacking.

Other writers in the ancient world also make use of similar techniques to similar ends. A number of examples are clearly evident in Philostratus's *The Life of Apollonius of Tyana*.[49] I have not attempted an exhaustive analysis of the text but have selected representative samples from Philostratus, some of which closely parallel the summary statements in Mark. In what follows I have broken down the summary statements by general type from the perspective of what they seemed designed to summarize. It will be noted that the categories are not rigid and some statements may fit into more than one category. There also appears to be a preference for the imperfect tense.

I. Statements that summarize events and activities over general periods of time in connection with summaries of the sage's usual or typical activities.

The statements seem designed to create an impression that these activities are typical of the sage, or they simply abbreviate a given period of the sage's life through the technique of describing in a general way the sorts of things he usually does.

A. Vol. I, Book III, Chap. XL, pp. 320-21.

With such lore as this, then, they surfeited themselves and were astonished at the many sided wisdom of the company. And day after day they asked all sorts of questions and were themselves asked many in return.[50]

B. Vol. I, Book III, Chap. L, p. 335.

In such conversations with the sages Apollonius spent the four months which he passed there, and he acquired all sorts of lore both profane and mysterious.

---

[49] *The Life of Apollonius* seems an appropriate text to search for such parallels, since many find it to have close parallels to Mark; see C. W. Votaw, "The Gospels and Contemporary Biographies," *American Journal of Theology* 19 (1915) 59-73 (repr. Philadelphia: Fortress, 1970, pp. 15-29); Charles Talbert, *What is a Gospel?* *The Genre of the Canonical Gospels* (Philadelphia: Fortress, 1977) 1-23; Moses Hadas and Morton Smith, *Heroes and Gods* (New York: Harper and Row, 1965). While Philostratus wrote in the third century A.D., similar compositional techniques may be found, for example, in the writings of Josephus.

[50] All translations of Philostratus are taken from F. C. Conybeare, *Philostratus: The Life of Apollonius of Tyana* (LCL; New York: G. P. Putnam, 1912).

C. Vol. II, Book VI, Chap. XLIII, p. 143.[51]

Such were the exploits of our sage in behalf of both temples and cities; such were the discourses he delivered to the public or in behalf of different communities, and in behalf of those who were dead or who were sick; and such were the harangues he delivered to wise and unwise alike, and to the sovereigns who consulted him about moral virtue.

D. Vol. II, Book VII, Chap. XXVIII, p. 227.

There followed other episodes in this prison, some of them insidiously contrived, and others of mere chance, and not of sufficient importance to merit my notice. But Damis, I believe, has recorded them in his anxiety to omit nothing; I only give what is to the point.

II. Statements that summarize the geographical movement of the sage over general periods of time, usually in connection with summaries of his usual or typical activities.

A. Vol. I, Book III, Chap. LVIII, p. 345.

And when they had sailed as far as the mouth of the Euphrates, they say that they sailed up by it to Babylon to see Vardan, whom they found just as they had found him before. They then came afresh to Nineveh, and as the people of Antioch displayed their customary insolence and took no interest in any affairs of the Hellenes, they went down to the sea at Seleucia, and finding a ship, they sailed to Cyprus and landed at Paphos, where there is the statue of Aphrodite. Apollonius marvelled at the symbolic construction of the same, and gave the priests much instruction with regard to the ritual of the temple. He then sailed to Ionia, where he excited much admiration and no little esteem among all lovers of wisdom.

B. Vol. I, Book IV, Chap. XI, p. 367.

Having purged the Ephesians of the plague, and having had enough of the people of Ionia, he started for Hellas. Having made his way to Pergamum, and being pleased with the temple of Asclepius, he gave hints to the supplicants of the god, what to do in order to obtain favourable dreams; and having healed many of them he came to the land of Ilium. And when his mind was glutted with all the traditions of their past, he went to visit the tombs of the Achaeans, and he delivered himself of many speeches over them, and he offered many sacrifices of a bloodless and pure kind.

C. Vol. I, Book IV, Chap. XXIV, pp. 399-401.

And he also visited all the Greek shrines, namely that of Dodona, and the Pythian temple, and the one at Abae, and he betook himself to those of Amphiaraus and of Trophonius, and he went up to the shrine of the Muses on Mount Helicon. And when he visited these temples

---

[51] This statement concludes Book VI, and may be intended as a concluding summary to the book.

and corrected the rites, the priests went in his company, and the
votaries followed in his steps, and goblets were set up flowing with ra-
tional discourse and the thirsty quaffed their wine.

D. Vol. I, Book V, Chap. XI, p. 487.

But as matters in the west were in such an inflamed condition
Apollonius and his friends returned thence towards Libya and the Tyr-
rhenian land; and, partly on foot and partly by sea, they made their
way to Sicily, where they stopped at Lilybaeum. Then they coasted
along to Messina and to the Straits, where the junction of the Tyrrhe-
nian Sea with the Adriatic gives rise to the dangers of Charybdis.

E. Vol. I, Book V, Chap. XX, p. 505.

Apollonius spent the winter in various Hellenic temples and towards
spring he embarked on the road for Egypt, after administering many
rebukes indeed, yet giving much good counsel to the cities, many of
which won his approval, for he never refused praise when anything
was done in a right and sensible way.

F. Vol. I, Book V, Chap. XLIII, p. 473.[52]

The companions of the sage understood his meaning, and about
twenty of them remained with Menippus; but the rest, ten in number,
I believe, offered prayer to the gods, and having sacrificed such an offering as men offer when they embark for a voyage, they departed
straight for the pyramids, mounted on camels and keeping the Nile on
the right hand. In several places they took boats across the river in
order to visit every sight on it; for there was not a city, fane or sacred
site in Egypt, that they passed by without discussion. For at each they
either learned or taught some holy story, so that any ship on which
Apollonius embarked resembled the sacred galley of a religious lega-
tion.

G. Vol. II, Book VI, Chap. XXXV, p. 125.

So many were the races which they say Apollonius had visited until
then, eager and zealous for others as they for him. But his subsequent
journeys abroad, though they were numerous, were yet not so many as
before, nor did he go to fresh districts which he was not already acquainted with; for when he came down from Ethiopia he made a long
stay on the sea-board of Egypt, and then he returned to Phoenicia and
Cilicia, and to Ionia and Achaea, and Italy, never failing anywhere to
show himself the same as ever.

H. Vol. II, Book VI, Chap. XLI, p. 139.

Now the sage determined not to allow the peoples of the Hellespont
to be imposed upon; so he visited their cities, and drove out the quacks
who were making money out of the misfortunes of others, and then he
divined the causes of the supernatural wrath, and by making such of-
ferings as suited each case averted the visitation at small cost, and the
land was at rest.

---

[52] This statement concludes Book V.

I. Vol. II, Book VIII, Chap. XXIV, p. 389.

After this, seeing that he had had enough of the people of Hellas, after living for two years among them, he set sail for Ionia, accompanied by his society; and the greater part of his time he spent teaching philosophy at Smyrna and Ephesus, though he also visited the rest of the cities; and in none of them was he found to be an unwelcome guest, indeed they all considered him to be worth their regret when he left them, and to the better class people he was a great boon.

III. Statements summarizing the widespread general popularity of the sage in connection with general descriptions of the typical activities of the sage.[53]

A. Vol. I, Book IV, Chap. I, p. 349.[54]

And when they saw our sage in Ionia and he had arrived at Ephesus, even the mechanics would not remain at their handicrafts, but followed him, one admiring his wisdom, another his beauty, another his way of life, another his bearing, some of them everything alike about him. Reports also were current about him which originated from various oracles; thus from the oracle at Colophon it was announced that he shared its peculiar wisdom and was absolutely wise, and so forth; from that of Didyma similar rumours emanated, as also from the shrine at Pergamum; for the God urged not a few of those who were in need of health to betake themselves to Apollonius, for this was what "he himself approved and was pleasing to the Fates." Deputations also waited upon him from various cities offering him their hospitality, and asking his advice about life in general as well as about the dedication of altars and images; and he regulated their several affairs in some cases by letter, but in others he said would visit them.

B. Vol. I, Book V, Chap. XXIV, pp. 515-17.

Such were his experiences in Rhodes, and others ensued in Alexandria, so soon as his voyage ended there. Even before he arrived Alexandria was in love with him, and its inhabitants longed to see Apollonius with the unique devotion of one friend for another; and as the people of Upper Egypt are intensely religious they too prayed him to visit their several societies. For owing to the fact that so many come hither and mix with us from Egypt, while an equal number pass hence to visit Egypt, Apollonius was already celebrated among them and the ears of the Egyptians were literally pricked up to hear him.

C. Vol. II, Book VIII, Chap. XV, p. 371.

But when the rumour of his arrival was confirmed, all flocked to see him from the whole of Greece, and never did any such crowd flock to any Olympic festival as then, all full of enthusiasm and expectation. People came straight from Elis and Sparta, and from Corinth away at

---

[53] See also: Vol. I, Book IV, Chap. XXXI, p. 419.
      Vol. I, Book III, Chap. LVIII, p. 345.
      Vol. II, Book VIII, Chap. XXIV, p. 389.
[54] This statement begins Book IV.

the limits of the Isthmus; and the Athenians too, although they are out-side the Peloponnese; nor were they behind the cities which are at the gates of Pisa, for it was especially the most celebrated of the Athenians that hurried to the temple, together with the young men who flocked to Athens from all over the earth. Moreover there were people from Megara just then staying in Olympia, as well as many from Boeotia, and from Argos, and all the leading people of Phocis and Thessaly.

D. Vol. II, Book VIII, Chap. XXVI, p. 393.

All Ephesus, for all Ephesus was at his lecture, was struck dumb with astonishment.

E. Vol. I, Book IV, Chap. XXXI, p. 419.

The conversations which Apollonius held in Olympia turned upon the most profitable topics, such as wisdom and courage and temperance, and in a word upon all the virtues. He discussed these from the platform of the temple, and he astonished everyone not only by the insight he showed but by his forms of expression. And the Lacedaemonians flocked round him and invited him to share their hospitality at their shrine of Zeus, and made him father of their youths at home, and legislator of their lives and the honour of their old men.

One of the striking features of this type of summary is the pro-pensity of the writer to exaggerate unabashedly in order to ensure the reputation of the sage. In A above he is described as being "ab-solutely wise." In B, it is related that "Alexandria was in love with him" and the "people of Upper Egypt" prayed for him to visit them; Apollonius was so celebrated that "the ears of the Egyptians were literally pricked up to hear him." In C, "all Greece" flocked to see the sage. Indeed it was the most excited crowd that had ever attended an Olympic festival. Young men came "from all over the earth," and the crowd included all "the leading people of Phocis and Thessaly." In D, "all Ephesus" attended his lecture. In E, he astonished "everyone" by his insight and speech.

The same type of exaggeration is also present in some of the Markan summaries: Mark 1:32-34—"all" sick or possessed of demons were brought to Jesus; the "whole city" was gathered about the door. 1:28—Jesus's fame spread "everywhere" through "all the surrounding region of Galilee." Mark 1:5—"all the coun-try of Judea and all the people of Jerusalem" came out to John; 6:33—"they ran on foot from all the towns."

IV. Statements summarizing the speeches of the sage.[55]
    A. Vol. II, Book VIII, Chap. XII, p. 365.

---

[55] See also Vol. II, Book VI, Chap. XLIII, p. 143.

And he proceeded to detail to them his own words, and above all at the end of them the citation: "For thou shalt not kill me," and he told them exactly how he vanished from the seat of judgment.

B. Vol. I, Book IV, Chap. XIX, p. 389.

Many were the discourses which according to Damis the sage delivered at Athens; though he did not write down all of them, but only the more indispensable ones in which he handled great subjects.

C. Vol. I, Book V, Chap. XVII, p. 503.

For in this way he continually ended up his discourses with useful and pious exhortations.

D. Vol. I, Book V, Chap. XXVI, p. 523.

And many other rebukes of the same kind he addressed to them as Damis informs us.

V. The writer's summary of a preceding or succeeding literary segment; it appears to be different from his summary of the activities of Apollonius.
Vol. II, Book VII, Chap. I, p. 147.[56]

I am aware that the conduct of philosophers under despotism is the truest touchstone of their character, and am in favour of inquiring in what way one man displays more courage than another. And my argument also urges me to consider the point; for during the reign of Domitian Apollonius was beset by accusations and writs of information, the several origins, sources and counts of which I shall presently enlarge upon; and as I shall be under the necessity of specifying the language which he used and the role which he assumed, when he left the court after convicting the tyrant rather than being himself convicted, so I must first of all enumerate all the feats of wise men in the presence of tyrants which I have found worthy of commemoration, and contrast them with the conduct of Apollonius. For this I think is the best way of finding out the truth.

It is striking that with possibly one exception the Markan summary statements fall neatly into these same categories!

I. Statements that summarize events and activities over general periods of time in connection with summaries of the sage's usual or typical activities: 1:21-22; cf. 3:7-12.

II. Statements that summarize the geographical movement of the sage over general periods of time usually in connection with summaries of his usual or typical activities: 1:39, 2:13, 5:21, 6:1, 6:6b, 6:12-13, (10:1?).

III. Statements summarizing the widespread general popularity of

---

[56] This statement begins Book VII, and seems to be intended as a literary summary of the contents of the book.

the sage in connection with general descriptions of the typical
activities of the sage: 1:5, 1:28, 1:32-34, 1:45, 2:1-2, 2:15,
3:7-12, 6:53-56, (6:30-33?).
  IV. Statements summarizing the speeches of the sage: 1:14-15,
      9:30-32.
  V. The writer's summary of a preceding or succeeding literary
     segment: 4:33-34, 10:1, 10:32.
What this analysis of Philostratus suggests is that Mark is
employing a literary device used by other authors in the ancient
world in order to expand the borders of his narrative beyond the
specific episodic events that he describes in detail. The summary
statements create an impression of animation and movement in the
narrative over broad geographical areas and general time frames.
As literary devices they give the narrative an expanded setting and
lengthened time frame.
  This analysis weakens, if not disproves, Perrin's argument that
the coincidence of geographical shifts and summary statements in
Mark serves as a key for identifying the divisions of Mark's literary
structure. If we follow Perrin's criteria, however, we find four additional potential structural divisions that fit Perrin's criteria but
which Perrin himself did not cite.[57]
  1. Geographical shift 4:35-36 plus summary 4:33-34
  2. Geographical shift and summary 5:21
  3. Geographical shift and summary 9:30
  4. Geographical shift and summary 10:1
There are at least three additional major geographical shifts that
appear in Mark apart from the summaries:
  5:1 – The trip to the county of the Geresenes
  7:31 – The return to Galilee
  8:27 – The trip to the villages of Caesarea Philippi
Another weakness of Perrin's argument that the summary
statements serve as "transitional" pieces from one major literary
section to another is the fact that generally the summary statements
have no immediately evident contact with the pericopae that
precede and follow the summary. It is, of course, probable that the
summary statements do serve additional functions in the narrative.
For example, Mark 1:14-15 provides cohesion by influencing the
reader's understanding of Jesus's message wherever he is described

---

[57] See above.

as preaching or teaching in the Gospel. And 10:1 provides part of
the literary structure for the trip to Jerusalem. Also the summaries
do sometimes serve as "bridges" that link episodes, as Schmidt also
has argued. And 4:33-34, as has been shown, does appear to summarize the content of the larger literary segment in 4:1-32, as well
as go beyond it. Subsidiary narrative functions, however, for the
other summaries must be worked out in individual cases.[58] In
general these statements summarize some new aspect of the
ministry of Jesus (or John) and seem to function as narrative
devices that broaden, expand and intensify the ministry of Jesus
and its effect. They are not summaries in the narrow sense that they
summarize specific literary segments that precede or follow in the
narrative. In short, they give the impression of a ministry that is
broader and more influential than the few brief examples of healings, debates and teaching episodes narrated by Mark. Without the
impression created by the summary passages, one is shocked at the
narrowness, brevity and sporadic character of Jesus' ministry
reflected in the Gospel.

---

[58] In a response to this paper for the Southwestern Regional Meeting of the
Society of Biblical Literature in Dallas, Texas, 12-13 March 1982, Joanna Dewey
has suggested additional specific functions for the summary statements in the
Markan narrative, other than those that I have noted. She argues that they also
provide general connective tissue for the narrative, build narrative suspense and
provide structure for individual pericopae.

DISCIPLES/CROWDS/WHOEVER:
MARKAN CHARACTERS AND READERS

by

ELIZABETH STRUTHERS MALBON
Blacksburg, VA

In recent years the portrayal of the disciples in Mark has received considerable scholarly attention.* Conclusions have ranged from Theodore Weeden's view that the disciples are representatives of Mark's historical opponents and thus negative in value[1] to Robert Tannehill's view that the disciples are, if one may put it thus, representatives of Mark's parishoners, the readers, and basically positive in value—not perfect, in fact problematic, but potential models nonetheless.[2] I find Tannehill's view more convincing, and I wish to extend it in two ways: by examining the relation between the disciples and the crowd within the Markan narrative and by considering the relation of these Markan characters to the hearers or readers of the Markan narrative. It is my threefold thesis that: (1) the disciples of Jesus are portrayed in the Gospel of Mark with both strong points and weak points in order to serve as realistic and encouraging models for hearers/readers who experience both strength and weakness in their Christian discipleship; (2) the crowd is also portrayed in the Gospel of Mark in both positive and negative ways in relation to Jesus and serves to complement the disciples in a composite portrait of followers of Jesus; (3) both separately and together, the disciples and the crowd serve to open the story of Jesus and the narrative of Mark outward to a larger group—whoever hears or reads the Gospel of Mark. My focus will be on part two of my thesis, part one having been argued per-

---

* I am pleased to thank the American Council of Learned Societies for a Research Fellowship in support of this research.

[1] "The Heresy that Necessitated Mark's Gospel," *ZNW* 59 (1968) 145-58; *Mark—Traditions in Conflict* (Philadelphia: Fortress, 1971).

[2] "The Disciples in Mark: The Function of a Narrative Role," *JR* 57 (1977) 386-405.

suasively by others,[3] and part three being offered here more as a suggestion than as a conclusion.

Two questions will orient my presentation. First: What parallels and distinctions between the disciples and the crowd does the Markan narrative manifest? Second: In light of these parallels and distinctions are the disciples and the crowd presented as basically competing or basically complementary character groups in the Markan narrative? In order to answer these questions, I wish to classify, compare, and contrast the kinds of activities that characterize each group's relationship with Jesus.[4] (Specific Markan references to the two groups are listed in the appendix.[5]) Whom does Jesus call, teach, heal, feed, command? Who follows Jesus, comes to Jesus, goes with Jesus, is amazed at Jesus, assists Jesus, hinders Jesus, abandons Jesus?

Calling and Following

Although we are accustomed to associating Jesus' activity of calling with the disciples, in fact the Markan Jesus calls to himself both the disciples and the crowd. After the inaugural statement of 1:14-15, the initial action of the Markan Jesus' ministry in Galilee is the calling of Simon and Andrew (1:16-18; 17, δεῦτε ὀπίσω μου)

---

[3] In addition to Tannehill, see Joanna Dewey, "Point of View and the Disciples in Mark," *1982 Seminar Papers* (SBLASP 118; Chico, CA: Society of Biblical Literature, 1982) 97-106.

[4] Ernest Best also compares and contrasts the kinds of activities that characterize the disciples' and the crowd's relationship with Jesus ("The Role of the Disciples in Mark," *NTS* 23 [1977] 390-93)—but with very different motives and conclusions. The crowd is examined as the "only possible candidate" for the "position as background 'good' group" against which the disciples as "bad" group could be set (390). But it is concluded that "the crowd possesses no unitary role in the gospel" (392), that the disciples and the crowd are two separate groups not "one group which is a sub-group of another" (392), and that "Mark's crowd is not 'religious' but the group from which those who will be religious are called" (393). See also n. 35 below.

[5] Μαθητής (disciple) always occurs in the plural, μαθηταί, and usually with a possessive (and J. Keith Elliot argues that other possessives have been dropped by copyists ["Μαθητής with a Possessive in the New Testament," *ThZ* 35 (1979) 300]). (Three referenes to μαθηταί are marked as the disciples of John, one as the disciples of the Pharisees.) Except at 10:1, ὄχλος (crowd) always occurs in the singular, indicating that the Markan author thinks of the crowd as, in Ernest Best's words, "a unified sociological entity," or, as I would rather say, a unified narrative entity, a "character." However, the frequent Markan reliance on pronouns used alone and on verb endings to indicate person limits the usefulness of a listing such as the appendix.

and James and John (1:19-20; 20, καλεῖν). Ernest Best limits the references in his category "They are called by Jesus" to 1:16-20.[6] Additional references to calling, although certainly not "call narratives" in the technical sense, might be investigated under the broader category of Jesus called them to himself, Jesus summoned them.[7]

At 3:13-19 Jesus "called to him (3:13, προσκαλεῖσθαι) those whom he desired" and appointed "twelve" (3:14, δώδεκα), "whom also he named apostles" (3:14, ἀπόστολος).[8] At 6:7 Jesus "called to him (προσκαλεῖσθαι) the twelve (δώδεκα)" in order to send them out on a mission of healing and teaching. The account of the feeding of the 4,000 opens with the notice (8:1) that Jesus "called his disciples (μαθηταί) to him (προσκαλεῖσθαι)"; and on four additional occasions the reader learns that Jesus called his disciples (or the twelve) to himself, and then said something to them concerning the demands of discipleship: 8:34, μαθηταί, προσκαλεῖσθαι; 9:35, δώδεκα, φωνεῖν; 10:42, them (the ten? the twelve?), προσκαλεῖσθαι; 12:43, μαθηταί, προσκαλεῖσθαι.

Twice in the Markan narrative Jesus is reported to have called the crowd to himself: at 7:14 (ὄχλος, προσκαλεῖσθαι) for the saying ("parable") on defilement, and at 8:34 (ὄχλος, προσκαλεῖσθαι) —together with his disciples—for the saying on taking up one's cross and following Jesus. At 10:46-52, Jesus, through the agency of the many (10:48, πολλοί) calls (φωνεῖν) Bartimaeus, who emerges from the many, is healed of his blindness, and follows Jesus on the way. One additional episode is clearly a calling but not so clearly a calling of either a disciple or one from the crowd. Jesus' interaction with Levi, the tax collector, at 2:14 parallels Jesus' interaction with Simon and Andrew and James and John, the fishermen, at 1:16-20: Jesus calls (2:14, Ἀκολούθει μοι), Levi follows. Levi, however, is not listed by Mark as one of the twelve disciples or apostles (3:13-19). Perhaps Levi, like Bartimaeus, is to be understood as

---

[6] "Role of the Disciples," 385.

[7] On the literary function of προσκαλέομαι, καλέω, and φωνέω in relation to the Markan disciples of Jesus, see Vernon K. Robbins, "Summons and Outline in Mark: The Three-Step Progression," *NovTest* 23 (1981) 97-114.

[8] There is, according to Kurt Aland et al., eds. (*The Greek New Testament* [3rd ed.; United Bible Societies, 1975]), a "considerable degree of doubt" whether the phrase οὓς καὶ ἀποστόλους ὠνόμασεν is the superior reading. Ernest Best regards the phrase as "not original" but coming from Lk. 6:13 (*Following Jesus: Discipleship in the Gospel of Mark* [JSNTSS 4; Sheffield: JSOT, 1981] 187, n. 18).

emerging from the crowd as a representative of the crowd or at least of the potential of the crowd. In reading 2:13-15 we note that the reference to Levi (2:14) follows immediately a reference to Jesus teaching the crowd (2:13) and is in turn followed by a reference to the many (2:15, πολλοί) who followed Jesus.

Thus the Markan Jesus called to himself both the disciples (or the twelve[9]) as a group (3:13-19; 6:7; 8:1; 8:34; 9:35; 10:42; 12:43) and individual disciples by name—Simon and Andrew and James and John (1:16-18; 1:19-20), and the crowd as a group (7:14; 8:34) and individuals from the crowd by name—Levi (2:13-14) and Bartimaeus (10:46-52). We will return later to the one occasion on which Jesus called to himself the crowd *with* his disciples and spoke to both groups concerning those who would follow him, whoever would save his life by losing it (8:34ff.).

Directly related to Jesus' calling to himself both the disciples and the crowd is the following of Jesus by both the disciples and the crowd. A careful examination of who is said to follow Jesus is revealing. Simon and Andrew follow him (1:18, ἀκολουθέω); James and John come after him (1:20, ἀπέρχομαι ὀπίσω); the disciples as a

---

[9] I find Best's reading of a distinction between "the twelve" and the "disciples" in Mark confusing. Best, whose basic concern is to separate tradition and redaction, concludes: "Mark distinguishes to some extent between the twelve [basically traditional] and the disciples [basically redactional], the latter being the wider group. . . . Yet Mark makes little distinction in the way in which he uses the twelve and the disciples . . ." ("Mark's Use of the Twelve," *ZNW* 69 [1978] 32). Mark "is not concerned to identify the Twelve and the disciples in such a way that when the disciples are mentioned we are to understand him to mean the Twelve and only the Twelve. It is, rather, the other way round: the Twelve is normally to be understood as signifying the wider group, the 'disciples'" ("Role of the Disciples," 380; cf. *Following Jesus*, 183, 188 n. 23, 204; cf. Heber F. Peacock, "Discipleship in the Gospel of Mark," *RevExp* 75 [1978] 556). Perhaps Gérard Genette's discrimination of three narrative levels is helpful at this point (*Narrative Discourse: An Essay in Method* [Ithaca: Cornell, 1980]). I judge that, *at the level of story*, "the twelve" and "the disciples" (and the "apostles") refer to the same group of characters. At the levels of the relation of story and narration and story and narrating, however, there is an expansive movement from this group, to additional characters (see esp. 4:10 and 10:32), to the implied readers; and at these levels "disciples" is a more flexible term than "the twelve." With my view compare Edward Lynn Taylor, Jr., "The Disciples of Jesus in the Gospel of Mark" (Ph. D. dissertation, Southern Baptist Theological Seminary, 1979), 91-93. R. P. Meye ("Messianic Secret and Messianic *Didachē* in Mark's Gospel," in *Oikonomia. Heilsgeschichte als Thema der Theologie*, ed. F. Christ [Hamburg: Herbert Reich, 1967] 63-65) and S. Freyne (*The Twelve: Disciples and Apostles. A Study in the Theology of the First Three Gospels* [London: Sheed and Ward, 1968] 107-19) also view "the twelve" and the "disciples" as identical.

group follow him (6:1, μαθηταί, ἀκολουθέω), as Peter later points out they have done (10:28, ἀκολουθέω). None of this surprises. But Jesus is also followed by many (2:15, πολλοί, ἀκολουθέω), a great multitude (3:7, πολὺ πλῆθος, ἀκολουθέω), a great crowd (5:24, ὄχλος πολύς, ἀκολουθέω), and by one who emerges from the crowd, Bartimaeus (10:48, πολλοί; 10:52, ἀκολουθέω).

In some cases, however, it is not possible to identify clearly the persons who are said to follow Jesus. At 10:32 those "on the road, going up to Jerusalem," those whom "Jesus was walking ahead of," appear to be Jesus' disciples (see 10:23, 24, μαθηταί). But "those who followed" appear to be an additional group because 10:32b seems to differentiate "the twelve" from the larger traveling group.[10] Are these additional followers drawn from the crowd? (At 10:46 Jesus leaves Jericho, still on the way to Jerusalem, "with his disciples and a great multitude.") At the entry into Jerusalem "those who went before and those who followed cried out, 'Hosanna! Blessed is he who comes in the name of the Lord!'" (11:9-10). Are these followers from the crowd? (At 11:8 "many [πολλοί] spread their garments on the road.")

In other cases, while individual followers are identified by name, it is not possible to determine clearly to which group (if any) they may belong. At 2:14 Jesus says to Levi, "Follow me" ('Ακολούθει μοι) as he had earlier said to Simon and Andrew, "Follow me" (1:17, δεῦτε ὀπίσω μου); and Levi leaves his tax office and follows Jesus as the four fishermen had left their nets and followed him. But Levi, unlike Simon and Andrew and James and John, is not listed as one of the twelve (3:13-19).[11] Immediately after the call of Levi, "Jesus and his disciples" are at table with "many tax collectors and sinners"—"for there were many (πολλοί) who followed him" (2:15). Presumably Levi is one of the tax collectors rather than one of the disciples. But since Levi did follow Jesus, he is presumably one of the "many (πολλοί) who followed him." Just before calling Levi (2:14), Jesus had been teaching the crowd (2:13, ὄχλος). Thus Levi seems to emerge from the crowd as a follower.[12]

---

[10] I find unconvincing Best's argument that "it is probable that Mark does not intend to depict separate groups" at 10:32 and his translation of the second clause as "and as they were following they were afraid" ("Twelve," 23, 24; cf. *Following Jesus*, 120).

[11] In Matthew's gospel the follower from the tax office is "Matthew" (9:9), who is listed among the "twelve apostles" (10:2) as "Matthew the tax collector" (10:3).

[12] Cf. Best: "The association of v. 13 with v. 14 implies that before he respond-

A second case of uncertain group identification of followers occurs at 15:40-41. Many women are said to have observed Jesus' crucifixion; three are named: "Mary Magdalene, and Mary the mother of James the younger and of Joses, and Salome, who, when he [Jesus] was in Galilee, followed (ἀκολουθέω) him, and ministered to (διακονέω) him" (15:40b-41a, *RSV*). ('Ακολουθέω and διακονέω are generally recognized as "discipleship" words in Mark.) These three women are part of a larger group since "also many other women (καὶ ἄλλαι πολλαὶ) . . . came up with him to Jerusalem" (15:41b). Have the three named women, then, emerged from the many, from the crowd?[13]

It would appear that following, while central to discipleship, is not limited to "disciples." The category of "followers" overlaps with the categories of "the disciples" and "the crowd." Additional references to ἀκολουθέω suggest a similar conclusion. At 9:38, John, speaking for the twelve (9:35), the disciples (9:31), reports to Jesus that they forbade a man casting out demons in Jesus' name "because he was not following us." John apparently expects Jesus' approval; Jesus, however, disapproves, stating that "no one who does a mighty work in my name will be able soon after to speak evil of me. For he that is not against us is for us" (9:39-40). Being "for" Jesus is not defined by membership among the twelve disciples; and followers of Jesus are characterized by action on behalf of others—whether a mighty work or the giving of a cup of water (9:41). At 10:17-22 action on behalf of others is again presented as a characteristic of followership. In the absence of his willingness to sell his possessions and give to the poor, neither the rich man's knowledge and observance of the Law nor Jesus' love for him enables the rich man to follow (10:21, ἀκολουθέω) Jesus.

Mark 8:34 is a pivotal verse concerning disciples, the crowd, and followers: "And, calling to himself the crowd with his disciples, he

---

ed to the call Levi was a member of the crowd, i.e., the unevangelised" (*Following Jesus*, 177). In Best's schema, however, Levi's response to Jesus breaks Levi's link with the crowd. When one from the crowd follows Jesus, so Best seems to assume, he or she relinquishes membership in the crowd; no matter how many of the crowd follow Jesus, the crowd as crowd is—by definition—never to be recognized as followers.

[13] Based on the significance of ἀκολουθέω and διακονέω and especially on the pattern of "a nucleus of three within an inner circle distinguished from the outer circle or crowd" (231), Winsome Munro regards the women mentioned at 15:40-41 as women disciples—the existence of whom, Munro argues further, Mark intentionally obscured ("Women Disciples in Mark?," *CBQ* 44 [1982] 225-41).

said to them, 'If anyone wishes to follow after me, let that one deny himself and take up his cross and follow me.'" "Anyone" can be a follower—one of the disciples, one of the crowd, one of the hearers or readers—as long as one is willing to deny oneself and take up one's cross.[14] Disciples, crowds, whoever—everyone is a potential follower. The demands of followership, however, make for a different actuality.

Not everyone is able to be a follower. And no followers, whether disciples or the crowd, find following easy. There is a profound irony in Peter's following (14:54, ἀκολουθέω) Jesus at a distance into the courtyard of the high priest, for while the house of the high priest is the scene of Jesus' trial, the courtyard is the scene of Peter's denial. A similar irony is manifest in the shift from the jubilation of the many (11:8, πολλοί) blessing Jesus and following (11:9, ἀκολουθέω) him into Jerusalem to the tumult of the crowd demanding his crucifixion there a few days later (15:8, 11, 15, ὄχλος). Perhaps the hearers/readers of Mark's gospel experienced the ironic tension of simultaneous desires to follow the crucified one and difficulties in denying themselves and taking up their own crosses.

Coming and Going

Jesus' activity of calling to himself both disciples and crowds and the activity of both disciples and crowds in following Jesus suggest certain parallels between the two groups. Other activities, however, distinguish them. Repeatedly the crowd is said to come to Jesus, the disciples are said to go with him. The crowd comes to Jesus seeking the healing (1:32, πᾶς; 2:2, πολλοί; 3:8, πλῆθος πολύ) that he offers. Jesus also offers the gathered crowd teaching (ὄχλος: 2:13; 3:32; 4:1 *bis*; 10:1; πολλοί: 2:2); and, even though the pursuing crowd hinders the freedom of Jesus and his disciples to eat (3:20, ὄχλος; 6:31, πολλοί), Jesus offers the crowd food (6:39, 41, 42, πᾶς; 8:1, ὄλλος). Wherever Jesus goes the crowd comes to him (ὄχλος: 5:21; 9:15; 9:25; εἷς ἐκ τοῦ ὄχλου: 9:17; πολλοί: 6:33; πολλαί: 15:41), or, when he is temporarily unreachable, to his disciples (9:14, ὄχλος). Even near the end, at Gethsemane, a crowd (14:43, ὄχλος)—this

---

[14] 8:34 presents something of a problem for Best (*Following Jesus*, 31-32), since he posits a definite distinction between the crowd ("the unevangelised mass") and the disciples ("the church") and 8:34 links the two groups.

time with Judas and from the chief priests, scribes, and elders—comes to Jesus. Unlike the earlier crowds who sought manifestations of Jesus' power in teaching, healing, and miraculous feeding, this final crowd seeks the restraint of Jesus' power in his arrest.

While the crowd continually comes to Jesus, the disciples continually go with him. Jesus withdraws with some of his disciples (the four—Peter and Andrew and James and John: 1:29; 13:3; the three—Peter, James and John: 5:37; 9:2; 14:33) or with his disciples as a group (μαθηταί: 2:15; 3:7; 4:34; 4:35-36 [they]; 6:31-32 [they]; 7:17; 8:10; 8:13ff. [they]; 8:27 *bis*; 9:28; 10:10; 10:32a [they]; 10:46; 14:32; δώδεκα: 4:10; 10:32b; 11:11; 14:17). Once, rather early in the narrative, Jesus asks his disciples to have a boat ready for him in case he needs to withdraw with them from the crowd (3:9, μαθηταί, ὄχλος). Another time, rather late in the narrative, Jesus withdraws (from Jericho toward Jerusalem) with his disciples and a great crowd together (10:46, μαθηταί, ὄχλου ἱκανοῦ). At the close of the narrative Jesus is reported to be "going before" his disciples to Galilee (16:7, μαθηταί, Πέτρος).

Often Jesus' withdrawal with his disciples is the setting for special instruction of them, instruction not offered the crowd (δώδεκα: 4:10; μαθηταί: 4:34; 7:17; 9:28; 10:10).[15] More often Jesus' withdrawal with his disciples is part of the overall pattern of their accompanying Jesus wherever he goes (μαθηταί: 2:15; 3:7; 3:9; 4:35-36 [they]; 6:31-32 [they]; 8:10; 8:13ff. [they]; 8:27 *bis*; 10:32a [they]; 10:46; 14:32; 16:7; δώδεκα: 10:32b; 11:11; 14:17).[16] Twice Jesus is alone with the four—Peter (Simon) and Andrew and James and John: once in Simon's house, where Jesus heals Simon's mother-in-law (1:29), and once on the Mount of Olives, where, at the initiative of the four, Jesus speaks of the end of time (13:3). Thrice Jesus takes the three—Peter, James and John—aside with him: at the raising of Jairus' daughter (5:37), at the transfiguration (9:2), at Gethsemane (14:33), giving these three episodes a special prominence in Jesus' story.

Like the disciples, the crowd is called by Jesus, and, like the disciples, the crowd follows Jesus. But although they continually

---

[15] These references are categorized by Best under "They are recipients of private instruction from Jesus" ("Role of the Disciples," 385-86.)

[16] Some of these references are categorized by Best as "They journey with Jesus" (Ibid.).

come to Jesus, the crowd, unlike the disciples, is not—with one significant exception (10:46, the close of the "way" section)—said to go with Jesus. While Jesus frequently withdraws *with* the disciples, he frequently withdraws *from* the crowd (3:9, ὄχλος, potential withdrawal; 4:36, ὄχλος; 6:31-33, attempted withdrawal from the many [6:31, 33, πολλοί];6:45, ὄχλος; 7:17, ὄχλος; 7:33, ὄχλος). The disciples are distinguished from the crowd as those *with* whom Jesus frequently withdraws; yet on occasion Jesus withdraws *from* the disciples as well as *from* the crowd. Of course, when Jesus withdraws with a small group of his disciples he withdraws from the majority (5:37; 9:2; 13:3; 14:33); but Jesus also withdraws from all of his disciples, either from all twelve at once (6:45-47, them [6:45, μαθηταί]) or first from the nine (14:33) and then from the three (14:35, 39, 41). At 1:35 Jesus withdraws by himself, and, since the twelve are not appointed until 3:13-19, Jesus cannot be said to have withdrawn specifically from the disciples; yet he is pursued by "Simon and those with him" (1:36). When Jesus withdraws from the crowd it is usually to be with his disciples (3:9; 4:36; 6:31-33; 7:17; 7:33 is exceptional—Jesus withdraws from the crowd with the deaf mute in order to heal him). But when Jesus withdraws by himself—from the crowd and his disciples (6:45-47), or from the three (14:35, 39, 41), or from unspecified people (1:35)—it is always for prayer.

To recapitulate: the disciples are called, and the crowd is called; the disciples follow, and the crowd follows; the crowd comes to Jesus, but the disciples go with him; yet sometimes Jesus is all alone. The multiple references to the crowd's coming appear to be the narrative manifestations of the Markan Jesus' understanding of why he "came out" (1:38); the multiple references to the disciples' going appear to be the narrative manifestation of his appointment of the twelve "to be with him" (3:14). Jesus comes out to preach and to cast out demons (1:38-39); Jesus appoints twelve apostles or disciples not only "to be with him" but also "to be sent out to preach and have authority to cast out demons" (3:14-15). Jesus journeys to Jerusalem with the disciples and the crowd (10:32, crowd?; 10:46), and, after his death and resurrection there, it is reported to the women who seem to emerge from the crowd and to act like disciples (15:40-41, ἀκολουθέω, διακονέω, πολλαί) that he is going before them to Galilee.

Teaching, Healing, Feeding

The people of the crowd are the chief beneficiaries, the disciples, the chief assistants, of Jesus' ministry of teaching and healing. Yet in order to assist in teaching (6:30, ἀπόστολοι), the disciples must first receive Jesus' teaching; thus the Markan Jesus teaches both the disciples and the crowd, as many passages throughout the narrative illustrate. Here those passages that employ διδάσκω or διδαχή specifically will serve as examples.[17] As has often been noted, the Markan narrator frequently refers to Jesus as teaching without giving—or even suggesting—the content of his teaching; this is especially the case in those scenes in which Jesus teaches the crowd (ὄχλος: 2:13; 4:1-2; 6:34;[18] 10:1; cf. 11:18; πᾶς: 1:21-27 [1:27, πᾶς]; πολλοί: 6:2; τὰς κώμας κύκλῳ: 6:7). The content of Jesus' teaching in the temple is specified—or at least exemplified; just how much of this teaching the crowd hears, however, is uncertain: 11:17? probably not, since 11:18 (ὄχλος) appears to be a general reference; 12:35-37? probably so, since 12:37 (ὄχλος) appears to conclude 12:35-37; 12:38-40? impossible to judge. Whether the crowd is intended as part of the audience at the flashback at 14:49 is also impossible to judge, and furthermore, 14:49 is a generalized reference to teaching. As noted above, when Jesus withdraws with his disciples it is often for private, more detailed teaching on a topic he has just covered more generally and more openly. When Jesus is explicitly said to be teaching (διδάσκω) the disciples, however, the content of his teaching is his coming passion and resurrection (8:31, they; 9:31, μαθηταί); this the crowd is not taught. Thus, the Markan Jesus teaches the disciples more about what the crowd is taught and more than the crowd is taught.[19]

Closely related to specific references to Jesus teaching (διδάσκω or διδαχή) the disciples or the crowd are references to Jesus commanding the disciples or the crowd to "hear," or statements reporting that they "heard" Jesus. The parable of the sower is framed by Jesus' exhortations to the very large crowd (4:1a, ὄχλος πλεῖστος),

---

[17] See R. T. France, "Mark and the Teaching of Jesus," *Gospel Perspectives: Studies of History and Tradition in the Four Gospels* (ed. R. T. France and David Wenham; Sheffield: JSOT, 1980), I: 101-136, esp. 105-106.

[18] Best regards ὄχλος at 6:34 as "a symbol for the instruction of Mark's church" and, thus, as an exception to Mark's "normal" use of the crowd to denote "the unevangelised mass" (*Following Jesus*, 210-11).

[19] See Best, *Following Jesus*, 235-36.

the whole crowd (4:1b, πᾶς ὁ ὄχλος): "Hear" (4:3, 'Ακούετε); "Whoever has ears to hear, let that one hear" (4:9, "Ός ἔχει ὦτα ἀκούειν ἀκουέτω). The interpretation of the parable of the sower is concluded by Jesus' exhortation to "those who were about him with the twelve" (4:10—a complex phrase apparently indicating more than the disciples and less than the whole crowd[20]): "If any one has ears to hear, let that one hear" (4:23, εἴ τις ἔχει ὦτα ἀκούειν ἀκουέτω). The "parable" (7:17) concerning defilement is introduced by Jesus' exhortation to the crowd (7:14, ὄχλος): "Hear me, all of you, and understand" (7:14, 'Ακούσατέ μου πάντες καὶ σύνετε). The paired feeding stories, as enacted parables, are concluded by Jesus' exclamation to the disciples (8:10, μαθηταί): ". . . having ears do you not hear? . . . Do you not yet understand?" (8:18, 21, . . . ὦτα ἔχοντες οὐκ ἀκούετε; . . . Οὔπω συνίετε;). Finally, the voice from the cloud speaks on behalf of Jesus at his transfiguration before Peter, James, and John: "hear him" (9:7, ἀκούετε αὐτοῦ). Thus both the disciples and the crowd are directly exhorted by Jesus to hear.

And both groups do hear—to a certain extent. Jesus questions the disciples' hearing—and understanding (8:18, 21; cf. 4:13)—and the hearing and understanding of "those outside" (4:10, the crowd?[21] part of the crowd?), who "may indeed *hear* but [do] not understand" (4:12).[22] The narrator comments that "with many such parables he [Jesus] spoke the word to them [the crowd? see 4:1-2, 10, 34], as they were able to *hear* it . . ." and that the

---

[20] Thus both Best and Synge oversimplify—in opposite directions. According to Best, "the twelve together with those about Jesus (4:10) are identical with the disciples (4:34) . . ." ("Twelve," 32; see n. 9 above). According to F. C. Synge, "the crowds were the 'arounders'" (53), "the publicans and sinners, Gentiles" ("A Plea for the Outsiders: Commentary on Mark 4:10-12," *Journal of Theology for Southern Africa* 30 [1980] 58).

[21] So Best, *Following Jesus*, 235.

[22] One could hardly find a view more distant from the view presented in this paper than David J. Hawkin's interpretation, based on 4:10-12, that "the disciples are made to be figures representative of the church, and the crowds are made to be figures representative of Israel" ("The Incomprehension of the Disciples in the Marcan Redaction," *JBL* 91 [1972] 497). Synge also regards the "outsiders" at 4:10-12 as "the orthodox" or "Israel," but he contrasts this group not with the disciples but with "the crowd": "The almost unanimity of commentators in equating the 'outsiders' with the crowds makes it necessary to reiterate that the 'outsiders' are those who disapproved of the crowds that encircled Jesus, that the crowds were the 'arounders,' and that the 'outsiders' were the orthodox" (53; see n. 20 above).

disciples *heard* (11:14, μαθηταί) Jesus curse the fig tree on his way into Jerusalem and into the temple. In addition, the many who *heard* Jesus in the synagogue (6:2, πολλοί) were astonished, and the great crowd who *heard* Jesus in the temple (12:37, πολὺς ὄχλος) "heard him gladly." But the latter phrase, ἤκουεν αὐτοῦ ἡδέως, is an ominous one: when Herod *heard* John, Herod "was much perplexed; and yet he heard him gladly" (6:20, ἡδέως αὐτοῦ ἤκουεν), but such gladness did not save John. Neither does the gladness of the crowd at hearing Jesus save him, although it does make the chief priests, scribes, and elders more circumspect in plotting his arrest (11:18; 12:12; 14:2). Yet Jesus was arrested and brought before the chief priests, scribes, and elders; there "many *heard* him say, 'I will destroy this temple that is made with hands, and in three days I will build another, not made with hands'" (14:58). This the Markan Jesus has not said; false speakers report a false hearing. Neither the disciples nor the crowd finds it easy to hear Jesus truly.

The response of the crowd or of individuals from the crowd to hearing about Jesus is more encouraging. In Capernaum, "many (πολλοί) gathered together" (2:2) when they *heard* that Jesus was at home (2:1); from all of Palestine and beyond, "a great crowd, *hearing* all that he did, came to him" (3:8) at the sea; at Gennesaret, they "ran about the whole neighborhood and began to bring sick people on their pallets to any place where they *heard* he was" (6:55). From amid the crowd the woman with the hemorrhage came to Jesus with faith after having *heard* reports about him (5:27); the Syrophoenician woman *heard* of Jesus and came with courage to him who "could not be hid" (7:24-25); Bartimaeus *heard* that Jesus was passing by and cried out, "Jesus, Son of David" (10:47), despite being rebuked by many (10:48, πολλοί). Hearing about Jesus, and especially about his healing power, the crowd gathers to him. To the gathered crowd and to the disciples Jesus says, "Hear—and understand." Both the crowd and the disciples hear; both have difficulty understanding.

Given the opportunity for hearing and the difficulty in understanding that the disciples and the crowd share, it is not surprising that they also share a response of amazement, astonishment, and even fear in relation to Jesus.[23] The crowd is amazed,

---

[23] Arguments can be made, of course, for analyzing reactions of fear separately from amazement and astonishment, and I have made such an analysis of the material presented here. For my present purpose, however, the results of the

astonished at Jesus' teaching (1:22, they [1:27, πᾶς], ἐκπλήσσεσθαι; 1:27, πᾶς, θαμβεῖσθαι; 6:2, πολλοί, ἐκπλήσσεσθαι; 11:18, ὄχλος, ἐκπλήσσεσθαι), at Jesus' healing (2:12, πᾶς, ἐξίστασθαι; 5:15, they [5:14, εἰς τὴν πόλιν καὶ εἰς τοὺς ἀγρούς], φοβεῖσθαι; 5:20, πᾶς, θαυμάζειν; 5:33, woman from crowd [ὄχλος: 5:24, 27, 30, 31], φοβεῖσθαι; 7:37, they [7:33, ὄχλος], ἐκπλήσσεσθαι), at Jesus himself (9:15, πᾶς ὁ ὄχλος, ἐκθαμβεῖσθαι). The disciples are amazed, astonished at Jesus' teaching (10:24, μαθηταί, θαμβεῖσθαι; 10:26, they [10:24, μαθηταί], ἐκπλήσσεσθαι), at Jesus' power over the sea (4:41, they [4:34, μαθηταί], φοβεῖσθαι; 6:50, they [6:45, μαθηταί; 6:50, πᾶς], ταράσσεσθαι; 6:51, they [6:45, μαθηταί], ἐξίστασθαι), at Jesus' transfiguration (9:6, they [the three; see 9:2], ἔκφοβος), at Jesus, prediction of his passion and resurrection (9:32, they [9:31, μαθηταί], φοβεῖσθαι).

Mark 10:32 is an especially important verse within the narrative pattern of amazement and fear of the disciples and the crowd. "And they [Jesus and the disciples; see 10:23, 24] were on the road, going up to Jerusalem, and Jesus was walking ahead of them [the disciples]; and they [the disciples] were amazed (θαμβεῖσθαι), and those that followed [from the crowd?] were afraid (φοβεῖσθαι)."[24] For both the disciples and the crowd Jesus' power is amazing; and, in light of that power, Jesus' suffering is amazing. Yet the reverse is also true. Jesus' suffering, his death, is amazing; and, in light of that death, his resurrection, his ongoing power, is amazing. It is no wonder that the three women who emerge from the crowd and act like disciples[25] (15:40-41, ἀκολουθέω, διακονέω, πολλαί) are amazed (16:5, ἐκθαμβεῖσθαι), astonished (16:8, ἔκστασις), and afraid (16:8, φοβεῖσθαι) at the empty tomb.[26] Amazement, astonishment, and even fear are not unknown by—and not inappropriate for—the followers of Jesus, whether these followers are disciples or the crowd. Not all who are amazed follow (12:17, ἐκθαυμάζειν), but all who follow are amazed.

---

twofold and the combined analyses did not differ significantly. (In my discussion I have listed the specific word/s for fear, astonishment, etc. employed in each relevant passage.) Best, seeking to distinguish tradition from redaction, does separate amazement and fear on the part of the disciples ("Role of the Disciples," 387-88).

[24] See n. 10 above.

[25] Best ("Role of the Disciples," 386) lists "16:8 (the women)" under the category of *the disciples* "are afraid at what he says or does or at what may happen to them" (Table 2. From the redaction.).

[26] Cf. David Catchpole, "The Fearful Silence of the Women at the Tomb: A Study in Markan Theology," *Journal of Theology for Southern Africa* 18 (1977) 8-9.

Whereas the disciples and the crowd share amazement and astonishment at Jesus' actions, the disciples' amazement is never (with the possible exception of the inclusion of the three at 5:42) and the crowd's amazement most frequently noted in response to Jesus' healing activity. It is, after all, the crowd and not the disciples who are healed by Jesus. Jesus does heal one member of one disciple's family, Simon's mother-in-law (1:29-31); but otherwise Jesus' healing is offered to the crowd and to members of the crowd (1:32, πᾶς; 1:34, πολλοί; 2:2-12, the paralytic [2:2, πολλοί; 2:4, ὄχλος; 2:12, πᾶς]; 3:10, πολλοί; 5:1-20, the Gerasene demoniac [5:20, πᾶς]; 5:24-35, the woman with a hemorrhage [5:24, 27, 30, 31, ὄχλος]; 7: 32-37, the deaf mute [7:33, ὄχλος]; 9:14-29, the epileptic boy [9:14, 15, 17, 25, ὄχλος; 9:26b, πολλοί]; 10:46-52, blind Bartimaeus [10:48, πολλοί]).

Jesus teaches, Jesus heals; the disciples and the crowd relate to Jesus somewhat differently in regard to these two actions, although both groups are amazed and astonished at Jesus. Jesus also feeds, and this activity also distinguishes the disciples and the crowd while uniting them as those for whom Jesus expresses concern. Jesus feeds the crowd bread in the desert (6:39, 41, 42, πᾶς; 8:2, 6a, 6b, ὄχλος) and asks the disciples to help him with the distribution (6:41, μαθηταί; 8:6, μαθηταί). Jesus feeds the disciples bread and wine in the upper room (14:22-25, they [14:23, πᾶς]). The feedings of the 5,000 and the 4,000 seem "miraculous"; the feeding of the twelve seems ordinary; but both are to be understood in relation to the kingdom of God (see especially 14:25) and neither is immediately understood by the participants (see especially 8:14-21). Since all three accounts—the feeding of the 5,000, the 4,000, the twelve—are marked by eucharistic language, those who particpate and those who need to understand include not only the disciples and the crowd but also the hearers/readers of the Markan narrative.

Assisting and Questioning

Jesus feeds both the disciples and the crowds, asking assistance of the disciples (6:41; 8:6). Jesus teaches both the disciples and the crowd, asking assistance of the disciples (3:14; 6:12, 30). Jesus heals the crowd, asking assistance of the disciples (3:15; 6:7, 13). Throughout the narrative the Markan Jesus enlists the assistance of his disciples, sometimes for a rather specific task involving arrangements for his ministry and movement throughout Palestine (3:9, μαθηταί; 6:37, you [6:35, μαθηταί]; 6:41, μαθηταί; 6:45, μαθηταί; 8:6, μαθηταί; 11:1, δύο τῶν μαθητῶν αὐτοῦ; 14:13 [and 16], δύο τῶν μαθητῶν αὐτοῦ; 14:32, μαθηταί; 14:33-42, the three, especially Peter [see 14:33, 37]), sometimes in more general terms that are often read as paradigmatic for later "disciples" of Jesus (particularly: 1:16-20, esp. 17, the four [see 1:16, 19]; 3:14-19, δώδεκα, [ἀπόστολοι], the twelve by name; 6:7, δώδεκα; but also: 6:41, μαθηταί; 8:6, μαθηταί; 14:32, μαθηταί; 14:33-42, the three).

Despite the recent emphasis on discipleship failure in Mark, the disciples frequently succeed in giving the assistance Jesus requests. Peter's statement that "we have . . . followed you" (10:28) fulfills Jesus' earlier command to "Follow me" (1:17). The apostles successfully preach and exorcise demons (6:12-13, 30), as Jesus appointed them to do (3:14-15). Jesus' disciples procure the boat (3:9), the colt (11:7), and the room (14:16) he requests. They are unable to multiply bread in the wilderness (6:37), but they do help Jesus distribute it (6:41; 8:6). They do not manage to go before Jesus to Bethsaida (6:45), but they do arrive there later with Jesus (8:22). They do wait with Jesus while he prays at Gethsemane (14:32), although Peter, James, and John cannot stay awake (14:33-42); yet, as the Markan Jesus notes, "the spirit indeed is willing but the flesh is weak" (14:38).[27]

Where the disciples get into real difficulty is in volunteering assistance that Jesus has not specifically requested. They are willing in their intentions, but their judgments are weak. The disciples

---

[27] It is not entirely clear whether the three women at the empty tomb, who are not quite disciples but are asked to speak to them, give the aid enlisted by the young man, who is not quite Jesus but speaks for him. It would appear that the narrator assumes that the hearer/reader assumes that the women did tell the disciples, because later someone surely told the narrator who now tells the hearer/reader! In addition, the phrase "they said nothing to any one" (οὐδενὶ οὐδὲν εἶπαν) may mean "they said nothing to any one else," or "they said nothing to any one in general." At 1:44 Jesus charged the healed leper to "say nothing to any one (μηδενὶ μηδὲν εἴπῃς); but go, show yourself to the priest, and offer for your cleansing what Moses commanded, for a proof to the people" (RSV). Surely in showing himself to the priest the former leper would say something to the priest; the priest, however, would not be just any one, but the very one the leper was instructed to inform. At the close of Mark, the disciples and Peter are not just "any one," but the very ones the women are instructed to tell. And in this case too, as at 1:45, the word does seem to have gotten out.

seem to mean well in volunteering assistance to Jesus and his ministry, but their exuberance must often be redirected by Jesus. It was not necessary for "Simon and those with him" (1:36) to pursue Jesus, for Jesus had not intended to withdraw for long (1:38). It was unnecessary for Peter to offer to build three booths for the transfigured Jesus, Moses, and Elijah (9:5), for Jesus would soon be on his way to Jerusalem. Yet Peter was eager to assist Jesus' ministry, to honor Jesus. It was inappropriate for John and the other disciples to forbid the unknown exorcist (9:38). It was inappropriate for the disciples to rebuke those bringing children to Jesus (10:13). But in each case the disciples intended to assist Jesus' ministry; they were surprised to learn their actions displeased Jesus.

The ten who were indignant at James and John probably thought to please Jesus in contrast to those two (10:41), but Jesus seems to have directed his correcting response to all twelve (10:42-45).[28] Peter's exclamation upon seeing the fig tree withered (11:21) seems to be offered as homage to Jesus, but Peter's surprise suggests as well his lack of faith in contrast to the faith Jesus calls for (11:22-24). The exclamation of one of the disciples upon coming out of the temple (13:1) is immediately reversed by Jesus (13:2), but certainly the disciple expected assent to his rhetorical remark. In each of these episodes, the disciples intend to do or say that which will please Jesus, but they misjudge Jesus' reaction. They do not yet realize what following Jesus entails.

At 9:18 we learn that the disciples have been asked to exorcise an unclean spirit, that they have been willing to do so, and that—although they have been successful in exorcisms previously (6:13)—this time they have failed.[29] It is not, however, their willingness that has failed, and they are eager to learn why they have

---

[28] So also Best, "Role of the Disciples," 380, and *Following Jesus*, 129.

[29] Friedrich Gustav Lang argues that the failure is to be attributed not to the disciples' lack of faith but to the father's lack of faith ("Sola Gratia im Markusevangelium: Die Soteriologie des Markus nach 9, 14-19 und 10, 17-31," *Rechtfertigung* [Käsemann festschrift; ed. J. Friedrich, W. Pöhlmann, P. Stuhlmacher; Tübingen: J. C. B. Mohr (Paul Siebeck), 1976] 321-37). More fruitfully, I think, Sharyn Dowd has suggested to me that "The story is ambiguous as to *whose* is the failure. At 9:18 the father blames the disciples. At 9:28 the disciples blame themselves. At 9:23 Jesus seems to blame the father." Perhaps the ambiguity is not to be resolved; perhaps the failure is not the father's alone or the disciples' alone but, as the Markan Jesus says in 9:19, the failure of this "faithless generation."

been unsuccessful (9:28). At 14:12 the disciples volunteer to make preparations for the celebration of the Passover with Jesus. In this case their voluntary assistance is directed by Jesus' specific commands (14:13-15), and their assistance is accepted and successful (14:16). Many of these references are categorized by Best under "They act as a foil to Jesus, giving him the opportunity to teach and act."[30] Each episode does contribute to a fuller understanding of the demands of discipleship.

At 14:29 and 14:31, Peter emphatically—and all the disciples as well—insist, against Jesus' warnings, that they will follow Jesus always. They volunteer their unfailing loyalty. Peter even makes an attempt to follow (14:54). But Jesus' judgment is right; their judgments are wrong—as they always are when not under the explicit direction of Jesus. When the disciples *respond* to Jesus' request for assistance they are often successful; when they *volunteer* assistance on their own, they are usually off course. Apparently, to follow Jesus, the disciples must follow Jesus' lead.

The crowd seems to err in the opposite direction: in following Jesus too closely; not in offering that which is not asked for, but in asking for continually that which is offered. The crowd seeks out Jesus' healing power (1:37, πᾶς—the crowd in addition to "Simon and those with him"?; 2:4, ὄχλος; 3:9, ὄχλος), sometimes obstructing by its very size those who seek healing (2:4, ὄχλος), sometimes obstructing them by direct rebuke (10:48, πολλοί). And sometimes the ever present crowd denies Jesus and his disciples the opportunity to eat (3:20, ὄχλος; 6:31, πολλοί), or even threatens Jesus' safety (3:9, ὄχλος). In short, the crowd crowds Jesus. For all its gathering to Jesus, however, the crowd does not always trust Jesus' healing power; "most of them" (9:26, τοὺς πολλούς) thought the epileptic boy had died when Jesus commanded the unclean spirit to come out of him.[31]

Yet the crowd over eager in its desire for healing from Jesus, like the disciples over eager in their desire to assist and please Jesus, does not in fact impede the ministry of Jesus. Rather, the interaction between Jesus and the crowd, like that between Jesus and the

---

[30] "Role of the Disciples," 385-86.

[31] In the future, Jesus warns, some of the crowd may be misled by others, perhaps also of the crowd, for many (πολλοί) will come in Jesus' name and lead many (πολλοί) astray (13:6).

disciples, helps illustrate the true nature of the ministry of Jesus and the discipleship of his followers. The crowd too is a foil for Jesus.[32]

Still, the disciples serve as the most significant foil for Jesus. And this is nowhere more clear than in the constant stream of questions Jesus asks his disciples and his disciples ask him. Generally accompanied by his disciples, Jesus naturally asks them questions throughout his ministry of teaching (4:21; 4:30; 9:12; 13:2), healing (5:30; 9:16, disciples?), and feeding (6:38; 8:5). But, more importantly, Jesus questions the disciples concerning their understanding of the parables (4:13; 7:18), of the feedings (8:17-21), of the demands of discipleship (8:36-37; 9:33; 9:50; 10:36, 38; 14:37, 41), of himself (8:27, 29). He questions their faith (4:40; 9:19). Jesus questions the crowd (or individuals amid the crowd) as well as the disciples, as he teaches (3:33; 4:13, those about him with the twelve; 4:30, crowd?; 8:36-37; 12:35; 37) and heals (5:30; 5:39; 9:16, 19, 21; 10:51). But Jesus' questions of the crowd are less frequent and—with the exception of 3:33—less profound at the metaphorical level than his questions of the disciples.

The contrast is even greater in regard to the questions the disciples and the crowd ask Jesus. Strictly speaking, no direct questions from the crowd to Jesus are reported by the Markan narrator; twice, however, the crowd questions itself concerning Jesus, and in his presence (1:27, πᾶς; 6:2, πολλοί). On the other hand, both indirect (4:10, those about him with the twelve; 7:17; 10:10) and direct questions from the disciples to Jesus are narrated, and twice the narrator notes that the disciples had questions they did not raise (9:10; 9:32). The disciples ask Jesus about parables (4:10; 7:17), teaching (9:11; 10:10), healing (9:28), feedings (6:37; 8:4), salvation (10:26), the signs of the end (13:4). They cannot bring themselves to ask about Jesus' death and resurrection (9:10; 9:32).[33] Almost always their questions betray their lack of faith and/or understanding (4:10; 4:38; 4:41, among themselves; 5:31; 6:37; 7:17; 8:4; 9:11; 9:28; 10:10; 10:26; 13:4; 14:4, disciples?; the exceptions are 14:12 and 14:19). But at least the disciples remain willing to question Jesus, and to be questioned by Jesus, and to question themselves (9:28; 14:19).

---

[32] *Contra* Best, ''Role of the Disciples,'' 392.

[33] As Best notes of 9:32, ''their failure to understand is only partial: they understand enough to be afraid to ask to understand more'' (*Following Jesus*, 73).

In some important ways the disciples and the crowd are distinguished from each other by their relation to Jesus. The crowd comes to Jesus and he heals them. But Jesus gives more time to his disciples: he frequently withdraws with them. And Jesus asks more in return from his disciples: he enlists their assistance (and they also volunteer their assistance); he questions them (and they also question him). Yet in other important ways the disciples and the crowd are parallel in their relation to Jesus: Jesus calls both to himself; both follow Jesus; Jesus teaches both and commands both to hear; both are amazed and astonished at Jesus; Jesus feeds both. And in two final ways the disciples and the crowd are also parallel: both find themselves, because of their relation to Jesus, in opposition with Jewish leaders; yet both, in the end, abandon Jesus to the opposition of Jewish leaders.

Abandoning

In the first half of the Markan narrative the disciples of Jesus find themselves in opposition with Jewish leaders, particularly the Pharisees (2:15-17, scribes of the Pharisees; 2:18, Pharisees and disciples of the Pharisees; 2:23-27, Pharisees; 7:1-8, Pharisees and scribes; 8:15, Pharisees and Herodians; 9:14, scribes).[34] On the surface the disputes have to do with eating and bread (2:15-17, eating with sinners; 2:18, not fasting; 2:23-27, plucking grain; 7:1-8, eating unwashed; 8:15, the leaven of the Pharisees and Herodians), but the more fundamental issues are purity and authority. In the second half of the Markan narrative the crowd that follows Jesus finds itself in opposition with Jewish leaders, particularly the chief priests and the scribes (11:18, chief priests and scribes; 11:32, chief priests, scribes, and elders; 12:12, chief priests, scribes, and elders; 14:2, chief priests and scribes). At this stage in the story the chief priests and scribes (and elders) hesitate to move against Jesus because they fear the crowd that supports him. After one of Jesus' disciples betrays him to the chief priests (14:10), however, they are able to stir up the crowd against Jesus (15:11).

---

[34] Thomas L. Budesheim points out, especially in regard to 9:14, that the Markan gospel presents a parallel between the disciples and their teacher in that both debate with the scribes ("Jesus and the Disciples in Conflict with Judaism," *ZNW* 62 [1971] 190-209, esp. 206-209).

Thus, both the disciples and the crowd, who were in opposition with Jewish leaders because they followed Jesus, abandon Jesus, who must then face the opposition of Jewish leaders alone. Judas betrays Jesus (14:10, Judas Iscariot, εἷς τῶν δώδεκα; 14:43, Judas, εἷς τῶν δώδεκα), as the narrator had noted (3:19, Judas Iscariot) and Jesus had implied (14:20, εἷς τῶν δώδεκα) he would. All the disciples forsake Jesus (14:50, πᾶς), as Jesus had warned (14:27, πᾶς) and the disciples had denied (14:31, πᾶς) they would. Peter denies Jesus (14:66-72), as Jesus had predicted (14:30) and Peter had denied (14:29, 31) he would. At Gethsemane Jesus faces a newly formed group: "Judas, one of the twelve, and with him a crowd with swords and clubs, from the chief priests and the scribes and the elders" (14:43). Presumably the many (14:56, πολλοί) who bear false witness against Jesus before the assembled chief priests and scribes and elders (14:53) emerge from this crowd. By the time Jesus is delivered to Pilate, the chief priests have the crowd well under their control (15:8, 11, 15). The crowd is coopted; the disciples have fled. His followers have failed him; Jesus is alone.

Conclusion

Both the disciples and the crowd follow Jesus. Both the disciples and the crowd are fallible. Yet the Gospel of Mark is not an allegory in which a group of characters in the story may be equated with a group of persons beyond the narrative. The disciples are equivalent to neither Mark's supposed opponents nor Mark's imagined hearers/readers.[35] The Gospel of Mark is, however, metaphoric and imagistic, and the disciples and the crowd—especially taken together—do evoke a composite image of the followers, the fallible followers, of Jesus. Were only the disciples depicted as followers, the demands of discipleship would be clear, but discipleship might appear restrictive. Were only the crowd depicted as followers, the outreach entailed in following Jesus would be clear, but follower-ship might appear permissive. With both disciples and the crowd

---

[35] Likewise Best's identification of the crowd as "the unevangelised mass" or "the uncommitted" (*Following Jesus*, 29, 101, 136, 154), the disciples as "the church" or "Christians" (29, 113, 136), and the twelve as "missionaries" (184, 195, 204-205) is over schematized. But with Best (*Following Jesus*, 46 n. 12) I reject Lohmeyer's identification of the crowd with the laity and the disciples with ecclesiastical officials.

depicted as followers, as fallible followers, the Markan narrative message is plain: discipleship is both open-ended and demanding; followership is neither exclusive nor easy.

In addition to the complementarity of the disciples and the crowd in this composite portrait of followers, there exists a kind of complementarity of the part and the whole within each group. The disciples, as the inner group specifically chosen and commissioned by Jesus, have a higher positive connotation as a group than does the crowd. But the individual disciples and groups of two, three, or four disciples set apart from the twelve generally have a negative connotation (see the appendix for references). On the other hand, when individuals are singled out of the crowd, their connotative value is highly positive (2:2-12, four men and paralytic [2:2, πολλοί; 2:4, ὄχλος; 2:12, πᾶς]; 2:13-14, Levi—from the crowd? [2:13, ὄχλος; 2:15b, πολλοί]; 5:1-20, Gerasene demoniac [5:20, πᾶς]; 5:24-34, woman with hemorrhage [5:24, 27, 30, 31, ὄχλος]; 7:32-37, deaf mute [7:33, ὄχλος]; 9:14-29, father of epileptic boy [9:17, εἷς ἐκ τοῦ ὄχλου; 9:14, 15, 25, ὄχλος; 9:26b, πολλοί]; 10:46-52, Bartimaeus [10:48, πολλοί]; 12:41-44, poor widow [12:41, ὄχλος; 12:43, 44a, πᾶς]; 15:40-41, three women—from the crowd? [15:41, πολλαί]). Perhaps this arrangement counters stereotyping; perhaps it challenges the assumptions of the hearers/readers. One expects disciples to be exemplary; their fallibility is surprising. One expects little of the crowd; their followership is surprising.

It hardly needs to be said that there are crucial differences between the disciples and the crowd—in terms of both narrative roles and theological significance. The concern here has been to illustrate the narrative and theological points of contact between the two groups. That both the disciples and the crowd are portrayed in positive and negative ways in relation to Jesus is indicated by the various—and parallel—kinds of activities that characterize each group's relationship with Jesus. That the disciples and the crowd are more complementary than competing groups in the Markan narrative, contributing to a composite portrait of followers of Jesus, is suggested by the distinctive—but compatible—kinds of activities that characterize each group's relationship with Jesus. The Markan extension of both the invitation and the demand of followership from the disciples to the crowd sets up its further extension—to the hearers/readers. The pattern of movement from the disciples to the

crowd to the hearers/readers is suggested especially by: (1) Jesus'
statements of the "whoever" type, addressed—within the story—to
the disciples and/or the crowd, but reaching beyond; and (2) Jesus'
statements about "many" and "all," addressed—within the
story—to the disciples, employing terms usually designating the
crowd, and pointing outward to the hearer/reader.[36]

Jesus addresses "whoever" type statements to his followers
—most frequently the disciples but also the crowd (8:34): whoever
has ears to hear (4:23; cf. 4:9), whoever would come after me
(8:34), whoever would save his or her life (8:35), whoever would be
first (9:35), whoever gives you a cup of water (9:41), whoever
causes a little one to sin (9:42), whoever does not receive the
kingdom of God like a child (10:15), whoever leaves house or family
or lands (10:29), whoever does not doubt in his or her heart (11:23).
Surely the twelve and members of the crowd are among the
"whoever," but so may be the hearers/readers. Here we can look
at but one example. Jesus' saying at 10:29-30, "there is no one who
has left (ἀφῆκεν) who will not receive . . .," echoes Peter's immediately prior statement, "we have left (ἀφήκαμεν) everything ..."
(10:28). Thus by their actions the disciples are linked with the
"whoever" of 10:29-30; the disciples, as the hearer/reader realizes,
are among those who have left families, houses, lands. But the
disciples alone do not necessarily comprise the "whoever" at
10:29-30, for not only does the "receiving" remain in the narrative
future, but also the way is left open for others to be included among
those who leave lands and regain lands for Jesus' sake "and for the
gospel" (10:29)—others including, if not especially, whoever hears
or reads Mark's "gospel of Jesus Christ, the Son of God" (1:1).

Other statements addressed by the Markan Jesus to the disciples
are centered on the words many (πολλοί) and all (πᾶς), familiar
Markan designations for the crowd. Jesus informs his disciples that

---

[36] On Mark's implied readers, see Robert M. Fowler, *Loaves and Fishes: The
Function of the Feeding Stories in the Gospel of Mark* (SBLDS 54; Chico, CA: Scholars,
1981) 149-79; and Idem, "Who Is 'the Reader' of Mark's Gospel?," *Society of
Biblical Literature 1983 Seminar Papers* (Chico, CA: Scholars, 1983) 31-53. On
Mark's hearers/readers, see Werner H. Kelber, *The Oral and the Written Gospel*
(Philadelphia: Fortress, 1983). Both Fowler's reading and Kelber's reading of the
disciples in Mark are different from mine, similar to each other's, and related to
Weeden's. See also H.-J. Klauck, "Die erzählerische Rolle der Jünger im
Markusevangelium," *Nov Test* 24 (1982) 1-26; K. Stock, *Boten aus dem Mit-Ihm-
Sein. Das Verhältnis zwischen Jesus und den Zwölf nach Markus* (Analecta Biblica 70;
Rome: Pontificio Istituto Biblico, 1975).

he gives his life, pours out his blood, for the many (10:45, πολλοί; 14:24, πολλοί). And, concerning followership, Jesus instructs his disciples that "many that are first will be last, and the last first" (10:31, πολλοί) and that "If any one would be first, he must be last of all and servant of all" (9:35, πᾶς, πᾶς) or "slave of all" (10:44, πᾶς). The Markan Jesus addresses the disciples, but the words he employs, many and all, are open-ended. The disciples are surely among the many for whom Jesus gives his life; the crowd is also among the many; but the many embraces as well the hearers/readers of the Markan narrative. Whoever—disciples, crowds, hearers/readers—would be first of all, must be servant of all. What the Markan Jesus says to the four disciples he says to all (13:37, πᾶς). What the Markan narrative says about discipleship it says to all. Both separately and together, the disciples and the crowd serve to open the story of Jesus and the narrative of Mark outward to the larger group—whoever has ears to hear or eyes to read the Gospel of Mark.

APPENDIX

	The Disciples (of Jesus)	The Crowd
1:16, 19	Simon, Andrew, James, John	
1:27		πᾶς
1:29	Simon, Andrew, James, John	
1:32		πᾶς
1:34		πολλοί
1:36	Simon	
1:37		πᾶς
2:2		πολλοί
2:4		ὄχλος
2:12a		πᾶς
2:12b		πᾶς
2:13		ὄχλος
2:15	μαθηταί	πολλοί
2:16	μαθηταί	
2:18d	μαηπταί	
2:23	μαθηταί	
3:7	μαθηταί	πλῆθος

3:8		πλῆθος
3:9	μαθηταί	ὄχλος
3:10		πολλοί
3:14	δώδεκα	
	[ἀπόστολοι]	
3:16	[δώδεκα]	
3:16-19	the twelve by name	
3:20		ὄχλος
3:32		ὄχλος
4:1a		ὄχλος
4:1b		ὄχλος
4:10	δώδεκα	
4:34	μαθηταί	
4:36		ὄχλος
5:20		πᾶς
5:21		ὄχλος
5:24		ὄχλος
5:27		ὄχλος
5:30		ὄχλος
5:31	μαθηταί	ὄχλος
5:37	Peter, James, John	
6:1	μαθηταί	
6:2		πολλοί
6:7	δώδεκα	
6:30	ἀπόστολοι	
6:31		πολλοί
6:33		πολλοί
6:34		ὄχλος
6:35	μαθηταί	
6:39		πᾶς
6:41	μαθηταί	πᾶς
6:42		πᾶς
6:45	μαθηταί	ὄχλος
7:2	μαθηταί	
7:5	μαθηταί	
7:14		ὄχλος
		πᾶς
7:17		ὄχλος
	μαθηταί	
7:33		ὄχλος

8:1		ὄχλος
	μαθηταί	
8:2		ὄχλος
8:4	μαθηταί	
8:6a		ὄχλος
	μαθηταί	
8:6b		ὄχλος
8:10	μαθηταί	
8:27a	μαθηταί	
8:27b	μαθηταί	
8:29	Peter	
8:32	Peter	
8:33	μαθηταί	
	Peter	
8:34		ὄχλος
	μαθηταί	
9:2	Peter, James, John	
9:5	Peter	
9:14	μαθηταί	ὄχλος
9:15		ὄχλος
9:17		εἷς ἐκ τοῦ ὄχλου
9:18	μαθηταί	
9:25		ὄχλος
9:26		πολλοί
9:28	μαθηταί	
9:31	μαθηταί	
9:35	δώδεκα	
9:38	John	
10:1		ὄχλος
10:10	μαθηταί	
10:13	μαθηταί	
10:23	μαθηταί	
10:24	μαθηταί	
10:28	Peter	
10:32	δώδεκα	
10:35	James, John	
10:41	δέκα	
	James, John	
10:46	μαθηταί	ὄχλος
10:48		πολλοί

11:1	δύο τῶν μαθητῶν	
11:8		πολλοί
11:11	δώδεκα	
11:14	μαθηταί	
11:18		ὄχλος
11:21	Peter	
11:32		ὄχλος
12:12		ὄχλος
12:37		ὄχλος
12:41		ὄχλος
12:43	μαθηταί	πᾶς
12:44		πᾶς
13:1	εἷς τῶν μαθητῶν	
13:3	Peter, James, John, Andrew	
13:6a		πολλοί
13:6b		πολλοί
14:2		λαός
14:10	Judas Iscariot, εἷς τῶν δώδεκα	
14:12	μαθηταί	
14:13	δύο τῶν μαθητῶν	
14:14	μαθηταί	
14:16	μαθηταί	
14:17	δώδεκα	
14:20	εἷς τῶν δώδεκα	
14:29	Peter	
14:32	μαθηταί	
14:33	Peter, James, John	
14:37	Peter (Simon)	
14:43	Judas, εἷς τῶν δώδεκα	ὄχλος
14:54	Peter	
14:56		πολλοί
14:66	Peter	
14:67	Peter	
14:70	Peter	
14:72	Peter	
15:8		ὄχλος
15:11		ὄχλος

15:15		ὄχλος
15:41		πολλαί
16:7	μαθηταί	
	Peter	

THE LITERARY STRUCTURE OF MARK 11:1-12:40

by

STEPHEN H. SMITH
Cambridge

I — *Assessing the Problems*

Despite the attention which has been focussed on Mark 11:1-13:2 during the past 35 years, a consensus on its literary structure has yet to be reached. One reason for this is inherent in the section itself: the pericopae which it embodies are, both formally and in content, much more disparate than the catena of five controversy stories in Mark 2:1-3:6 which has frequently been observed to be the counterpart of the Jerusalem conflict cycle in Mark 11, 12. The 'actors' are more varied, and the issues in question more diverse than in the Galilean controversies. This factor alone would be enough to explain the lack of agreement among scholars. Unfortunately there are also unwarranted factors whose unwelcome intervention could perhaps be eradicated if only more attention were paid to the application of method. Most serious of these factors, in my opinion, is the tendency to divorce structural from theological concerns. Too often scholars have drawn conclusions about gospel theology from a purely redactional or linguistic analysis, or even by adopting a blanket approach in which the gospel is understood from a literary-critical perspective, regardless of other methodologies. Surely it is time to take stock of current critical scholarship on Mark, and to heed the advice issued some 16 years ago by the late Norman Perrin[1] that our understanding of Mark's theology — or that of the other synoptists, for that matter — can be enhanced only by synthesising the methodologies at our disposal. In that light, the study of gospel structure must be treated as a genuine critical methodology in its own right, every bit as essential as the more widely accepted ones. If theology is made the

---

[1] N. Perrin, ''The Evangelist as Author: Reflections on Method in the Study and Interpretation of the Synoptic Gospels and Acts'', *BR*, 17 (1972) 5-18.

procrustean bed of structural and other considerations, the conclusions drawn will inevitably be distorted. Only when the gospel
structure itself has been properly understood — and understood, if
possible, from the viewpoint of its own first-century milieu — can
we begin to appreciate the theological notions to which it points.

We do not have to search far for studies of Mark 11:1-13:2 whose
conclusions have been distorted by a reliance on one critical method
at the expense of all others. Several scholars have argued that the
structure of this section is dependent largely on some hypothetical
pre-Markan controversy collection underlying it.[2] But this is to
reduce Mark to a mere stringer of pearls when the trend today is to
acknowledge in our Evangelist a creative, theological mind. On the
other hand, to be too heavily dependent on redaction-criticism is to
lay oneself open to the danger of subordinating structure to
theology.

Joanna Dewey goes to the opposite extreme. Despite claiming to
unlock the door to Mark's theology with the key of rhetorical and
structural criticism, which I think she does with some sensitivity in
the case of Mark 2:1-3:6,[3] she fails to allow Mark his true
theological voice in the case of Mark 11, 12, because her chief concern is to force these chapters into the same structural mould as the
Galilean controversies.[4] There seems to me to be a serious flaw in
the reasoning that if Mark 2:1-3:6 is chiastic, so too must Mark 11,
12 be. There is no reason why the Evangelist could not have chosen
a totally different rhetorical structure for his second controversy
catena, and I believe he did.

Much more sensitive to the situation is Klemens Stock[5] who
genuinely acknowledges the importance of the narrative structure
as a key to the Markan theology. He rightly perceives the
significance of the temporal and geographical rubrics within the

---

[2] So M. Albertz, *Synoptischen Streitgespräche* (Berlin: Trowitzsch & Sohn, 1921)
16-36; W.L. Knox, *The Sources of the Synoptic gospels: I-Mark* (ed. H. Chadwick;
Cambridge: CUP, 1953) 77-102; M.J. Cook, *Mark's Treatment of the Jewish Leaders*
(NovTSup LI; Leiden: E.J. Brill, 1978); R. Pesch, *Das Markusevangelium* (2 vols.;
Freiburg-Basel-Wien: Herder, 1976-77) 2.1-27, esp. 15-17. For an approach
based on the canons of rabbinic forms, see D. Daube, *The New Testament and Rabbinic Judaism* (London: Athlone, 1956) 158-69.

[3] J. Dewey, *Markan Public Debate: Literary Technique, Concentric Structure and
Theology in Mark 2:1-3:6* (SBLDS 48; Chico: Scholars, 1980) 109-22.

[4] Dewey, *Markan Public Debate*, 156-63.

[5] K. Stock, "Gliederung und Zusammenhang in Mk 11-12", *Bib* 59 (1978)
481-515.

section, especially the celebrated three-day scheme. Although we cannot promise to echo his conclusions, we believe that this method of approach is fundamentally sound, and well worth consideration.

Our task in the remainder of this paper is fourfold: to delineate the section (we cannot simply *assume* that 11:1-13:2 is the delineation as originally intended); to establish the structure of the section itself; to ascertain the theological implications of this structure; to determine its function in the Markan community.

II — *Delimiting the Section*

a) *Mark 10:46-52*

Does our literary unit commence at 10:46 or at 11:1? Scholars are divided on the issue.[6] Those who argue the latter case tend to do so on a geographical basis. In 10:46-52 Jesus is leaving Jericho, but in 11:1-11 he is in the immediate vicinity of Jerusalem, the scene of the Gospel's final chapters. It is noticed, too, that the preceding section, 8:27-10:45, is on discipleship. In this context, 10:46-52 may be regarded as a call to follow through healing, for after his recovery Bartimaeus follows Jesus ἐν τῇ ὁδῷ. This compares with the third passion prediction and its setting (10:32-34) where Jesus is on the road to Jerusalem with those who are following.

Both these arguments can be countered. Since Jesus does not enter Jerualem until 11:11, the journey from the Mount of Olives to the city can be regarded as the final stage of his journey from Galilee, and thus as the climax to a travel narrative which begins · at 9:30. Also, the end of the section on discipleship does not terminate the disciples' activity; they continue to play a significant rôle in Mark 11-16. Thus, the treatment of Bartimaeus as a follower does not necessarily mean that 10:46-52 must be appended to the preceding section. Moreover, the title 'Son of David' (10:47, 48) is found elsewhere in Mark only in Mark 11, 12 where it is clearly of messianic significance. In this manner, 10:46-52 could be seen as a prologue to the account of Jesus' messianic activity in 11:1-11 rather than as an epilogue to the section on discipleship.

---

[6] Compare V. Taylor, *The Gospel According to St. Mark* (London: MacMillan 1952) 447-49; W.L. Lane, *The Gospel According to Mark* (Grand Rapids: Eerdmans, 1974) 390, with Dewey, *Markan Public Debate*, 56, 57.

We cannot, however, discount the notion that it is actually a transitional passage which serves both purposes.[7]

Joanna Dewey, who regards 10:46-52 as part of a prologue to 11:12-12:40, attempts to show that it is related to 11:1-11 both temporally and theologically. The inclusion of the Bartimaeus pericope in the first day of Mark's three-day scheme, however, cannot be argued on the evidence of the text; the absence from 11:1 of a time rubric like those found in 11:12, 20 does not entitle us to assume that temporally 10:46-52 and 11:1-11 must belong together. Nevertheless, Mark may have intended such an arrangement. Dewey's theological point, that both pericopae develop the theme of Davidic messianism—at precisely the point where Jesus is about to enter David's city—has rather more force behind it. It is further noticed that in both narratives the rôle of the crowd is significant.

The perspective of V.K. Robbins on the matter is that if 10:46-52 is a transitional episode it must function as a means of drawing together the theologies of two major sections. In effect, the "suffering-rising christology" of 8:27-10:45 and the authoritative Son of David image in 11:1-12:40 are fused together and correlated with the theme of discipleship. All these elements are interrelated in the Bartimaeus narrative where the healing aspect recalls Jesus' earlier "healing-through-faith" activity (see 2:5; 5:34, 35; 6:5, 6; 9:23, 24). Although the title 'Son of David' is never mentioned by Mark prior to 10:47, the healing of the man on whose lips it is first found demonstrates that such behaviour is essentially "Son of David activity". Moreover, the question of Jesus, Τί σοι θέλεις ποιήσω (10:51), and the fact that Bartimaeus followed ἐν τῇ ὁδῷ, indicates that this story has something in common with the earlier discipleship episodes (10:32, 35, 36). Thus, in the light of 10:46-52, it becomes evident that all aspects of Jesus' ministry, both in 8:27-10:45 and in 11:1-12:40, constitute "Son of David activity".

We would agree with Robbins that 10:46-52 is a transitional passage which in one sense stands independently of both the major

---

[7] T.A. Burkill, "Strain on the Secret: An Examination of Mark 11:1-13:37", *ZNW* 51 (1960) 31; S.E. Johnson, *A Commentary on the Gospel According to Mark* (London: A. & C. Black, ²1972) 181; N. Perrin, "Towards an Interpretation of the Gospel of Mark", *Christology and a Modern Pilgrimage* (ed. H.D. Betz; Claremont, Ca.: New Testament Colloquium, 1971) 4; V.K. Robbins, "The Healing of Blind Bartimaeus (Mk. 10:46-52) in the Markan Theology", *JBL* 92 (1973) 238.

sections either side of it. The statement καὶ ἔρχονται εἰς Ἰερειχω is akin to other such statements which introduce a new unit,[8] and the allusion in 11:1 to Bethany initiates the three-day sequence in which Jesus travels from Bethany to Jerusalem and back, and of which 10:46-52 is not geographically a part. On the other hand, the healing of Bartimaeus is reminiscent of the recovery of the blind man in 8:22-26, and these two pericopae effectively frame the section on discipleship. Further, the fact that Jesus "calls"[9] Bartimaeus (10:49) and that the latter's response is to follow (10:52) is not simply a call to be healed, but to discipleship, and Bartimaeus follows Jesus along the road to Jerusalem as surely as those in 10:32, if not more so. The faith of the man, too, is seen not only in terms reminiscent of that shown by others who Jesus healed, but also in anticipation of Jesus' remarks on faith in 11:23, 24. Again, Bartimaeus' reference to Jesus as 'Son of David' is meant to indicate that as Jesus approaches and enters Jerusalem, his activity should, as noted above, be understood as "Son of David activity" within the vicinity of David's city.

b) *Mark 13:1, 2*

If, then, Mark 10:46-52 signifies the beginning of the section, how should we delimit its conclusion? Since the appearance of Marc Lauverjat's article on Mark 12:37b-13:2[10], no consideration of this question would be complete without critical reference to that work. Lauverjat regards 12:37b-13:2 as a literary unit, adducing the following evidence for his conclusion:

i) The Temple is quite markedly the scene of 11:11-13:2 (11:11, 15, 27; 12:35-41), but in 13:1 Jesus leaves that edifice, never to return. Mark 13:1 contains the prophecy of the Temple's destruction as the departure is made. This would seem to establish the conclusion of the unit and of the entire section. The beginning of the unit may be 12:37b, for the use there of πολὺς ὄχλος may correspond to the ὄχλος in v. 41. The word occurs nowhere else in this chapter except 12:12. The substance of the unit is a debate on the Temple and its values which is concluded by the example of the poor widow (12:41-44). The behaviour of this woman stands in

---

[8] See Mark 1:21; 2:1; 3:20; 5:1; 6:1; 7:24,31; 8:22,27; 9:33; 10:1.

[9] The word used here, however, is not καλέω as in 1:20, but φωνέω.

[10] M. Lauverjat, "L'autre regard: Marc 12:37b-13:2", *ETR* 55 (1980) 416-20.

direct contrast to that of the vendors (11:15) or the scribes (12:38-40).

ii) The arrangement of the characters and their respective rôles forms a loose rhetorical, symmetry, thus reinforcing the evidence for the unitary nature of the passage:

12:37b-----pleasure of the crowd
12:38-40---scribes...... condemnation
12:41,42---rich people/poor widow
12:43,44---she with nothing/they with abundance
13:1,2------Temple...... destruction
13;1,2------reflection (pleasure?) of a disciple

iii) The unit is characterised by various references to looking and seeing. This is implicit in 12:38-40 where the activities of the scribes are determined by their desire to be seen and admired by all. In v. 41 Jesus 'looks at' (θεωρεῖν) people dropping money into the treasury. Again, the rich wish to be seen for their 'generosity'. In 13:1 the disciple, remarking on the splendour of the Temple, says, 'Behold!' (ἴδε), while Jesus, predicting its destruction, replies, 'You see...' (βλέπεις) (13:2).

iv) The theme of 12:37b-13:2, according to Lauverjat, is the contrast between the falsehood of appearances and the right attitude to God that proceeds from within. The scribes wish to be honoured by men, but Jesus condemns them; the disciple marvels at the Temple, the ultimate symbol of Jewish institutionalism, but Jesus predicts its destruction; the scribes offer long prayers, but it is really the widow's example of practical giving that pleases God; the rich contribute great sums to the treasury—again, in an ostentatious display—but it is the widow who, having sacrificed all, is truly honoured, for her motives are internal, not external.

Lauverjat demonstrates adequately enough that 13:2 denotes the end of the section. It is there that the setting changes. In 13:3 Jesus, though still within sight of the Temple, is now sitting "over against" (κατέναντι) it on the Mount of Olives. Moreover, in place of the one disciple singled out in 13:1, four disciples are identified now.

But how convincing are Lauverjat's arguments for the literary unity of 12:37b-13:2? Quite clearly, he is right in his judgement that Jesus' condemnation of the scribes' behaviour (12:38-40) is antithetically related to his commendation of the widow's behaviour (12:41-44), and the Temple setting, certainly, shows that what is at issue is the attitude that one adopts in his devotion to God; but all this should be accepted on a less formal basis than Lauverjat avers. Language and theme may indeed interlock the sub-units here (12: 37b-40, 41-44; 13-1,2), but they also serve to relate this material both to what precedes and to what follows.

One of the most debatable points is Lauverjat's insistence that 12:37b be regarded as part of his literary unit. If it is agreed that the statement καὶ ὁ πολὺς ὄχλος ἤκουεν αὐτοῦ ἡδέως belongs to the Markan redaction, it is likely that its position is dictated by the rôle it plays in the literary structure of its context. Rationally, however, it would not make sense to say that the crowd heard Jesus gladly before the message of his teaching had been given. Further, the words καὶ ἐν τῇ διδαχῇ αὐτοῦ ἔλεγεν (12:38a) form a new redactional beginning to Jesus' condemnation of the scribes. Thus, 12:37b is surely intended to describe the reaction of the people to the *Davidssohnfrage* (12:35-37a). It is really the only place in 12:37b-13:2 where gladness is mentioned; Lauverjat's proposal that the reaction of the disciple in 13:1 is similar to this can be no more than speculation.

A further blow to Lauverjat's thesis is dealt by the presence of the adverb κατέναντι in 12:41. It is a term used just three times by Mark. At least twice, it stands at the head of a new section (as opposed to standing in the preceding transitional passage). In 11:2 Jesus instructs two of his disciples to go into the village "opposite". Since the village in question is probably Bethany, the reader is to understand that Mark is embarking on a new section in which Jesus is seen to shuttle between that village and Jerusalem. In 13:3 κατέναντι reappears. Its use here, to depict Jesus sitting "over against" the Temple, is perhaps meant to be symbolic of his final severance from institutionalised Judaism. In view of the above occurrences, it is no surprise to find the third appearance of the term at the beginning of another (sub-)unit. In 12:41 Jesus sits "opposite" the treasury. Again, the symbolism is clear: Jesus and his disciples are set over against the scribes and the rich, who make an ostentatious display of their religiosity. But κατέναντι also appears to indicate a pause in the action. Its use here and in 13:3 seems to mark off 12:41-44 as a self-contained unit, and 13:1,2, which is heavily redactional, would then serve as a short transition between major sections.

Finally, Lauverjat's precise symmetrical arrangement of 12:37b-13:2 according to its actors and their attitudes may not be as sound as he would claim. Certainly, the inclusion of 12:37b in his scheme weakens his case. The various antithetic relationships are present, to be sure, but 12:37b-13:2 is quite strongly related to the material in Mark 11, 12 generally. Mark 13:1,2, in particular, is not simply the conclusion to Lauverjat's unit; rather, it is, like 10:46-52, a transitional passage[11] which both recalls and anticipates material beyond itself. In 12:10,11 Jesus quotes Ps. 118:22,23: the stone which the builders rejected has become the head of the corner—Jesus is the stone on which the security of the entire building depends. In 13:2 the stones of the Temple which are to be cast down represent the religious authorities whose legalistic system is to be destroyed along with the Temple itself. It is these very leaders who are themselves to become fallen stones since they have rejected the one stone on which the whole building depends.

Another backward glance is cast by the disciple's use of the vocative διδάσκαλε. Uttered in the vicinity of the Temple, it reminds us of the opponents' use of that term to address Jesus as he taught in the Temple precincts (12:14,19,32).

Equally, 13:1,2 looks ahead, for its reference to the destruction of the Temple and its prophetic nature prepare the ground for the apocalyptic discourse (13:5-37) and prompt the disciples to ask, "Tell us, when will these things be....?" (13:4). And, of course, the Temple itself remains in view throughout the discourse (13:3,14). Further, the double reference to 'seeing'—ἴδε, βλέπεις (13:1,2)—anticipates the stern, repeated warning of the apocalypse itself: Take heed! Watch! (13:5,9,23,33,35,37).

Thus, we agree with Lauverjat that the story of the poor widow is antithetically related to the material on the scribes, especially 12:38-40, but we do not regard 12:37b-13:2 as an independent literary unit. It is more likely, as will be shown, that, along with 12:35-37, 38-40, Mark 12:41-44 constitutes a triad. Mark 13:1,2 then stands as a redactional *Sammelbericht*, effecting a transition from one major section to the next.

---

[11] So also V.K. Robbins, *Jesus the Teacher: A Socio-Rhetorical Interpretation of Mark* (Philadelphia: Fortress, 1984) 44.

III — *The Literary Structure of Mark 11:1-12:44*

a) *Mark 11:1-12:12*

Within the limits set by 10:46-52 and 13:1,2 Mark arranges the pericopae at his disposal, broadly-speaking, on the basis of a three-day temporal scheme. The first sub-unit of this arrangement is 11:1-11, a passage which a few scholars—rather unnecessarily, in my opinion—sub-divide into two or three units.[12] As we have noted, it represents the final stage of the journey from Galilee which begins at 9:30. Mark 11:9a, καὶ οἱ προάγοντες καὶ οἱ ἀκολουθοῦντες, is reminiscent of 10:32a where Jesus is said to be on the way to Jerusalem with his followers. In 11:1-10 he is still accompanied by "those who followed" as distinct from "the disciples" or "the twelve" with whom he leaves the city. Bethany, however, does mark a new and final stage in the journey. Mark makes it clear that the journey from Galilee is an "ascent" to Jerusalem, but physiographically, as he no doubt realised, the way from Bethany into the city is essentially a descent (cf. Luke 19:37).

In both Matthew and Luke the 'cleansing' of the Temple follows directly upon the triumphal entry. Matthew adds the story of the fig tree as an undivided pericope, while Luke omits it altogether. Matthew, therefore, has a two-day scheme, while Luke's chief concern appears to be with historical accuracy: he says simply that, after the 'cleansing' of the Temple on the *first* day, Jesus was daily in the Temple teaching (Luke 19:47; cp. Mark 14:49). In its Lukan context, this gives credence to the view that between his entry into Jerusalem and his crucifixion, Jesus actually spent far longer in the city than is superficially apparent from Mark. In the Second Gospel, the first day is brought to a close immediately after the triumphal entry because the theological significance of 11:1-10 is not identical with that of 11:12-25.[13] That 11:11 is redactional is apparent not only from the use of Markan terminology, but from the fact that once Jesus has entered Jerusalem nothing happens: he simply enters the Temple, looks around (περιβλεψάμενος—a characteristically Markan word) and leaves.

Mark 11:1-10 develops the use of the title Υἱὸς Δαυείδ, first found in the Bartimaeus episode. Bartimaeus is among those who follow

---

[12] See Stock, *Bib* 59 (1978) 488; E. Lohmeyer, *Das Evangelium des Markus* (Göttingen: Vandenhoeck & Ruprecht, [12]1953) 228.
[13] So also Stock, *Bib* 59 (1978) 500-04.

ἐν τῇ ὁδῷ (10:52), and it is some of those same disciples who recognise Jesus as the one who comes with the βασιλεία τοῦ πατρὸς ἡμῶν Δαυειδ (11:9,10). The double use of the word ἔρχομαι in 11:10 suggests that ''he who comes in the name of the Lord'' and the coming kingdom of David are synonymous. Jesus is God's representative who establishes this kingdom as he enters the city of David. The followers, in referring to David as πατήρ, naturally regard themselves as sons. This makes all the more pointed the argument in 12:35-37 which the reference here apparently anticipates. The people are sons of David, but Jesus is the one whom David himself calls 'Lord'.

The second day follows a similar pattern. Jesus comes again from Bethany (11:12) to Jerusalem (11:15), condemning the fig tree on the way. He is accompanied by the disciples, but when he enters the Temple they mysteriously disappear.[14] Indeed, Jesus' controversy with his adversaries in Mark 11,12, in marked contrast to 2:1-3:6, is consistently conducted in the absence of any followers.

The 'cleansing' of the Temple ends the second day (11:19). In 11:20 it is implicit that Jesus is once more journeying from Bethany with his disciples. The resumption of the fig tree episode suggests this. Mark 11:12-25 is a clear instance of the Evangelist's intercalation technique. The fact that the narrative extends over two days draws together the events of the second and third days at a theological level. The interposition of the Temple 'cleansing' shows that the condemnation of the fruitless fig tree is really symbolic of the rejection of fruitless Israel, of which 11:15-18 is an anticipation. The withering of the fig tree demonstrates that Jesus has the authority to destroy the old Judaic order. Both these questions are developed in the following pericopae—on Jesus' authority (11:27-33) and Israel's rejection (12:1-12). It is to be noted, too, that a further connection exists in the linguistic similarity between the redactional 11:18 and 12:12. In both cases the authorities (chief priests, scribes) wish to arrest or destroy Jesus, but are prevented from doing so by their fear of the crowd with whom Jesus enjoys popularity.

---

[14] The ἐξεπορεύοντο of 11:19 (ABW 28 565 700al itᶜ·ᵈ) indicates that when Jesus leaves for Bethany that evening, he is rejoined by his disciples. 01 D Θ f¹ f¹³ pm it, however, read the singular, ἐξεπορεύετο.

Mark 11:18
καὶ ἤκουσαν οἱ ἀρχιερεῖς
καὶ οἱ γραμματεῖς, καὶ ἐζήτουν
πῶς αὐτὸν ἀπολέσωσιν.
ἐφοβοῦντο γὰρ αὐτόν, πᾶς
γὰρ ὁ ὄχλος ἐξεπλήσσετο
ἐπὶ τῇ διδαχῇ αὐτοῦ.

Mark 12:12
καὶ ἐζήτουν αὐτὸν
κρατῆσαι καὶ ἐφοβήθησαν
τὸν ὄχλον.

The verb ἀπόλλυμι in 11:18 underscores Mark's insistence that Jesus is on an inevitable collision course with his opponents which can result only in destruction—his or theirs (cp. 2:22; 3:6; 12:9).

The third day adopts the same pattern as the other two: Jesus enters Jerusalem with his disciples, but is found alone in the Temple. At this point there occurs the first in a series of direct confrontations (11:27-33). The double question on authority (11:28) marks the climax to an on-going theme in the gospel: Does Jesus possess divine ἐξουσία? (1:22,27; 2:10; 3:15; 6:7). The ταῦτα of the opponents' question may refer specifically to Jesus' action in the Temple, but it may also embrace his activity in general.

Mark 12:1-12 belongs structurally to the preceding material rather than to what follows. First, it is implied that the opponents against whom Jesus tells the parable are those of 11:27—the chief priests, scribes and elders. This composite group does not reappear until 14:1. The opponents of 12:13-40, being predominantly scribal in nature, have an interest in legal matters which, in the case of the scribes and the Pharisees, has been their concern all along. But the chief priests work in quite a different way: they are determined to bring about the destruction of Jesus by as direct a means as possible. This is clear from their reaction to Jesus' 'cleansing' of the Temple, and their question in 11:28 is posed with this in mind; it is hoped to frame Jesus on a charge of blasphemy—the very charge by which he is finally condemned (14:61-64). Jesus' response is to tell the Parable of the Wicked Tenants (12:1-9) in which the religious leaders' own condemnation is asserted.

We find that in 12:13-40, where the chief priests are absent, these efforts to destroy Jesus are relaxed. The one episode here in which Jesus could conceivably have incriminated himself is the tax question (12:13-17), and in that instance we are informed at the outset that the Pharisees and Herodians were "sent" (ἀποστέλλουσιν), presumably by the chief priests. When the chief priests, scribes (and

elders) reappear in 14:1,2, the language of destruction is rein-
troduced. Indeed, these verses are linguistically akin to both 11:18
and 12:12. By 14:10,11, thanks to the assistance of Judas, the
priests have already achieved their objective; all that remains is to
make the arrest at the appointed time.

On the basis of these leadership-group patterns and their respective functions it is clear that Mark intends a sub-division between
12:12 and 12:13, for the rôle of the chief priests, scribes and elders
is quite different from that of the opponents in 12:13-40. The
priests manage to achieve within a few verses what the scribes and
Pharisees have failed—and perhaps never even intended—to do
throughout the entire Gospel. It is significant, indeed, that the story
of Jesus' final conquest over the legalists is actually interpolated
into the growing campaign of the chief priests to secure Jesus' condemnation.

Second, 12:10-12 recalls certain material from Mark 11. We
have mentioned already ἀπόλλυμι in this regard. To this we should
add the observation that the citation from Ps. 118:22,23 in Mark
12:10,11 is taken from virtually the same point in the psalm as the
citation in Mark 11:9,10 (cf. Ps. 118:26). The scripture by which
Mark shows how Jesus enters Jerusalem in the name of the Lord
is also that by which he shows that he whom the authorities have
chosen to reject has become the head of the corner by the Lord's
consent. These two quotations, in effect, present the entire passion
story in cameo form: Jesus enters Jerusalem as the Lord's
viceregent, bringing in the kingdom of David; he is rejected by the
Jewish leaders, but is raised to prominence by God.

Third, both 11:12-21 and 12:1-12 share the same theological
theme—the rejection of Israel. Just as the fig tree is destroyed
because it bears no fruit, and 11:15-18 applies this to all that the
Temple symbolises for Jewish institutionalism, so the tenants are
destroyed because they bear no fruit (καρπός—12:2; cf. 11:14) for
the vineyard owner. The action of God's Son in the Temple
foreshadows the destruction of the old order; the death of the son
in 12:8 spells destruction for the Jewish leaders.

At this point it will be convenient to summarise the conclusions
reached thus far:

i) Mark 11:1-12:12 contains two instances of the Markan intercalation technique—11:12-14/15-19/20-25 and 11:12-25/27-33/
12:1-12. The first of these is spread over two days of Mark's tem-

poral programme. According to Johnson,[15] this is due to the time-lapse necessary for the fig tree to wither, but Matt. 21:18-22 can do without it, and it appears more likely that by placing the Temple 'cleansing' at the end of the second day, Mark establishes this pericope as the climactic episode in the 'sandwich'. A similar climax is achieved at the end of the first day (11:10).

ii) The fig tree pericope is designed to interpret 11:15-18 (and *vice versa*, according to Lane).[16] The sayings on faith and prayer are not essentially part of this purpose,[17] but Mark possibly seized the opportunity here to show, by means of Jesus' teaching, what faith could achieve, and there may be a deliberate contrast between the faith advocated here and the Jewish leaders' implied lack of faith in the same chapter. Schweizer[18] suggests that these sayings may have been intended to serve as a midrash on the phrase 'house of prayer' (11:17).

iii) The second 'intercalation' is introduced by 11:12-25. I do not mean to suggest that Mark intended to apply the technique here as strictly as in the case of 11:12-14/15-19/20,21; nevertheless, there are points of relationship between the first intercalation and 12:1-12. There is, as we have seen, the stereotyped reaction of Jesus' adversaries (11:18; 12:12), but of especial significance is the use of καιρός/καρπός imagery. In both cases, the term καρπός is symbolic of the religious leaders whom God expects to bear fruit. Moreover, this fruitfulness is expected to occur at the appropriate time (καιρός—11:13; 12:2).[19] The theological implication is that the time has come with Jesus' arrival—an acclamation stressed by Mark as early as 1:15—but that the Jewish authorities have not borne the fruit expected of them, and so can expect only condemnation (11:20,21; 12:9). Common to both passages also is a hint of universalism. In 11:17 Jesus quotes from Isa. 56:7 to show that God intended the Temple as a place of worship for "all nations" (πᾶσιν

---

[15] Johnson, *Mark*, 191.

[16] Lane, *Mark*, 402.

[17] So E. Best, "Mark's Preservation of the Tradition", *L'Évangile selon Marc: Tradition et rédaction* (BETL 34; ed. M. Sabbe; Louvain: Leuven U.P., 1974) 30; but contra C.W.F. Smith, "No Time for Figs", *JBL* 79 (1960) 322.

[18] E. Schweizer, *Das Evangelium nach Markus* (Göttingen: Vandenhoeck & Ruprecht, 1968) 134.

[19] This correspondence between the fruit and its season in 12:2 makes more likely the view that the problematic ὁ γὰρ καιρὸς οὐκ σύκων (11:13) is original also. Space limitations will not permit a discussion of that thorny issue here, however.

τοῖς ἔθνεσιν), while in his parable he suggests that if the Jews cannot justify themselves as worthy tenants the vineyard must be given over "to others" (12:9).

The interposition of 11:27-33 is intended to show that the rejection of Israel in 11:12-21/12:1-9 occurs primarily because the leaders refuse to accept the divine authority of Jesus. In his reply to the question on authority Jesus presents the opponents with two clear alternatives regarding the baptism of John—was it from God, or was John only a self-styled baptist? It is clear that the authorities do not accept the first alternative, and since, by implication, it is suggested that Jesus' authority emanates from the same source as that of John it is hardly likely that the religious leaders would accept Jesus any more than they had accepted John. In refusing to believe in God's own messengers, they were bringing about their own condemnation.

iv) It is not likely that Mark intended his third day to extend to the end of Chapter 12[20] or 13. In 13:3 we do find Jesus back on the Mount of Olives, it is true, but that reference is more probably intended to introduce the apocalyptic discourse than to delimit the third day of the Markan scheme. We notice that in 11:17,18 the climactic scriptural citation followed by the redactional comment on the opponents' resolve to destroy Jesus effectively ends the second day. In 12:10-12, as already shown, the same pattern occurs. The change of leadership group after 12:12 may likewise indicate the conclusion there of the three-day scheme. Finally, we have the internal evidence of 14:49 that Jesus was teaching daily (καθ᾽ ἡμέραν) in the Temple, which would suggest that Mark never intended this part of the Jerusalem ministry (12:13-44) to belong to his three-day format.[21]

b) *Mark 12:13-44*

It remains for us to consider the structure of the material in 12:13-44. There is apparently no tight concentric structure here as in the corresponding controversy catena in 2:1-3:6. There exists instead a greater freedom of literary relationships in which may be

---

[20] So Lohmeyer, *Markus*, 238, but contra Stock, *Bib* 59 (1978) 485, 504.

[21] See Lohmeyer, *Markus*, 227; Smith, *JBL* 79 (1960) 316; F.J. Matera, *The Kingship of Jesus: Composition and Theology in Mark 15* (SBLDS 66; Chico: Scholars, 1982) 67, 68.

found overlapping patterns operating at different levels and on the basis of various criteria:

i) On the basis of Jesus' relationship with his opponents we can detect a loose five-pericope structure (12:13-40) corresponding in the broadest possible manner to 2:1-3:6.

ii) On the basis of the context of the locality data we can identify two triads (12:13-17/18-27/28-34 and 12:35-37/38-40/41-44) in which the first pericope of the first triad and the final pericope of the second are related.[22]

The first of these schemes takes into account the pattern suggested by the tenor of the controversies themselves. Mark 12:13-17 is by far the most malicious confrontation. Since the Galilean controversies end with the Pharisees and Herodians conspiring to destroy Jesus (3:6) it is appropriate that they should be the ones to raise the curtain on the Jerusalem conflict stories with the most hostile encounter of the catena. The Sadducees (12:18-27) are restricted to an attempt to ridicule Jesus' beliefs; they could not have hoped by this means to bring about his destruction. In 12:28-34, since even a scribe must acknowledge Jesus' wisdom, Jesus' triumph over his scribal opponents is assured. Next, he takes the offensive. The *Davidssohnfrage* (12:35-37) corresponds to 12:18-27, for it has a touch of *boruth* about it. Just as the Sadducees ridicule a belief which Jesus regards as being essentially correct, so now Jesus disparages—superficially, at any rate—a belief of the scribes which they acknowledge to be based on scriptural authority. Mark 12:38-40 is pure polemic against the scribes and their practices. The prediction by Jesus that they will receive judgement makes this pericope correspond to 12:13-17 where it is hoped that Jesus' own

---

[22] An alternative scheme could be arrived at by taking account of the proposals of Daube (*Rabbinic Judaism*, 158-69; idem, "Four types of Question", *JTS* ns 2 (1951) 45-48; idem, "The Earliest Structure of the Gospels", *NTS* 5 (1958-59) 180-84) and Lauverjat (*ETR* 55 (1980) 416-20). Daube argues that the four questions in Mark 12:13-37 may correspond formally to a rabbinic tradition underlying both the four-question form outlined in b. *Niddah* 69b-71a and the Passover Haggadah in which questions about the meaning of the festival are posed by different types of son (see j. *Pesah* 37d; Mek.R.Ish.Exod. 13:8,14). The four units suggested by Daube and those delineated by Lauverjat could be conveniently juxtaposed:

12:13-17/18-27/28-34/35-37 (Daube)
12:37b-40/41-42/43-44/13:1,2 (Lauverjat).

However, the four-element form in Mark, if it exists at all, is not common, and the proposals of both the aforenamed scholars are open to question.

judgement will be secured. On this level, then, we have, in essence, an informal chiastic arrangement:

a-12:13-17:   Opponents' attempt to condemn Jesus
b-12:18-27:   Opponents' attempt to ridicule Jesus
c-12:28-34:   An 'opponent' acknowledges Jesus. Jesus triumphs over the opposition.
b'-12:35-37:   Jesus attempts to ridicule his opponents
a'-12:38-40:   Jesus warns of his opponents' condemnation.

On a different level it may be possible to argue for a double triadic arrangement.[23] In 12:13-34, Jesus is assailed by various Jewish leaders, each of whom addresses him as διδάσκαλε (12:14,19,32) and poses some kind of question. We assume from the context (cf. 11:27) that the setting is the Temple. It is not until 12:35-44, however, that Jesus is presented as teaching of his own volition (12:35,38). Moreover, in the second triad, the scene is reset: we learn that his teaching occurs specifically in the Temple (12:35,41). In 12:35-40 Jesus denounces the scribes, but there is no direct encounter here as in 12:13-34.[24] Mark 12:41-44 certainly belongs to the second triad, for the widow's behaviour is deliberately set in antithetic relation to that of the scribes at whose hands widows suffer (cf. 12:40,42). Dewey's arguments, too, indicate that 12:13-34 should be distinguished from 12:35-44.[25]

---

[23] See Burkill, ZNW 51 (1960) 42. Mark 12:13-34, he contends, stresses the wisdom of Jesus in replying to his opponents, while 12:35-44 is characterised by Jesus as the assailant of his opponents. The first triad is concluded by the statement, καὶ οὐδεὶς οὐκέτι ἐτόλμα αὐτὸν ἐπερωτῆσαι. In the second triad the redactional embellishments tend to associate the pericopae with the Temple (12:35,41). The statement, καὶ ἐκπορευομένου αὐτοῦ ἐκ τοῦ ἱεροῦ... in 13:1 effectively concludes this sequence. Although the proposed triadic arrangement appears to work well enough in the present case, it is possible to be too rigorous in this respect. Lohmeyer (Markus) regards the entire Gospel as a series of triads, and in more recent years R. Pesch (Markusevangelium 2.1-27; idem, Das Evangelium der Urgemeinde (Freiburg-Basel-Wien: Herder, 1979)) has advanced a similar view with regard to his proposed pre-Markan Passion source. But rigid structure should not be made the procrustean bed for all other considerations any more than vice versa.

[24] In the Matthean parallel to Mark 12:35-37 the adversaries are specified as being present (Matt. 22:41), and the use of the second person pronoun in the scribal denunciation which follows (Matt. 23) suggests their presence on that occasion, too.

[25] Dewey, Markan Public Debate, 158-59. Her argument rests chiefly on form. Both 12:13-17 and 12:28-34 contain a double question/statement-response sequence, thus enveloping 12:18-27 which has but a single version of that form. The pericopae in 12:35-44, of course, have a different form entirely.

It is all the more likely that 12:13-34, 35-44 should be taken as two triads when it is recognised that a similar arrangement occurs in 11:12-12:12. And just as the first two triads are interlinked by means of 11:12-25, so those in 12:13-34,35-44 are likewise related. We saw that the image of fruit in its season (καρπός/καιρός) stood at the extremities of the double triad in 11:12-12:12, and the same phenomenon is to be found in its counterpart, 12:13-44. In 12:13-17 Jesus advises that what belongs to Caesar should be rendered to Caesar, and what belongs to God should be rendered to God. Since the census coin bears Caesar's image and inscription, it follows that it is part of his property. But what belongs to God? To some extent, that question is answered in 12:30 where Deut. 6:5 is cited, but it is not specified there what "love of God" means in practice. In 12:41-44 it is! Just as 12:13-17 concerns the poll tax, so the story of the widow's mite concerns the Temple tax. The widow demonstrates her love and devotion to God by using the Temple in the manner for which it was intended. It is not so much the widow's coins which belong to God as her sacrificial attitude in giving them. In rendering to Caesar one's attitude is of no account; because Caesar's coin bears his stamp, it must necessarily return ultimately to its source. What belongs to God, however, is precisely man's right attitude towards him. He neither requires nor accepts the external 'religious' trappings which the Jewish leaders use to glorify themselves.

If we are able to connect 12:13-17 and 12:41-44 in this manner, it is possible also that the two λίθος passages (12:10,11; 13:1,2) may form a frame around the double triad.

It is possible now to summarise the results of our enquiry in the following table:

The Structure of Mark 11:1-13:2

10:46-52: Healing of Bartimaeus (transitional)
DAY 1- 11:1-11:   Triumphal entry
                      Citation: Ps. 118:26
DAY 2- 11:12-14:   Condemnation of the fig tree
                      καιρός/καρπός terminology
        11:15-19:   'Cleansing' of the Temple
DAY 3- 11:20-25:   Withered fig tree
                      Faith/prayer
        11:27-33:   Question on authority
        12:1-12:   Parable of Wicked Tenants
                      καιρός/καρπός terminology
                      Citation: Ps. 118:22,23 (λίθος)

End of Three-Day Scheme

12:13-17:	Question on taxes
	Poll-tax
	What belongs to God?
12:18-27:	Question on resurrection
12:28-34:	Question on first commandment
12:35-37:	*Davidssohnfrage*
12:38-40:	Condemnation of the scribes
12:41-44:	Widow's mite
	Temple-tax
	Love/devotion belong to God

13:1,2: Temple prophecy (λιθός) (transitional)

IV — *The Relationship Between Structure and Theology in Mark 11:1-13:2*

We have argued that Mark 11:1-12:44 consists of various subsections. The first of these, 11:1-12:12, contains an introduction in which Jesus is presented as the messianic king coming in triumph to his holy city and Temple. Much of the journey appears to be a re-enactment of the prophecies in Zechariah, notably Zech. 9:9; 14:4, and it is evident that this Markan presentation of Jesus as a Davidic deliverer is intended to contrast sharply with the next movement of the narrative (11:12-12:12) in which Jesus' rôle as judge of his people confounds the traditional Jewish notion of messiahship. The two closely related citations from Ps. 118 (Mark 11:9,10; 12:10,11) actually form a kind of *inclusio*, marking off these judgement pericopae from the remainder of the section.

In each of the narratives in 11:12-12:12, apart from 11:27-33, Jesus is presented as the judge who indicts his people through symbolism and parable. His condemnation of the fig tree is really a condemnation of fruitless Israel, while the so-called 'cleansing' of the Temple directs this condemnation to the cultic heart of Jewish institutionalism. Unlike the performance of similar rituals in bygone days (2 Kgs. 22:3-23:25; 2 Chr. 29:12-36; 34:3-35:19; Neh. 13:4-9; I Macc. 4:36-61; 2 Macc. 10:1-8) Jesus' act was not for resanctification, but for destruction: the cultic régime of the Jewish leaders was coming to an end. A specific reason for this judgement is suggested in the parable in 12:1-9 where, although Jesus may have been rebuking the leaders for their treatment of God's prophets, Mark clearly regards their treatment of God's own Son as the prime reason for their judgement.

Within the context of the adjacent pericopae, the question on authority (11:27-33) takes on a significance beyond that which is superficially evident. The question, 'Εν ποίᾳ ἐξουσίᾳ ταῦτα ποιεῖς; refers not only to Jesus' 'cleansing' of the Temple, nor even only to the work and words of Jesus in general, but to the rôle of Jesus as judge of Israel. This narrative represents the sum total of all other questions about authority because, in a sense, it transcends them all. For Jesus to act as judge of his people would be to claim the divine prerogative more openly and more boldy than ever before, and, of course, this is precisely what Mark intends to assert: for him Jesus is God, no less.

The next sub-section consists of three narratives—12:13-17,18-27,28-34. The first two distinguish sharply between the beliefs of the religious leaders and those of Jesus who is at this point presented as a sage deftly side-stepping the devious designs of his adversaries. In 12:13-17 he turns the question of the Pharisees and Herodians on its head, showing that the emphasis placed by the opponents on whether or not one should pay taxes to Caesar should be transferred to the matter of what is due to God. When one has made a response to the latter issue, the initial question answers itself.

In 12:18-27 Jesus appears to be siding with the Pharisees against the Sadducees on the resurrection issue, and in 12:28-34 the favourable response of a scribe indicates, as we have seen, that Jesus has finally triumphed in his long struggle with the legalists. In his offensive against the scribes (12:35-40) the note of judgement (κρίμα) returns. Having already served as judge against cultic· Israel, Jesus now condemns legal Israel for her misconceptions of messiahship (12:35-37) and abuse of the law (12:38-40). True obedience to the law as epitomised by *a* scribe in 12:28-34, and particularly in the double citation from Deut. 6:4; Lev. 19:18, is sharply contrasted with the legal deception of the scribes as a group; so, too, is the example of the poor widow in 12:44.

In all this, we can appreciate that the structure of Mark 11,12 reveals an image of a Jesus who assumes the rôle of God as both plaintiff and judge of his people—a symbolism which is ultimately deutero-Isaianic.[26] Cultic stagnation and abuses of the Law—and, of course, from Mark's own perspective, the crucifixion of Jesus—

---

[26] See, for instance, Isa. 41:1-5,21-29; 43:8-13; 44:6-8; 45:18-25.

bring condemnation, but glimpses of the true road to God, through loving obedience and devotion, are provided, in marked contrast, by a scribe and a widow.

V — Mark and His Community

Why is the theme of judgement so prominent in 11:1-12,44? The answer may lie in the political and religious milieu of the Markan Gospel. Although we cannot argue our case here, there is a strong possibility that Mark was written shortly before the fall of Jerusalem in A.D. 70, and probably in Rome. The Jews were the butt of Roman hostility, and the onset of the Jewish war suggested to our Evangelist that the destruction of the old cultic centre was inevitable. Thus, the Gospel as a whole, and 11:1-12:44 in particular, represents a rallying-cry to the Markan community. It is a call, especially, to the Jewish (or Judaising-) Christians of that community who may still have felt tempted to adopt the cultic and legalistic stance of their 'orthodox' brethren. Mark's message to them is to abandon the old Jewish institutionalism on which decisive and irrevocable judgement is about to be passed, and to fully embrace the community of the New Age which symbolises a new, sanctified Temple characterised by the obedience of that community to God. The inertia of Jewish institutionalism and the nature of Jewish disobedience is spelled out (11:12-22; 12:1-9,35-40), and it is suggested that the one means of escape from God's condemnation is true obedience to him. This sentiment is developed in three stages: Christians must render to God what they owe him (12:13-17); that which is owed to him is the believer's love and devotion (12:28-34); the self-sacrificial attitude of the poor widow provides a practical example of what this love and devotion implies (12:41-44).

Jesus' affirmation of the Pharisaic doctrine of the resurrection in 12:18-27 may have been located here by Mark to reassure his readers that the resurrection promise still held good—a consideration which would have been of some importance in view of the troubled times which the community would have been forced to endure. For the same reason, Mark may have found it expedient to tone down the political implications of messiahship. Thus, the title 'Son of David' in 12:35-37 is intentionally divorced from its traditional politico-nationalist associations (πῶς λέγουσιν οἱ γραμματεῖς ὅτι ὁ Χριστὸς υἱὸς Δαυειδ ἐστιν;). Mark decided to accord the title a more ethical interpretation, insisting that it could be understood only in the light of other christological terms—Lord, Son of man and Son of God. To have presented Jesus as a nationalist Messiah in a mixed Jewish-Roman community, c.A.D. 68-69, would have been disastrous—hence the need for the Evangelist to commend to his community an ethical universalism rather than a political nationalism.

One final point! Doubt has sometimes been cast on the suggestion that the message of Mark 11:1-12:44 was primarily for Jewish-Christians. Might not the Evangelist's polemic have been aimed at the Jews as a whole? There was, after all, a large contingent of them in Rome. I would make just two points here. First, Mark would hardly have expected Jewish non-Christians to read his Gospel, so he could not have been appealing to them, only polemicising against them. This polemic would have been effective only for those *inside* the community—in effect, Do not follow those Jewish outsiders on the road to condemnation! Secondly, Mark appeals throughout his Gospel to the ἐξουσία of Jesus: Christians have the authority to act and believe as they do precisely because Jesus possessed that authority first (see especially 11:27-33). But such an appeal would have fallen on deaf ears had it been intended for the 'orthodox' Jewish sector of the populace. The authority of Jesus would have meant nothing to the ordinary Jew, for unlike the 'insider' he would not have accepted it. For these reasons, I suggest that Mark was appealing passionately to those Jewish-Christians in his community who, bewildered by the turn of political events, were wavering on the precipice of apostasy.

MARKAN SANDWICHES
THE SIGNIFICANCE OF INTERPOLATIONS
IN MARKAN NARRATIVES

by

JAMES R. EDWARDS

Jamestown, North Dakota

1. *Introduction*

Readers of the Gospel of Mark are familiar with the Second Evangelist's convention of breaking up a story or pericope by inserting a second, seemingly unrelated, story into the middle of it. A good example occurs in chapter 5 where Jairus, a ruler of the synagogue, importunes Jesus to heal his daughter (vv 21-24). A woman with a hemorrhage interrupts Jesus *en route* to Jairus' house (vv 25-34), and only after recording the woman's healing does Mark resume with the raising of Jairus' daughter, who had died in the meantime (vv 35-43). Another example occurs in chapter 11 where Mark separates the cursing of the fig tree (vv 12-14) and its subsequent withering (vv 20-21) with Jesus' clearing of the temple (vv 15-19). This technique occurs some nine times in the Gospel: Mark begins story A, introduces story B, then returns to and completes story A.

These inserted middles have been variously indentified as intercalations,[1] interpolations,[2] insertions,[3] framing,[4] or, in German, as

---

[1] E.B. Redlich, *St. Mark's Gospel. A Modern Commentary* (London: Gerald Duckworth & Co. Ltd, 1948) 35; T.A. Burkill, *Mysterious Revelation. An Examination of the Philosophy of St. Mark's Gospel* (Ithaca: Cornell University Press, 1963) 121; J.R. Donahue, *Are You the Christ? The Trial Narrative in the Gospel of Mark* (SBLDS 10; Missoula: Scholars Press, 1973) 42; J. Dewey, *Markan Public Debate. Literary Technique, Concentric Structure, and Theology in Mark 2:1-3:6* (SBLDS 48; Chico: Scholars Press, 1980) 21; R. Fowler, *Loaves and Fishes. The Function of the Feeding Stories in the Gospel of Mark* (SBLDS 54; Chico: Scholars Press, 1981) 165.

[2] H.C. Kee, *Community of the New Age. Studies in Mark's Gospel* (London: SCM Press, 1977) 54.

[3] D.E. Nineham, *The Gospel of St Mark* (Pelican Gospel Commentaries; Penguin Books, 1963) 112.

[4] D. Rhoads, "Narrative Criticism and the Gospel of Mark," *JAAR* 50 (3, 1982) 424.

Schiebungen[5] or *Ineinanderschachtelungen*.[6] A more graphic description, and one I prefer, is to refer to Mark's A-B-A literary convention as a sandwich technique.[7]

Until recently commentators on the Gospel of Mark have paid relatively little attention to this convention. This neglect is largely due to the influence of the form-critical method, the chief objectives of which are to recover, as far as possible, the units of oral tradition which became the building blocks of the later written Gospels.[8] The quest includes the recovery of a possible *Urmarkus*, a written source which lay beneath the Second Gospel. As long as interest was directed to the sources of the Gospel of Mark (i.e., oral units and forms, historical background, earlier prototypes, etc.) rather than the canonical text, the Gospel of Mark *as a literary product* was judged rather like one of Cinderella's ugly stepsisters. Günther Dehn decreed that Mark was "neither a historian nor an author. He assembled his material in the simplest manner thinkable."[9] Bultmann said that "Mark is not sufficiently master of his material to be able to venture on a systematic construction himself."[10] Etienne Trocmé scoffed at Mark's literary achievement: "The point is settled: the author of Mark was a clumsy writer unworthy of mention in any history of literature."[11]

The past two decades have witnessed the rise of new methods in Gospel interpretation. These have not supplanted form criticism,

---

[5] E. von Dobschütz, "Zur Erzählerkunst des Markus," *ZNW* 27 (1928) 193.

[6] E. Klostermann, *Das Markus-Evangelium*[4] (HNT; Tübingen: J.C.B. Mohr [Paul Siebeck], 1950) 36, or "Verschachtelungen," so H.-W. Kuhn, *Ältere Sammlungen im Markusevangelium* (Göttingen: Vandenhoeck & Ruprecht, 1971) 200-01. J. Schniewind (*Das Evangelium nach Markus*[4] [NTD; Göttingen: Vandenhoeck & Ruprecht, 1949] 148) calls them "Verschmelzungen."

[7] So F. Neirynck, *Duality in Mark: Contributions to the Study of the Markan Redaction* (BETL 31; Leuven: Leuven University Press, 1973) 133; R. Stein, "The Proper Methodology for Ascertaining a Markan Redaction History," *NovT* 13 (1971) 193; E. Best, *The Temptation and the Passion: the Markan Soteriology* (SNTSMS 2; Cambridge: The University Press, 1965) 74, 83.

[8] According to R. Bultmann these oral units can be classified variously as apophthegms, Jesus logia, prophetic and apocalyptic sayings, 'I' sayings, legal sayings and church rules, miracle stories, and historical stories and legends. See *The History of the Synoptic Tradition* (Rev. ed.), trans. J. Marsh (New York and Evanston: Harper and Row, 1968).

[9] G. Dehn, *Der Gottessohn. Eine Einführung in das Evangelium des Markus* (Hamburg: Im Furche-Verlag, 1953) 18.

[10] *Hist. Syn. Trad.*, 350.

[11] E. Trocmé, *The Formation of the Gospel According to Mark*, trans. P. Gaughan (London: SPCK, 1975) 72.

but they have brought alternative perspectives to bear which have broadened and deepened our understanding of the Gospels. Of significance for this study is the structuralist approach. Structuralism is indebted to redaction criticism which rightly perceived that the authors of the canonical gospels were not witless water boys schlepping water from a spring (a creative oral tradition) to thirsty hordes (the readers). They were themselves creative theologians who molded the tradition which they received for their individual purposes. Structuralism, however, goes a step further and examines the literary patterns or structures which the Evangelists employed in the construction of their narratives. Not surprisingly, structuralists have had the most to say about Mark's sandwich technique.

The current state of research on this issue reminds one of a scene in Wilson Rawls's *Where the Red Fern Grows*. Night after night the hounds chase a raccoon to the same big oak, only to find that the "phantom coon" has eluded them. Similarly, not a few scholars have found their way to the right tree, but they have yet to produce the coon. That is to say, they recognize that Mark intentionally sandwiches one account into another, but they cannot agree what he achieves by doing so. Some scholars, for example, simply note Mark's sandwiches without discussing their purpose.[12] Others believe that Mark employs his sandwich technique to heighten suspense or allow for the passage of time.[13] Still others, particularly American rhetorical critics, believe that the sandwiching of two stories together intends to establish a relationship between the stories, even if the exact nature of the relationship cannot be identified.[14] Finally, a few scholars suggest that the purpose of Mark's

---

[12] Redlich, *St. Mark's Gospel*, 35-37; D. Rhoads, "Narrative Criticism," 424.

[13] Von Dobschütz ("Erzählerkunst," 193) says that "The art of a good narrator...intends to awaken in his listeners the illusion of a longer period of time or a larger spatial distance." D. Nineham (*The Gospel of St Mark*, 112) says "(St Mark is fond of insertions between two halves of a single story, time being thus given for the initial action to develop.)" Also, Bultmann, *Hist. Syn. Trad.*, 301-02. A time lapse, to be sure, plays a role in some sandwiches (e.g., 5:21-43; 11:12-21), but it is not itself the reason for the sandwich. If the creation of a time lapse were Mark's intent, it would be necessary to address the question why Mark, who uses the word "immediately" some 40 times, and who narrates his Gospel in an otherwise rapid-fire fashion, would need to create the illusion of a passage of time at these particular points?

[14] Dewey says, "Intercalation is primarily a literary device and should be studied first in terms of rhetorical terms, to see how the intercalation affects the

sandwich technique is not in itself literary but *theological*.[15] In this respect John Donahue's conclusions are the most specific. He argues that "Mark uses the technique of intercalation to underscore two major themes of his gospel, the way of suffering of Jesus, and the necessity of the disciples to follow Jesus on this way."[16]

2. Thesis

The purpose of this study will be to argue that Mark sandwiches one passage into the middle of another with an intentional and discernible *theological purpose*. The technique is, to be sure, a literary technique, but its purpose is theological; that is, the sandwiches emphasize the major motifs of the Gospel, especially the meaning of faith, discipleship, bearing witness, and the dangers of apostasy. Moreover, I shall endeavor to show that *the middle story nearly always provides the key to the theological purpose* of the sandwich. The insertion interprets the flanking halves. To use the language of medicine, the transplanted organ enlivens the host material.

The establishment of this thesis will require three investigations. First, we shall attempt to define as precisely as possible the characteristics of a Markan sandwich. Second, we shall investigate whether there are any precedents for Mark's sandwich technique in

---

progression of the narrative" (*Markan Public Debate*, 22). R. Fowler says the technique "demands that the reader view these episodes together as a whole" (*Loaves and Fishes*, 165). E. Klostermann sees the technique as a "literary intention to place related material together" (*Markus-Evangelium*, 36). More specifically, T.A. Burkill thinks the technique serves either to stress a parallel or a contrast between the two stories (*Mysterious Revelation*, 121). L. Gaston notes a relationship but cannot decide whether the surrounding story or the inserted story provides the interpretive key (*No Stone on Another. Studies in the Significance of the Fall of Jerusalem in the Synoptic Gospels* [Leiden: E.J. Brill, 1970] 83, fn 1).

[15] See R. Stein: "It is quite evident that when the Evangelist inserts a statement into some tradition that he does so in order to comment upon or explain that tradition to his readers. The investigation of this comment will therefore reveal something of the Evangelist's particular theology..." ("Proper Methodology," 184). Less specifically, H.C. Kee suggests that interpolations heighten dramatic impact of the material, but also that they make the material more acceptable to Mark's community, or make Jesus' trial and death better conform to what God ordained in scripture (*Community of the New Age*, 56).

[16] *Are You the Christ?*, 62. Again, "[Mark] uses [the intercalated material] to cast over the whole gospel the shadow of the cross, and all intercalations contain some allusion to the suffering and death of Jesus," *Ibid*, 60.

pre-Christian literature, particularly in the Hebrew Bible. And third, each of the sandwich units in the Gospel will require individual examination.

3. *Characteristics of Markan Sandwiches*

Each Markan interpolation concerns a larger (usually narrative) unit of material consisting of *two* episodes or stories which are narrated in *three* paragraphs or pericopes. The whole follows an A^1-B-A^2 schema, in which the B-episode forms an independent unit of material, whereas the flanking A-episodes require one another to complete their narrative. The B-episode consists of only one story; it is not a series of stories, nor itself so long that the reader fails to link A^2 with A^1.[17] Finally, A^2 normally contains an allusion at its beginning which refers back to A^1, e.g., repetition of a theme, proper nouns, etc.[18]

On the basis of these criteria it is possible to identify nine sandwiches in the Gospel of Mark:

1. 3:20-35
   A Jesus' companions try to seize him, vv 20-21
   B The religious leaders accuse Jesus of being in league with Beelzeboul, vv 22-30
   A Jesus' family seeks him, vv 31-35
2. 4:1-20
   A Parable of the Sower, vv 1-9
   B Purpose of parables, vv 10-13
   A Explanation of the Parable of the Sower, vv 14-20

---

[17] Redlich (*St. Mark's Gospel*, 35) suggests that the five conflict stories between Mark 2:1 and 3:6 are an insertion, but this constitutes a unit of material so long that few readers would think of linking 3:7 back with 1:45.

[18] The sandwich phenomenon under consideration here is not to be confused with smaller units of sayings-material, sometimes referred to as "insertions." See, for example, the lists of such brief parenthetical units, and the attempts to categorize them, in F. Neirynck, *Duality in Mark*, 131-33; J. Donahue, *Are You the Christ?*, 241-43; and F.C. Synge, "Intruded Middles," *ExpT* 92 (11, 1981) 329-33. R. Fowler's list in *Loaves and Fishes*, 164-65, follows Donahue's. While not wishing to deny that Mark may have employed a sandwich technique on a smaller scale, the criteria for identifying insertions, often depending on the mere repetition of a word or phrase, seem to me notoriously subjective. Of a combined total of 58 "insertions" listed in Neirynck and Donahue, for example, the authors agree on only two!

3. 5:21-43

   A Jairus pleads with Jesus to save his daughter, vv 21-24

   B Woman with a hemorrhage touches Jesus, vv 25-34

   A Jesus raises Jairus's daughter, vv 35-43

4. 6:7-30

   A Mission of the Twelve, vv 7-13

   B Martyrdom of John the Baptist, vv 14-29

   B Return of the Twelve, v 30

5. 11:12-21

   A Cursing of the fig tree, vv 12-14

   B Clearing of the temple, vv 15-19

   A Withering of the fig tree, vv 20-21

6: 14:1-11

   A Plot to kill Jesus, vv 1-2

   B Anointing of Jesus at Bethany, vv 3-9

   A Judas's agreement to betray Jesus, vv 10-11

7. 14:17-31[19]

   A Jesus predicts his betrayal, vv 17-21

   B Institution of the Lord's Supper, vv 22-26

   A Jesus predicts Peter's betrayal, vv 27-31

8. 14:53-72

   A Peter follows Jesus to the courtyard of the high priest, vv 53-54

   B Jesus' inquisition before the Sanhedrin, vv 55-65

   A Peter's denial of Jesus, vv 66-72

9. 15:40-16:8[20]

   A Women at the cross, vv 15:40-41

   B Joseph of Arimathea requests Jesus' body, vv 15:42-46

   A Women at the empty tomb, vv 15:47-16:8

A comparison of these passages within the synoptic tradition reveals that in two instances both Matthew and Luke follow Mark's

---

[19] The material in 14:1-31 can be viewed variously. E. Best (*Temptation and Passion*, 91) sees in it a "double sandwich." I view it otherwise. The instructions for the preparation of the passover in 14:12-16 appear to me as a neutral or buffer unit between sandwich 6 and 7.

[20] Kee (*Community of the New Age*, 54), Neirynck (*Duality in Mark*, 133), and Fowler (*Loaves and Fishes*, 165) identify 15:6-15/16-20/21-32 as a sandwich. The material, however, fails to display the characteristics of a sandwich listed above and appears to be simply a part of the passion progression in 15:1-39.

A-B-A order,[21] in two instances neither follows Mark,[22] and in five instances either Matthew[23] or Luke[24] follows Mark's pattern. In other words, of Mark's nine sandwiches, Matthew retains Mark's A-B-A pattern five times and Luke retains it four times. That is not to say, however, that Matthew and Luke reproduce 50% of Mark's sandwiches. Even though Mark's A-B-A sequence is retained by one or the other, his intention is often lost.

The above comparison demonstrates that, over against Matthew and Luke, Mark shows a distinct proclivity for the sandwich technique. Given this fact, it may not be irrelevant to recall the *testimonium Papiae*. As recorded by Eusebius,[25] Papias said that Mark "wrote accurately, though not actually in order" (*akribōs egrapsen, ou mentoi taxei*). Moreover, continued Papias, it was not Mark's purpose to produce a catena of dominical sayings (*all' ouch hōsper suntaxin tōn kuriakōn poioumenos logiōn*). Three times in the brief *testimonium* Papias attests that the reliability of Mark's Gospel derives from the authority of Peter, thus assuring Papias's readers that the *content* of the Gospel is apostolic. With regard to *form*, however, Papias says that Mark followed his own designs—and that "he did no wrong" in doing so.[26] The stylistic liberty, or artistry, as I should like to call it, of Mark's sandwich technique appears to corroborate Papias's testimony of Mark's literary design.

4. *Precedents for the Sandwich Technique in Pre-Markan Literature?*

Before turning to Markan sandwiches it is worth inquiring whether the inserting of one story into the middle of another,

---

[21] Mark 4:1-20//Matt 13:1-23//Luke 8:4-15; Mark 5:21-43//Matt 9:18-26//Luke 8:40-56.

[22] Mark 3:20-35: see Matt 12:22-32 and 12:46-50, and Luke 11:14-23; 12:10, 8:19-21. Mark 11:12-22: see Matt 21:12-20 and Luke 19:45-48.

[23] Mark 14:1-11//Matt 26:1-16; Mark 14:17-31//Matt 26:20-35; Mark 14:53-72//Matt 26:57-75.

[24] Mark 6:7-30//Luke 9:1-10; Mark 15:40-16:8//Luke 23:49-24:8.

[25] *Hist. eccl.* 3, 39, 15.

[26] On the relationship between Petrine authority and Markan style, see J. Kürzinger, "Die Aussage des Papias von Hierapolis zur literarischen Form des Markusevangeliums," *BZ* 21 (1977) 245-64. For a positive assessment of the Papias testimony, see M. Hengel, *Studies in the Gospel of Mark*, trans. J. Bowden (London: SCM Press, 1985) 47-50. Hengel says, "The main objection against the note in Papias, advanced by the representatives of the form-critical school, namely that the Second Gospel is not a literary work but a conglomerate of anonymous, popular and collective Jesus tradition, has now proved invalid"(47).

wherein the middle story provides the hermeneutical key for the understanding of the whole, can be found in literature prior to Mark. The question is relevant to determine whether Mark followed a prior precedent, or whether his sandwich technique may be said to originate with himself.

There are many examples in ancient literature where an author interrupts one story with another in order to achieve a desired effect. A good example is the story of the scar of Odysseus in the 19th book of the *Odyssey*. Odysseus has been away from Ithaca for twenty years and on his return home he had disguised himself as a beggar in order to size up the opposition which has beset the faithful Penelope in his absence. So effective is his disguise that Penelope fails to recognize him. She nevertheless takes pity on the beggar and orders her maidservant and Odysseus's old nurse, Euryclea, to bathe the stranger...whereupon Euryclea recognizes Odysseus by a scar on his leg. The scar provides Homer with the occasion for a (three-page) digression how Odysseus had received the wound by a wild boar, and information relating to his youth and parents. The insertion creates a momentary retardation of the plot, as E. Auerbach noted,[27] and heightens suspense. The interruption is, however, a *suspension* of the plot, not an interpretation of it. It is an effective flashback by which Homer baits his readers at a crucial part of the story.

A similar though less effective digression is found in the *Iliad* (16. 155ff), where Homer describes the aid brought by the Myrmidons in the midst of the ship burning scene. As the flames leap the poet compares the heroic arrival of the Myrmidons with a pack of wolves, and even describes their troop formations and background on their leaders. Homer again makes dramatic use of the flashbach to create suspense as well as to provide information which he felt necessary. From a literary-critical perspective, however, the insertion interrupts the plot, it does not interpret it.

It is sometimes difficult to judge if a pericope contains an insertion or not. In the sixth chapter of 2 Maccabees, for example, we read of Gentile atrocities in Jerusalem narrated in the third person (vv 1-11). This is followed by a theodicy in the first person in which the author avers that God's punishment is for the purpose of

---

[27] *Mimesis. Dargestellte Wirklichkeit in der abendländischen Literatur* (Bern: A. Francke Verlag, 1946) 7-11.

disciplining the Jews, not destroying them (vv 12-17). Thereafter the Gentile atrocities resume with the story of the martyrdom of Eleazar, again narrated in the third person. Another example occurs in 2 Maccabees 14-15. Nicanor pursues Judas Maccabeus to the temple (vv 31-36), this is followed by the martyrdom of Razis, a member of the Jewish senate (vv 37-46), and then the story of Nicanor's sabbath attack on Judas in Samaria is recounted (15:1-5). Is the middle story in these instances an insertion, or not? One *might* argue in the affirmative, particularly in the account in 2 Maccabees 6. On the other hand, it seems more plausible that in the author's mind the above episodes represented consecutive events which were related without transitions between them.

There is an insertion, however, in 2 Maccabees 8. Verses 23-29 describe the Jewish battle with Nicanor, the same encounter being resumed in verses 34-36. The continuity is broken, however, with the unexplained interjection of a Jewish battle against Timothy and Bacchides in verses 30-33. At the very least we have here a jumbled chronology. But why the author included verses 30-33 at this point, and what he intended in doing so, if anything, is difficult to say.

The case for interpretive insertions improves somewhat in the Hebrew Scriptures. There, in selected instances, we encounter something resembling the Markan sandwich technique, wherein a host pericope receives new meaning by a second pericope inserted into it.

The best example is perhaps the story of Hosea and Gomer (Hos 1-3). God commands Hosea "to take a harlot ($z^e n\hat{u}n\hat{\imath}m$) for a wife and raise up harlot's children ($z^e n\hat{u}n\hat{\imath}m$), because the land has played the harlot (*zanoh*) and is unfaithful to Yahweh" (Hos 1:2). But the narrative of Gomer and her three children is interrupted in chapter two by a prophetic speech. Speaking as a wronged husband, God proclaims both the judgment and restoration of his faithless wife, Israel. The prophecy reaches its climax in 2:14ff with God's gracious renewal of the covenant with Israel. "And I will say to 'Not-my-people,' 'You are my people, ' and he will say, 'You are my God'" (2:25). The story of Hosea and Gomer then resumes in chapter three with Hosea's redeeming Gomer from slavery and restoring her as his wife. "[Hosea] said to her, 'Many days you shall live with me, neither playing the harlot nor knowing another man'" (Hos 3:3).

In a skillfully constructed A-B-A narrative the prophet celebrates

the triumph of Yahweh's grace over fallen Israel. The effect is
enhanced by a prose (ch 1)–poetry (ch 2)–prose (ch 3) alternation
in style. The restoration of Gomer from a harlot (ch 1) to a faithful
wife (ch 3) depends on the divine decree in chapter two, namely,
that love—and not damnation—will be God's final word with
faithless Israel. In other words, the resolution of the Hosea-Gomer
story is contingent on the middle oracle which gives meaning to and
restores a broken relationship.[28]

Another example of sandwiching is the David-Bathsheba story,
into which the Nathan prophecy is inserted (2 Sam 11:1-12:25). In
suspenseful narration the author recounts David's intrigue and
adultery with Bathsheba and the order of Uriah's death (ch 11). In
one episode David has broken three of the Ten Commandments—
covetousness, adultery, murder—and has succeeded in avoiding
detection. Or so it seems, until the narrator adds, "But what David
had done was wrong in the eyes of the Lord" (11:27). Then comes
Nathan's parable about the rich shepherd who robbed his neighbor
of his dear ewe lamb—and its devastating conclusion, "You are the
man" (12:1-7). Thereafter follows a story of judgment (in the death
of the child) and grace (in the birth of Solomon, vv 7-25). Central
to the whole is Nathan's parable, which breaks the continuity of the
narrative yet provides the key to its understanding, for the parable
allows David to see his action from God's perspective.

There may be other examples of sandwiching in the Hebrew
Scriptures. Auerbach suggests that the death of Absalom in 2
Samuel 18:9-15 functions in such a manner.[29] It is not clear to me,
however, how Joab's killing of Absalom in the forest of Ephraim
sheds light on the rebellion or its suppression. It seems simply to
elaborate an element in a narrative rather than to interpret the narrative, much as we saw in Homer.

By way of summary on the sandwich technique prior to Mark,
we might say that although the suspension of a narrative for one
reason or another was not uncommon in ancient literature, the use
of an inserted middle to give new meaning or to resolve a tension
in a host passage can be seen, to the best of my knowledge, only

---

[28] For helpful analyses of Hosea 1-3, see F. I. Andersen and D.N. Freedman,
Hosea (The Anchor Bible 24; Garden City: Doubleday, 1980) 61-62, 115-27; J.L.
Mays, *Hosea* (OTL; London: SCM Press, 1969) 15; and especially H.W. Wolff,
Dodekapropheton I, Hosea (BKAT; Neukirchener Verlag, 1961) 74.

[29] *Mimesis*, 14.

in the Hebrew Scriptures, and there seldomly. The clearest examples of such a technique are the Hosea-Gomer and David-Bathsheba stories. But these stories differ from Mark's sandwiches in one important respect: their B-episodes are intentional commentaries on the flanking A-episodes, whereas in Mark the B-episode is (with the exception of 4:1-20) always an independent narrative. Whether Mark is indebted to these stories (or others like them) for his sandwich technique, is doubtful, for neither of the stories is quoted or alluded to in Mark's Gospel, and none of Mark's sandwich units alludes to earlier precedents. We are thus left to examine Mark's material on its own.

5. *Considerations of the Markan Sandwiches*

Scholars concerned with Markan interpolations generally recognize the following five: 3:20-35; 5:21-43; 6:7-30; 11:12-21; 14:1-11. I shall begin with these passages and then consider four others which in my judgment exhibit sandwich characteristics: 4:1-20; 14:17-31; 14:53-72; and 15:40-16:8.

5.1. *The Woman with the Hemorrhage and the Healing of Jairus's Daughter, 5:21-43.*

This is one of two Markan sandwiches preserved by both Matthew (9:18-26) and Luke (8:40-56), although both abbreviate Mark's version. In the Greek the narrative of the woman with the hemorrhage (vv 24b-34) differs somewhat in style from the Jairus-narrative (vv 21-24a; 35-43) Jairus's story is a straight-forward narrative related in the (historical) present tense, and most of the sentences begin with *kai*. The woman's story, however, is narrated in the imperfect tense, there are fewer instances of initial *kai*, and in verses 25-27 there is a long complex sentence woven around six aorist participles. We cannot judge for certain on the basis of this evidence, but the central section appears somewhat less Markan stylistically. If so, Mark may have utilized a separate unit of material for the woman's story, and the pericope would be a Markan composition.[30]

---

[30] See V. Scippa, ''Ricerche preliminari per uno studio su Mc 5,21-43 secondo la *Redaktionsgeschichte*,'' *RivistB* 31 (4, 1983) 385-404.

More important is the juxtaposition of the stories. Jairus and the woman share only one thing in common: they both are victims of desperate circumstances, and apart from Jesus they have no hope. Otherwise their stories diverge. Jairus has a name and holds an important position. He is a ruler of the synagogue and hence a respected member of the community. He has enough prestige to ask Jesus to come to his house, and his presumption is not disappointed, for Jesus goes with him. The woman can claim none of these. Her name is not given (or known) and she has no position in society. Her only identification is her shame, a menstrual hemorrhage. Whereas Jairus approaches Jesus face-to-face, she approaches Jesus unaware and from behind.

Jairus apparently holds a religious advantage. But with typical Markan irony, Jesus reverses their roles, for it is the woman who displays the greater faith. Despite her embarrassing condition she pushes through the crowd, even past the disciples, hoping only to touch the back of Jesus' garment.[31] Is there an element of superstition in her faith? Perhaps. She is determined, however, to let nothing prevent her from reaching Jesus, and to this undaunted woman Jesus says, "Daughter, your faith has healed you; go in peace" (v 34).

The woman's interruption has, of course, worked to Jairus's disadvantage, for in the meantime his daughter has died. With that announcement Jairus's hope fails him. Surely his servants are right, why trouble the Master further (v 35)? It is as though Mark were asking his readers, 'Is there any hope for Jairus now?' And his answer—coming from the mouth of Jesus—is a resounding 'Yes,' if Jairus does "Not fear, but believe" (v 36). But what kind of belief must Jairus have in a situation in which all human hopes are exhausted? The answer is given in Jesus' command to believe (*pisteuein*, v 36): Jairus must have the kind of faith (*pistis*, v 34) the woman had! Faith knows no limits, not even the raising of a dead child, as Jesus goes on to demonstrate.[32]

---

[31] M. J. Selvidge ("Mark 5:25-34 and Leviticus 15:19-20. A Reaction to Restrictive Purity Regulations," *JBL* 103 [4, 1984] 619-23) says the woman's behavior ran counter to the prescriptions preserved in Lev 15:19, 28. Jesus, she maintains, saw the woman's faith, not her ritual uncleanness. See also J. D. M. Derrett, "Mark's Technique: the Haemorrhaging Woman and Jairus' Daughter," *Bib* 63 (4, 1982) 474-505.

[32] C.H. Bird ("Some *gar* Clauses in St. Mark's Gospel," *JTS* (NS) 4 [1, 1953] 179-82) sees Jairus's daughter and the hemorrhaging woman linked by the

The insertion of the woman with the hemorrhage into the Jairus story is thus not an editorial strategem whose primary purpose is to create suspense or "to give time for the situation in the main incident to develop".[33] The woman's faith forms the center of the sandwich and is the key to its interpretation. Through her Mark shows how faith in Jesus can transform fear and despair into hope and salvation. It is a powerful lesson for Jairus, as well as for Mark's readers.

5.2. *The Mission of the Twelve and the Martyrdom of John the Baptist,* 6:7-30.

This sandwich is one of Mark's more instructive, for the return of the Twelve (A²) is contained in a single verse (v 30). Matthew rearranges Mark's account radically (10:1, 5-15; 14:1-13). Luke (9:1-10) follows Mark's order, but the interrelation between the mission and the martyrdom is largely lost because Luke is more interested in Herod's anxiety (vv 7-9) than in the Baptist's martyrdom.

On literary-critical grounds the martyrdom of the Baptist (vv 14-29) exhibits several unique features. It is the only narrative in the Gospel which is not about Jesus.[34] It is narrated in the simple aorist instead of Mark's preferred historical present (although the flashback may account for this). There are, as Lohmeyer noted,[35] several *hapax legomena* in the narrative, and its language is more cultivated than is characteristic of Mark. It is not improbable that Mark took over a preformed narrative of the Baptist's death and used it for his purposes in chapter six.

There is surely more than one motif at work in the Baptist's martyrdom. The most obvious and important is the parallel between the death of the Baptist and the death of Jesus. Mark clearly intends

---

number "twelve." Twelve, moreover, may signify Israel to Mark's readers, indeed, Israel coming to faith in Jesus.

[33] So Nineham, *The Gospel of St Mark*, 157. Von Dobschütz ("Erzählerkunst," 195) and Klostermann (*Markus-Evangelium*, 50) also regard its purpose solely as the creation of a suspenseful pause.

[34] Unless one considers 1:2-8, although in this passage John is related to Jesus as forerunner.

[35] E. Lohmeyer, *Das Evangelium des Markus* (MeyerK 17. Auflage; Göttingen: Vandenhoeck & Ruprecht, 1951) 117-21.

to show that as John was the forerunner of Jesus' message and ministry, so too is he the forerunner of his death.[36] John is righteous and suffers silently, and the same will be true of Jesus. Both Herod and Pilate are Roman officials, both are vacillating and pusillanimous in the face of social pressure, and both condemn innocent men to death.

All this was surely in Mark's mind in the Herod-Baptist narrative, but it does not answer the question why he bracketed it with the sending (vv 7-13) and return (v 30) of the Twelve?[37] The rather awkward appending of the return of the Twelve (in only one verse!) to the story of the Baptist's death must mean that Mark saw a relationship between missionaries and martyrdom, between discipleship and death. This is precisely Jesus' teaching in 8:34, "If someone wishes to come after me, let him deny himself, take up his cross and follow me." The cross, of course, was an instrument of death. According to Mark, Jesus addressed that word to his *disciples* (*tois mathētais*, v. 34). Mark says the same thing in sandwiching the Baptist's death into the mission of the Twelve: discipleship may lead to martyrdom. The disciple of Jesus must first reckon with the fate of John. Thus, John's martyrdom not only prefigured Jesus' death, it also prefigures the death of anyone who would follow after him!

5.3. *The Cursing of the Fig Tree and the Clearing of the Temple*, 11:12-21.

The cursing of the fig tree and the clearing of the temple have a long and controversial history of interpretation.[38] The interpretation begins already in the synoptic tradition, for Matthew (21:12-22) reduces Mark's sandwich (A-cursing of the fig tree; B-clearing of the temple; A-withering of the fig tree) to a simple sequence (clearing the temple–cursing the tree); and Luke replaces the fig

---

[36] So 9:11-13. See C. Wolff, "Zur Bedeutung Johannes des Täufers im Markusevangelium," *TLZ* 102 (2, 1977) 857-65, and D. Losada, "La muerte de Juan el Bautista. Mc 6,17-29," *RivistB* 39 (2, 1977) 143-54.

[37] R. Fowler (*Loaves and Fishes*, 114-32) rightly asks why Mark sandwiched the death of the Baptist between the sending and return of the Twelve. Unfortunately, he fails to recognize that Mark relates the Baptist's martyrdom to the Twelve as well as to Jesus' impending crucifixion.

[38] See W. R. Telford, *The Barren Temple and the Withered Tree. A Redaction-Critical Analysis of the Cursing of the Fig-Tree Pericope in Mark's Gospel and Its Relation to the Cleansing of the Temple Tradition* (JSNT Supplement Series 1; Sheffield: JSOT Press, 1980) 1-38.

tree miracle with a parable (13:6-9). Here also the oft-repeated opinion that Mark's sandwich technique simply affords a necessary time lapse for events to occur fails to account for the creative and symbolic interrelation of the sandwich.[39]

The interrelation of the clearing of the temple (vv 15-19), and the cursing (vv 12-14) and withering (vv 20-21) of the fig tree, is established at several points. For one, all the material between Mark 11:1 and 13:37 is oriented around the temple; this is itself a cue that there is a relationship between the fig tree and temple. There is also a clear parallel between "his disciples were hearing" (v 14) and "the chief priests and the scribes heard" (v 18). Above all, the fig tree is often in the Old Testament a symbol for Israel, and more than once Israel is judged under this symbol.[40] "There will be no figs on the tree, and their leaves will wither," said Jeremiah (8:13). In connection with this is the intriguing statement that "it was not the season for figs" (v 13). This statement surely has less to do with horticulture than theology. The word for "season" (*kairos*) is used at the opening of the Gospel, "'The time (*kairos*) has come,' said Jesus, 'the kingdom of God is near'" (1:14). *Kairos* means a special, critical moment. There is no fruit on the tree because its time has passed. The leafy fig tree, with all its promise of fruit, is as deceptive as the temple, which, with all its bustling activity, is really an outlaw's hideout (v 17).[41]

Verses 15-19 have often been called the 'cleansing' of the temple. Cleansing, however, implies a removal of impurities and restoration to a rightful function, as envisioned, for example, in Isaiah 55:1-8 or Psalms of Solomon 17:30: "He [Messiah] will purge Jerusalem (and make it) holy as it was even from the beginning,

---

[39] Lohmeyer (*Evangelium des Markus*, 234-35) was one of the first to discuss the symbolic import of the sandwich. In a personal conversation Prof. Martin Hengel drew my attention to a double sandwich in chapter 11: temple (1-11), fig tree (12-14), temple (15-19), fig tree (20-21).

[40] Isa 34:4; Jer 5:17; 29:17; Hos 2:12; 9:10; Joel 1:7; Mic 7:1-6. See the material gathered in Telford, *Barren Temple and Withered Tree*, 132-37, and his conclusion: "Enough has now been said about the fig-tree's use in image and symbol to justify the conclusion that Mark's readers, steeped in the Old Testament tradition, would readily have understood Jesus' cursing of the barren fig-tree as at the very least a judgment upon Israel" (136).

[41] Important discussions of these points can be found in H. Giesen, "Der verdorrte Feigenbaum—Eine symbolische Aussage? Zu Mk 11,12-14," *BZ* 20 (1, 1976) 95-111; E. Best, *Temptation and Passion*, 83; and C.H. Bird, "Some *gar* Clauses," (already cited, fn 32) 177-79.

(for) nations to come from the ends of the earth to see his glory."
But Jesus is not restoring the temple; he is pronouncing its doom![42]
The fig tree, symbolizing Israel (see 13:28!), has been found want-
ing and judged. Like the fig tree, the temple's function is now
"withered from the roots" (v 20: see Hos 9:16). Here more than
elsewhere the A-episodes admittedly also interpret the B-episode,
for the cursing and withering of the fig tree do, in fact, foreshadow
the destruction of the temple. But on a deeper level the B-episode
remains the key, for apart from the clearing of the temple the cursing and withering of the fig tree remain an enigma.[43] The cursing
and withering of the fig tree, in other words, are a symbolic or
enacted prophecy[44] which can only be understood in light of Jesus'
activity in the temple. Jesus himself has replaced the temple as the
center of Israel's faith (15:38-39); salvation is found in him, not in
the temple.[45]

5.4. The Betrayal of Jesus and the Anointing at Bethany, 14:1-11.[46]

The dividing of the plot to betray Jesus by the anointing at
Bethany creates bitter irony at the beginning of the Markan pas-
sion. Matthew (26:1-16) retains the sandwich and its effect, but
Luke (22:1-6) recounts only the betrayal and omits the anointing.
John (11:55-12:11) also maintains the semblance of Mark's A-B-A
schema, and identifies the woman as Mary, sister of Lazarus.

---

[42] W. Kelber, *The Kingdom in Mark. A New Place and a New Time* (Philadelphia:
Fortress Press, 1974) 101-102.

[43] It was the fig tree story (among others) taken *by itself* which led Bertrand
Russell to accuse Jesus of "vindictive fury." In *Why I Am Not a Christian, and Other
Essays on Religion and Related Subjects* (New York: Clarion Books, Simon and
Schuster, 1957) Russell wrote: "This is a very curious story, because it was not
the right time of year for figs, and you really could not blame the tree. I cannot
myself feel that either in the matter of wisdom or in the matter of virtue Christ
stands quite as high as some other people known to history" (17-19).

[44] For other enacted prophecies, see Isa 20:1-6; Jer 13:1-11; 19:1-13; Ezek
4:1-5.

[45] Telford rightly notes that the clearing of the temple "was intended to provide, by virtue of its odd position, [Mark's] commentary on these traditions of
chapter 11," *Barren Temple and Withered Tree*, 49. See also R. Stein, "Proper
Methodology," 184, fn. 1.

[46] Recent periodical literature includes J. Suggit, "An Incident from Mark's
Gospel," *JournTheolSAfric* 50 (1985) 52-55; F. Schnider, "Christusverkündigung
und Jezuserzählungen. Exegetische Überlegungen zu Mk 14, 3-9," *Kairos* 24 (3-4,
1982) 171-80; C.-P. März, "Zur Traditionsgeschichte von Mk 14,3-9 und
Parallelen," *StudNTUmwelt* 6-7 (1981-1982) 89-112.

Mark hones a keen edge of contrast between the A and B parts of the sandwich. Judas, "one of the Twelve" (v 10), is in collusion with the religious leaders to betray his master. The betrayal plot reeks with intrigue: "the chief priests and the scribes were seeking how they might seize him by treachery and kill him" (v 1). In the Gospel of Mark the word "seek" (*zētein*) occurs 10 times, always in pejorative contexts. "To seize" (*kratein*) occurs some 15 times and carries predominantly negative connotations. Coupled with "treachery" (*dolos*) and "killing" (*apokteinein*), the description seethes with deception and violence. By contrast, "a woman came having an alabaster flask of nard ointment, extremely valuable, which she broke and poured on [Jesus'] head" (v 3). Mark stumbles over himself in Greek to emphasize the extent of her devotion by the expense of the ointment, which, to the chagrin of the disciples, was roughly estimated at a year's wages! (v 5). This unnamed woman performs an act of devotion which results in a solemn pronouncement, "Truly I tell you, wherever the gospel may be preached in the whole world, even that which she has done shall be spoken in remembrance of her" (v 9).

The bracketing of the woman's devotion by the betrayal plot creates an acid contrast between her faith and Judas's treachery. Sacrificial faith or scheming betrayal? Tender devotion or intrigue? Is not Mark saying that in Jesus' "hour" (14:35) there can be only one of two responses to him, that of the woman or that of Judas? Mark places the woman in the middle as the ideal.

5.5. *Jesus, His Companions, and Beelzeboul, 3:20-35.*

This unit is less obviously a sandwich. Neither Matthew nor Luke recognized Mark's technique here, or, if they did, regarded it worth preserving, for both alter his sequence.[47] The A-parts are only loosely connected and it is unclear whether Jesus' mother and brothers in A² (vv 31-35) are the same as his ambiguous "intimates" (*hoi par' autou*) in A¹ (vv 20-21). Uncials D and W, in fact, identify *hoi par' autou* with the scribes of verse 22. Moreover, it appears that verses 20-30 are a separate unit, the linking idea being the charge that Jesus was *mad*, both from his companions

---

[47] Matt 12:22-32, 46-50; Luke 11:14-23; 12:10; 8:19-21.

(*exestē*, v 21), and from the religious leaders (*Beelzeboul echei*, v 22).[48]

Closer examination, however, reveals a sandwich in verses 20-35. The setting for both A parts is the "house" of verse 20, and in both Jesus is surrounded by the "crowd" (vv 20, 32). More importantly, in both A parts the companions of Jesus (whether or not *hoi par' autou* = Jesus' mother and brothers) try to suppress him. Mark says expressly in verse 21: "[Jesus'] intimate companions went out to *seize* him." The verb "to seize" (*kratein*) is often in Mark used in the sense of preventing Jesus from fulfilling his mission, and the same is implied in A[2] by the use of "calling" (*kalein*, v 31) and "seeking" (*zētein*, v 32).[49] Equally telling is the contrast between "insiders" and "outsiders" in A[2]. Jesus' mother and brothers are "standing outside" (v 31); they are not "with Jesus" (*peri auton kuklō kathēmenous*, v 34) nor "doing the will of God" (*hos gar an poiēsē to thelēma tou theou*, v 35), which, according to Mark, is the chief characteristic of discipleship (see 3:14-15)!

If 3:20-35 is a sandwich, what does Mark intend by breaking up the attempts of Jesus' most intimate circle to straight-jacket him by the story of Jesus and Beelzeboul (vv 22-30)? The answer is a hard one: the attempt to restrain Jesus from his mission or redirect him to another course, even though it comes from his most intimate associates, nay, even from his mother and brothers,[50] is ultimately as mistaken and blasphemous as confusing Jesus with Satan! To avert Jesus from his mission is satanic. This, of course, is precisely the point of Jesus' stinging rebuke when Peter tried to prevent him from going to the cross. "Get behind me, Satan, for you do not understand the things of God but only the ways of man" (8:33).

---

[48] See the discussion of this pericope, and the literature noted, in H.-W. Kuhn, *Ältere Sammlungen*, 201.

[49] There is a difference in Mark between misunderstanding (e.g., 8:14-21), which is regrettable, and opposition, which is damnable. In 3:20-35 Jesus' companions exert pressure against his fulfilling his mission. Of 15 instances of *kratein* in Mark, 11 are negative (e.g., 6:17; 12:12). Of 10 occurences of *zētein* in Mark, all are negative. Even *kalein* is likely negative in v 31, for it is the only instance in Mark where someone other than Jesus is its subject.

[50] See J. Fenton ("The Mother of Jesus in Mark's Gospel and its Revisions," *Theology* 86 [714, 1983] 433-37), who argues that Mark's harsh portrayal of Mary (which was softened by the later Evangelists) was part of his insistence that not even the privilege of flesh-and-blood relation to Jesus guaranteed—or was a substitute for—*faith* in Jesus.

5.6. *Predictions of Betrayal and the Lord's Supper*, 14:17-31.

Mark's account of the Lord's Supper (vv 22-26) is flanked by two predictions of Jesus that the disciples will deny him. Matthew (26:20-35) follows the Markan order whereas Luke (22:14-23, 31-34) disrupts it. In both the Markan predictions Jesus is alone with the Twelve. The first prediction comes at the beginning of the Supper (vv 17-21); the second occurs after the meal *en route* to the Mount of Olives (vv 27-31). Both predictions are met with disbelief by the disciples. In the first it is incredulity (v 19) and in the second outright disavowal (vv 29-31). With not-so-subtle irony Mark contrasts the theoretical fidelity of the disciples ('' and they all said the same thing'' [i.e., agreed with Peter not to leave Jesus], v 31) with their actual flight (''and they all left him and fled,'' v 50).

What significance does Mark intend by placing the Lord's Supper (vv 22-26) between accounts of denial and cowardice? The answer can only be to contrast the faithlessness of Jesus' disciples to the covenant faithfulness of God. Eduard Schweizer rightly notes that A provides the background or relief against which B gains its specific character: ''so immensely gracious is God and so limitless his gift.''[51] It is a familiar theme from the prophets. Where human faithfulness fails, God's covenantal love stands. We see substantially the same picture with Jesus praying alone in Gethsemane while the disciples sleep, dying alone on Calvary after the disciples have fled. God's salvific covenant depends on *his* faithfulness, and it stands in spite of the faithlessness of his people. ''Let God be true, even though everyone be a liar'' (Rom 3:4).

5.7. *Peter's Denial and Jesus' Trial before the Sanhedrin*, 14:53-72.[52]

A similar sandwich occurs at the end of chapter 14 where Mark brackets Jesus' trial before the Sanhedrin (vv 55-65) with Peter's denial (vv 53-54, 66-72). Luke (22:54-62, 66-71) breaks Mark's A-B-A sequence, but both Matthew (26:57-75) and John (18:15-27) maintain it. Mark and John contain two similar references to

---

[51] Personal letter, 8 June 1988.

[52] For recent literature, see Anonymous, ''Analyse de la véridiction. Procès de Jésus devant le Sanhédrin (Marc 14,55-65),'' *SemiotBib* 27 (1982) 1-11; J. Ernst, ''Noch Einmal: Die Verleugnung Jesu durch Petrus (Mk 14,54. 66-72),'' *Catholica* 30 (3-4, 1976) 207-26.

Peter's warming himself (Mark 14:54//John 18:18; Mark 14:67//John 18:25), "a startling seam," in the words of C. A. Evans.[53] Three of the four Evangelists thus agree on an A-B-A sequence. Evans is probably correct that John's agreement with Mark's order is due to common oral tradition rather than reliance on Mark.[54] This passage, therefore (along with 14:1-11 and 5:21-43), may be evidence that some application of the sandwich technique already existed in the tradition which Mark received.

Luke's order of relating Peter's denial (22:54-62) and Jesus' trial (22:66-71) as two separate episodes is certainly simpler. Mark, on the other hand, opens the account of Jesus before the council with a tantalizing reference to Peter's standing "in the courtyard of the high priest...warming himself by the fire" (14:54). He proceeds to Jesus' trial before the Sanhedrin (vv 55-56), and then returns to the sorry account of Peter's denial (vv 66-72). What does Mark's sandwich arrangement accomplish?

Two accents emerge sharply from the sandwich. First, Peter's equivocation before the servant girl is the first time in Mark that Jesus is openly denied. Coming from the chief apostle it is all the more bitter. The disciples have misunderstood Jesus (8:14-21), Judas has *secretly* betrayed him (14:10-11), but Peter's repudiation is the first open denial of Jesus. By contrast, Jesus' confession before the chief priest, "I am [the Christ, the Son of the Most Blessed]" (v 62), is the first time in Mark that Jesus drops the veil of silence and openly confesses his identity. Jesus' identity is thus revealed at the moment of his deepest humiliation and weakness. The juxtaposition of bold confession and cowardly denial forces upon the reader the terrible gap between Jesus and Peter. The stage is set for chapter 15 which also is built around the poles of denial (mockery in vv 16-32) and confession (v 39). This sandwich thus intensifies the truth of the previous one: the Son of God is faithful

---

[53] C.A. Evans, "'Peter Warming Himself': The Problem of an Editorial 'Seam'" *JBL* 101 (2, 1982) 245.

[54] "It would appear...that the appearance of a few details of agreement (many of them quite general) such as Jesus inside before the High Priest, Peter outside by the fire, and Peter's three denials are not too complicated and involved for preservation within oral tradition which at some points branched out into various streams that became written traditions" ("Peter Warming Himself," 249). For a somewhat stronger reliance of John on Mark, see R. T. Fortna, "Jesus and Peter at the High Priest's House: A Test Case for the Question of the Relation between Mark's and John's Gospels," *NTS* 24 (3, 1978) 371-83.

and true where his disciples are not, and their failure can only be
seen for what it is in light of his suffering righteousness.[55]

5.8. *Joseph of Arimathea and the Women*, 15:40-16:8.

A sandwich of less importance occurs at the end of the Gospel.
Mark records that "women were watching [the crucifixion] from a
distance" (*gunaikes apo makrothen theōrousai*, 15:40). These same
women are found again on Easter morning making their way to the
tomb, having prepared spices for Jesus' burial (16:1). They are
anxious about who will roll the stone away (16:3), and their
meeting with the angel at the tomb finds them bewildered and
distressed (*exethambēthēsan*, 16:5) and fearful (*ephobounto*, 16:8).

In between the crucifixion and resurrection Mark inserts the
story of Joseph of Arimathea. Mark's order is retained by Luke
(23:49-24:8), but not by Matthew (27:55-28:8). Whereas the
women watch the events (*theōrein*, 15:40, 47), Joseph *acts*. "Joseph
of Arimathea came...and dared to go to Pilate and request the body
of Jesus" (15:43). Joseph, in fact, is the first individual since the
woman at Bethany who acts from courage and conviction. In this
oft-unnoticed sandwich Mark reminds his readers that courage and
conviction, not by-standing and beholding, are the characteristics
of true discipleship.

5.9. *The Parable of the Sower and the Purpose of Parables*, 4:1-20.

The most important and most difficult sandwich in Mark occurs
in chapter four where Mark divides the parable of the sower (vv 1-
9) and its interpretation (vv 14-20) by the purpose of parables (vv
10-13). Both Matthew (13:1-23) and Luke (8:4-15) follow Mark's
arrangement. The literature on the enigmatic explanation of
parables in verses 10:12 is extensive.[56] It is curious how few

---

[55] Nineham (*The Gospel of St Mark*, 399) says the story of Peter's denial serves
as a foil for Jesus' self-revelation.

[56] Recent periodical literature includes C. A. Evans, "On the Isaianic
Background of the Sower Parable," *CBQ* 47 (3, 1985) 464-68; *Id.*, "The Function
of Isaiah 6:9-10 in Mark and John," *NovT* 24 (2, 1982) 124-38; *Id.*, "A Note on
the Function of Isaiah VI, 9-10 in Mark IV," *RB* 88 (2, 1981) 234-35; M.
Wojciechowski, "Sur *hina* dans Mc 4,12," *BibNotizen* 28 (1985) 36-37; J. Marcus,
"Mark 4:10-12 and Marcan Epistemology," *JBL* 103 (4, 1984) 557-74; B.
Hollenbach, "Lest They Should Turn and be Forgiven: Irony," *BT* 34 (3, 1983)

scholars recognize this as a sandwich.[57] One indication of a sandwich is the artificial arrangement of chapter four. The parable of the sower is set beside the sea (v 1), but the explanation takes place privately (*kata monas*, v 10). Without informing his readers of a change of location, Mark has Jesus again beside the sea in verse 35, which constitutes something of a contradiction.

If we have a sandwich here, and if the middle episode provides the key to understanding its flanking halves, what does this sandwich mean? The question continues to puzzle exegetes. Some scholars argue that the difficulty of verses 10-12 is due either to a mistranslation (from Aramaic to Greek), or to a mistaken arrangement of material.[58] There is, however, no textual evidence of mistranslation. Moreover, the Isaiah 6:9-10 quotation occurs always in the New Testament, as here, in contexts of unbelief and hardness of heart (Acts 28:26-27; John 12:40; also 1QIsa 6:4). This leads us to favor the text as it stands.

Mark and the early church stood before the enigma why the Jews disbelieved Jesus as the Messiah. Verses 10-12 address this enigma. The crucial observation in these verses is the distinction between insiders and outsiders. "To you the mystery of the reign of God has been given; but to those outside all things become in parables," says Jesus to the disciples (v 11). "Mystery" (*mystērion*), which occurs only here (and synoptic parallels) in the Gospels, means the secret truths of God which, apart from divine revelation, are hidden

---

312-21; G. Sellin, "Textlinguistische und semiotische Erwägungen zu Mk. 4.1-34," *NTS* 29 (4, 1983) 508-30; G.K. Falusi, "Jesus' Use of Parables in Mark with Special Reference to Mark 4:10-12," *IndJournTheol* 31 (1, 1982) 35-46; F. C. Synge, "A Plea for the Outsiders: Commentary on Mark 4:10-12," *JournTheolSAfric* 30 (1980) 53-58; T.J. Weeden, "Recovering the Parabolic Intent in the Parable of the Sower," *JAAR* 47 (1, 1979) 97-120; J.R. Kirland, "The Earliest Understanding of Jesus' Use of Parables: Mark IV,10-12 in Context," *NovT* 19 (1, 1977) 1-21.

[57] But see von Dobschütz ("Erzählerkunst," 193) and especially E. Haenchen (*Der Weg Jesu. Eine Erklärung des Markus-Evangeliums und der kanonischen Parallelen* [Berlin: Alfred Töpelmann, 1966] 31), who says the inserted verses 10-12 and the added verse 34 serve Mark's secrecy theory; and E. Best (*Temptation and Passion*, 74), who correctly notes that "iv. 11f...are Markan insertions into the parables with the intention of explaining their use."

[58] E.g., T.W. Manson, *The Teachings of Jesus. Studies of its Form and Content* (Cambridge: At the University Press, 1955) 75-80; T.J. Weeden, "Recovering the Parabolic Intent," 97-120; J.R. Kirkland, "The Earliest Understanding," 1-21. See the critique of Manson's argument in M. Black, *Die Muttersprache Jesu. Das Aramäische der Evangelien und der Apostelgeschichte*, trans. G. Schwarz (Stuttgart: Kohlhammer Verlag, 1982), 211-16.

from human understanding.[59] The disciples are thus insiders, albeit misunderstanding insiders (8:14-21), but insiders nonetheless. The mystery has been committed to them (v 11), they belong to Jesus' fellowship (3:13-15), and they partake of his authority and mission (6:7-13). Nowhere in Mark are they called "outsiders".

Surprisingly, it is Jesus whom Mark portrays as an "outsider".[60] He fits none of the social categories of his day, and since the beginning of his ministry he has faced misunderstanding, hardness and rejection. This is abundantly clear in chapters 1-3, and the parables of chapter four cannot be understood apart from this. To speak openly of his person and mission would be to invite termination of both from the religious leaders (2:7-8; 3:6), and perhaps from others (3:21). If Jesus is to give insight into his person and mission it must come from a standpoint of hiddenness. Concealment is thus essential to revelation. Here is where parables serve their function. In verses 14-20 Jesus lays critical emphasis on the "word" (*logos*, 8 times) and "hearing" (*akouein*, 4 times). The response to parables, in other words, determines whether one is an insider or outsider. Parables can only be understood 'from within,' by allowing oneself to be taken up into the story and there experience the challenge and promise of God's way. So too is Jesus, the teller of parables, also to be understood, not by a title or report, but by intimate experience (*hina ōsin met' autou*, 3:14). As Jesus' person divided people into insiders and outsiders in the previous story (3:31-35), so too his message divides them here into insiders and outsiders (v 11).

The purpose of parables, and above all the parable of the sower (v 13!), is like the cloud which separated the fleeing Israelites from the pursuing Egyptians. It brought "darkness to the one side and light to the other" (Exod 14:20). The same cloud which condemned the Egyptians to their hardness of heart also protected Israel and made a way for her through the sea. That which was blindness to Egypt was revelation to Israel. And so are the parables. For those outside they are opaque; for those inside they are light and revelation.

---

[59] *BAG*, 532.
[60] *exō*: 1:45; 8:23; 11:4, 19; 12:8; 14:68.

6. *Conclusion*

The foregoing discussion demonstrates that in some nine instances Mark sandwiches one story into the middle of another in order to underscore the major motifs of his Gospel. In some cases the inserted narrative *illustrates* an ideal (e.g., faith, 5:21-43), and in others, particularly in the Passion, it functions by creating a *contrast* between the ways of God and the ways of humanity. Almost always the insertion is the standard by which the flanking material is measured, the key to the interpretation of the whole. J. Donahue is correct in regarding the purpose of Markan sandwiches as theological and not solely literary, although, as our investigation evinces, their purpose cannot be limited, as Donahue supposes, to the way of Jesus' suffering and the necessity of discipleship.[61] They are equally concerned with the meaning of faith, bearing witness, judgment, and the dangers of apostasy. Our examination of pre-Markan sandwiches did not indicate that Mark patterns his sandwiches after an earlier design. Nevertheless, 5:21-43, 14:1-11, and 14:53-72 may indicate that some sandwiching existed in the tradition which Mark received. It is clear, at any rate, that among the Evangelists Mark employs the sandwich technique in a unique and pronounced manner. This appears to corroborate Papias's testimony that the Second Evangelist was uniquely responsible for the design of the Gospel. Finally, the subtlety and sophistication of Markan sandwiches effectively dismisses the judgments of earlier scholars that Mark was a clumsy writer who produced an uncouth Gospel.[62] It is increasingly recognized today that Mark was not only a skilled and purposeful theologian, but that he crafted a new genre of literature in his Gospel to narrate his theological understanding. Both his literary and theological craftsmanship converge in his sandwich technique.[63]

---

[61] See footnotes 15-16.

[62] See footnotes 9-11.

[63] I wish to express my appreciation to Professors Otto Betz, Martin Hengel, and Eduard Schweizer for their helpful critiques of this study.

THOSE OUTSIDE (MK. 4:10-12)

by

MICHAEL D. GOULDER
Birmingham

The massive inconsistency in which Mark is involved by including 4:10-12 is now widely recognized[1]. The inconsistency is both theological and practical. On the theological side we have an apparent statement that Jesus taught in parables to prevent those who were not disciples from turning and being forgiven. William Wrede already spoke of this as an exercise "whose cruelty vies with its oddity and pointlessness"[2]. It is in sharp contrast with the general attitude of Mark, who frequently speaks of Jesus teaching the crowds, and they hear him gladly[3]. In particular Mark fosters the impression that Jesus had a successful ministry communicating with sinners. Further, the theory that the *crowds* had their hearts hardened (by God) sits uncomfortably alongside the later Marcan statements that the *disciples* had their hearts hardened (6:52, 8:17). Nor does this tension have to wait for a few chapters, where it might be overlooked, for the disciples do not understand the Sower parable (4:10), and are reproached for this in 4:13.

The inconsistency is the more glaring because of the practical setting which Mark has given it. In 4:1f a very large crowd gathers, forcing Jesus to go on board a boat; "and he *taught* them many

---

[1] W. Wrede, *The Messianic Secret* (ET Cambridge/London 1971 = *Das Messiasgeheimnis in den Evangelien*, 1901), 56-63; H. Räisänen, *The 'Messianic Secret' in Mark's Gospel* (Edinburgh 1990, a revised edition of *Das 'Messiasgeheimnis' im Markusevangelium*, Helsinki, 1976), 76-143; R. Pesch, *Das Markusevangelium* (Herders ThK 2/1, Freiburg/Basel/Wien, 1976), 236-241; H.-J. Klauck, *Allegorie und Allegorese in Synoptischen Gleichnistexten* (NTA 13, Münster, 1978), 240-259; J. Gnilka, *Das Evangelium nach Markus* (EKK, 3rd edn. Zürich, Brunswick, Neukirchen-Vluyn, 1989), I, 162-172, D. Lührmann, *Das Markusevangelium* (HNT 3, Tübingen, 1987), 85-88; R. A. Guelich, *Mark 1-8:26* (Word Biblical Commentary 34A, Dallas, 1989), 198-215.

[2] *Messianic Secret*, 62; cited by Räisänen, *'Messianic Secret'*, 79 (Greig's translation has "purposelessness").

[3] Klauck, 243f. In *Die Verstockung Israels*, (StANT 3, Munich, 1961), 83-86, J. Gnilka minimised Mark's inconsistency in attitude to the crowd.

things in parables, and he said to them in his *teaching*". To teach
people means to communicate with them meaningfully; J.L. Austin
called the verb a "performative"[4]. At 4:3 he calls on the crowd to
hear, and at 4:9 he says, "he who has ears to hear, let him hear";
which seems to imply that some of the crowd do have ears to hear
in some effective sense. But 4:11f says that those outside understood nothing. In 4:33 "with many such parables he spoke the word
to them as they were able to hear"; apparently the crowd *is able* to
hear the word in part—a distinction is made between "them" and
"his own disciples", who receive a full explanation privately[5]. In
addition, there seems to be a confusion over the location. In 4:1-9
Jesus is speaking to the crowd from a boat, and 4:35ff imply that
he goes straight on "as he was in the boat" across the lake. But in
4:10 "when he was κατὰ μόνας those about him with the twelve
asked him the parables". No explanation is given of how Jesus can
be on his own with his followers if he is still in the boat, nor at what
point he resumes teaching the crowd from the boat again.

The natural resource of a scholar faced with this battery of
difficulties is to hypothesize a "tradition" which will them account
for all the contradictions. Mark found 4:10-12 already in his
source[6], and that is why Jesus is sometimes at sea and sometimes
on land, sometimes seeing the crowds as hardened, sometimes the
disciples, understanding parables sometimes as a means of
teaching, sometimes of procuring damnation. It is, of course,
impossible to prove such hypotheses to be wrong; but it has to be
confessed that they are not very satisfying. For one thing, they
make Mark out a pretty good fool, for which we lack other
evidence. Naturally, an author who is rewriting traditions will often
betray his activity by small oversights and inconsistencies. But we
do not expect to find Mark including a text like Matt:23.2f, "The
scribes and Pharisees sit on Moses' seat..."; nor does he do so. On

---

[4] *Philosophical Papers* (Oxford, 1979), 233-252.

[5] Räisänen, 'Messianic Secret', 105, observes that 4.33 has to be understood
positively, as the phrase "speak the word" "belongs to the terminology of
evangelization"; while 4.34 contains the more negative idea of the explanation of a
coded message, which derives from a second idea of the function of parable as
riddle.

[6] Räisänen, 'Messianic Secret', 130-137, Gnilka, *Markus*, I, 163, Guelich, *Mark*,
199f. Lührmann, 87f, attributes 4.11f to Marcan redaction, and the surrounding
material to the source. For other opinions see Guelich, ibid.

major issues, like his attitude to the disciples, or to Jesus' family, or the controversies which the Paulines had with Jerusalem over the sabbath, the food-laws, etc., Mark is remarkably consistent. On less important issues, like the supposed settings of his pericopae, it would be wise to concede that he may nod. But a hypothesis that Mark simply overlooked *all* the tensions implied in 4:10-12 would be better avoided if we can manage it. It would be better if we could say that, whether he has taken the verses over from tradition or not, he has taken responsibility for them, and that they make general sense.

A problem often passed over rather quickly is the translation of ἐκείνοις τοῖς ἔξω, usually rendered "those outside", or something similar. ἐκείνοις is then said to be pleonastic[7]; though the word recurs 23 times in Mark, and is never pleonastic elsewhere. If it is given its proper demonstrative meaning, it will refer to the crowds[8]—"those people, those outside"; but then, if Mark is thinking of Jesus as in the boat, τοῖς ἔξω is a very curious expression. Outside the boat? Paul does speak of οἱ ἔξω on occasion (1 Cor. 5:12f, 1 Thess. 4:12, Col. 4:5) meaning non-believers, but then it is clear that they are ἔξω τῆς ἐκκλησίας, and this is a way of thought which Mark is not likely to have attributed to the historical Jesus. Similar expressions in Jewish tradition[9] refer to those outside Israel, and cannot be helpful.

It is often noticed, however, that the same word occurs in 3:31-35, and in the same contrast with οἱ περὶ αὐτόν which we find in 4:10f: "And his mother and his brothers come and standing ἔξω

---

[7] J. Jeremias, *The Parables of Jesus* (ET London 1972 = *Die Gleichnisse Jesu*, 8th edn., Göttingen, 1970), 15, calls it redundant, and takes this as an indication of an Aramaic origin (*inter alia*); but cf. Räisänen, *'Messianic Secret'*, p. 78, n. 2. It is said to be pleonastic by Pesch, 231, Gnilka, 163, and Guelich, 207.

[8] So Räisänen, *'Messianic Secret'*, 78. It would be a happy solution if ἐκείνοις could refer to the scribes, or some similar hardened opposition; and this is opted for by Klauck, 247: "im Makrotext des MkEv sind die οἱ ἔξω die entschiedenen Gegner Jesu", cf. 251, "verschiedene jüdische Gruppierungen die sich als erbitterte Gegner Jesu erweisen"—cf. P. von der Osten-Sacken, "Streitgespräche und Parabel als Formen markinischer Christologie", in G. Strecker ed. *Jesus Christus in Historie und Geschichte* (Fs. H. Conzelmann, Tübingen, 1975), 386-388, and C. Breytenbach, *Nachfolge und Zukunftserwartung nach Markus* (ATANT 71, Zürich, 1984), 157. Von der Osten-Sacken comes nearest to the solution offered in this article, but shies away, assimilating Jesus' relatives to the scribes.

[9] Strack-Billerbeck, II, 7: especially Minim.

sent to him calling him. And a crowd was sitting περὶ αὐτόν, and they say to him, Lo, your mother and your brothers ἔξω are seeking you... And looking round at those sitting in a circle περὶ αὐτόν...'' It might be helpful therefore to follow this hint rather more single-mindedly than has been customary.

It is usually thought, and correctly, that 3:20f are the introduction to 3:31-35, with the Beelbezul controversy of 3:22-30 as the Marcan sandwich[10]. The view of Jesus' family is not favourable. Jesus' healing ministry has evoked such enthusiasm in 3:7-12 that he has nearly been mobbed; in 3:13-19 he has called twelve disciples to leave their livelihoods to be with him, and they have done so (ἀπῆλθον πρὸς αὐτόν); a crowd has gathered outside his house in 3:20 so insistent to hear his preaching that he has not leisure to eat. His relatives (οἱ παρ' αὐτοῦ)[11], however, are untouched by any such positive feelings: ''they went out to lay hold of him; for they said that he was out of his mind''. This total failure to understand the great truth which Mark has confided to his hearers, that Jesus is the Christ, the Son of God (1:1), shows up again in 3:31 where his family cannot wait till Jesus has finished teaching his followers, but stand outside calling him away from his ministry. The scene is a symbol of the Church in Mark's mind. There is Jesus with his disciples sitting *round him*, listening to his teaching. His family are *outside* the circle. Jesus asks who are his [true] mother and brothers, and then answers his own question: whoever does the will of God, he is his brother and sister and mother. He says this looking round at *those round him*. The Church consists of those who do the will of God, or, as the parable will express it, those who hear the word and receive it and bring forth fruit. His natural family are *outside* this circle of salvation.

Mark shows his teeth again at 6:4. Jesus is rejected at his home

---

[10] E. Best, ''Mark iii.20,21,31-35'', *NTS* 22 (1976), 309-319, argues that 3:20f ''provides the background against which vv. 31-35 get their bite''; that the sandwich is a familiar Marcan structure; and that the combination is in accord with Mark's total purpose. The last point is correct, although Best has, in my view, misunderstood the overall purpose of the Gospel. A similar position is taken by Taylor, 235ff, Pesch, 211ff, Gnilka, 143-155, Lührmann, 73-78, Guelich, 168-172.

[11] H. Wansbrough defended a translation ''his followers'' in ''Mark iii.21—Was Jesus out of his Mind?'', *NTS* 18 (1972), 233-235; but he was effectively answered by Best (see previous note).

town, Nazareth, and says wryly, "A prophet is not without honour save in his home town, and ἐν τοῖς συγγενεῦσιν αὐτοῦ καὶ ἐν τῇ οἰκίᾳ αὐτοῦ". Jesus' συγγενεῖς are in the first place his brothers and the rest of his family; and it is they who live in his οἰκία too.

The significance of these verses has been steadily undervalued, for a reason perhaps not too far to seek. But reflection should assure us that neither a biographical[12] nor a pastoral[13] explanation is adequate. *The family of Jesus had been the leaders of the Jerusalem church since the 40s. Everybody in Mark's community knew that James had been its most influential figure (Gal. 1:18; 2:9; Acts 12:17; 15:13; 21:18); that other brothers shared in this influence (1 Cor. 9:5); and that the dynasty had now continued in Jesus' cousin Simeon ben Clopas*[14]. It is really unimaginable that continuously adverse comments on so well-known a group of Christian leaders should not be significant[15].

It is not as if the New Testament were short of signs that there were tensions between the Jerusalem church and the Pauline mission. We have an actual incident described in Gal. 2:11-14 which makes it clear that Peter was given to weak compromise where he could, and that James was the backbone of the Jerusalem require-

---

[12] Taylor, 236, deplores Lagrange's reference to the family's "affectionate restraint", and maintains instead that "their deep personal concern is combined with a lack of sympathy for his aims". M. Hengel, *The Charismatic Leader and His Followers* (Edinburgh, 1981 = Berlin, 1968), 64, says, "Jesus' behaviour, breaking as it did the bounds of the conventions, had among his closest relatives given cause for offence and annoyance". Gnilka, I, 148, continues the biographical approach: "The activity of the revealer meets with incomprehension, which includes even his family".

[13] Pastoral emphasis has been made popular through the writings of Ernest Best—"Mark iii.20,21,31-35" (n. 10), *Following Jesus* (Sheffield, 1981), *Mark as Story* (Edinburgh, 1986), "The Role of the Disciples in Mark", *NTS* 23 (1977), 377-401. Cf. Richard Bauckham, *Jude and the Relatives of Jesus in the Early Church* (Edinburgh, 1990), 49, "it is more likely that Mark is interested in portraying Jesus as a precedent for his followers, who have to face opposition and misunderstanding from their families". But if so, it would have been helpful if Jesus had made some such comment as Mk. 10:29f after 3:21 or 3:35.

[14] Hegesippus, apud Eusebius, *H.E.* 3.11, 4.22.4.

[15] Their significance is argued by E. Schweizer, *Das Evangelium nach Markus* (NTD 1 [12]Göttingen, 1968), 48; J.D. Crossan, "Mark and the Relatives of Jesus", *NT* 15 (1973), 81-113; Pesch, *Markus* I, 224; and is hinted by J.B. Tyson in a famous article. "The Blindness of the Disciples in Mark", *JBL* 80 (1961), 261-268. Crossan's argument is marred by too close an association of Jesus' family with Peter and his christological error; and also by doubtful matter about Mary the mother of Joses. But it included important points, and it is unjust of Gnilka to call it absurd, I, 148.

ment that the law be observed[16]. Hegesippus[17] and Josephus[18]
preserve evidence that James was an ascetic, respected by Pharisees
in Judaism. John, whose Gospel is sharply anti-Jewish-Christian
(Jn 8:31-59; 2:23-3:21), and whose attitude to the Law is
dismissive, says that Jesus' brothers did not believe in him; that
they harassed him to go to Jerusalem before his time; that their
time was always ready; and that the world could not hate them (7:3-
7)[19]. Matthew, whose loyalty is not merely to the Law (5:17-19) but
to Jewish scribal interpretation of the Law (23:2f, 23), omits Mk.
3:21[20], and so weakens the force of Mk. 3:31-35, and leaves out the
συγγενεῖς at Mk. 6:4. Luke, whose aim is the reconciliation of the
Church, also omits Mk. 3:21. Instead of standing outside calling
Jesus, his family now "could not reach him because of the crowd"
(8:19). Mk. 6:4 has become "No prophet is acceptable in his own
home town", without either συγγενεῖς or οἰκία. All four Gospels are
involved in this battle.

Mark, like John, is firmly on the Pauline side. For the practical
Pauline controversies with the Jacobites, Mark stands shoulder to
shoulder with Paul[21]; over eating with "sinners" (2:15ff), keeping
Jewish fasts (2:18ff), seceding from Judaism (2:21f), observing sab-

---

[16] James is sometimes felt to have been less of a hard-liner than Paul might suggest: cf. W. Pratscher, *Der Herrenbruder Jakobus und die Jakobustradition* (FRLANT
139, Göttingen, 1987), 59-92. But Pratscher too easily credits the Gospel picture
of Jesus as a Pauline liberal; and his plea that James claimed authority only over
the Jewish Christians at Antioch is misleading. If James could divide the
Antiochene church (as he did), then he could force Paul either to accept Jerusalem
terms or to found a sect of his own. Paul resolved the dilemma by taking the gospel
to Europe.

[17] Ap. Eus., *H.E.*, 2.23.10-16: James was called "the Just"; he was devoted
to prayer and fasting, he wore no wool, his knees became like camels' knees from
constant intercession, etc.: the Jewish Pharisees came to him to ask him to speak
against the Messiaship of Jesus.

[18] Ant. 20:9.1: "those in the city who had a reputation for greater fairness, and
strict observance of the laws" protested over James' murder in 62.

[19] Pratscher, *Herrenbruder*, 24ff, reaches the surprising conclusion that in the
Semeia-Quelle Jesus' family were behind him; he thinks Barnabas Lindars' comment that in 7:3-10 "they appear to be positively hostile" "weit übertrieben".

[20] Bauckham, *Jude*, 49, says that Matthew's picture is not significantly different
from Mark's: "Mark 3:19b-21 is probably simply a casualty of Matthew's conflation of his sources". But Mk. 3:21 has not just been a casualty. Matthew has
carefully amended Mark's "(Jesus) ἐξέστη" to "all the crowds ἐξίσταντο" (12:23).
Pratscher, *Herrenbruder*, 22, thinks Matthew felt the tension was too great with the
picture of Mary in Matt. 1.

[21] See my "A Pauline in a Jacobite Church", in the forthcoming *Festschrift* for
Frans Neirynck (Leuven, 1992).

bath (2:23-3:6), following the food-laws (7:1-23), refusing the
demand for signs (8:11f), forbidding divorce (10:2-12), and requir-
ing the payment of taxes (12:13-17). Each time the Jacobites are
represented by "the Pharisees", and the Marcan Jesus speaks with
the voice of Paul. On other matters Mark is equally Pauline. He
thinks Jesus is the Son of God; that the standard understanding of
Christ as son of David is inadequate; that the disciples did not
understand this profound truth; and that it was first seen by a Gentile centurion. He believes in the Gentile mission, in the cross, in
a postponed Coming and a future Kingdom. We cannot always
prove that the Jacobites were against the Paulines on these issues,
though the evidence often points that way[22]. But we do know what
Paul thought, and Mark is steadily with Paul.

The matter of the Beelzebul controversy is not quite so straight-
forward, but there is wide agreement that its position is likely to be
significant between the two parts of the story of Jesus' family[23]. The
latter said that he was out of his mind; the Jerusalem scribes said
that he had Beelzebul. Although the "sandwiched" passages in
Mark are not always related to the enveloping matter, they sometimes are; and it is easy to think that Jesus' family are being in some
way *aligned* with the scribes[24]. Perhaps one might think of a church
like Antioch where "those of James" *came down from Jerusalem* and
delivered authoritative rulings on the local observance of the food-
laws, very like *the scribes*. It is noticeable how bitter the Marcan
church feels towards such people: anything else people do can be
forgiven, but the assertion that Jesus is possessed by an unclean
spirit is permanently unforgivable. The theory that he was possessed by even a good spirit is perhaps not so much better. We are
not told precisely what blasphemy against the Holy Spirit involves,
only that it includes saying that Jesus has an unclean spirit. In other
contexts blaspheming against the Holy Spirit is done only from
within the Church (Matt. 12:31ff, Lk. 12:10, Heb. 6:4ff).

The limits of forgiveness take us back to Mk. 4:11f. It is more
than half a century since T.W. Manson attempted to save Jesus'

---

[22] This matter is discussed at length in my "The Jewish-Christian Mission, 30-
130", forthcoming in *Aufstieg und Niedergang der römischen Welt*, expected in 1992.

[23] See above n. 10.

[24] Crossan, "Relatives", 110-113, says no more than this, and is wrongly
criticised by Gnilka, I, 148, for making the scribes the family's *cipher*.

reputation by introducing the suggestion that the text was a mistranslation of the Targum of Isa. 6:9f[25]; and this unfortunate evasion is still repeated in some modern commentaries[26]. Mk. 4:12 runs:—

ἵνα βλέποντες βλέπωσιν καὶ μὴ ἴδωσιν,
καὶ ἀκούοντες ἀκούωσιν καὶ μὴ συνιῶσιν,
μήποτε ἐπιστρέψωσιν καὶ ἀφεθῇ αὐτοῖς.

The Targum of Isa. 6:9f has, in Bruce Chilton's translation[27]:—

Go and speak to this people that hear indeed but do not understand, and who see indeed but do not know. Make the heart of this people dull and their ears heavy and shut their eyes, lest they see with their eyes and hear with their ears and understand with their heart, and they repent, and it be forgiven them.

The Septuagint, Mark's normal Bible, has:—

πορεύθητι καὶ εἰπὸν τῷ λαῷ τούτῳ·
  ἀκοῇ ἀκούσετε καὶ οὐ μὴ συνῆτε
καὶ βλέποντες βλέψετε καὶ οὐ μὴ ἴδητε·
  ἐπαχύνθη γὰρ ἡ καρδία τοῦ λαοῦ τούτου
καὶ τοῖς ὠσὶν βαρέως ἤκουσαν
  καὶ τοὺς ὀφθαλμοὺς αὐτῶν ἐκάμμυσαν·
μήποτε ἴδωσιν τοῖς ὀφθαλμοῖς
  καὶ τοῖς ὠσὶν ἀκούσωσιν
καὶ τῇ καρδίᾳ συνῶσιν
  καὶ ἐπιστρέψωσιν καὶ ἰάσομαι αὐτούς.

There are three striking agreements with the LXX: βλέποντες βλεπ- followed by μὴ ἰδ- in the subjunctive (against the Targum's וחזין ומחזא ולא ידעין); μήποτε, where ἵνα μὴ would be normal (μήποτε occurs only twice elsewhere in the whole prophetic canon, Isa. 8:12 and Jer. 47:15, both readings being doubtful); and ἐπιστρέψωσιν for שׁוב, where a free Marcan rendering of the Targum would have given μετανοήσωσιν. It is thus virtually certain that the primary dependence is on the LXX. Nor is it fair to say that Mark agrees with the Targum against the LXX in using the third person[28]: he

---

[25] *The Teaching of Jesus* (Cambridge, 1943), 77-79. For Manson's less effective predecessors, cf. Klauck, 249, n. 321.
[26] Attribution to the Targum is nearly universal—Gnilka, I, 163, Guelich, 209-212; even Räisänen, *'Messianic Secret'*, 81.
[27] *A Galilean Rabbi and his Bible* (London 1984), 91.
[28] Contra Chilton, 91.

has much abbreviated the quotation, combining lines 2f and 7f of the latter, as may be seen from his placing the eyes before the ears, as in lines 7f, where the third person is used—ἴδωσιν, συνῶσιν; and in any case the quotation is not intended to be exact, and the third person is required by his ἵνα. So the *only* agreement with the Targum is "it be forgiven them".

But it needs to be asked whether this is significant. Isaiah prophesied that God had hardened Israel "lest they turn and one heal them (וְרָפָא־לוֹ)/ I heal them (LXX)"—that is, *deliver them from their enemies*. But this yields no sense in Mark's context: he is concerned with eternal "healing", viz. forgiveness, and this interpretation is necessary if his hearer/reader is to follow. Mk. 1:2f shows no less than five divergences from a basic LXX text, Mal. 3:1, including the insertion of the totally alien verb κατασκευάσει for ἐπιβλέψεται (פנה); and it is quite believable that he has deliberately amended the LXX here also. He has just said that every sin and blasphemy *will be forgiven to* (ἀφεθήσεται) the sons of men, apart from the blasphemy against the Holy Spirit. He now interprets the unclear "and I heal them" with the same locution in the subjunctive, ἀφεθῇ αὐτοῖς[29]. The impersonal third person with the dative is suggested by both Mk. 3:28, ἀφεθήσεται τοῖς, and by the Hebrew וְרָפָא־לוֹ, once the healing theme of ἰάσομαι has been displaced. We do not require the Targum at all, and it would never have won such a following but for the spurious hopes of the mistranslation hypothesis.

We have thus a triple link between 4:10-12 and 3:20-35—ἔξω, περὶ αὐτόν and ἀφεθη- + dat. — and are led to treat the connection substantively. Somehow there has been a crossing of the wires over the setting of ch. 4, for one cannot be in a boat addressing a crowd and suddenly find oneself κατὰ μόνας. Perhaps we may think that Mark revised his account of the scene with the scribes and Jesus' family, and inserted 4:1-9, where he teaches the *parable* of the Sower from the boat, in a story where he had been speaking in *parables* in a house[30]. He came into the house at 3:20, and the crowd gathered;

---

[29] Lührmann, 87, draws the further parallel to ἐπιστρέψωσιν...ἀφεθῇ of Mk. 1.4, μετάνοιαν εἰς ἄφεσιν, where μετάνοια is a synonym of ἐπιστρέφειν.

[30] Cf. Gnilka, *Verstockung*, 30: "Wenn die Jünger hier in Vers 11 'denen draussen' gegenübergestellt werden, ist anzunehmen, dass sie sich mit Jesus im Haus befinden".

"they", that is Jesus and the newly called disciples, have not leisure
to eat. The scribes appear with their carping, and Jesus addresses
them ἐν παραβολαῖς. While he is still speaking to them, his family
appear outside: "For they were saying, He has an unclean spirit.
And his mother and his brothers come, and standing outside they
sent to him, calling him." The crowd of 3:20 is mentioned again
in 3:32 as "a crowd sitting round him", so "those sitting in a ring
round him" in 3:34 are in fact the ὄχλος and his disciples, who are
not specified.

3:31-35 tells the incident of his family's attempt to interrupt from
outside, but the family are left in the air; the story is then completed
in 4:10-22. "And when he was alone", that is, *when the scribes and
the family have gone away*, "those around him", that is, τοὺς περὶ αὐτὸν
κύκλῳ καθημένους, of 3:34, "with the Twelve", that is the αὐτούς of
3:20, "asked him τὰς παραβολάς", that is the παραβολαί of 3:23-30.
Jesus said that the mystery of the kingdom of God was given to the
questioners, but "to those people, those outside" the whole thing
comes in riddles (ἐν παραβολαῖς τὰ πάντα γίνεται). The kingdom has
not been referred to in 4:1-9, whereas in 3:24 it was not divided.
ἐκείνοις has its normal demonstrative force, and means the family,
who have just been twice spoken of as ἔξω, and the scribes, who
have been aligned with the family, and have now departed. The
trouble with both groups is that they see and hear on one level, but
entirely miss the deeper meaning; and this is in fact their destiny,
prophesied by Isaiah, for God has hardened their hearts *lest they
should turn and it be forgiven them*. The unforgivable sin of the scribes
has been set forth in a difficult saying (παραβολή) at 3:29, and this
is now reflected upon as the divine intention. The fact that it is a
sin against the Holy Spirit suggests that some *Christians* are
involved in it too.

I have suggested that Mark might be thought to be out of sympathy with Jesus' family, as leaders of the anti-Pauline Jerusalem
church; and that this hostility might express itself in aligning them
with the Jerusalem scribes, insofar as they came from the same city
and were enthusiasts for applying the same Law. But such activities
on their own would scarcely evoke the Marcan charge of a destiny
to damnation. For this we should expect a *christological* difference,
for it is the christological issue which drives 1 John to associate his
opponents with the Antichrist (4:1-3), and John to speak of "the
Jews who had believed in" Jesus as sons of the devil (8:31-59).

Irenaeus tells us that Ebionite (i.e. Jewish) Christians held a possessionist christology (*A.H.* 1.26.1f); and it is plausible to associate this with the Jewish Christian opposition in John[31]. Indeed, the Jewish Christians of 2 Cor. 11:22 preach "another Jesus" (11:4), and there seem to have been Christians who cursed Jesus in Corinth too (1 Cor. 12:3), perhaps because they "confessed" the possessing Christ only. So it is certainly possible that the differences in christology go back a long way, and that the family's ἐξέστη in Mk: 3.21 is an unsympathetic reflection of the Jerusalem christology of the 60s[32]. James and Jude and Simeon thought that from his baptism Jesus had been possessed by Christ, a spirit from heaven; and this seemed to the Paulines to be beyond the Pale.

It is no surprise if Mark has got himself into a muddle over the setting; commentaries are full of arguments from such muddles, alleging distinctions between Mark's tradition and his redaction on the basis of them. There is a notorious instance in 2:1-12, where the paralytic is let down through the roof in 2:1-5a and enabled to take up his bed and walk in 2:11f. The words λέγει τῷ παραλυτικῷ are repeated at the end of 2:10 in an anacoluthon. It turns out in 2:6 that there are some scribes sitting in the house (as well as the πολλοί of 2:2, and the owner, presumably, and his family): they seem to have turned up early and taken the best places. Furthermore, the reader has been expecting that 2:5 will read "And Jesus, seeing their faith, said to the paralytic... Arise, take up your mattress...", which is what Mark does say in 2:11; but instead we have the totally new matter of the man's sins, which are not mentioned in 2:1-5a nor in 2:11f. It is a widely held conjecture that Mark has inserted alien material in 2:5b-10. Another famous instance is 16:1-8, where the news of Jesus' physical resurrection depends on the women delivering the word to the disciples, a thing which Mark tells us they were too frightened to do. There has certainly been some similar muddling in ch. 4: the proposal above merely suggests *how* the muddle took place and affected 3:20-35, 4:10-12.

---

[31] M. Hengel, *The Johannine Question* (London, 1990), 57ff, brings together the opposition in the Johannines and the evidence of Irenaeus, *A.H.* 1.26.1; but he takes Cerinthus to be an educated Greek, and ignores the second paragraph aligning him with the Ebionites.

[32] Gnilka, *Verstockung*, 34-44, argues convincingly that the μυστήριον of 4:11 given to the disciples is the secret of who Jesus is. Gnilka thinks that this is the Messiah, but Mark means more than that, that he is the Son of God.

This would leave Mark with the remainder of 4:1-20 as a presumed unit, and there would have to be some request at 4:10 for Jesus to respond to in 4:13[33]. Mark will have decided to cut the repetition by transferring 4:10-12 to its present position. It is not remarkable that he failed to notice the contradiction he was letting himself into, because the same term παραβολαί is being used in the two stories, first as a riddle and second as an illumination. Matthew, who is in general a clear-headed author, falls into a similar contradiction in ch. 5 with πληροῦν, which over most of the chapter means to radicalise the law from action to disposition, but at two points (divorce, *talio*) to change the law. Luke does it often.

It strikes the modern commentator as plausible that Mark should feel hostile towards the scribes, whom he sees as Jesus' principal enemies, and the engineers of his crucifixion; what he has found unlikely is that Jesus' family, and in particular his *mother*, should be thought of in this way[34]. But such pre-judgements are not only sociologically naive; they are also contradicted by our NT evidence. For the former, one needs only to have lived through the sad drama of the Social Democratic Party in Britain in the 1980s, or to have an acquaintance with the history of the Trotskyites in the Communist Party, to be aware that the most savage feelings are reserved for deviants *within* a movement. It is they who are felt to be traitors, and they are hated and persecuted with a vengefulness quite different from the cool dislike felt for the Tories or the capitalists. This is especially true when it is feared that the opposing faction is in danger of taking the whole movement over; as is the case with Mark's minority Gentile churches under pressure from delegates from the metropolitan church at Jerusalem. We should not allow ourselves to be deceived by the prestige we give to St Paul; in Mark's day Jerusalem had the edge over the Paulines in authority, in numbers, in organization and in logic.

Paul himself was a generous hearted man who did not often feel hardly towards the unbelieving Jews, and then not for long. In Rom. 9:1-3 he speaks of the great grief and persevering pain he

---

[33] Cf. Räisänen, *'Messianic Secret'*, 115, "if the parable and its explanation were connected in some way, then there must also have been a request for an explanation, or something similar".

[34] Protestant Christian authors like Guelich, 209-215, are just as defensive as Catholic commentators like J. Fitzmyer, *The Gospel according to Luke I-IX. 50* (Anchor Bible 28A, Garden City, New York, 1981), 722-725.

feels for them. By 9:18 he has concluded that their unbelief is caused by divine hardening, to make them vessels of wrath for destruction; but this does not stop him praying for them in 10:1, and by 11:25 he has had the vision that the hardening is only partial, and is a phase in the grand divine plan for the salvation of the fulness of the Gentiles as well as all Israel. He can tell of the five thrashings which he has suffered at the hands of synagogue authorities without the least bitterness: such "weaknesses" are his glory.

But with the Jerusalem leaders' attempts to enforce their discipline on his converts, even Paul is less charitable. He withstands them to the face, and does not yield to them for a moment. If they destroy the temple of God, God will destroy them (1 Cor. 3:17); they are οἱ ἀπολλύμενοι, whose smell is from death to death[35] (2 Cor. 2:15f, cf. 4:1-6, 1 Cor. 1:18); their end is ἀπώλεια, their God is their belly and their glory in their private parts (Phil. 3:19). They are dogs, evil workers (Phil. 3:2), and he wishes they would castrate themselves (Gal. 5:12). They are false apostles, ministers of Satan (2 Cor. 11:13ff). But most significant of all, salvation is beyond them. Paul writes in 2 Cor. 4:4 of the opposition as τοῖς ἀπολλυμένοις: "the god of this age blinded the minds of the faithless (ἀπίστων), lest the light of the gospel of the glory of Christ shine on them". In 2 Thess. 2:10f it is God himself who has predestined them[36]: "And for this reason God is sending on them a force of heresy (πλάνη) that they should believe a lie, so that all who have not believed in the truth and who have approved ungodliness may be judged". Under pressure Paul (or his disciple) thinks that those who follow πλάνη in the Church have been

---

[35] The ἀπολλύμενοι are often understood to be those who refuse the gospel, e.g. C.K. Barrett, *The Second Epistle to the Corinthians* (London 1973), 100f; but the context requires that they be the same as the πολλοί of 2:17 who water down the word of God and commend themselves in 3:1. Barrett is clear that the same expression means the unconverted again in 4:3, while seeing that "the adversaries" are referred to in the preceding verse (pp. 128ff). For 1 Cor. 1:18 see my "Σοφία in 1 Corinthians", forthcoming in *NTS* (1991).

[36] E. Best, *A Commentary on The First and Second Epistles to the Thessalonians* (London, 1972), 306f, sees that the "signs and wonders" are the healings performed by the Church, but thinks that it is the non-Christians who believe the lie; so also W. Trilling, *Der Zweite Brief an die Thessalonicher* (EKK 14, Zürich/Neukirchen-Vluyn, 1980), 109ff. But πλάνη is always used elsewhere of *the corruption of true religion*, and 2 Thess. 2:2 supplies this context (μή τις ὑμᾶς ἐξαπατήσῃ (v. 3) ...ἐν πάσῃ ἀπάτῃ (v. 10)).

destined thereto by God for their damnation—the same doctrine which Mark holds of the leaders of the Jerusalem church, ἐκείνοις τοῖς ἔξω, in 4:10ff.

Mark distinguishes Jesus' family, who ruled the Jerusalem church with their Pharisaic ways[37] from the 40s, from Peter and the Zebedaids, who had been their vacillating supporters, but had at least believed in the Lord in his lifetime. "The disciples" in his Gospel do not understand a lot when it comes to Christology, and are unreliable in many other ways; but they did leave all and follow him, and Jesus made them large promises. Nevertheless, the Marcan Jesus speaks to them in tones strongly reminiscent of 4:10-12. They *did not understand* about the loaves, but *their heart was hardened* (6:52). "And he said to them, *Are you thus also without understanding?*" (7:18). "Do you *not* yet know nor *understand?*", asks Jesus at 8:17ff, "*Have you your heart hardened? Having eyes do you not see, and having ears do you not hear?...* And he said to them, *Do you not yet understand?*" It is the same basic feeling which the orthodox Pauline holds for all who refuse the truth, and is very different from the attitude he holds to the Jewish crowds who heard Jesus gladly, and were so keen on his message they nearly pushed him into the sea. But for all their bone-headedness the disciples were all right in the end: it was only James and Jude and Simeon and the others who were outside the circle of faith, and whom God had willed to obduracy and destruction. The question of divine hardening could be asked of the disciples rhetorically, but with Jesus' family it was an unhappy fact.

---

[37] Cf. my "A Pauline in a Jacobite Church", in the forthcoming Festschrift for Frans Neirynck.

A DIVINE TRAGEDY: SOME OBSERVATIONS ON THE DRAMATIC STRUCTURE OF MARK'S GOSPEL

by

STEPHEN H. SMITH

Tunbridge Wells, England

At various times during the past 65 years the question has been posed as to whether the structure of Greek tragic drama might not be evident in some parts of the Bible. Sarah Halperin[1] has claimed to detect in the Samson narrative a comparable structure, while the dramatic possibilities of Job have also been examined.[2] But it is the Gospel of Mark whose structure has been found to conform more closely than any other biblical work to dramatic literature.[3] Despite the gathering momentum of interest in this field, however, the superficiality of much of the work has given rise to certain inconsistencies, and most certainly to the need for further study. Many writings merely touch upon the matter as a means to other ends, and Bilezikian's volume remains the only readily accessible systematic study of the subject.

Although we shall be making critical reference to particular scholars as occasion requires, we should mention at this stage two points which, if not universal in their scope, at least have a more general application. The first is that Aristotle's *Poetics* always seems to be made the yardstick with regard to what the ideal structure of

---

[1] S. Halperin, "Tragedy in the Bible", *Semitics*, 7 (1980) 28-39.

[2] Job, indeed, has been treated as a drama since the fourth century A.D. See M.H. Pope, *Job* (AB; Garden City: Doubleday, 1965) xxx-xxxi, and the literature cited there.

[3] E.W. Burch, "Tragic Action in the Second Gospel: A Study in the Narrative of Mark", *JR*, 11 (1931) 346-358; C. Beach, *The Gospel of Mark: Its Making and Meaning* (New York: Harper & Row, 1959) 48-51; G.G. Bilezikian, *The Liberated Gospel: A Comparison of the Gospel of Mark and Greek Tragedy* (Grand Rapids: Baker Book Ho., 1977); T. Moser, "Mark's Gospel—A Drama?" *BibTod*, 80 (1975) 528-533; F.G. Lang, "Kompositionsanalyse des Markusevangeliums", *ZTK*, 74 (1977) 1-24, esp. 19-22; B. Standaert, *L'Évangile selon Marc: Composition et genre littéraire* (Zevenkerken-Brugge, 1978) esp. 30-34, 82-108. On Mark as comedy, see D.O. Via, *Kerygma and Comedy in the New Testament* (Philadelphia: Fortress, 1975); idem, *The Ethics of Mark's Gospel—In the Middle of Time* (Philadelphia: Fortress, 1985) 27-59.

a tragic drama ought to be rather than the plays themselves. Some writers, indeed, have managed to pronounce at length on the issue with hardly more than a passing reference to any of the dramatic texts. Now there is no doubt that Aristotelian precepts do make for an obvious point of departure, and the broad structural principles elucidated there are in general conformity with what we find to be the case in the extant plays. Nevertheless, we ought to appreciate that the standardisation of such principles as an expression of literary-dramatic theory arose out of the historical development of drama in fifth-century Athens, and not from the fourth-century pen of Aristotle. He, at best, can be no more than a literary adjudicator or critic passing opinion upon the principles that had already been established. As Standaert[4] has rightly observed, some of the subtleties behind Aristotle's assessment of the 'ideal' play might better be ascribed to the sublety of his own thinking.

On the other hand—and here is our second point—there is a sense in which some scholars have not read Aristotle closely enough in that they fail to make a clear distinction between the structure and the plot of the drama. Standaert,[5] for instance, treats 'prologue', 'recognition' and 'epilogue' in direct sequence, as if they all operate at the same structural level. We may accept as fundamentally sound Standaert's desire to demonstrate that in Mark the prologue is related in substance to the epilogue, and both these elements to the central recognition scene (8:27-30): this is to be faithful to Aristotle's dictum that every literary whole must have a beginning (ἀρχή), a middle (μέσον) and an end (τελευτή).[6] But on further examination of the *Poetics* we discover that 'recognition' is regarded as part of the *plot* (complication—δέσις; recognition—ἀναγνώρισις; dénouement—λύσις),[7] whereas 'prologue' and 'epilogue' properly belong to the dramatic *structure* (prologue—πρόλογος; episode—ἐπεισόδιον; exode—ἔξοδος; parode—πάροδος; stasimon—στάσιμον)[8] which, of course, extends beyond the limits of the plot.

---

[4] Standaert, *Marc*, 33.

[5] Standaert, *Marc*, 83-106.

[6] *Poetics*, VII.2-3. This and all subsequent references to this work are to the Loeb edition (Cambridge, Ma.: Harvard University Press; London: Heinemann, 1927).

[7] *Poetics*, X.3-4; XVIII.1-3.

[8] *Poetics*, XII.1-3. Chapter XII as a whole, which discusses the various elements comprising the drama, appears to be something of a misfit in its present context, since it interrupts the discussion of plot. The fact that, but for one word, the opening and closing sentences are identical also suggests an interpolation.

In the remainder of this paper it is hoped to demonstrate how and why the structure of Mark's Gospel conforms to the principles of tragic drama. First we shall outline the tripartite plot pattern, and also the various dramatic elements or, as Aristotle puts it, "the separable members into which [the text] is quantitatively divided." We shall suggest that the Markan model need not have been the tragedies of classical Greece only, but more particularly the inferior Roman imitations which abounded in Mark's own day. Finally, we shall enquire as to the Evangelist's purpose in adopting the tragic structure as his model for a work which, in all other respects, was a new departure in literature.

Of course, it would be possible to further support our thesis by showing that Mark met the requirements or expectations of other salient features of the tragic genre—the ideal character of the tragic hero, the concept of 'tragic error' (*hubris*), the use of irony and of diction commensurate with oral presentation. But since these matters have been treated by others,[9] and our concern is exclusively with structure, we need not pursue them.

I

In an attempt to maintain a degree of homogeneity in our discussion it is intended, as far as possible, to focus chiefly on Sophocles' *Oedipus Rex* to illustrate our arguments, while referring more briefly to other plays which might more appropriately be used in specific instances. Our choice of the *Oedipus* is not arbitrary: its plot structure was much admired by Aristotle, and its text cited by him more than any other. The characterisation is exceedingly powerful, and the recognition scene one of the most striking of all Greek tragedy.[10]

The myth behind the play needs little introduction. The exposure of Oedipus at birth because it had been prophesied that he would kill his father, the king of Thebes; his salvation by a shepherd and subsequent upbringing in the royal household at Corinth; his unwitting murder of his true father on the road to Thebes, and his marriage to Jocasta, his real mother, after he had saved the city from the Sphinx's curse—these are the well-known events

---

[9] Burch, *JR*, 11 (1931) 353-358; Bilezikian, *Liberated Gospel*, esp. 107-138.

[10] Further, the motif of physical and metaphorical blindness in the *Oedipus* finds a clear echo in Mark. We are not, however, at liberty to enquire further into that parallel here.

which the dramatic plot assumes. The action itself opens, years later, with Thebes in the grip of a plague. It transpires that the only way to lift this curse is to identify and banish the man who killed Laius. Of course, it turns out that Oedipus himself is the unsuspecting culprit, and the dramatic plot works towards the self-recognition of his crime.

Complication

The complication (δέσις) straddles the mythological presuppositions of the play and its internal action. That is to say, the action embodied in the complication is founded on and develops the spectator's understanding of events which occur prior to the opening of the drama. Against this background, the protagonist is presented at the outset as a humane monarch who cares deeply for the welfare of his subjects, but he is also something of a 'know-all',[11] and this turns out to be the tragic flaw that leads to his demise, for as he strives to discover the identity of the murderer, so he is drawn inevitably into an obsessive quest for his own identity. Other characters are reluctant to divulge information, or try to dissuade the protagonist from delving any deeper into the question: but Oedipus must *know*, and it is that thirst for knowledge which leads inexorably to the catastrophe.

The Markan complication (1:14-8:26) follows a somewhat similar course. Jesus' Galilean ministry, with its popular teaching, its healings and exorcisms, undoubtedly has a wide appeal, and Jesus soon gathers a popular following. But as with Oedipus, so with Christ: the more resolutely he engages in his task, the nearer he draws to catastrophe; for it is precisely this teaching and healing activity which causes the authorities to begin plotting his downfall (3:6). Unlike the *Oedipus* there is no clearly definable tragic flaw in the Markan Jesus other than that he refuses to be deflected from his course, despite the inevitability of the fate to which it leads.

---

[11] Although the name Oedipus ("swell-foot") is derivative of the child's being discovered with his feet pinned together, it can also be taken as a pun on the verb οἶδα—"to know".

Recognition

In turning to the recognition scene (ἀναγνώρισις) we aim to discuss, albeit briefly, four matters which have received little attention in the past, taking issue, where occasion demands, with other presentations.

1) Typically in Greek tragedy, the recognition is anticipated in the preceding scenes. This is particularly striking in the *Oedipus* where, piece by piece, the puzzle is solved as the protagonist interacts with the characters around him. The seeds of doubt are first implanted in the mind of the super-confident Oedipus by Tiresias, the blind prophet who accuses him of the murder of Laius for which the city is plagued (l. 362). A change comes over the king; he becomes tetchy and suspicious of those around him (l. 378). Before long, in dialogue with Jocasta, Oedipus learns that the place where he once killed a man in an argument matches the spot where Laius was murdered. The king must know the truth. He seeks confirmation—or exoneration—from a shepherd who witnessed the incident... the very shepherd, indeed, who will eventually provide the vital clue to the king's true identity (ll. 765, 1119-1185).

Meanwhile, a messenger arrives from Corinth with news of the death of Oedipus' foster father, Polybus. In the course of the scene (ll. 924 ff.) Oedipus discovers that the old king and his wife were not his true parents after all, but had reared him after receiving him from a shepherd of Laius' household who had saved him from exposure. Jocasta now perceives that Oedipus is not only her husband but her son, and the remainder of the scene is dominated by her frantic efforts to prevent him from discovering the truth.

Now the shepherd arrives on the scene. He had been called originally to establish whether or not Oedipus was Laius' murderer: by identifying him as Laius' son the whole horrific situation is made clear; Oedipus is guilty of both parricide and incest—all that was prophesied of him has come to pass. Thus, we see how, in this play, the entire complication is concerned to collate, from various independent character-sources, the information necessary for leading the protagonist to his self-recognition. The climactic power of this ἀναγνώρισις is dependent upon the gradual revelation to Oedipus of the circumstances behind the dramatic situation.

In certain other plays the recognition scene is emphasised by the device of repeated postponement. Euripides' *Electra* provides a good example here.[12] The ἀναγνώρισις itself occurs in ll. 509-584, but for some 300 lines prior to that it threatens to happen as likely circumstances come and go. Orestes and Electra first meet in l. 215. There follows a long stichomythic dialogue in which Orestes enquires into his sister's circumstances, yet conceals his own identity. One wonders whether he is about to do so as he asks if the chorus can be trusted (l. 272), but the opportunity goes begging. Nevertheless, this scene does anticipate the real recognition scene by introducing the old servant who will eventually effect it (ll. 285 ff.). The possibility of recognition appears to recede until in ll. 332-338, Electra stresses the urgency with which so many desire Orestes' return. Perhaps now he may disclose his identity out of pity, if nothing else, but any such possibility is curtailed by the return of Electra's husband. He invites Orestes to stay at his house, and sends for supplies by a servant—the one man who can recognise him. Even then the recognition is in jeopardy as the servant hesitates over entering the house where Orestes is waiting (ll. 500). After the ἀναγνώρισις has been frustrated so many times (and, for brevity's sake, we have not been able to tease out every detail of the sequence) we almost despair of arriving at that point. But then the old servant asks to see the stranger and recognises him by means of a scar above his eye (l. 573).

In the Gospel of Mark the recognition scene is both anticipated and delayed in just the same way as in Greek tragedy. People begin to recognise the distinctiveness of Jesus from the beginning of his ministry (1:27-28). The disciples, in particular, are privy to his 'inside' teaching (4:10-12; 7:17-23; 8:14-21) and marvellous signs (1:29-31, 4:35-41; 5:35-43; 6:45-52). Potentially, each such episode provides them with an opportunity to recognise who Jesus is, but they fail to do so, and Jesus becomes increasingly exasperated at their lack of understanding (4:13,40; 7:18; 8:17-21). Indeed, the very exhortation to understand is a heartfelt plea for an understanding of Jesus' messianic identity. Just as in the *Oedipus*, every unit in Mark 1:14-8:26 has its fixed place and purpose in pointing to the recognition scene, but two in particular may presage it more than any other. First, the fact that in 6:14-16 some are identifying

---

[12] Examples of other Euripidean plays containing the same kind of device are *Ion, Helen,* and *Iphigenia in Tauris.* The recognition scenes in these plays, along with that in *Electra,* are thoroughly discussed in F. Solmsen, "Euripides' Ion im Vergleich mit anderen Tragödien", *Hermes,* 69 (1934) 390-419.

Jesus with John the Baptist, or Elijah or one of the prophets, clearly foreshadows 8:28 where the disciples deliver the same report. Again, the Pharisees in 8:11-12 attempt to do what the disciples do in 8:27-30—namely, establish who Jesus really is. But both Herod and the Pharisees get it wrong: no wonder they are juxtaposed in Jesus' logion about the leaven (8:15)! The failure of these two contrasts sharply with Peter's assessment at Caesarea Philippi, thus making the recognition there all the more striking.

2) It is common enough for recognition scenes in Greek tragedy to be preceded by some preparatory scene. In the *Oedipus*, for instance, the messenger from Corinth makes the important double disclosure that Oedipus' real parents were not Polybus and his wife, and that he was handed over by a shepherd in Laius' employment. At once Jocasta realises the awful truth that Oedipus is her son (ll. 1056-1071), as we have seen.

Similarly, in Sophocles' *Electra* there is the urn scene (ll. 1098-1173) in which Electra receives what she believes to be Orestes' ashes from the man himself. The long, poignant speech over the urn (ll. 1126-1170) is in stark contrast to the joy that will be generated by the recognition. Her mourning the death of the man who is, in fact, standing before her is powerful drama indeed.

Although in Mark there are no preparatory speeches as there are in these and other plays, there is, nonetheless, a preparatory episode. It is not, as has been suggested by some,[13] the discussion about Jesus' identity in 8:27-28—that is properly part of the ἀναγνώρισις—but the healing of the blind man in 8:22-26. It is commonly observed that the two phases of the healing in this pericope is paradigmatic of Peter's imperfect recognition of Jesus;[14] he sees that Jesus is the Messiah, but does not appreciate what messiahship entails. The paradigm assures us that, like the blind man, Peter and the other disciples will one day see clearly, but that phase of understanding is projected beyond the parameters of the action.

3) Next, how well does Mark 8:27-30 correspond to Aristotle's view of what a good recognition scene should be like? In one sense it fares rather well because, as in the *Oedipus*, recognition and rever-

---

[13] So Burch, *JR*, 11 (1931) 352.

[14] W.L. Lane, *The Gospel of Mark* (Grand Rapids: Eerdmans, 1974) 286-287, and n. 54. On the structural relationships between 8:22-26 and 8:27-30, see M.A. Beavis, "The Trial before the Sanhedrin (Mark 14:53-65): Reader Response and Greco-Roman Readers", *CBQ*, 49 (1987) 581-596, see especially 589-590.

sal (περιπέτεια) coincide.[15] In the first 'act' of Mark, Jesus' teaching and healing make him a popular figure, although his religious opponents are lurking in the wings. As soon as he is recognised, however, he is compelled to teach what true messiahship means—suffering and death prior to glory, a fate which the followers are expected to share (8:34-38). Of course, this teaching does not go down so well; many adherents fall away, even the inner circle finds it hard to accept, and the authorities redouble their efforts to bring Jesus down. At the end, he is left desolate, having been deserted by all—even, it seems, by God (15:34).

But if the coincidence of ἀναγνώρισις and περιπέτεια conforms to Aristotelian recommendations, the manner by which the recognition scene is constructed is less satisfactory. According to Aristotle the most effective of such episodes arises directly from the plot;[16] again, the *Oedipus* is a fine example. But the Markan recognition scene, like that in Euripides' *Iphigenia in Tauris* where Orestes reveals himself to Iphigenia (ll. 800 ff.), which Aristotle criticises, is contrived by the author, and does not emerge effortlessly from the preceding section. Jesus, in fact, has to initiate the scene by asking the disciples about people's opinion of his identity. Only then is the discovery made!

4) It has been contended by both Burch and Standaert[17] that Mark's recognition scene is a double one, comprising 8:27-30 and 9:2-8. It is true enough that some of the Greek plays do have such double scenes. In the *Oedipus* the dialogue which prepares for Oedipus' recognition of his own identity (ll. 911-1085) also contains Jocasta's realisation that she is the king's mother. Similarly, in Euripides' *Iphigenia in Tauris* Orestes recognises Iphigenia before she recognises him (ll. 725-833). In Mark, on the other hand, the situation is rather different, a fact which even Standaert unwittingly anticipates when he refers to the Transfiguration as "un moment supplémentaire de révélation et de reconnaissance". This is precisely the point: the Transfiguration *is* a revelation—an epiphany of messianic glory—but it is not a recognition in the sense of a typical tragic ἀναγνώρισις; that has already occurred in 8:27-30. Double recognitions in Greek tragedy tend to arise out of reciprocal

---

[15] *Poetics*, XI.5.
[16] *Poetics*, XVI.11.
[17] Burch, *JR*, 11 (1931) 350, 352; Standaert, *Marc*, 93, 94.

situations, such as the one in *Iphigenia* to which we have just
alluded. But Mark 8:27-30 and 9:2-8 supposedly involve recognition on the part of the same character, Peter. Surely, once he has
recognised who Jesus is he does not need to do so again. The
Transfiguration is a manifestation of the true nature of the messianic identity which has just been recognised, and even then,
Peter, with his peculiar comment in 9:5, seems unable to grasp it.

The above comments remind us that, despite the obvious
similarities between 8:27-30 and the recognition scenes in Greek
tragedy, we should not underplay the differences. It is as well to
note that in the latter we generally find that it is the protagonist who
experiences the ἀναγνώρισις, and the disclosure which he himself
makes results in a change in his own fortune. But in Mark it is the
protagonist who invites others to recognise *him*, and his change of
fortune comes about chiefly because, once recognised, he finds that
he must adapt his teaching about himself to meet the new situation.

Dénouement

The dénouement, that part of the action which follows the
recognition scene and leads to the resolution of the plot, has been
adequately treated by others, so little need be said here. In Greek
tragedy the extent of the dénouement depends, of course, on the
position of the recognition scene. In the *Oedipus* it is comparatively
short (ll. 1223-1530): we are simply told of the effects of the
ἀναγνώρισις—the suicide of Jocasta, the self-blinding of Oedipus,
his poignant farewell to his children before he is banished. The real
centre of interest in the play lies not so much in the dénouement
as in the complication where it is shown exactly how the oracle
given to Oedipus regarding his incest and parricide is fulfilled. In
Aeschylus' *Choephoroi*, on the other hand, the ἀναγνώρισις occurs
very early in the play (ll. 164-263) because the centre of interest in
that work lies in the dénouement where the conspiracy of Orestes
and Electra to murder Aegisthus and Clytaemnestra is developed.

In Mark, however, the complication (1:1-8:26) and the dénouement (8:31-16:8) are virtually co-extensive, and equal weight is
given to both 'acts' of the drama. We have seen already how the
recognition itself forces Jesus to adopt a style of messianic teaching
which causes him to lose popular support, thus giving his
opponents fresh impetus. They harbour a more malicious intent

now (8:11; 10:2; 11:18; 12:12,13; 14:1,2), and the elders/chief priests/scribes, who are to be instrumental in Jesus' downfall, appear, significantly, for the first time as a composite group in the very first verse of the dénouement (8:31). The shadow of the cross looms large over these chapters (8:31,34-38; 9:12, 30-32; 10:32-34, 45; 12:1-9).

II

Independently of the plot structure, Aristotle enumerates the elements which comprise the structure of the play (*Poetics*, XII.1-3). Fundamentally, these can be reduced to prologue, epilogue and episode. The chorus, which has a structural function in Greek tragedy, is used quite differently by Mark. Something must now be said about each of these features.

Prologue

The prologue, that part of the play which precedes the entry of the chorus (Aristotle), can be spoken by one or more of the human characters integral to the action, or by one of the gods.[18] Of course, this element varies from one play to another, especially with regard to its purpose, but a number of general observations can be made, using Euripides' *Ion* as an illustration:

1) There is no firm rule as to who the speaker should be. In some cases he/she is the protagonist, in others some kind of messenger (like the watchman in Aeschylus' *Agamemnon*) or a god. In the *Ion* Hermes, appearing on behalf of Apollo, speaks as both god and messenger.

2) The speaker often declares his own pedigree or credentials. Hermes, for instance, begins by telling us what function he performs, and of his parentage.

3) He may set the scene not only by informing the audience where the action takes place (*Ion*, l. 5), but also by filling in the necessary background detail, especially if an understanding of the plot requires foreknowledge of a specific myth. In the *Ion* Hermes tells how Apollo raped Creusa, how Ion was born of the union and

---

[18] Gods feature in the prologue in several cases—so Sophocles', *Ajax*; Euripides', *Ion*, *Women of Troy*, *Hippolytus*, *Bacchae*.

how, when Ion had been exposed by his mother, Hermes was sent by Apollo to rescue the child and deposit him in his temple at Delphi where he would be raised by the priestess. It is in performing his duties there that Ion is introduced to us. It may be, too, that any other necessary information is given to the audience at this point, especially if it helps explain the presence of certain characters. Thus, we learn of Xuthus' appearance in the *Ion* as the husband of Creusa.

4) Foreshadowing of certain events or motifs which are to occur within the body of the drama is frequently found in the prologue. Euripides' *Hecuba, Hippolytus* and *Bacchae* are examples chosen at random. The *Ion* goes so far as to provide us with an outline of the plot (ll. 69-75), even though it is not strictly adhered to.

5) Sometimes, as in Aeschylus' *Agamemnon* and Euripides' *Woman of Troy* and *Ion*, the speaker, having fulfilled his function, leaves the stage at the end of the prologue, never to return.

A glance at the Markan prologue (1:1-13)[19] shows that it conforms to these principles rather well. To begin with, Mark himself exploits his position as omniscient author to disclose to his readers information of which most of the characters are unaware. Within the parameters of his rôle as messenger he introduces to us two others, John the Baptist and God, both of whom are given speaking parts. All the speakers have something momentous to disclose about Jesus—that he is the Son of God (1:1,[20] 11), and so is

---

[19] The extent of the Markan prologue has been much debated. The suggestion of Mark 1:1-20 by J. Sargeant (*Lion Let Loose: The Strucutre and Meaning of St. Mark's Gospel* [Exeter: Paternoster, 1988] 93) can safely be dismissed. More realistically, the choice lies between 1:1-13 (so Standaert, *Marc*, 82-89; Lang, *ZTK*, 74 [1977] 10, 12; D.-A. Koch, "Inhaltliche Gliederung und geographischer Aufriess im Markusevangelium", *NTS*, 29 [1982-83] 157; D.E. Nineham, *St. Mark* [Harmondsworth; Penguin, 1963] 55; Lane, *Mark*, 29; M.D. Hooker, *The Gospel According to St. Mark* [London: A. & C. Black, 1991] 27); and 1:1-15 (so L.E. Keck, "The Introduction to Mark's Gospel", *NTS*, 12 [1965-66] 352-370; H. Anderson, *The Gospel of Mark* [London: Oliphants, 1976] 58; S.E. Johnson, *The Gospel According to St. Mark* [London: A. & C. Black, ²1972] 23; J. Gnilka, *Das Evangelium nach Markus* [EKK II/I; Zürich/Neukirchen: Benziger/Neukirchener, 1978] 32; R.A. Guelich, *Mark 1-8:26* [Dallas, Tx.: Word Books, 1989] xxxvii). But if we accept the dramatic structure of Mark, we have to say that the prologue must conclude at v. 13, for the following verse initiates the action by introducing the activity of the protagonist.

[20] There is, of course, the textual problem regarding the inclusion of Ὑιοῦ θεοῦ, which cannot be engaged here. Suffice it to say that the phrase is well and reliably attested; thus, BDW and (reading Ὑιοῦ τοῦ Θεοῦ) A f¹ f¹³ 565 700, etc.

mightier than any human, even prophetic figure (1:7,8). The chief character in the prologue is John and, like the speaker in certain other prologues, he never appears after this as a character in his own right, even though we still hear *about* him (1:14; 2:18; 6:14-29; 8:28; 11:27-33; and, implicitly, 9:11-13).

As with the speaker in many a Greek tragic prologue, we learn here something about John's own activity as well as his mission (1:4-6). We may recall the presence of Hermes in the *Ion*, who informs us of both his pedigree and his function in the play. He also sets the action against its background, just as Mark does in his gospel. There, we learn that John's messenger rôle, and the one to whom the message points, have already been foretold in the Old Testament (Mark 1:2, 3), the upshot being that the gospel story can be understood only against that background—in particular against the myth of a God who openly intervenes in the history of his people, transforming history *per se* into salvation history.

Finally, like the prologue of Greek tragedy, that in Mark 1:1-13 is characterised by foreshadowing. Themes and motifs which are to appear and be developed throughout the narrative are introduced there. Thus, the messenger (ἄγγελος) motif, which appears at the outset (1:2), is found also to bring the gospel to a close (16:5-7). Part of the quotation, "Prepare the way of the Lord", not only testifies to John's rôle as the one who is preparing for the coming of Jesus, but also anticipates the whole central section of the gospel (8:27-10:52) where the ὁδός motif is of paramount importance.[21] The description of John in 1:6 and his function as herald (1:8) is intended to cast him in the rôle of Elijah (cf. 2 Kgs. 1:8), so it is no surprise to find him appearing again in that guise in 9:11-13. Again, the words of the divine voice in 1:11 not only find an echo in Ps. 2:7, but serve as a foreshadowing of that same voice at the Transfiguration (9:7). Finally, the story of Jesus' temptation in the wilderness (1:12,13) sets the scene for a sustained conflict between Jesus and the forces of evil (1:23-26, 34, 39; 3:11, 15, 22-27; 5:1-20; 6:13; 7:24-30; 8:31-33; 9:14-29, 38-39),[22] and in particular

---

[21] The phrase ἐν τῇ ὁδῷ appears in the central section five times; 8:27; 9:33, 34; 10:32, 52.

[22] On Jesus' conflict with Satan and his entourage (including human opponents) as a predominant concern of the narrative, see J.M. Robinson, *The Problem of History in Mark* (SBT 21; London: SCM, 1957); E. Best, *The Temptation and the Passion: The Markan Soteriology* (SNTSMS 2; Cambridge: CUP, 1965); F.W. Danker, "The Demonic Secret in Mark: A Re-examination of the Cry of Dereliction (15:34)", *ZNW*, 61 (1970) 48-69.

presages the aftermath of the recognition scene where Peter endeavours to tempt Jesus away from his divinely appointed course and is given the name Satan (8:31-33).

Thus, we see that the form and purpose of the Markan prologue is in basic conformity with those typical of Greek tragic drama.[23]

Epilogue

The different forms of Greek tragedy give rise to various types of ending, yet here, too, there appears to have developed a convention which many plays, especially those of Euripides, followed. Aristotle defined the ἔξοδος as "that part of a tragedy which is not followed by a song of the chorus",[24] and since, in some plays, the final song occurs little more than half way through, it is clear that Aristotle's definition and our more usual understanding of the term ἐπίλογος may not be the same thing. Nevertheless, the typical form of the dramatic ἔξοδος and the epilogue in Mark 16:1-8 are sufficiently homogeneous in form and purpose to bear comparison.

In many plays of Sophocles and Euripides[25] we find that the final ode is followed by the arrival of a messenger who relates the fate of the protagonist. This fate, of course, depends on the type of play: it may be the death or demise of the hero/heroine, or in tragicomedy the success of some cunning plan (so Euripides, *Helen*, ll. 1512-1692; *Iphigenia in Tauris*, ll. 1284-1499). But what matters above all is that the plot is brought to a satisfactory conclusion, and not left hanging in mid-air.

To provide us with an example of this form of ἔξοδος we may turn once more to Sophocles' *Oedipus*. After the prelude to the recognition scene (ll. 911-1085) Jocasta, realising who Oedipus is, rushes off stage with an agitated cry. By the end of the recognition scene itself Oedipus, too, understands his identity and departs in like manner. The chorus sings its final ode, dwelling upon the lamentable facts which have just been brought to light. Then comes the

---

[23] A readily accessible discussion of the relationship of the Markan prologue to the rest of the gospel can be found in M.D. Hooker, *The Message of Mark* (London: Epworth, 1983) 4-16.

[24] *Poetics*, XII.6.

[25] Sophocles, *Oedipus Rex*, ll. 1237-1284; *Antigone*, ll. 1192-1243; *Oedipus at Colonus*, ll. 1585-1666; Euripides, *Electra*, ll. 774-858; *Ion*, ll. 1122-1228; *Helen*, ll. 1526-1618; *Iphigenia in Tauris*, ll. 1327-1419; *Bacchae*, ll. 1043-1152.

messenger scene in which Jocasta's suicide and Oedipus' self-blinding—events too gruesome to take place on stage—are described in grim detail. Finally, Oedipus himself appears. After his initial anguish, when his speech gushes forth in irregular, anapaestic rhythms, a quiet air of resignation takes over—a mood found in several other tragedies.

Some dramas use the *deus ex machina* device to draw them to a close. Aristotle much objected to its use simply as a means of unravelling the plot when the action itself was unable to do so by the process of cause and effect. It was, however, permissible to use it, as in Euripides' *Iphigenia in Tauris* and *Ion*, as a means of divulging information about events which lay beyond the parameters of the dramatic action.[26]

After the trauma of the Passion, the Gospel of Mark draws quietly to a close. The appearance of the young man (νεανίσκος) at the tomb recalls the *deus ex machina* device of Greek tragedy, and one might think that his presence here may violate the Aristotelian principle that such a device should not be used to unravel the plot,[27] for once Jesus is in the tomb there seems to be no alternative but to use this technique in order to announce his resurrection. Perhaps, indeed, the Markan ending may lack the dramatic subtlety of one created by a professional playwright, but this simply serves to remind us that, in the last analysis, Mark's Gospel is *not* a play, and was never written for performance by actors. Had that been the case the crucifixion, too, would have been announced by a messenger whereas, of course, the gospel genre allows it to be presented by the author himself, and not on the lips of one of the characters. Moreover, the messenger device, while conforming incidentally to dramatic precedent, is used at this point primarily to counterbalance the same kind of scene in 1:2-8: on both occasions a messenger appears in order to deliver a message of paramount importance.

Nevertheless, the Markan epilogue is dramatic enough, and recalls tragic convention. If the crucifixion arouses in the reader a sense of pity (ἔλεος), the empty tomb leads to a sense of fear (φόβος)—twin emotions which every tragedian sought to draw out

---

[26] *Poetics*, XV. 10.

[27] Although there is no need of a *deus ex machina* to unravel the plot, because Jesus' resurrection is anticipated throughout the dénouement (8:31; 9:9-10, 31; 10:34). See Bilezikian, *Liberated Gospel*, 134-135.

of his audience! In addition, Bilezikian has rightly noted that, like many Greek dramas, Mark's Gospel ends on a note of departure—the women flee in fear from the tomb.[28]

We are left with the question as to how far the Markan ending is truly tragic, and our response to it depends on the credence we give to the resurrection as part of the dramatic narrative. Both Burch and Beach[29] stress that this event is external to the dramatic action, and that Mark can still be regarded as inherently tragic while pointing to new life beyond itself. Dan Via,[30] on the other hand, takes the resurrection to be an integral part of the plot, and argues that comedy or tragicomedy is a better model than tragedy for the gospel. But 16:6, on which his reasoning is largely based, is external to the dramatic action since it concerns what takes place beyond the end of Mark, and so is entirely appropriate as an announcement of the *deus ex machina*. Bilezikian, while denying Via's view that Mark resembles tragicomedy, yet shares his opinion regarding the happy ending. Tragedy, he alleges, does not always end in doom, and he provides examples to prove his point.[31] What he fails to consider, however, is that tragedies were written to be performed as part of a tetralogy in which three successive tragedies were followed by a satyric play which tended to parody the tragic theme. The first two tragedies would be open-ended to some degree because they would be treating successive episodes within an epic narrative which would only reach a settled conclusion at the end of the third play. This is suggested by our only surviving trilogy, Aeschylus' *Oresteia*. The relatively happy ending of the final play in the series, the *Eumenides*, is likely to be due to its position in the trilogy, and is not representative of the tragic ἔξοδος in general.

In the last analysis, it seems that we can maintain the tragic nature of Mark's Gospel without the need to recognise a happy ending. The plain fact is that the epilogue is *not* happy, but

---

[28] Bilezikian, *Liberated Gospel*, 135-136. Among the plays that end in this way are: Aeschylus, *Choephoroi; Eumenides;* Sophocles, *Oedipus Rex*; Euripides, *Electra; Trojan Women; Ion; Helen; Iphigenia in Tauris; Bacchae;* Seneca, *Oedipus; Trojan Women*. That so many plays close like this may be due to the fact that departure acts as a convenient device by which the actors may make their final exit.

[29] Burch, *JR*, 11 (1931) 355-356; Beach, *Mark*, 50.

[30] Via, *Kerygma and Comedy*, 45-46, 98-101; idem, *Ethics*, 34.

[31] Bilezikian, *Liberated Gospel*, 27, n. 52.

mysterious: the overriding mood is one of fear, in the sense of awe. And this is a response which is entirely appropriate to tragic drama.

Episode

According to Aristotle,[32] "an episode is the whole of that part of a tragedy which falls between whole choral songs". In effect, the songs delimit the intervening material which really constitutes "scenes". They provide the characters with the opportunity to enter or exit from the action. Some scholars, notably F.G. Lang,[33] have made much of the supposition that Greek tragedy was conventionally divided into five scenes. On this basis Lang has suggested that Mark, too, constitutes five episodes (1:14-3:6; 3:7-8:26; 8:27-10:52; 11:1-13:37; 14:1-16:8) plus a prologue (1:1-13); and Standaert[34] also has hinted at a possible five-part structure, given that both prologue and epilogue are regarded as part of it (1:1-13; 1:14-6:13; 6:14-10:52; 11:1-15:47; 16:1-8).[35] Both these scholars are indebted to the seminal work of H. Lausberg.[36]

It is true enough that some Greek dramas do fall into five sections, depending on the method used to delineate them, and, following Horace's advice that anyone who wished to have his play performed more than once should ensure that it comprised five acts,[37] many Latin dramas, including those of Seneca, certainly adopted this pattern quite clearly. Nevertheless, many Greek plays, particularly those of Euripides, are structurally idiosyncratic. The number of choral odes, and hence of scenes, tends to vary from play to play. Moreover, the use of odes as scene-markers need not conform to any hard-and-fast rule. Sometimes the ode is sung by an actor instead of the chorus, or may be shared by the two, as in Euripides' *Ion* (ll. 82-236). Even in those plays where five-part structure does seem likely scholars disagree over the criteria to be used. Sophocles' *Oedipus*, for instance, can be reckoned to contain five scenes if we exclude the prologue, but *include* the ἔξοδος (ll. 123-

---

[32] *Poetics*, XII.5.

[33] Lang, *ZTK*, 74 (1977) 20.

[34] Standaert, *Marc*, 106-108.

[35] It should be noted that in Standaert's case the Markan structural scheme is established rhetorically as well as dramatically.

[36] H. Lausberg, *Handbuch der literarischen Rhetorik* (Band I: München: Hueber, 1960) esp. 565-571.

[37] Horace, *Ars Poetica*, 189.

1530). But this procedure seems somewhat inconsistent, for both of these contain long verbal exchanges between the characters of the drama, and the prologue initiates the action just as surely as the ἔξοδος concludes it. Similarly, Euripides' *Bacchae*, which is often held up as an example of "textbook" structure, can be taken as a play of five scenes framed by a prologue and ἔξοδος, or as one of six scenes preceded by a prologue (which, unlike that of the *Oedipus*, is a static announcement of the circumstances upon which the plot depends, but external to the action itself).

Thus, the disparity found between the respective presentations of Markan structure afforded by Lang and Standaert is symptomatic of the ambiguity which has underlain the various efforts to establish a standard model to which all Greek tragic dramas might, to varying degrees, be expected to conform. Because of the structural diversity of Greek tragedy, then, we should not feel obliged to shackle Mark to a five-part dramatic structure if alternative schemes seem more plausible on textual grounds. Neither Lang nor Standaert appear to appreciate that Mark 13, being radically different in character from its context, should be viewed as a short scene in its own right; neither have they given sufficient credence to the existence of transitional passages which, in the absence of choral odes, serve to effect changes of scene. My own analysis of the Markan structure which, of course, I am unable to defend here,[38] would be as follows:

> 1:1-13—Prologue
>   1:14, 15—Transitional
> 1:16-3:6—Growing controversy over Jesus' authority
>   3:7-12—Transitional
> 3:13-6:6—Jesus' true family in contrast to those outside
>   6:7-13—Transitional
> 6:14-8:26—Mission to the Gentiles; the disciples' lack of understanding
>   8:27-30—Transitional (pivotal)

---

[38] A similar outline appears in N. Perrin, "Towards an Interpretation of the Gospel of Mark", *Christology and a Modern Pilgrimage* (ed. H.-D. Betz; Claremont, Ca.: New Testament Colloquium, 1971) 5. Other works of relevance include D.-A. Koch, *NTS*, 29 (1982-83) 145-166; C.W. Hedrick, "The Role of 'Summary Statements' in the Composition of the Gospel of Mark: A Dialogue with Karl Schmidt and Norman Perrin", *NovT*, 26 (1984) 289-311.

8:31-10:45—The true messianic nature; the way of self-sacrifice
for Jesus and his disciples
10:46-52—Transitional
11:1-12:44—The Son of David claims his city; conflict with the
authorities.
13:1, 2—Transitional
13:3-37—The Apocalyptic Discourse
14:1, 2—Transitional
14:3-15:47—The Passion
16:1-8—Epilogue.

It will be seen that this is a seven-part scheme, with the addition
of a prologue and epilogue.

Chorus

The chorus in Greek tragedy was used in a variety of ways and
for a variety of purposes. Again, we can do no more than generalise
on a matter which really demands much closer attention, but it can
safely be said that by the time of Euripides the choral odes had
become well-established as scene-markers, and also as a means of
passing comment or judgement upon the action. Indeed, in a few
cases the chorus becomes directly involved in it. In the *Oedipus* it
anticipates the arrival of the various characters (l. 1416)[39] and
prompts dialogue between them by raising questions or inciting
responses (ll. 1367-68).[40] Significantly, the choral writing is sometimes designed to arouse in the audience the desired emotions of
fear and pity. Thus, in the *Oedipus*, the chorus seeks to stress, in the
form of brief, anguished ejaculations, the tragedy and pity of the
sight of the blind king as he emerges from his palace (ll. 1297-1307,
1312, 1319-20, 1347-48).

In Mark choral odes are not used—transitional passages instead
serve to denote scene changes; nor is the rôle of the chorus represented, as in Greek tragedy, by a homogeneous body of

---

[39] A line which the Loeb edition (vol. 1; Cambridge, Ma.: Harvard University
Press; London: Heinemann, 1912/1981, p. 129) ascribes to Creon.

[40] Thus, in Aeschylus' *Choephoroi*, ll. 770-774, the chorus leader advises the
nurse to persuade Aegisthus to come without his bodyguards so that Orestes' plan
to kill him may be fulfilled all the more easily. It should be noted that Aristotle
favoured the Sophoclean device of involving the chorus in the action rather than
the Euripidean one of setting it apart (*Poetics*, XVIII.19-20).

individuals. Nevertheless, some of the utterances of the minor characters—the disciples as a group, the bystanders—do conform to the kind of choral comment we might expect to find in Greek tragedy. They do not foreshadow the action—the protagonist and Mark himself do that (2:20; 3:4, 6; 8:31; 9:31; 10:32-33, 45; 11:18; 12:12)—but they do pass comment upon it, thereby exciting the reader's emotions. The method is normally that of appealing to the relevant emotion in the light of an event which has just been reported, and the emotion most frequently appealed to is that of awe (1:27, θαμβέω; 2:12, ἐξίστημι; 4:41, φοβέω; 7:37, ἐκπλήσσω). Thus, in response to Jesus' stilling of the storm, the disciples remark, "Who, then, is this, that even the wind and the sea obey him?" (4:41). It will be seen that this question about Jesus' person is directly evoked by the miracle which precedes it, just as in the *Oedipus* the sight of the blind king emerging from the palace calls forth from the chorus a mixed reaction of pity and revulsion. Another of the choral comments in Mark, "He has done all things well" (7:37, καλῶς πάντα πεποίηκεν), even finds a linguistic precedent in Euripides' *Ion* (l. 1595), where a similar compliment is paid to Apollo by Athene (καλῶς δ' 'Απόλλων πάντ' ἔπραξε).

It is noticeable that ejaculations of the kind under discussion, which urge the reader to consider who Jesus really is, are confined to the first 'act' of the gospel because, following 8:27-30, the reader's knowledge of his messianic identity is shared with some of the characters. The question then is no longer, "Who is Jesus?" but, "What does his messianic identity mean?" Any choral comments found after the recognition scene, therefore, are of a different order from those prior to it. Thus, the disciples' perplexed question in 10:26, "Then who can be saved?", which is directed as much to the reader as to themselves, focuses not on the person of Jesus, but on the Christian community. If it is so hard to enter the kingdom (10:17-25), what hope for the Christian? The author wants his audience to groan in despair—but only so that Jesus' word of salvation, by contrast, will make all the more impact: with men salvation is, indeed, impossible; but with God!... *all* things are possible with him! (10:27).

III

Even some of those scholars who have previously drawn attention to the similarity between the form and structure of Mark on

the one hand, and that of ancient Greek tragedy on the other, fight
shy of asserting that the Evangelist consciously modelled his work
on such literature.[41] But why should it seem strange that Mark and
his readers could have been aware of their own literary environ-
ment? There are good grounds for arguing that they were conscious
of their dramatic legacy, particularly if, as tradition suggests, their
world was that of first-century Rome.

First, Greek tragedy was still regarded in the first century as part
of the staple diet of Greco-Roman education. Just as Homer lay at
the heart of study in epic literature, and Menander was the model
comedian, so Euripides took pride of place in the curriculum as far
as tragedy was concerned.[42] After textual criticism (διόρθωσις),
which involved the pupil homogenising his copy of the text with
that of his teacher, there followed the expressive reading which, in
the case of plays, may have been done in dialogue form. The
absence of punctuation in the text meant that the pupil had first to
establish an adequate understanding of it. He was then taught the
art of delivery[43]—when to raise or lower the volume and pitch of
the voice, how to master rhythm, and so on. Reading was very
much a matter of declamation. Many of Mark's addressees, then,
would have been familiar not only with the content of Greek
tragedy, but also with its literary analysis and presentation. This
observation holds good even if they had never attended a public
performance.[44]

Secondly, Mark's audience my have been acquainted as well
with the Roman closet drama which was much in vogue at that
time. A closet drama was a work written in dramatic form, but
intended for private recitation rather than for public performance.
The surviving plays of Seneca belong to this genre.[45] Possibly

---

[41] Beach, *Mark*, 50-51.

[42] H.I. Marrou, *A History of Education in Antiquity* (trans. G. Lamb; New York:
Sheed & Ward, 1956) 163.

[43] See Quintilian, *InstOr*, I.viii.1 ff.

[44] On reading in the ancient world, see W.B. Sedgewick, "Reading and Writing in Classical Antiquity", *Contemporary Review*, 135 (1929) 90-94; Beavis, *CBQ*,
49 (1987) 592-596.

[45] Among those who think that the Senecan tragedies were written for recitation
rather than performance, see R.J. Tarrant, *Seneca's Thyestes* (APATS 11; Atlanta:
Scholars, 1985) 13-15; E.F. Watling, *Seneca: Four Tragedies and Octavia* (Harmonds-
worth: Penguin, 1966) 19. Lack of theatrical direction is one of the reasons given
for this conclusion. Moreover, according to the ancient sources, the practice ascribed to Seneca appears to have been rather widespread (see Ovid, *Tristia*, 5.7.27;

Mark's Gospel was written with just this kind of situation in mind—to be read expressively by a lector before a closed circle of Christians in the setting of a private house. It has even been suggested that the cryptic comment "Let the reader understand" in 13:14 can be explained as a directive to the lector to read the following passage with particular feeling or emphasis. Who knows? Certainly there is evidence enough, on the whole, to justify the suggestion that Mark consciously intended to cast his gospel, albeit rather broadly, in the form of tragic drama, and that the members of his audience would have understood this, even if the extent of their formal education was not very great.

IV

Finally, once it has been established that Mark was probably conscious of composing a work formally and structurally akin to tragic drama, and that he intended it to be presented to a specific audience in the manner of a closet drama, two further factors must be taken into account. First, Mark's source material was drawn from the historical traditions handed down to him by the early Church, which, despite the presence in it of certain mythological elements, was by no means pure mythology of the kind so accessible to the Greek tragedians. Yet even here Mark is not totally distinctive. Although Aeschylus' *Persae* is the only historical drama to have survived from fifth-century Athens[46] it is enough to betray the fact that such plays were being produced from that time onwards. Further, the *Octavia*, at one time attributed to Seneca but now thought to be spurious, shows that the historical play was still current in first-century Rome. Comparison of these surviving examples with the corresponding sections in Herodotus and Tacitus respectively[47] reveals significant differences which may be due in large measure to distinctions between the dramatist's and the historian's purpose.

Pliny, *Epist.*, 7.17; Tacitus, *Dial.*, 2.1-3.3). But F. Ahl, (*Seneca*: Three Tragedies [Ithaca/London: Cornell University Press, 1986] 26) feels that performance—private rather than public—was possible. He finds a nugget of evidence for his view in a passage from Suetonius (*Domitian*, 7) where the emperor forbids actors to use the public stage, but allows them to perform in private houses.

[46] The comedies, of course, tended to parody current political situations which were history in the making.

[47] Herodotus, Book VIII; Tacitus, *Annals*, XIV.59-64.

Similarly, Mark has an ulterior motive in view: he is not writing history, but using historical traditions dramatically in order to achieve his ultimate purpose which is to proclaim to his audience the divine sonship of Jesus Christ.

The second point is that the Greco-Roman system laid stress on the study of literature for moral purposes.[48] The art of public reading did, of course, lead to proficiency in declamation, and so was necessary for preparing a student for public life; but in the last analysis its aim was to facilitate the student's understanding of the passage which was being read,[49] thus enabling him to read in an informed manner and, where possible, to underscore the meaning of the passage by modulating the pitch and volume of the voice. Only when the passage had been fully comprehended in this way could its underlying moral intent (if it had one) be grasped.

The purpose of Mark's Gospel reflects this situation rather well. Although the Evangelist made use of the many rhetorical and dramatic devices available to him, his overriding aim was not aesthetic, but theological and ethical.[50] There is no doubt that, despite the degree to which his work was informed by the literary conventions of his day, particularly formal and structural ones, Mark was also an innovator. In the term εὐαγγέλιον we find something radically new. For Mark's audience the newness lay in the dynamic gospel message, but it was a message that would have been unintelligible to it had the literary genre in which it was presented been totally unfamiliar. Thus, Mark chose to present his gospel in terms of tragic dramatic conventions which would already have been a part of his audience's cultural heritage. In this way, he was able not only to preserve his message in all its radical newness, but to ensure that, given an adequate reading, its dynamism would emerge from the oral presentation itself. That is to say, the new dynamic of the gospel, latent in the text, would be fully realised only in the spoken word. Thus, not the parenthetical "asides" alone, [51] but the struc-

---

[48] Marrou, *History of Education*, 169-170.

[49] Quintilian (*InstOr*, I.viii.2) counted understanding as the "golden rule" of reading (*Unum est igitur quod in hac parte praecipiam, et omnia ista facere possit: intellegat*).

[50] The ethical element in Mark has been seriously neglected in the past, but now see Via, *Ethics*. Via stresses the importance of narrative as the primary means of driving home the ethical message.

[51] So 2:10, 28; 3:30; 7:19b; 8:32a; 13:14b. Beavis (*CBQ*, 49 [1987] 593) takes the "reader" (ὁ ἀναγινώσκων) of 13:14b to be the lector who delivered the gospel orally to the gathered church.

ture of the entire work became indispensable aids to the lector, advising him how to read it in such a manner as to draw the most meaningful response from his audience.[52]

Despite the fact that further progress may yet be made in the field of oral dynamics and reader-response criticism in the gospels, it is hoped that in this paper we have at least opened up some possibilities for a reading of Mark which might help us to understand more clearly the processes by which a first-century audience would have sought to understand the text when it was received orally for the first time.

---

[52] It may be objected that since many members of the Markan community would have been slaves, there is some doubt as to how well educated they would have been. Nevertheless, the fact that some slaves became techers or tutors shows that education was not necessarily dependent on status. In any case, even the uneducated Christian, who may not have understood the hermeneutic subtleties behind a proper oral presentation of Mark, would surely have perceived its narrative immediacy.

INDEX OF AUTHORS

INDEX OF BIBLICAL REFERENCES

BRILL'S READERS
IN BIBLICAL STUDIES

Selected Studies from
NOVUM TESTAMENTUM

1. *The Composition of Luke's Gospel.* Compiled by D.E. Orton. 1999.
    ISBN 90 04 11157 3
2. *The Composition of John's Gospel.* Compiled by D.E. Orton. 1999.
    ISBN 90 04 11158 1
3. *The Composition of Mark's Gospel.* Compiled by D.E. Orton. 1999.
    ISBN 90 04 11340 1
4. *The Synoptic Problem and Q.* Compiled by D.E. Orton. 1999.
    ISBN 90 04 11342 8